Cultural and Heritage Tourism in the Middle East and North Africa

This is the first book to provide a comprehensive account of cultural and heritage tourism in the Middle East and North Africa (MENA) region and the many complexities that heritage sites and tourist attractions face.

The MENA region has long been regarded as the cradle of Western and Arab civilisation and is the home of many of the world's major religions. Because of this, the region is rich in heritage sites that serve as major tourist attractions and as icons of national, cultural and religious identity. However, as this book examines, heritage in the region is simultaneously highly contested and has even become a target for terrorism creating a situation that brought major challenges for heritage management and sustainable tourism development. Many of the region's innumerable cultural sites are threatened, in some cases by overuse, in others by neglect and, in many, simply by the pressures of economic development.

This book is therefore of interest not only to heritage managers and policy makers but those academics who seek to address the delicate balance between tourism development, communities and the tourists who visit such sites in a turbulent but highly significant region of the world.

C. Michael Hall is a Professor in the Department of Management, Marketing and Entrepreneurship at the University of Canterbury, New Zealand; Docent in Geography, University of Oulu, Finland; a Visiting Professor in Tourism at Linnaeus University, Kalmar, Sweden; and a Guest Professor in the Department of Service Management and Service Studies, Lund University, Helsingborg, Sweden. He has written widely on tourism, regional development, heritage, food and global environmental change.

Siamak Seyfi is an Assistant Professor at the Geography Research Unit of the University of Oulu, Finland. Using an interdisciplinary and multidisciplinary approach, his research interests focus on tourism politics and geopolitics with a primary focus on the MENA region, cultural heritage, resilience, sustainability as well as qualitative sociological/ethnographic research methods in tourism.

Contemporary Geographies of Leisure, Tourism and Mobility

Series Editor: C. Michael Hall
Professor at the Department of Management, College of Business and Economics, University of Canterbury, Christchurch, New Zealand

The aim of this series is to explore and communicate the intersections and relationships between leisure, tourism, and human mobility within the social sciences.

It will incorporate both traditional and new perspectives on leisure and tourism from contemporary geography, e.g. notions of identity, representation, and culture, while also providing for perspectives from cognate areas such as anthropology, cultural studies, gastronomy and food studies, marketing, policy studies and political economy, regional and urban planning, and sociology, within the development of an integrated field of leisure and tourism studies.

Also, increasingly, tourism and leisure are regarded as steps in a continuum of human mobility. Inclusion of mobility in the series offers the prospect to examine the relationship between tourism and migration, the sojourner, educational travel, and second home and retirement travel phenomena.

The series comprises two strands:

Contemporary Geographies of Leisure, Tourism and Mobility aims to address the needs of students and academics, and the titles will be published in hardback and paperback. Titles include:

Tourism and Innovation, 2nd Edition
C. Michael Hall and Allan M. Williams

Routledge Studies in Contemporary Geographies of Leisure, Tourism and Mobility is a forum for innovative new research intended for research students and academics, and the titles will be available in hardback only. Titles include:

Cultural and Heritage Tourism in the Middle East and North Africa
Complexities, Management and Practices
Edited by C. Michael Hall and Siamak Seyfi

For more information about this series, please visit: www.routledge.com/Contemporary-Geographies-of-Leisure-Tourism-and-Mobility/book-series/SE0522

Cultural and Heritage Tourism in the Middle East and North Africa

Complexities, Management and Practices

Edited by C. Michael Hall and Siamak Seyfi

LONDON AND NEW YORK

First published 2021
by Routledge
2 Park Square, Milton Park, Abingdon, Oxon OX14 4RN

and by Routledge
52 Vanderbilt Avenue, New York, NY 10017

Routledge is an imprint of the Taylor & Francis Group, an informa business

© 2021 selection and editorial matter, C. Michael Hall and Siamak Seyfi; individual chapters, the contributors

The right of C. Michael Hall and Siamak Seyfi to be identified as the authors of the editorial material, and of the authors for their individual chapters, has been asserted in accordance with sections 77 and 78 of the Copyright, Designs and Patents Act 1988.

All rights reserved. No part of this book may be reprinted or reproduced or utilised in any form or by any electronic, mechanical, or other means, now known or hereafter invented, including photocopying and recording, or in any information storage or retrieval system, without permission in writing from the publishers.

Trademark notice: Product or corporate names may be trademarks or registered trademarks, and are used only for identification and explanation without intent to infringe.

British Library Cataloguing-in-Publication Data
A catalogue record for this book is available from the British Library

Library of Congress Cataloging-in-Publication Data
Names: Hall, Colin Michael, 1961- editor. | Seyfi, Siamak, editor.
Title: Cultural and heritage tourism in the Middle East and North Africa : complexities, management and practices / edited by C. Michael Hall and Siamak Seyfi.
Description: Abingdon, Oxon ; New York, NY : Routledge, 2021.
| Series: Contemporary geographies of tourism, leisure and mobility
| Includes bibliographical references and index.
Identifiers: LCCN 2020015497 (print) | LCCN 2020015498 (ebook)
Subjects: LCSH: Heritage tourism--Middle East. | Heritage tourism--Africa, North. | Sustainable tourism--Middle East.
| Sustainable tourism--Africa, North.
Classification: LCC G155.M66 C85 2021 (print) | LCC G155.M66 (ebook) | DDC 338.4/7915604--dc23
LC record available at https://lccn.loc.gov/2020015497
LC ebook record available at https://lccn.loc.gov/2020015498

ISBN: 978-0-367-23271-9 (hbk)
ISBN: 978-0-429-27906-5 (ebk)

Typeset in Times New Roman
by MPS Limited, Dehradun

Contents

List of illustrations	vii
List of contributors	ix
Preface and acknowledgements	xi
List of abbreviations	xiv

1 **Cultural heritage tourism in the MENA: introduction and background**   1
SIAMAK SEYFI AND C. MICHAEL HALL

2 **Tourism and the multi-faith heritage of the Middle East and North Africa: a resource perspective**   34
DALLEN J. TIMOTHY

3 **Contesting religious heritage in the Middle East**   54
DANIEL H. OLSEN AND CHAD F. EMMETT

4 **Making a sense of place for Safranbolu World Heritage Site: an analysis of *Safranbolu: Reflections of Time***   72
ENIS TATAROGLU

5 **Cultural heritage and tourism in Tunisia: evolution, challenges, and perspectives**   87
NAJEM DHAHER, SIAMAK SEYFI, AND C. MICHAEL HALL

6 **Touring 'our' past: World Heritage tourism and post-colonialism in Morocco**   102
BAILEY ASHTON ADIE

7 **National park or urban green space: the case of [Tel] Ashkelon**   115
YAEL RAM

8 Cultural heritage in Palestine: challenges and opportunities 129
RAMI K. ISAAC

9 Visitors' expectation and experience in a World Heritage Site: evidence from ancient Göbekli Tepe, Sanliurfa, Turkey 141
ALI RIZA MANCI

10 Theme park Arabism: Disneyfying the UAE's heritage for Western tourist consumption 157
SALMA THANI AND TOM HEENAN

11 Integrated cultural heritage planning in Egypt: a catalyst for tourism after the Arab Spring? 170
EMAN M. HELMY

12 UNESCO's World Heritage Sites: the interplay between international and local branding for the Gonbad-e Qābus Brick Tower, Iran 187
BARDIA SHABANI, HAZEL TUCKER, AND AMIN NAZIFI

13 Factors influencing residents' perceptions toward heritage tourism: a gender perspective 202
S. MOSTAFA RASOOLIMANESH, BABAK TAHERI, MARTIN GANNON, AND HAMID ATAEISHAD

14 Climate change threats to cultural and heritage tourism in Iran 218
JENNIFER M. FITCHETT AND GHOLAMREZA ROSHAN

15 Conclusion: the futures of cultural heritage tourism in the MENA countries 239
C. MICHAEL HALL AND SIAMAK SEYFI

Index 253

Illustrations

Figures

2.1	Types of religious heritage attractions in MENA	38
14.1	Map of Iran indicating the location of the 38 cities of interest for this study	220
14.2a-b	UTCI calculated risk maps for heat and cold thermal stress for Iran: a) Heat stress b) Cold stress	232

Tables

1.1	MENA country profiles	3
1.2	International visitation by type of tourism activities in Morocco in 2014	7
1.3	Morocco: tangible heritage inscribed on the UNESCO Heritage List	8
1.4	Morocco: representative List of the Intangible Cultural Heritage of UNESCO	8
1.5	Location and nature of the main monuments popular with tourists	9
1.6	Number of World Heritage Sites in MENA region by countries as of January 2020	14
1.7	International tourist arrivals in MENA countries, 2000–2018 (million)	20
1.8	International tourist receipts in MENA countries, 2000–2018 (million)	21
1.9	The travel and tourism competitiveness of MENA countries in 2019	22
2.1	A sample of faith traditions and religions originating in the Middle East	37
2.2	Religion-associated archaeological UNESCO World Heritage Sites in MENA	40
2.3	Sample of religious history-oriented museums in MENA	42

viii *Illustrations*

2.4	Examples of sacred hills and mountains in MENA	43
5.1	Historical and archaeological sites in Tunisia	92
7.1	Descriptive statistics of the study's variables	120
7.2	Regression coefficient for the study variables	121
7.3	Detailed information about the interviewees	123
9.1	Demographic characteristics of the visitor	145
9.2	Statements of the modified HISTOQUAL scale – dimensions and descriptive statistics	147
9.3	Test results of the hypotheses	152
12.1	Total number of visitors per year	196
13.1	Measurement model assessment results	209
13.2	Hypothesis testing results	211
14.1	Heritage and cultural tourism attractions at the 38 Iranian locations of interest in this study	221
14.2	Mean annual and monthly TCI scores for 38 locations in Iran, calculated from historical data spanning the period 1961–2010 and future projections for 2020–2040	230

Case studies

1.1	Tourism and heritage in Morocco – Mimoun Hillali	6
1.2	The Syrian armed conflict and its impact on the country's cultural heritage	15
1.3	Cultural heritage and conflict in the Western Sahara	23

Contributors

Bailey Ashton Adie, School of Business, Law and Communications, Solent University, East Park Terrace, Southampton, SO14 0YN, UK; bailey.adie@solent.ac.uk

Hamid Ataeishad, Department of Urban and Regional Planning, Tarbiat Modares University, Tehran, Iran; hamid.ataei@yahoo.com

Najem Dhaher, National School of Architecture and Urban Design, Tunis (ENAU), Avenue de la République, University of Carthage, P. O. Box 77, 1054, Amilcar, Tunisia; najem_dhaher@yahoo.fr

Chad F. Emmett, Department of Geography, Brigham Young University, 622 KMBL, Provo, Utah, 84660, USA; Chad_Emmett@byu.edu

Jennifer M. Fitchett, School of Geography, Archaeology and Environmental Studies, University of the Witwatersrand, South Africa

Martin Gannon, Edinburgh Napier Business School, 219 Colinton Road, Edinburgh, EH14 1DJ, Scotland, UK; gannonmartinj@gmail.co

C. Michael Hall, Department of Management, Marketing and Entrepreneurship, University of Canterbury, Christchurch, New Zealand; Linnaeus University School of Business and Economics, Kalmar, Sweden; Department of Service Management and Service Studies, Lund University, Helsingborg, Sweden; Geography, Oulu University, Finland; michael.hall@canterbury.ac.nz

Tom Heenan, School of Languages, Literature, Culture & Linguistics, Faculty of Arts, Building 11, Monash University, Clayton, VIC 3800, Australia; Tom.Heenan@monash.edu

Eman M. Helmy, Faculty of Tourism & Hotel Management, Helwan University, 1 Abd El-Aziz Al-Soud Street, Manial, Orman Post Office, 12612 Cairo, Egypt; eman_helmy@hotmail.com

Mimoun Hillali, The Higher International Institute of Tourism of Tangier, Baie de Tanger, B.P: 1651, Tanger 90060, Morocco; mimohill@yahoo.fr

Contributors

Rami K. Isaac, Centre for Sustainability, Tourism & Transport, P.O. Box 3917 – 4800 DX Breda, Mgr Hopmansstraat 2, 4817 JT Breda, The Netherlands; & Institute of Hotel Management and Tourism, Bethlehem University, Palestine; Isaac.r@buas.nl

Ali Rıza Manci, Harran University, School of Tourism and Hotel Management, Kat Mardin Yolu 22 Km, Osmanbey Kampüsü 63200, Şanlıurfa, Turkey; armanci@harran.edu.tr

Amin Nazifi, Department of Marketing, University of Strathclyde, Glasgow, Scotland, UK

Daniel H. Olsen, Department of Geography, Brigham Young University, 622 KMBL, Provo, Utah, 84660, USA; dholsen@byu.edu

Yael Ram, Department of Tourism Studies, Ashkelon Academic College, Ashkelon, Israel; ramy@edu.aac.ac.il

S. Mostafa Rasoolimanesh, School of Hospitality, Tourism and Events, Taylor's University, No. 1, Jalan Taylor's, Subang Jaya, 47500, Malaysia; rasooli1352@yahoo.com, mostafa.rasoolimanesh@taylors.edu.my

Gholamreza Roshan, Department of Geography, Golestan University, Gorgan, Iran

Siamak Seyfi, Geography Research Unit, University of Oulu, Finland; siamak.seyfi@oulu.fi, siamak.seifi@yahoo.com

Bardia Shabani, UMR 5281 ART-Dev, Paul Valery Montpellier 3 University, France

Babak Taheri, Room 24b, Esmee Fairbairn Building, Edinburgh Business School, Heriot-Watt University, Edinburgh, Scotland, UK; B.Taheri@hw.ac.uk

Enis Tataroglu, Department of Tourism and Hotel Management, Atilim Universites, Kizilcasar Mahallesi, 06830 Incek Golbasi, Ankara, Turkey; enis.tataroglu@atilim.edu.tr

Salma Thani, Monash Intercultural Lab, Faculty of Arts, Building 11, Monash University, Clayton, VIC 3800, Australia; Salmathani@gmail.com

Dallen J. Timothy, School of Community Resources and Development, Arizona State University (MC 4020), 411 N. Central Avenue, Suite 550, Phoenix, AZ 85004, USA; dtimothy@asu.edu

Hazel Tucker, Tourism Department, University of Otago, Dunedin, New Zealand; hazel.tucker@otago.ac.nz

Preface and acknowledgements

Heritage is regarded as one of the more significant components of tourism. For many countries, World Heritage Sites serve as cultural icons, a means for destination and place promotion, and are regarded as a means of increasing tourist visitation. Besides its role in economic development, heritage tourism is widely accepted as an effective way to achieve the educational function of tourism by helping government influence public opinion and gain support for national ideological objectives, promoting national ambitions, developing a positive national image, and producing national identities.

Heritage is extremely important for tourism and identity in the Middle East and North Africa (MENA). Over 12 per cent of World Heritage Sites are located in this region. The term MENA covers an extensive region stretching from Morocco to Iran, including all Mashriq and Maghreb countries. The MENA region is the cradle of the world's major monotheistic religions and is a region encompassing approximately 22 countries in the Middle East and North Africa. The MENA region accounts for approximately 6 per cent of the world's population, 60 per cent of the world's oil reserves, and 45 per cent of the world's natural gas reserves and is of immense geopolitical significance.

Tourism in the MENA region has received limited but growing interest in recent years. The wealth of cultural heritage endowments of the MENA countries has therefore increasingly become part of the tourism economy of the region. Despite this wealth of heritage sites, the MENA region as a whole remains one of the world's least developed tourism regions, and the region's share of international tourism remained one of the lowest in the world. However, in addition to the region's geo-strategic importance, tourism is of growing economic significance as an alternative to energy-based economies and as a means of diversification. Yet, the whole region remains extremely underrepresented in the tourism literature. The image of the Middle East and North Africa is one that has been portrayed as a theatre of war and conflict, from the Arab–Israeli conflicts and civil war in Algeria, Lebanon, and Syria to the more recent war against Islamic extremists in Syria and Iraq, Syria's civil war, Turkish aggression against the Kurds, conflict in Western Sahara, Saudi Arabian-led intervention in Yemen, regional competition between Saudi Arabia and Iran, and the nuclear issues and sanctions in Iran. Hence, all these issues have presented significant challenges to the inbound flows of international tourists to the region.

The recent 'Arab Spring' with its new round of regional leadership competition and the advent of Islamic radical groups has also had significant negative impacts on the tourism industry and more importantly the cultural heritage in the Middle East. The escalation of the conflicts in the region since early 2011 has caused, and is still causing, dramatic human suffering. Cultural heritage destruction has become an important and irreversible collateral damage in those conflicts; extremely rich and varied cultural heritage buildings, sites, and cities are either eliminated or severely damaged to the point of devastation, while looting and trafficking of antiquities has reached unprecedented levels. In such a context, tourism may present an opportunity to positively contribute to conservation and management of heritage in the region by providing an economic value for retaining heritage. Nevertheless, tourism is also recognised as creating its own issues with respect to heritage management, while both state and non-state actors use cultural heritage for their own ends. Nevertheless, we hope that this book provides a long overdue exploration of cultural heritage tourism in the region in terms of both its significance as well as its complexities, conflicts, and practices.

Michael would like to thank a number of colleagues with whom he has undertaken related conversations and research over the years. In particular, thanks go to Bailey Adie, Alberto Amore, Dorothee Bohn, Tim Coles, Hervé Corvellec, David Duval, Alexandra Gillespie, Martin Gren, Stefan Gössling, Johan Hultman, Maria Juschten, Dieter Müller, Girish Prayag, Yael Ram, Anna Laura Raschke, Jarkko Saarinen, Dan Scott, Anna Dóra Sæþórsdóttir, Allan Williams, and Maria José Zapata-Campos for their thoughts on tourism, as well as for the stimulation of Agnes Obel, Ann Brun, Beirut, Paul Buchanan, Nick Cave, Bruce Cockburn, Elvis Costello, Stephen Cummings, David Bowie, Ebba Fosberg, Aldous Harding, Father John Misty, Mark Hollis, Margaret Glaspy, Aimee Mann, Larkin Poe, Vinnie Reilly, Henry Rollins, Matthew Sweet, Henry Wagon, and *The Guardian*, BBC6, JJ, and KCRW – for making the world much less confining. Special mention must also be given to the Malmö Saluhall; Balck, Packhuset, and Postgarten in Kalmar; and Nicole Aignier and the Hotel Grüner Baum in Merzhausen. Finally, and most importantly, Michael would like to thank the Js and the Cs who stay at home and mind the farm.

Nobody has been more important to me in the pursuit of this project than the members of my family. I would like to thank my parents, and especially my late father whose love and guidance are with me in whatever I pursue. And, most importantly, I wish to thank my loving and supportive wife, Mina, for her enduring love and patience. My thanks are extended to various friends and colleagues for their advice and warm encouragement at times of despair. I won't mention their names; I am just thinking about them. – Siamak

We also wish to gratefully acknowledge the help and support of Jody Cowper for proofreading and editing. Finally, we would both like to thank Emma Travis, Lydia Kessell, and all at Routledge for their continuing support.

Abbreviations

GCC	Gulf Cooperation Council
GDP	Gross domestic product
ICCIMA	Iran Chamber of Commerce, Industries, Mines and Agriculture
ICCROM	International Centre for the Study of the Preservation and Restoration of Cultural Property
ICHTO	Iran Cultural Heritage, Handcraft and Tourism Organization
ICOMOS	International Council on Monuments and Sites
IMF	International Monetary Fund
ITTO	Iran Touring and Tourism Organization
JCPOA	Joint Comprehensive Plan of Action
MASL	metres above sea level
MENA	Middle East and North Africa
MENAP	Middle East, North Africa, Afghanistan, and Pakistan
MENAT	Middle East, North Africa, and Turkey
NAWA	North Africa-West Asia
NGO	non-governmental organisation
OECD	Organisation for Economic Co-operation and Development
OIC	Organisation of Islamic Cooperation
OPEC	Organization of Petroleum Exporting Countries
SADR	Sahrawi Arab Democratic Republic
SCTH	Saudi Commission for Tourism and National Heritage
SCI	Statistical Center of Iran
SCO	Shanghai Cooperation Organisation
UNDP	United Nations Development Programme
UNEP	United Nations Environmental Programme
UNESCO	United Nations Education, Scientific and Cultural Organization
UNITAR	United Nations Institute for Training and Research
UNWTO	United Nations World Tourism Organization
USAID	United States Agency for International Development
VFR	Visiting friends and relatives/relations
WANA	West Asia and North Africa
WEF	World Economic Forum
WTO	World Trade Organization
WTTC	World Travel and Tourism Council

1 Cultural heritage tourism in the MENA

Introduction and background

Siamak Seyfi and C. Michael Hall

Understanding the Middle East and North Africa

The concept of a 'Middle East' is one that often appears and is of considerable importance in contemporary geopolitics (Amanat, 2012; Bilgin, 2019). Indeed, as Bilgin (2019, p. 1) observes,

> In the early twenty-first century, 30 years after the end of the Cold War, the Middle East comes across as an arena of incessant conflict attracting global attention. As evinced by accelerating South-to-North human mobility in the Mediterranean and the rise (and fall) of ISIS in Syria and Iraq, it is difficult to exaggerate the centrality of Middle Eastern insecurities to world politics.

Yet, the notion of the Middle East developed from Eurocentric and imperial coinage of the international strategic diplomacy of the early twentieth century to demarcate a strategic middle ground between the 'Near' and 'Far' East, the 'Middle East' (Koppes, 1976; Sidaway, 1994; Culcasi, 2012), and is therefore a relatively new geographical and geopolitical category whose history, as Green (2014, p. 556) suggests, 'has been far less stable than its hard rhetoric might suggest'. Bilgin even observes that 'Middle Eastern insecurities' are even 'portrayed as consequences of the "artificiality" of the "Middle East" as a region and/or the borders of Middle Eastern states' (2019, p. 2). However, he goes on to argue that 'inquiring into the relationship between (inventing) regions and (conceptions and practices of) security offers an appropriate starting point' to understand the region (Bilgin, 2019, p. 2).

Despite its Eurocentric and often contested nature (Culcasi, 2010), the notion of a Middle East still plays an important role in the academic, geopolitical, social, and environmental imaginings of the world (Amanat, 2012; Green, 2014; Evered, 2017), and continues to frame regional and policy considerations, including with respect to tourism (Hazbun, 2004, 2006; Daher, 2007; Steiner, 2010; Morakabati, 2013; Timothy, 2019a; Zandieh & Seifpour, 2020). Such a situation reflects that models of geographical space are empowered by a hard rhetoric that, in suggesting the concrete stability of the longue durée, lends the aura of geological fixity. But while places might themselves be sheer facts, our conceptions of them both in themselves and in relation to other places are cultural constructions born in particular moments in time (Green, 2014, p. 556).

Such socio-cultural and political considerations are central to understanding the heritage, and therefore heritage tourism in the region, given that ideas of heritage and place, as well as their commoditisation for tourism, are inherently connected to issues of identity (Daher, 2005; Al-Oun & Al-Homoud, 2008; Samuels, 2009; Jacobs, 2010; Mills, 2012; Campos, 2014; Makhzoumi, 2016; Özkan, 2018; Hammond, 2019; Zandieh & Seifpour, 2020). Therefore, in this particular volume, we have sought to frame the region through the lens of MENA in part because it better reflects some of the geopolitical framing that occurs from within the region and therefore connects to some of the common cultural heritage, and heritage tourism management problems, that exist (see also Timothy, 2019a).

The MENA region

MENA is an acronym and a popular geographical term used by international institutions, media, and academic and economic organisations, including those in the region itself. However, there are a number of other terms that are also used, including WANA (West Asia and North Africa) or the less common NAWA (North Africa–West Asia) or MENAT (Middle East, North Africa, and Turkey) which adds Turkey to the MENA countries. More recently, a new term was used by the International Monetary Fund (IMF) in its report – MENAP (Middle East, North Africa, Afghanistan, and Pakistan) – which adds Afghanistan and Pakistan to MENA countries (International Monetary Fund, 2019). The MENA acronym is also often considered interchangeable with the term 'greater Middle East' and in some cases the 'Arab World', with these classifications typically being based upon the mandates of each agency involved (Timothy, 2019b). In the case of the United Nations Development Programme (UNDP) (2019), the Arab World statistical category includes the MENA countries discussed here along with the Sudan, Somalia, and Djibouti and excludes Iran, Israel and Turkey.

The MENA is a large, complex, and diverse region and given there is no standardised list of countries included in the MENA region, the region typically covers an extensive region stretching from Morocco to Iran, including all Mashriq and Maghreb countries and is a huge centre of cultural and travel influence. The MENA region is the cradle of the world's major monotheistic religions and encompasses 20 countries in the Middle East and North Africa (Table 1.1). Moreover, the high ethnic diversity and large numbers of identity groups in the region also has substantial implications for cultural heritage tourism. Five of the largest ethnic groups in the region

Table 1.1 MENA country profiles

Countries	International economic and political associations	Area (km²)	Population	UNDP Human Development Index (HDI) (2018)	HDI rank (2018)	GDP per capita (USD) (2018) (IMF, 2018)	Largest ethnic groups	Main language	Main religion
Algeria	AL, OIC	2,381,741	43,053,054	0.759	81	15,440	Arab, Berber	Arabic (with Berber)	Islam (Sunni)
Bahrain	AL, GCC, OIC	760	1,641,172	0.838	45	50,057	Arab, Asian	Arabic	Islam (Shia, Sunni)
Egypt	AL, OIC	1,001,450	100,388,073	0.700	116	13,366	Arab, Copt	Arabic	Islam (Sunni)
Iran	OIC	1,648,195	82,913,906	0.797	63	19,557	Persian, Azeri, Kurds	Persian	Islam (Shia)
Iraq	AL, OIC	438,317	39,309,783	0.689	120	17,659	Arab, Kurds	Arabic (with Kurdish)	Islam (non-denominational)
Israel	OECD	20,770	8,519,377	0.906	22	37,972	Jewish, Arab	Hebrew (with Arabic)	Judaism (de-facto)
Jordan	AL, OIC	89,342	10,101,694	0.723	99	9,433	Arab, Circassian, Armenian	Arabic	Islam (Sunni)
Kuwait	AL, OIC	17,818	4,207,083	0.808	57	67,000	Arab, Asian	Arabic	Islam (Shia, Sunni)
Lebanon	AL, OIC	10,400	6,855,713	0.730	93	14,684	Arab, Armenian	Arabic	
Libya	AL, OIC	1,759,540	6,777,452	0.708	111	11,469	Arab, Berber	Arabic	Islam (Sunni)
Morocco	AL, OIC	446,550	36,471,769	0.676	121	8,933	Arab, Berber	Arabic (with Berber)	Islam (Sunni)
Oman	AL, GCC	309,500	4,974,986	0.834	47	46,584	Arab, Baluchi	Arabic	Islam (Ibadi)
Palestine	AL, OIC	6,220	4,981,420	0.690	119	3,199	Arab, Jewish	Arabic (Hebrew also in occupied territories)	Islam (Sunni, non-denominational)
Qatar	AL, GCC, OIC	11,586	2,832,067	0.848	40	130,475	Arab, Asian	Arabic	Islam (Sunni)
Saudi Arabia	AL, GCC, OIC	2,149,690	34,268,528	0.857	36	55,944	Arab, Asian	Arabic	Islam (Sunni)
Syria	AL (suspended), OIC (suspended)	185,180	17,070,135	0.549	154	2,900	Arab, Kurds, Armenian	Arabic	Islam (Sunni, Alawite)

(Continued)

Table 1.1 Continued

Countries	International economic and political associations	Area (km²)	Population	UNDP Human Development Index (HDI) (2018)	HDI rank (2018)	GDP per capita (USD) (2018) (IMF, 2018)	Largest ethnic groups	Main language	Main religion
Tunisia	AL, OIC	163,610	11,694,719	0.739	91	12,372	Arab, Berber	Arabic	Islam (non-denominational)
Turkey	OECD, OIC	783,562	82,003,882	0.806	59	*9,370	Turkish, Kurds	Turkish (with Kurdish)	Islam (Sunni)
UAE	AL, GCC, OIC	83,600	9,770,529	0.866	35	69,382	Arab (Emirati), South Asian, Egyptian	Arabic	Islam (non-denominational)
Yemen	AL, OIC	527,968	29,161,922	0.463	175	2,377	Arab	Arabic	Islam (Shia, Sunni)

Source: UN World Population, 2019; International Monetary Fund, 2019; UNDP, 2019.

Notes
* World Bank figure for 2018.
AL: Arab League; GCC: Gulf Corporation Council, formally known as Cooperation Council for the Arab States of the Gulf, and is a transnational political and economic union of Arab countries surrounding the Persian Gulf; OECD: Organisation for Economic Co-operation and Development; OIC: Organisation of Islamic Cooperation.

are included: Arabs, Azerbaijanis, Kurds, Persians, and Turks. The majority of the population in the Middle East adhere to the two main variants of Islam: Sunni Islam, which has the greater following in most countries, and Shia Islam, centred on Iran and Iraq, although in some countries there are also a significant number of Muslims who identify as non-denominational, while Oman is primarily Ibadi Islam. In addition, there are Christian and Jewish minorities in a number of countries, while Israel is obviously primarily Jewish.

The MENA region accounts for approximately 6 per cent of the world's population, 60 per cent of the world's oil reserves, and 45 per cent of the world's natural gas reserves (Khatib, 2014). Many of the 12 OPEC (The Organization of the Petroleum Exporting Countries) members are within the MENA region. Together with the region's substantial petroleum and natural gas reserves, this makes the region an important contributor to global economic stability, and clearly demonstrates the centrality of the region to the global oil and gas market. Nevertheless, while oil and gas are very significant for economic growth in the region (Al-Mulali, 2011) and indirectly contribute to tourism demand, dependency on these products has historically limited the development of the tourism sector as well. Therefore, there is a growing focus on tourism as a means of economic diversification in the oil- and gas-rich states of the region (Morakabati, 2013; Tang & Abosedra, 2014), although its development in Saudi Arabia and Iran remains primarily guided by conservative Islamic values and religious perspectives, especially as each country aspires to present itself as the epitome of Muslim society (Seyfi & Hall, 2019). In Saudi Arabia, which has begun to seek to encourage heritage and cultural tourism by non-Muslims as well as increase domestic tourism (Saudi Commission for Tourism and National Heritage (SCTH), 2018a, 2018b), the growing emphasis on developing tourism outside the *hajj* pilgrimage and building an entertainment city 'not subject to [the] conservative kingdom's rules' is still a source of domestic political contention (Madden, 2018).

It is not just the states in the region with carbon-based economies that are trying to diversify through tourism. Nearly every MENA country has begun to see tourism as a means of economic diversification and private-sector employment generation (O'Sullivan, Rey, & Mendez, 2011) (see Case study 1.1 on Morocco). And, in those countries that are experiencing war and political instability, tourism will undoubtedly become a focus once relative peaceful stability resumes, as has already been demonstrated in the region with respect to Lebanon (Ladki & Dah, 1997; Ladki & Sadik, 2004; Issa & Altinay, 2006; Rowbotham, 2010), Iran (Seyfi & Hall, 2018, 2020a), Israel (Mansfeld, 1999), Palestine (Isaac, Hall, & Higgins-Desbiolles, 2016). Indeed, in some cases war sites have become tourist attractions and become locations of national and secular pilgrimage.

Case study 1.1 Tourism and heritage in Morocco

Being bordered by two seas, the Mediterranean and the Atlantic, and straddling mountain ranges, oases, and the Sahara, Morocco's geography and history have some significant differences to those of other MENA countries which have significantly influenced its cultural heritage and tourism. First, Morocco is a thousand-year-old monarchy consolidated by dynastic alternation. Second, the kingdom escaped Ottoman domination in 1512 when the eastern Maghreb was occupied and this has led to some important historical differences compared to much of the MENA area. Third, it was spared the wave of coups d'état that eliminated the last African kingdoms in the twentieth century. Finally, Morocco put up resistance to the colonial expansionism of France and Spain, before undergoing a short-lived tripartite protectorate (1912–1956). The 44 years of occupation did not greatly alter the country's culture, much less its heritage. On the contrary, the protectorate favoured tourism as a means of economic development, certainly modern and colonial, but nevertheless primarily cultural in nature.

As soon as it was established, the administration of the protectorate assigned a symbolic dimension to the conservation of Morocco's monuments and cities (Hillali, 2007a, 2007b; Berriane, 2009). After independence in 1956, Moroccan tourism went through a period of stagnation (1956–1964) before benefiting from the effects of a targeted liberal orientation with respect to tourism development. The geographical resources and the cultural heritage of the kingdom provided planners with the necessary arguments to give tourism an important role, second only to agriculture, among the national economic priorities (Hillali, 2007a; Moudoud & Ezaïdi, 2005; Bouzahzah & El Menyari, 2013). However, the inexperience of the tourism actors and the persistence of internal and external crises disrupted the evolution of this sector, once described as the 'engine of development' for Morocco (Hillali, 2007a).

Tourism has received a major boost with the reign of Mohammed VI since 1999, via a series of large-scale development plans (e.g. Vision 2010 and 2020), substantial investment in infrastructure, and increasing foreign investment in the sector (Almeida-García, 2018). As a consequence, tourism has become the main factor of economic growth and is the second biggest contributor to GDP and the second largest source of employment generation (Bilali, 2016). In 2018, over 12 million tourists visited Morocco and made Morocco the top African tourist destination

Introduction 7

and the 30th most popular in the world (UNWTO, 2019b; WTTC, 2019). Hilali (2007a) argues that for Morocco, the choice of tourism is above all an option compatible with the monarchical doctrine and its heritage and politics being suitable for the continued evolution of the moderate liberalism desired by Morocco.

In the case of Morocco, heritage in general, and the commoditisation of culture for tourism in particular, has evolved in a social and political climate where tradition and modernity seek to coexist. The museums in Morocco are primarily visited by international tourists rather than domestic ones. Data from Morocco's Tourism Observatory Office shows French tourists as the main market for tourism in Morocco, representing 27.6 per cent of the total foreign tourists during 2018. The other major markets for Moroccan tourism are Spain, followed by the United Kingdom, and Belgium. Culture, museums, and the history of Morocco are key elements for more than 34 per cent of French students who make cultural visits to Morocco (Kasraoui, 2019). The 13 museums managed by the Ministry of Culture and the 20 historic sites open to the public bring in about 15 million dirhams in revenue per year, reflecting the fact that the entrance fees are very low (10 dirhams (approximately a little under one euro, to which the currency is pegged) for public museums and 20 dirhams for private ones). A study by Kasraoui (2019) showed that visits to monuments and museums were undertaken by 40 per cent of international tourists, with 12 per cent participating in cultural and artistic events (Table 1.2). In comparison, walks in the city/beach accounted for 19 per cent of the activities undertaken by foreign tourists in 2014.

Table 1.2 International visitation by type of tourism activities in Morocco in 2014

Activities	*Percentage*
Visits to monuments, museums	40%
City/beach walks	19%
Calm, rest, idleness	17%
Hiking	16%
VFR and wedding	15%
Cultural and artistic events	12%
Beach	11%
Gastronomy	10%
Business and professional activities	9%

Source: Observatoire du tourisme Maroc, 2014.

Table 1.3 Morocco: tangible heritage inscribed on the UNESCO Heritage List

World Heritage Sites	Year	Sites on the Tentative List	Year
Ksar of Ait-Ben-Haddou	1987	Moulay Idriss Zerhoun	1995
Medina of Essaouira (formerly Mogador)	2001	Taza and the Great Mosque	1995
Medina of Fez	1981	Tinmel Mosque	1995
Medina of Marrakech	1985	Lixus (ancient city)	1995
Medina of Tétouan (formerly known as Titawin)	1997	El Gour	1995
Rabat, Modern Capital and Historic City: A Shared Heritage	2012	Taforalt (Grotte des Pigeons)	1995
Archaeological Site of Volubilis	1997	Talassemtane National Park	1998
Historic City of Meknes	1996	Aire du Dragonnier in Ajgal	1998
Portuguese City of Mazagan (El Jadida)	2004	Khnifiss lagoon	1998
		Dakhla National Park	1998

Source: UNESCO, 2019.

Table 1.4 Morocco: representative List of the Intangible Cultural Heritage of UNESCO

Name	Location or city	Year
Jemaa el-Fnaa square (market)	Marrakech	2008
Tan-Tan Moussem (tribal gathering)	Tan Tan	2008
The Mediterranean Diet	Morocco	2013
The art of falconry	El Jadida	2012
Practices and know-how concerning the argan tree	Popular areas	2014

Source: Morocco's Ministry of Culture, 2019 (http://www.patrimoineculturel.ma/).

The income generated by visits to monuments and museums is significant for heritage conservation as well as the wider destinations (Observatoire du tourisme Maroc, 2014). As with many MENA countries, World Heritage listing is regarded as important for tourism as well as being a source of national prestige. The inscription of nine heritage sites by UNESCO on the World Heritage List contributes both to the protection and recognition of these properties (Table 1.3). There are five items inscribed on UNESCO's representative list of intangible cultural heritage (UNESCO, 2015) (Table 1.4) which also serve to reinforce the importance of several location as tourism sites. This is especially the case with respect to Jemaa el-Fnaa square in Marrakech which is a market as well as a space within which traditional storytelling, music, and performance occurs. Nevertheless, it is important to recognise that the UNESCO-listed sites are only a very small part of the many sites of national significance.

Although tourism growth remains a major focus of the government, tourism strategies such as Vision 2011–2020 have attempted to correct the mistakes of the past by emphasising the protection of the environment and heritage. In its Vision 2020, the Ministry of Tourism has drawn up a plan for the development of national culture, entitled 'Legacy and Heritage', which aims to put forward the cultural identity of Morocco through the structuring and the upgrading of the physical and non-physical legacies of the Kingdom and the building of coherent and attractive tourism products (Ministry of Tourism, Air Transport, Handicrafts and Social Economy, 2018). As a part of this plan and in the first instance, two world-class museums are being developed, the African Museum of Tangier and the Moroccan Museum of History of Meknes, to allow tourists to discover and interpret the historical and cultural inheritance of the Kingdom in a manner similar to major contemporary European museums (Ministry of Tourism, Air Transport, Handicrafts and Social Economy, 2018). These high-profile projects aim to promote tourism by enhancing culture while many other heritage sites remain important for tourism (Table 1.5).

Nevertheless, coastal development remains a major focus. For example, Plan Azur 2020 focuses on strengthening the Morocco seaside resort industry on both the Atlantic and Mediterranean shores, and seeks additionally to develop new tourist destinations in the Souss and Sahara (Bilali, 2016). Overall, it aims to build a competitive Moroccan offer on an international basis and seeks to raise Morocco to be one of

Table 1.5 Location and nature of the main monuments popular with tourists

Monuments	Characteristics	Location
Palace	Royal residences and residences associated with the members of a royal household	Imperial cities or locations frequented by the royal family
Riads	Traditional multilevel houses of the wealthier members of society	Grandes villes du Bled el Makhzen
Kasbahs	Adobe fortresses	Oases and on trading routes
Ksour	Fortified villages	Oases and palm groves
Attics	Fortified collective granaries	Anti-Atlas and surroundings
Madrasahs	Old religious educational institutions /universities	Imperial cities and surroundings
Medinas	Ancient cities	All over Morocco

the world's top 20 tourist destinations by 2020 and a model of sustainability among Mediterranean destinations (Bilali, 2016).

Cultural tourism in Morocco is constantly increasing; culture and heritage tourism accounts for 80 per cent of tourism activities in the country, despite the desire of government authorities to develop seaside resorts, often at the expense of other forms of tourism. The historical heritage elements, whether tangible or intangible, old or recent, dispersed or concentrated, are sensitive products requiring great care. The inscription of nine historic properties on the World Heritage List, between 1981 and 2019, has certainly helped to anchor this type of tourism in the country. And yet, beyond the idyllic image of tourism advertising, the relationship between tourist activity and cultural heritage in Morocco is highly complex. While the contribution of Moroccan-built and intangible heritage to tourism is visible in the form of attractions, foreign exchange, revenue, and employment, the opposite, the contribution of tourism to the conservation and maintenance of heritage, remains to be proven. It is true that, in terms of safeguarding or protection, historic sites and monuments have often been enhanced to serve as a platform for socio-cultural events of a seasonal nature. Moreover, craft products (weaving and porcelain), traditional activities (cooking and gastronomy), and popular arts (songs and dances) have experienced a certain renaissance, or at least have been maintained, at the cost of only limited change. Nevertheless, opinions differ on this point: optimists believe that tourism is an excellent saviour of heritage, while pessimists see it, instead, as an agent of its long-term annihilation.

Mimoun Hillal

That tourism is of growing economic significance to the region should not be surprising. MENA represents a market of 389 million consumers which has a combined GDP of USD 2.4 trillion (2017), accounting for 3 per cent of the world's economy (UNWTO, 2019a). The growing middle class in many countries, especially in the Gulf region, as well as significant international diasporas, means that there are substantial international outbound markets for VFR (visiting friends and relatives) travel as well as leisure markets. Given the central role of the Abrahamic religions in the region, religious tourism and pilgrimage is clearly important (Zamani-Farahani & Eid, 2016; Seyfi & Hall, 2019), while there is also a small but possibly growing Islamic tourism market (Hall & Prayag, 2020). The Organisation of Islamic Cooperation's (OIC) (2017) perspective on Islamic tourism is significant for some forms of cultural heritage tourism in that it argues:

Islamic tourism includes visions and ideas that outline the inclusion of Islamic religious cultural sites in tourism programs with 'pedagogical' and self-confidence building elements. It tries to encourage a reorientation inside the tourist destinations towards less consumption and 'western culture' loaded sites towards more Islamic historical, religious and cultural sites (OIC, 2017, p. 28).

However, the OIC goes on to explicitly describe Islamic tourism as a 'religious conservative' concept:

> The religious conservative concept for Islamic tourism is based on the conservative interpretation and understanding of Islam. Merging elements of the extremely conservative Islamic lifestyle with the modern tourism industry could indeed present new tourism options, spaces, and spheres. For a growing conservative intra Arab and intra Muslim tourism market, the implementation of a religious conservative concept in tourism planning as an extra option and as an insertion into the existing mainstream tourism could indeed have a positive economic and social effect (OIC, 2017, p. 28).

While there is undoubtedly a religious conservative element in some forms of tourism within the region, that is particularly reflected in the tourism policies of Iran and Saudi Arabia (Seyfi & Hall, 2019, 2020a); less conservative members of society are increasingly likely to engage in leisure-oriented domestic and international tourism. Indeed, in a study of domestic tourist camping in Israeli national parks, Ram and Hall (2020) reported that religiously conservative individuals, whether Jewish or Muslim, show little engagement in leisure camping. Heritage tourism there need not be regarded as implicitly conservative, although the recognition of intangible heritage and the cultural dimensions of heritage undoubtedly call on appropriate sensitivity by tourists and in the development of heritage tourism. Significantly, international heritage tourists may potentially offer higher yields than more conventional coastal resort tourism and may also offer significant returns for more peripheral areas (Wright & Eppink, 2016; Lak, Gheitasi, & Timothy, 2019). Therefore, given the rich cultural heritage of the MENA countries, it is perhaps unsurprising that the economic value of heritage tourism is gaining greater attention from governments as they face the challenge of generating employment at a time of substantial economic, social, and environmental change.

This chapter provides an introduction and background to the MENA region in general and the cultural and heritage tourism in the region in particular and the challenges it faces given the current conflict in the region. It also outlines the development of tourism in the MENA region and identifies key issues in the region in relation to the chapters in the book. These issues and their respective implications for heritage tourism will set the context for the chapters to come.

The geopolitics of the MENA region

Heritage and tourism in the MENA is very much affected by the region's geopolitics. The rivalry between major powers in the region, namely Saudi Arabia and Iran, which is played out in Lebanon, the West Bank and Gaza Strip, and post-war Iraq, along with Iran's sophisticated interventions in Bahrain and other countries in the region and, more recently, Saudi-led intervention in Yemen has shaped the geopolitics of the region since the 2003 US invasion and occupation of Iraq (Salloukh, 2013). The popular uprisings of the Arab Spring intensified this geopolitical confrontation and the regional struggle which spread to Syria and Yemen (Dalacoura, 2012; Malmvig, 2014). The fall of a number of the region's long-time dictatorships as a result of the Arab Spring has intensified awareness of the geopolitical significance of the region (Aras & Yorulmazlar, 2016). Salloukh (2013, p. 33) commented that:

> The sectarianisation of the region's geopolitical battles, and the instrumental use of some of the uprisings for geopolitical ends, has hardened sectarian sentiments across the region, complicated post-authoritarian democratic transitions, and, at least in Syria's case, transformed its popular uprising into a veritable civil war.

In addition, the extremely volatile oil market of the producing countries in the region has had an influence on international markets and, for many, oil is seen as particularly sensitive to sudden shifts in the geopolitical climate (Kausch, 2015). Iran's threat to block the Strait of Hormuz in response to US sanctions on the country's oil industry and exports, as well as several attacks on tankers clearly, demonstrates the geopolitics of oil and the significance of the region in shaping the global oil market (Kausch, 2015; Cordesman, 1999). Such issues affect not only global energy markets but also affect perceptions of the region in terms of safety and security, including the major aviation hubs that have been developed by some of the Gulf states.

Civil war in Syria has generated a new wave of geopolitical manoeuvring in the political geography of the Middle East and has brought the US and Russia into direct military competition, along with significant regional interventions by Turkey and Iran. Clearly indicating the MENA's position in global affairs and in geopolitical and geostrategic equations, Rashed (2019) argued that:

> For most of its modern history, the Middle East has been besieged by international conflicts. Since the early nineteenth century, European powers have competed to colonise the Middle East's territories in an attempt to control its natural resource and geostrategic location. Almost two centuries later, the region finds itself embattled in another round of intense crises in which both superpowers and regional powers compete for territorial influence. The once stable region became an arena for violence in the aftermath of the popular uprisings of the 2010s, and what

started as peaceful demands for democracy and freedom soon metamorphosed into civil and regional wars in many areas. The rise of violent change and the counter violent quest to maintain the status quo has been closely tied to the region's resources.

Moreover, the broken diplomatic and commercial ties in the aftermath of the sanctions against Qatar by the Saudi-led coalition has forged a new series of relations among countries in the region. Visitors from the rest of the Gulf Cooperation Council (GCC) usually account for approximately half of all tourists to Qatar. Therefore, the decision by Saudi Arabia, the UAE, Bahrain, and Egypt to cut diplomatic and transport ties in 2017 had a substantial impact on the country's tourism industry along with its role as an aviation hub for Qatar Airlines (Reuters, 2017). As of February 2020, the governments of Bahrain, Comoros, Egypt, Mauritania, Saudi Arabia, the United Arab Emirates, and Yemen had still not restored diplomatic ties with Qatar. The number of visitors to Qatar fell by more than a third in the first half of 2018, with 945,000 visitors arriving in the first six months of 2018, compared to 1.5 million in the same period in 2017. Key to the change in the number of arrivals was an 84 per cent drop in visitors from the GCC and a 45 per cent drop in visitors from other Arab countries (Dudley, 2018). Hassan Al-Ibrahim, the acting chairman of the QTA, said Qatar had been faced with a situation where 'other countries are weaponizing tourism' and said that Qatar was going to follow a strategy of trying to diversify its source markets (Dudley, 2018).

These geopolitical upheavals in the region along with the United States' unilateral withdrawal from the Iran nuclear agreement (known as the Joint Comprehensive Plan of Action – JCPOA) and imposition of further stringent sanctions against Iran (Seyfi & Hall, 2019, 2020b); the targeted killing of the Iranian general Qassem Soleimani in Baghdad by a US drone and the subsequent accidental missile attack on Ukraine International Airlines Flight 752 (Hubbard, 2020); President Trump's 'peace plan' for Israel and Palestine (Beaumont & Proctor, 2020); and ongoing tensions between Iran and major powers in the region, particularly Saudi Arabia and Israel (Guzansky & Shapiro, 2019) demonstrate the level of political uncertainty and potential instability in the region, with subsequent direct and indirect implications for tourism and heritage.

Cultural and heritage tourism in the MENA region

Heritage is regarded as one of the more significant and fast-growing components of tourism in many developed economies (Richards, 2018; Timothy & Boyd, 2015), with much of the focus placed on World Heritage Sites (Adie, 2019). Since the adoption of the *Convention Concerning the Protection of World Natural and Cultural Heritage* in 1972, as of January 2020, some 1,121 sites (869 cultural, 213 natural, and 39 mixed) throughout the world have been designated as World Heritage Sites (UNESCO, 2020). Many significant sites in the region grace this list (Shackley, 1998). For many countries, World Heritage Sites serve as cultural icons and a means for developing a positive national image and increasing international visitation (Adie & Hall, 2017). Heritage tourism is also an important sector of domestic tourism in many countries. Besides its role in economic development, heritage tourism is widely accepted as an effective way to achieve the educational function of tourism by helping government influence public opinion and gain support for national ideological objectives and ambitions, developing a positive national image, and contributing to national and regional identities (Adie, Hall, & Prayag, 2018; Timothy & Boyd, 2015; Bourdeau, Gravari-Barbas, & Robinson, 2016).

The MENA are home to 129 UNESCO World Heritage Sites (119 cultural, five natural, and five mixed) which are of outstanding universal value; 325 sites are also tentatively listed, which shows the huge potential of the region. As Table 1.6 shows, around 12 per cent of World Heritage Sites are

Table 1.6 Number of World Heritage Sites in MENA region by countries as of January 2020

Country	Cultural sites	Natural sites	Mixed sites	Total sites	Sites on the tentative list	UNESCO region
Iran	22	2	–	24	56	Asia and the Pacific
Turkey	16	–	2	18	78	Europe and North America
Morocco	9	–	–	9	13	Arab States
Tunisia	7	1	–	8	13	Arab States
Algeria	6	–	1	7	6	Arab States
Egypt	6	1	–	7	33	Arab States
Israel	7	–	–	7	18	Europe and North America
Iraq	5	–	1	6	11	Arab States
Syria	6	–	–	6	12	Arab States
Jordan	4	–	1	5	15	Arab States
Lebanon	5	–	–	5	10	Arab States
Libya	5	–	–	5	0	Arab States
Oman	5	–	–	5	7	Arab States
Saudi Arabia	5	–	–	5	11	Arab States
Bahrain	3	–	–	3	6	Arab States
Palestine	3	–	–	3	13	Arab States
Qatar	1	–	–	1	1	Arab States
Yemen	3	1	–	4	10	Arab States
UAE	1	–	–	1	8	Arab States
Kuwait	–	–	–	0	4	Arab States
Total	119	5	5	129	325	

Source: Authors' compilation, UNESCO, 2020.

located in the MENA region together with sites recognised under national heritage legislation.

The wealth of cultural heritage endowments of the MENA countries reflects the importance of the region's contributions to humanity's history (Timothy, 2019a). Nevertheless, despite the growing significance of heritage to tourism in the region, substantial contestation remains over its conservation and recognition which, at its most extreme, can result in its deliberate destruction.

Cultural property destruction and representation in the MENA region

The destruction of cultural heritage and attacks on cultural property has been the subject of war crimes and international outcry and has received increasing international focus (Cunliffe, Muhesen, & Lostal, 2016). Cultural property has suffered and continues to suffer severe damage during the recent upheaval and armed conflicts in the Middle East and North Africa (Al Quntar, 2013). Munawar (2019, p. 157) observes, 'The targeting of cultural heritage, which has taken place during the current political instability in the Middle East and North and West Africa, has evidently had a direct impact on the collective memory and cultural identity of the nations concerned'. The escalation of the conflicts in the region since early 2011 has caused, and is still causing, dramatic human suffering. Cultural heritage destruction has become an important and irreversible collateral damage in those conflicts. Extremely rich and varied cultural heritage buildings, sites, and cities in Syria, Iraq, Yemen, and Libya are either eliminated or severely damaged to the point of devastation, e.g. the Old City of Aleppo and Nineveh (Iraq), some of which have been deliberately targeted (see Case study 1.2). The looting and trafficking of antiquities in the Middle East and North Africa has also reached unprecedented levels since the rise of ISIS, with subsequent substantial effects on the heritage values of some sites.

> **Case study 1.2 The Syrian armed conflict and its impact on the country's cultural heritage**
>
> The Arch of Triumph in Palmyra ... has been part of Syria's heritage ever since it was first constructed during the third century CE, regardless that the intention behind its construction was to commemorate a victory for the Romans who, in a later period, humiliated Palmyra's queen Zenobia when the Roman emperor Aurelian brought her back to Rome in golden chains. Today, and after the destruction of the monumental arch, it represents a permanent scar in Syrian history, a symbol of violence, and a reminder of the intolerance and brutality of Daesh (Munawar, 2019, p. 157).

Syria, home to some of the oldest and culturally rich cities and archaeological sites in the world, has witnessed damage to much of its heritage. UNITAR (United Nations Institute for Training and Research, 2014) assessed the status of 18 larger cultural heritage areas that contained the country's six World Heritage Sites: 290 locations were found to have been affected in the 2011–2014 period, of which 24 were destroyed, 104 severely damaged, and 85 moderately damaged.

The country's six World Heritage Sites have all been placed by UNESCO on the List of World Heritage in Danger, namely: the Ancient City of Damascus, the Ancient City of Bosra, the Site of Palmyra, the Ancient City of Aleppo, Crac des Chevaliers and Qal'at Salah El-Din, as well as the Ancient Villages of Northern Syria, so as to draw attention to the risks they are facing because of the situation in the country. Moreover, many sites tentatively listed by UNESCO, including the Ebla, Apamea, Dura Europos, and Mari sites, have also witnessed extensive looting. The danger listing is intended to mobilise all possible support for the safeguarding of these properties which are recognised by the international community as being of outstanding universal value for humanity as a whole (UNESCO, 2013). The World Heritage Centre, the International Council of Monuments and Sites (ICOMOS), and the International Centre for the Conservation and Restoration of Monuments (ICCROM) have reached the conclusion that, in some places, the extent of the damage is such that the outstanding universal value of these sites, a feature that is necessary for these properties to retain the special status of World Heritage, may have been permanently compromised.

Escalating violence in Syria has had devastating effects on the country's cultural heritage sites since 2011 and these sites continue to be casualties of the ongoing Syrian Civil War and have also been damaged and/or looted during the conflict (Buffenstein, 2017). The looting and destruction of cultural heritage in armed conflicts have been features of war for many decades and have received increasing international focus (Cunliffe, Muhesen, & Lostal, 2016). Cunliffe et al. (2016, p. 2) commented that:

> While cultural heritage is threatened during peacetime, the severest damage takes place during social disorder and conflict, not only resulting in the loss of something unique and irreplaceable but also psychologically affecting the communities linked to it and potentially causing increased violence.

Due to escalation of the conflicts in the region and to the significant destruction of cultural heritage in the light of rising Islamic extremism,

UNESCO has stressed the issue of post-conflict reconstruction in the Middle East context, and in the Ancient City of Aleppo in particular as part of a wider approach to post-conflict reconstruction in the Middle East. Many of the region's innumerable cultural sites are threatened, in some cases by overuse, in others by neglect, and in many simply by the pressures of economic development.

The increase in the prospects of criminal accountability for the destruction of heritage has also been a driving force in the adoption of international laws for the protection of cultural heritage. However, many have criticised the ineffectiveness of such laws for protecting the cultural properties of international value. For instance, Lostal (2015, p. 17) concluded that:

> This is especially frustrating if one takes into consideration that the driving force behind the adoption of conventional laws for the protection of cultural property has mostly been motivated by a desire to hold individuals accountable. The accountability gap shown in the case of Syria should serve those involved in the implementation of cultural heritage laws (e.g., UNESCO, the World Heritage Committee at the international level) as a warning that the 2003 UNESCO Declaration, or any other instrument before that, did not manage to have consequences for Bamiyan or beyond.

Moustafa (2016) has also argued that preserving cultural heritage in conflict zones presents a number of challenges. The level of expertise is low among those who work to preserve cultural heritage in the Middle East. However, deliberate and direct destruction of cultural heritage is by no means a new phenomenon, particularly during armed conflict. Noyes (2013, p. 1) argues that 'the destruction of religious and cultural icons has gone hand in hand with the political construction of the modern State'. Indeed, such a situation raises some extremely important points with respect to the potential reconstruction of heritage sites and the relationship to memoricide. As Munawar (2019, p. 158) cogently argues, 'the ongoing destruction of cultural heritage in Syria is writing new episodes of Syrian collective memory and how the inclusion of wartime memories in post-war heritage reconstruction could help the healing process':

> The destruction of monuments, including those considered to be material representations of a nation's identity, does not inevitably mean the end of the lifecycle of those monuments. Rebuilding cultural heritage in the aftermath of war should not be taken

> for granted, and the focus should first be on the semantics and motives of the destruction—i.e. how and why these heritage sites and monuments were built and later damaged, and what reasons lay behind the targeting of historic cities by state or non-state actors.
>
> Pursuing the same approach that was implemented to reconstruct Palmyra's Arch of Triumph as it was before the war could result in erasing a significant portion of the collective memory of wartime or ... 'political amnesia', something that could bury and/or erase specific histories for the sake of forgetting the memories of Syria's war. Establishing a just and healthy society in the aftermath of war, where displaced people will be able to live together in harmony, would require a reconstruction plan that relies mainly on public engagement and negotiating individual and collective memories so as to be inclusive in the formation of post-war Syrian heritage (Munawar, 2019, pp. 157–158).

However, it should also be noted that some cultural property destruction may be state-sanctioned, or ignored, particularly as a result of unrestrained urban development. Naccache (1998), for example, writing in the context of heritage in post-civil war Lebanon (see Sandes, 2013), writes of Beirut's 'memoricide' in terms of a mutual forgotten memory as archaeological projects that were aimed at finding common historical ground of all Lebanese (Kaufman, 2004), from all sects and ethnicities, were halted due to politics. Nevertheless, archaeology and heritage conservation and management have always been tied to advancing political (imperialist, colonialist, nationalist, racist, religious) and economic objectives (Hamilakis & Duke, 2007).

In the case of Lebanon, Heinz (2008, p. 464) notes that archaeology focused on Phoenician, Greek, and Roman history has been useful at times 'for many divergent interests. Politicians and residents used archaeology in order to create a common identity, the building industry and the Department of Tourism to attract visitors and to make money with the "visibility of the past".' Yet different interests will take different views on heritage and may not be willing to give up their view of history and identity. For example, in the case of the Beqa'a Valley in Lebanon, which is inhabited by Muslims and Maronite Christians, Heinz (2008, p. 466) notes that 'visible evidence for a community from Islamic times would be politically desirable for one group, reinforcing their identity, and be politically exploitable as a proof for the long history of Islamic history and culture in the area'. As a result, so long as archaeology and heritage management and interpretation with their specific ways of producing knowledge 'supports the locally dominant worldview, it is considered helpful.

However, where the archaeological evidence foils the political concepts of the local authorities, it runs the risk of becoming troublesome' (Heinz, 2008, p. 466). In such a context heritage management and tourism may deliberately focus on one aspect of history and ignore others. In the Beqa'a Valley:

> the desire to keep Islamic evidence visible on the site at the same time implied the impossibility of excavations of any older levels. In addition, exposing older settlements would qualify the Islamic culture as only one part in a long cultural development of various traditions and complicate the construction of local identity and its use for political purposes by one of the concerned groups. Thus, a differently interested approach to the past, the archaeological one which ideally tends not to 'favor' specific periods, runs counter to local views of the value of the past (Heinz, 2008, p. 466).

In Israel archaeology and heritage management is used to reinforce certain narratives of the Israeli state and its establishment (Bauman, 2004; Rego, 2012; Rashed, Short, & Docker, 2014; Hijazi, 2016; Jubeh, 2018), especially with respect to the state's creation and highlighting the idea that Palestine has been the land of Israel from ancient times (Okada, 2012). In both Israel and Jordan, substantial attention is given to focusing on Christian archaeology and heritage, often to the neglect or damage of other heritage because of the economic benefits that it can bring, including with respect to tourism, as well as donations, investment, and aid especially from the United States. For example, Addison (2004) noted that USAID (United States Agency for International Development) investment in road-building and tourist signage was undertaken in Jordan almost entirely for Christian sites, adding that 'the Hashemite regime in particular has worked overtime [in its relations with the West] to configure itself as a secular, Western-identified state' (Addison, 2004, p. 246). Indeed, this theme is also picked up by Abu-Khafajah, Al Rabady, and Rababeh (2015) in their examination of World Bank funding for urban heritage projects in Jordan. They argue that the World Bank approach, particularly its emphasis on conventional 'readings' of urban space that highlight universal values and histories, serves to neglect and marginalise local values and understandings and suggest that 'local sociocultural and economic contexts as assets to enrich development projects, rather than obstacles to be "fixed" and "fitted" for tourism' (Abu-Khafajah et al., 2015, p. 441; see also Abu-Khafajah & Miqdadi, 2019). Of course, marginalisation can occur not only in the conservation, development, and management of heritage sites, but also in interpretation. For example, in the cases of the City of David (Jerusalem Walls) National Park interpretive centre in Jerusalem and the Yigal Allon Center, the 'Jesus boat' museum in Ginosar, separate interpretive introductions to the heritage of the sites are available from Christian perspectives that ignore other historical identities, memories, and interpretations. The City of David site is particularly controversial, as since 1997 it:

has been run by an Israeli NGO called El-Ad (acronym for 'To the City of David' in Hebrew), making it the only national park in Israel to be operated by an organization whose aim is to promote a particular ideology. The decision to entrust the City of David to El-Ad was made contrary to the position of the Israel Antiquities Authority, namely that the site should be operated by the Israel Nature and Parks Authority (B'Tselem – The Israeli Information Center for Human Rights in the Occupied Territories, 2015).

Tourism in the MENA region

The MENA region comprises a wide range of destinations, including established and emerging destinations in the Mediterranean (e.g. Morocco, Tunisia) and the Arabian Peninsula, and high-spending outbound markets from the Gulf Cooperation Council (GCC) (UNWTO, 2019). The MENA region has vast natural, historical, and cultural resources, with an abundance of tourist sites, diverse climates, different exotic food, and hospitable hosts (Mansfeld, 1999; Bassil, 2014; Isaac, 2013; Morakabati, 2011, 2013; Seyfi & Hall, 2019; Hall & Prayag, 2020). Despite the wealth of tourism sites and resources and positive global tourism trends, the MENA region as a whole remains one of the world's least developed tourism regions (Stephenson & Al-Hamarneh, 2017; Isaac et al., 2016; Seyfi & Hall, 2018;

Table 1.7 International tourist arrivals in MENA countries, 2000–2018 (million)

Country	UNWTO region	2000	2010	2016	2017	2018
Bahrain	Middle East	0.8	1.0	4.0	4.4	–
Egypt	Middle East	5.1	14.1	5.3	8.2	11.3
Iraq	Middle East	0.1	1.5	–	–	–
Jordan	Middle East	1.6	4.2	3.6	3.8	4.1
Kuwait	Middle East	0.1	0.2	0.2	–	–
Lebanon	Middle East	0.7	2.2	1.7	1.9	2
Libya	Middle East	0.2	–	–	–	–
Oman	Middle East	0.6	1.4	2.3	2.4	–
Palestine	Middle East	0.3	0.5	0.4	0.5	0.6
Qatar	Middle East	0.4	1.7	2.9	2.3	1.8
Saudi Arabia	Middle East	6.6	10.9	18.0	16.1	15.2
Syria	Middle East	2.1	8.5	–	–	–
UAE	Middle East	3.1	7.4	14.9	15.8	15.9
Yemen	Middle East	0.1	1.0	–	–	–
Algeria	North Africa	0.9	2.1	2.0	2.5	–
Morocco	North Africa	4.3	9.3	10.3	11.3	12.3
Tunisia	North Africa	5.1	7.8	5.7	7.1	8.3
Iran	South Asia	1.3	2.9	4.9	4.8	
Turkey	Southern/Mediterranean Europe	10.4	28.6	25.3	37.6	45.7
Israel	Southern/Mediterranean Europe	2.4	2.8	2.9	3.6	4.2

Source: Compiled from data in UNWTO (2019a, 2019b); the World Bank (2020).

Table 1.8 International tourist receipts in MENA countries, 2000–2018 (million)

Country	UNWTO region	2000	2010	2015	2016	2017
Bahrain	Middle East	0.6	1.4	1.6	3.8	3.6
Egypt	Middle East	4.3	12.5	6.1	2.6	7.8
Iraq	Middle East	0.0	1.7	4.1	2.4	–
Jordan	Middle East	0.7	3.6	4.1	4.0	4.6
Kuwait	Middle East	0.1	0.3	0.5	0.6	0.3
Lebanon	Middle East	–	8.0	6.9	7.0	7.6
Libya	Middle East	0.1	0.1	–	–	–
Oman	Middle East	0.2	0.8	1.5	1.6	1.7
Palestine	Middle East	0.3	0.7	0.3	0.2	0.2
Qatar	Middle East	0.1	0.6	–	5.4	6.0
Saudi Arabia	Middle East	–	6.7	–	11.1	12.1
Syria	Middle East	1.1	6.2	–	–	–
UAE	Middle East	1.1	8.6	–	19.5	21.0
Yemen	Middle East	0.1	1.2	–	0.1	–
Algeria	North Africa	0.1	0.2	0.3	0.2	0.1
Morocco	North Africa	2.0	6.7	6.3	6.5	7.4
Tunisia	North Africa	1.7	2.6	1.4	1.2	1.3
Iran	South Asia	0.7	2.6	4.7	3.9	4.8
Turkey	Southern/Mediterranean Europe	7.6	26.3	35.5	26.7	31.8
Israel	Southern/Mediterranean Europe	4.6	5.6	6.5	6.6	7.6

Source: Compiled from data in UNWTO (2019a, 2019b); the World Bank (2020).

Timothy, 2019a), and the region has generally failed to capitalise on its resources to reap the benefits of international tourism. The region's share of international visitor arrivals therefore remains one of the lowest in the world, estimated at about only 6 per cent (UNWTO, 2019). For instance, the MENA region welcomed 87 million international tourist arrivals in 2018 (Table 1.7), equivalent to 6 per cent of the world's total arrivals, and the region earned USD 77 billion in international tourism receipts in 2017 (Table 1.8), an estimated 6 per cent of the world's receipts (UNWTO, 2019). As a result, tourism is emerging as a major economic pillar in many MENA countries and is regarded as an alternative to entirely energy-based economies and as a means of diversification (Daher, 2007). Accordingly, it has been put at the core of the long-term development vision of the countries in the region (e.g. Saudi Arabia's Vision 2030, Iran's 20 Year National Vision, Oman's clustering system to 2040, or Sharjah's Tourism Vision 2021 for the United Arab Emirates) and is increasingly becoming integral to notions of regional competitiveness (Table 1.9).

The region also attracts significant numbers of corporate travellers with its vast financial and corporate growth opportunities, and estimates show that the influx to the region is expected to continue to increase to reach over 150 million tourists by 2030, with an increase from the current 6 per cent to

Table 1.9 The travel and tourism competitiveness of MENA countries in 2019

Country	Global rank*	Natural resources	Cultural resources and business travel
Bahrain	64	140	113
Egypt	65	69	22
Iraq	–	–	–
Jordan	84	119	101
Kuwait	96	137	127
Lebanon	100	130	93
Libya	–	–	–
Oman	58	108	54
Palestine	–	–	–
Qatar	51	136	92
Saudi Arabia	69	133	58
Syria	–	–	–
UAE	33	103	45
Yemen	140	135	109
Algeria	116	126	51
Morocco	66	63	47
Tunisia	85	90	90
Iran	89	99	33
Turkey	43	77	17
Israel	57	111	64

Source: Compiled from data in World Economic Forum, 2019.

Notes
* Among 140 countries.

8 per cent of all global tourists (UNWTO, 2019). Cultural heritage is still the major reason for travel to the region; however, leisure travel to countries in the region, such as the UAE, reflects the growing significance of leisure-oriented destinations and the development of intercontinental transport hubs. According to the UNWTO (2019), improved political stability and security measures, market and product diversification, visa facilitation policies, lifting of travel restrictions, new routes and air capacity enhancement, expansion in accommodation, and marketing and promotion in key source markets are some of the factors that have helped MENA tourism to perform positively.

The MENA region – a turbulent legacy

Despite positive tourism growth, geopolitical tensions, instability, conflict, and religious extremism and military interventions will undoubtedly prove critical for future tourism development. Since the early twentieth century, the turbulent political climate of the MENA region has led to a negative image of the region in many potential markets in which it has been principally portrayed as a theatre of war (Hazbun, 2004, 2006; Morakabati, 2011, 2013; Cohen &

Cohen, 2015; Isaac et al., 2016; Seyfi & Hall, 2018, 2020a). Events such as the 1947–1949 Palestine war (known also as the War of Independence in Israel and al-Nakba or the Catastrophe in Palestine) and the subsequent Arab–Israeli wars have created political tensions, military conflicts, and disputes between the Arab countries and Israel (Seyfi & Hall, 2020a).

During the Cold War, major oil discoveries in the Persian Gulf and the growing demand at international level made the region an economically significant geostrategic area. Perhaps a major consequence of this oil discovery was the overthrow of a democratically elected Iranian Prime Minister Mohammad Mossadegh in a coup orchestrated by the CIA and British intelligence in 1953 following his aim to nationalise Iran's oil industry (Goldsmith, 2005; Israeli, 2013). The Six-Day War (also known as the Third Arab–Israeli War) in 1967 between Israel and the neighbouring states of Egypt, Jordan, and Syria also contributed to the displacement of civilian populations, and had long-term consequences for the region in general and for its tourism industry in particular (Gharaibeh, 1985; Isaac et al., 2016). The Arab Spring and the subsequent political transitions in the region, along with the more recent civil wars in the region and the competition between the major powers in the region, have created fertile ground for further violence, especially given that many of the underlying issues that led to the Arab Spring have yet to be significantly addressed (Campante & Chor, 2012; Malik & Awadallah, 2013). This has hindered political and economic development and has meant that the region has some of the lowest levels of intra-regional trade and political cooperation in the world in spite of its relative close cultural and historical ties. This long history of political instability along with ongoing security events and crises has negatively affected the development of tourism in the Middle East and has presented significant challenges to the inbound flows of international tourists to the region and, more importantly, the cultural heritage in the region (Avraham, 2015; Tomazos, 2017).

Case study 1.3 Cultural heritage and conflict in the Western Sahara

Located on the north-western coast of Africa, between Mauritania and Morocco, the Western Sahara (formerly known as the Spanish Sahara), has been the subject of a territorial conflict between Morocco (which occupies some 80 per cent of the territory) and the indigenous Polisario Front (the independence movement of Western Sahara forming the Sahrawi Arab Democratic Republic (SADR) – which is composed largely of the indigenous nomadic inhabitants, the Sahrawis) backed by Algeria (which administers the remainder of the territory known as the 'Free Zone' or 'Liberated Territories' from the Saharawi refugee camps in southwestern Algeria) since the withdrawal of Spain (the colonial power) in 1975. Western Sahara, and its indigenous Berber ethnic group, has been described as the 'last colony in Africa', and its situation has often been compared with that of East Timor before the latter's recent independence from Indonesia (Brooks, 2005).

The former Spanish colony is one of the most sparsely populated territories in the world, mainly consisting of desert flatlands although it is also home to significant phosphate and iron ore reserves and is believed to have untouched offshore oil deposits (Gaffey, 2016). The region depends mostly on pastoral nomadism, fishing, and phosphate mining as the principal sources of income for the population, while incomes and standards of living in Western Sahara are substantially below the Moroccan level. Nevertheless, over the last years, there is some evidence that tourism is providing modest additional income for locals (Brooks, 2005; Bhatia, 2001) with much of this tourism focused on archaeological sites. The Sahara embodies an immensely rich natural and cultural heritage, both prehistoric and living, much of which has been recognised as warranting UNESCO World Heritage status (Keenan, 2005). Archaeology is believed to be an economic resource for Sahara in the long term (Brooks, 2005) and the Polisario have encouraged archaeological research in the Free Zone to be undertaken by the international research community. Brooks (2005, p. 174) commented that: 'A greater appreciation and more detailed understanding of the archaeology within the Saharawi community, and care stewardship of the region's cultural heritage, thus has some very tangible benefits'.

Given the ongoing political and territorial conflict with Morocco and the security situation in neighbouring Algeria, archaeology is believed to be less vulnerable as it addresses issues of cultural identity and sheds light on the history of human occupation in the region. Because of its political past and isolated desert location, this disputed area of the Sahara is mainly attractive for more adventurous tourism markets. Against the long-running background of international contention over the governance of Sahara, more recently there have been some efforts to develop the occupied territory into a tourist destination, and a small group of pioneering expatriates are developing eco-aware and low-impact tours exploring the lagoon, rocky landscape, and surrounding desert in the SADR-controlled areas (Le Monde, 2019; Lonely Planet, 2017). However, given that the vast majority of Western Sahara is administered by Morocco, independent travel in the region is restricted and Western countries have warned their citizens about travelling to this disputed area (Minvielle & Minvielle, 2010; Le Monde, 2019).

Introduction 25

Structure of the book

This book consists of 14 chapters that examine a number of significant themes surrounding cultural heritage tourism in the MENA region. Chapters 2 and 3 provide a broad overview of some of the religious heritage issues in the region. Timothy (Chapter 2) examines the multi-faith heritage of the region, while Olsen and Emmett (Chapter 3) detail some of the ways in which religious heritage has become a source of contestation.

Issues of contestation over representations of heritage, both religious and secular, is a recurring theme in a number of chapters. Chapter 4 by Tataroglu discusses how the Safranbolu World Heritage Site has been used to present certain interpretations of Turkish national identity and political narrative, a theme also taken up in more touristic terms in Chapter 9 by Rıza Manci on Göbekli Tepe, Sanliurfa, Turkey. Chapter 5 by Dhaher, Seyfi, and Hall also details how cultural heritage in Tunisia is increasingly commoditised to serve tourism as well as national narratives, although they note that local opposition to such narratives provides opportunities for the formation of new relationships with heritage and identity. Adie (Chapter 6) focuses on the use of heritage as a tourist attraction in post-colonial Morocco and the disconnect that can occur between tourist and local interpretations of heritage and its significance. Ram (Chapter 7) also examines differences between official and local narratives and understanding of heritage in Ashkelon in Israel. However, here the official heritage narratives of the national park stand in stark contrast to that of local users who see the park more as somewhere to have a picnic and barbeque.

Chapters 8 to 11 look at heritage more as a tourism resource. Chapter 8 by Isaac focuses on how cultural heritage is an important source of tourism income as well as national identity. Chapter 9 also notes the significance of identity, but here Thani and Heenan note how the commodified theme park Arabism of the UAE has been primarily undertaken to attract the Western tourist and convey certain narratives of national identity, a theme also raised in earlier chapters in the book. The potential lack of inclusion of such an approach is also touched on in Chapter 11 in which Helmy highlights the integrated cultural planning approach in Egypt as a means to respond to the economic impacts of the Arab Spring on Egyptian tourism. While the Egyptian strategy has been developed to try and boost employment and economic growth, whether the heritage of Ancient Egypt is relevant to many present-day Egyptians potentially remains a moot point.

The final series of chapters deal with further emerging issues in cultural heritage tourism in the region. Chapter 12 by Bardia Shabani Hazel Tucker, and Amin Nazifi continues some of the themes of earlier chapters in terms of the nexus between local, national, and international understandings, and uses of heritage in the case of the Gonbad-e Qābus Brick Tower World Heritage Site in Iran. Chapter 13 by Rasoolimanesh, Taheri, Gannon, and Ataeishad discuss issues of gender in heritage tourism, while Fitchett and Roshan look at the emerging threat of climate change and its effects on heritage sites in Iran given temperature increases at peak visitation times. The final chapter by Hall and Seyfi (Chapter 14) discusses emerging research issues.

Conclusion

The MENA region is one of the most significant areas for cultural heritage in the world, especially in the context of the Abrahamic religions and Western and Islamic civilisation. Tourism in the region has long been driven by its cultural heritage resources. However, tourism is also increasingly problematic in the way it is serving to commoditise heritage and reinforce certain narrow narratives of identity, history, and place. Indeed, the chapters in this book serve to reinforce Hammond's (2019) observation that cultural heritage in the Middle East provides two key insights with much broader relevance:

> First, examining how heritage is made (and unmade) shows one way that regions are constructed through the articulation of material and symbolic connections. Second, these regions might be better understood not as containers but as complexes in and in relation to which people articulate and communicate shared meanings.

Significantly, the chapters in this book also highlight the incredibly dynamic nature of heritage in the MENA countries. This is not just as a result of the way in which heritage has been deliberately destroyed, thereby creating new layers of meaning on the past, but also how heritage and its interpretation is multilayered with different levels of attachment and understanding depending on the nature of the relationship between viewer/commodifier and the heritage resource. Such concerns are especially important given the way that heritage is commonly used in the region to service national political, economic, and religious agendas. Nevertheless, this process of heritage-making demonstrates how heritage is in a constant process of transformation which, positively, may potentially contribute to rebuilding identities in the aftermath of war and political violence (Munawar, 2019), as well as, when undertaken appropriately, return positive economic and social benefits from cultural heritage tourism. It is with such a hope that we commend the various chapters in this book.

References

Abu-Khafajah, S., Al Rabady, R., & Rababeh, S. (2015). Urban heritage 'space' under neoliberal development: A tale of a Jordanian plaza. *International Journal of Heritage Studies, 21*(5), 441–459.

Abu-Khafajah, S., & Miqdadi, R. (2019). Prejudice, military intelligence, and neoliberalism: Examining the local within archaeology and heritage practices in Jordan. *Contemporary Levant, 4*(2), 92–106.

Addison, E. (2004). The roads to ruins: Accessing Islamic heritage in Jordan. In Y. Rowan & U. Baram (eds), *Marketing heritage: Archaeology and the consumption of the past* (pp. 229–248). Walnut Creek, CA: Rowman Altamira.

Adie, B. A. (2019). *World Heritage and tourism: Marketing and management.* Abingdon: Routledge.

Adie, B. A., & Hall, C. M. (2017). Who visits World Heritage? A comparative analysis of three cultural sites. *Journal of Heritage Tourism, 12*(1), 67–80.

Adie, B. A., Hall, C. M., & Prayag, G. (2018). World Heritage as a placebo brand: A comparative analysis of three sites and marketing implications. *Journal of Sustainable Tourism, 26*(3), 399–415.

Almeida-García, F. (2018). Analysis of tourism policy in a developing country: The case of Morocco. *Journal of Policy Research in Tourism, Leisure and Events, 10*(1), 48–68.

Almuhrzi, H., Alriyami, H., & Scott, N. (eds) (2017) *Tourism in the Arab World: An industry perspective.* Bristol: Channel View Publications.

Al-Mulali, U. (2011). Oil consumption, CO_2 emission and economic growth in MENA countries. *Energy, 36*(10), 6165–6171.

Al-Oun, S., & Al-Homoud, M. (2008). The potential for developing community-based tourism among the Bedouins in the Badia of Jordan. *Journal of Heritage Tourism, 3*(1), 36–54.

Al Quntar, S. (2013). Syrian cultural property in the crossfire: Reality and effectiveness of protection efforts. *Journal of Eastern Mediterranean Archaeology & Heritage Studies, 1*(4), 348–351.

Amanat, A. (2012). *Is there a Middle East? The evolution of a geopolitical concept.* Stanford: Stanford University Press.

Aras, B., & Yorulmazlar, E. (2016). State, region and order: Geopolitics of the Arab Spring. *Third World Quarterly, 37*(12), 2259–2273.

Avraham, E. (2015). Destination image repair during crisis: Attracting tourism during the Arab Spring uprisings. *Tourism Management, 47*, 224–232.

Bassil, C. (2014). The effect of terrorism on tourism demand in the Middle East. *Peace Economics, Peace Science and Public Policy, 20*(4), 669–684.

Bauman, J. (2004). Tourism, the ideology of design and the nationalized past in Zippori/Sepphoris, an Israeli national park. In Y. Rowan & U. Baram (eds), *Marketing heritage: Archaeology and the consumption of the past* (pp. 205–228). Walnut Creek, CA: Rowman Altamira.

Beaumont, P., & Proctor, K. (2020). Doubts raised over workability of Trump's Middle East peace plan. *The Guardian*, 29 January. Retrieved from https://www.theguardian.com/world/2020/jan/29/middle-east-analysts-question-workability-of-trump-peace-plan.

Berriane, M. (2009). *Tourisme des nationaux, tourisme des étrangers : Quelles articulations en Méditerraneé? [Tourism for nationals, tourism for foreigners: Which articulations in the Mediterranean?]* Rabat: Université Mohamed V, Faculté des Lettres et des Sciences Humaines.

Bhatia, M. (2001). The Western Sahara under Polisario control. *Review of African Political Economy, 28*(88), 291–298.

Bilali, B. (2016). Tourism: Morocco keeps its vision 2020 plan in sight. *Morocco World News.* Retrieved from https://www.moroccoworldnews.com/2016/09/197454/tourism-morocco-keeps-its-vision-2020-plan-in-sight/.

Bilgin, P. (2019). *Regional security in the Middle East: A critical perspective*, 2nd edn. Abingdon: Routledge.

Bourdeau, L., Gravari-Barbas, M., & Robinson, M. (eds) (2016). *World Heritage Sites and tourism: Global and local relations*. Abingdon: Routledge.

Bouzahzah, M., & El Menyari, Y. (2013). International tourism and economic growth: The case of Morocco and Tunisia. *The Journal of North African Studies, 18*(4), 592–607.

Brooks, N. (2005). Cultural heritage and conflict: The threatened archaeology of Western Sahara. *The Journal of North African Studies, 10*(3–4), 413–439.

B'Tselem – The Israeli Information Center for Human Rights in the Occupied Territories (2015). *Jerusalem Walls National Park*. Retrieved from https://www.btselem.org/jerusalem/national_parks_jerusalem_walls.

Buffenstein, A. (2017). A monumental loss: Here are the most significant cultural heritage sites that ISIS has destroyed to date. *Artnet news*. Retrieved from https://news.artnet.com/art-world/isis-cultural-heritage-sites-destroyed-950060.

Campante, F. R., & Chor, D. (2012). Why was the Arab World poised for revolution? Schooling, economic opportunities, and the Arab Spring. *Journal of Economic Perspectives, 26*(2), 167–188.

Campos, M. U. (2014). Between others and brothers. *International Journal of Middle East Studies, 46*(3), 585–588.

Cohen, E., & Cohen, S. A. (2015). A mobilities approach to tourism from emerging world regions. *Current Issues in Tourism, 18*(1), 11–43.

Cordesman, A. H. (1999). Geopolitics and energy in the Middle East. *Center for Strategic and International Studies*.

Culcasi, K. (2010). Constructing and naturalizing the Middle East. *Geographical Review, 100*(4), 583–597.

Culcasi, K. (2012). Mapping the Middle East from within: (Counter-)cartographies of an imperialist construction. *Antipode, 44*(4), 1099–1118.

Cunliffe, E., Muhesen, N., & Lostal, M. (2016). The destruction of cultural property in the Syrian conflict: Legal implications and obligations. *International Journal of Cultural Property, 23*(1), 1–31.

Daher, R. F. (2005). Urban regeneration/heritage tourism endeavours: The case of Salt, Jordan 'Local actors, international donors, and the state'. *International Journal of Heritage Studies, 11*(4), 289–308.

Daher, R. F. (ed.) (2007). *Tourism in the Middle East: Continuity, change and transformation*. Clevedon: Channel View Press.

Dalacoura, K. (2012). The 2011 uprisings in the Arab Middle East: Political change and geopolitical implications. *International Affairs, 88*(1), 63–79.

Dudley, D. (2018). Qatar's tourism chief accuses neighboring countries of 'weaponizing' tourism. *Forbes*, 15 October. Retrieved from https://www.forbes.com/sites/dominicdudley/2018/10/15/qatar-tourism-weaponizing-tourism/#6df44da8b6e0.

Evered, K. T. (2017). Beyond Mahan and Mackinder: Situating geography and critical geopolitics in Middle East studies. *International Journal of Middle East Studies, 49*(2), 335–339.

Gaffey, C. (2016). Western Sahara: What is the 40-year dispute all about? *Newsweek*. Retrieved from https://www.newsweek.com/western-sahara-morocco-algeria-polisario-front-435170.

Gharaibeh, F. A. (1985). *The economies of the West Bank and Gaza Strip*. Boulder, CO: Westview Press.

Goldsmith, D. (2005). Confronting threats before they materialize: The United States and the overthrow of the Iranian government. *McGill Journal of Middle East Studies*, *8*, 81–99.

Green, N. (2014). Rethinking the 'Middle East' after the Oceanic turn. *Comparative Studies of South Asia, Africa and the Middle East*, *34*(3), 556–564.

Guzansky, Y., & Shapiro, D. B. (2019). Friends with caveats: Will Israel and the Gulf States form a united front against Iran? *Foreign Affairs*, 5 August. Retrieved from https://www.foreignaffairs.com/articles/israel/2019-08-05/friends-caveats.

Hall, C. M., & Prayag, G. (Eds.), (2020). *The Routledge handbook of Halal hospitality and Islamic tourism*. Abingdon: Routledge.

Hamilakis, Y., & Duke, P. (Eds.). (2007). *Archaeology and capitalism: From ethics to politics*. Walnut Creek, CA: Left Coast Press.

Hammond, T. (2019). Heritage and the Middle East: Cities, power, and memory. *Geography Compass*, https://doi.org/10.1111/gec3.12477.

Hazbun, W. (2004). Globalisation, reterritorialisation and the political economy of tourism development in the Middle East. *Geopolitics*, *9*(2), 310–341.

Hazbun, W. (2006). Explaining the Arab Middle East tourism paradox. *The Arab World Geographer*, *9*(3), 201–214.

Heinz, M. (2008). Archaeological research in conflict areas: Practice and responsibilities. *Archaeologies*, *4*(3), 460–470.

Hijazi, A. (2016). Toward spacio-cide: Building the Museum of Tolerance over the Mamilla Cemetery in Jerusalem. *Jerusalem Quarterly*, *67*, 97–109.

Hillali, M. (2007a). Du tourisme et de la géopolitique au Maghreb : le cas du Maroc [Tourism and geopolitics in the Maghreb: The case of Morocco], *Hérodote*, *4*, 47–63.

Hillali, M. (2007b). *La politique du tourisme au Maroc : diagnostic, bilan et critique [Tourism policy in Morocco: Diagnosis, assessment and criticism]*. Paris: Harmattan.

Hosni, E. (2000). *Strategy for sustainable tourism development in the Sahara*. Paris: UNESCO.

Hubbard, B. (2020). Iran admits firing 2 missiles at jet and says it's studying effect. *New York Times*, 21 January. Retrieved from https://www.nytimes.com/2020/01/21/world/middleeast/iran-plane-crash-missiles.html.

International Monetary Fund (2019). *Regional economic outlook: Middle East and Central Asia*. Retrieved from https://www.imf.org/en/Publications/REO/MECA/Issues/2019/10/19/reo-menap-cca-1019.

Isaac, R. K., Hall, C. M., & Higgins-Desbiolles, F. (eds) (2016). *The politics and power of tourism in Palestine*. Abingdon: Routledge.

Isaac, R. K. (2013). Palestine: Tourism under occupation. In R. Butler & S. Wantanee (eds), *Tourism and war* (pp. 143–158). London: Routledge.

Israeli, O. (2013). The circuitous mature of Operation Ajax. *Middle Eastern Studies*, *49*(2), 246–262.

Issa, I. A., & Altinay, L. (2006). Impacts of political instability on tourism planning and development: The case of Lebanon. *Tourism Economics*, *12*(3), 361–381.

Jacobs, J. (2010). Re-branding the Levant: Contested heritage and colonial modernities in Amman and Damascus. *Journal of Tourism and Cultural Change*, *8*(4), 316–326.

Jubeh, N. (2018). The Bab al-Rahmah Cemetery: Israeli encroachment continues unabated. *Journal of Palestine Studies*, *48*(1), 88–103.

Kasraoui, S. (2019). Morocco remains main destination for French tourists. *Morocco World News*. Retrieved from https://www.moroccoworldnews.com/2019/10/283957/morocco-main-destination-french-tourists/.

Kaufman, A. (2004). *Reviving Phoenicia. The search for identity in Lebanon*. London: I.B. Tauris.

Kausch, K. (2015). Competitive multipolarity in the Middle East. *The International Spectator, 50*(3), 1–15.

Keenan, J. (2005). Looting the Sahara: The material, intellectual and social implications of the destruction of cultural heritage (Briefing). *The Journal of North African Studies, 10*(3–4), 471–489.

Keenan, J. (ed.) (2013). *The Sahara: Past, present and future*. Abingdon: Routledge.

Khatib, H. (2014). Oil and natural gas prospects: Middle East and North Africa. *Energy Policy, 64*, 71–77.

Khirfan, L. (2014). *World Heritage, urban design and tourism: Three cities in the Middle East*. Farnham: Ashgate.

Koppes, C. R. (1976). Captain Mahan, General Gordon and the origin of the term 'Middle East'. *Middle East Studies, 12*, 95–98.

Ladki, S. M., & Dah, A. (1997). Challenges facing post-war tourism development: The case of Lebanon. *Journal of International Hospitality, Leisure & Tourism Management, 1*(2), 35–43.

Ladki, S. M., & Sadik, M. W. (2004). Factors affecting the advancement of the Lebanese tourism industry. *Journal of Transnational Management Development, 9*(2–3), 171–185.

Lak, A., Gheitasi, M., & Timothy, D. J. (2019). Urban regeneration through heritage tourism: Cultural policies and strategic management. *Journal of Tourism and Cultural Change*. Retrieved from https://doi.org/10.1080/14766825.2019.1668002.

Le Monde (2019). Sahara occidental: Dakhla, du poste militaire au spot de kitesurf [Western Sahara: Dakhla, from military post to kitesurf spot]. Retrieved from https://www.lemonde.fr/afrique/article/2019/11/14/sahara-occidental-dakhla-du-poste-militaire-au-spot-de-kitesurf_6019124_3212.html.

Lonely Planet (2017). *Lonely Planet Morocco travel guide*. Melbourne: Lonely Planet Publications.

Lostal, M. (2015). Syria's world cultural heritage and individual criminal responsibility. *International Review of Law, 2015*(1), 3.

Madden, D. (2018). Saudi Arabia signals tourism intent with release of leisure tourist visas. *Forbes*. Retrieved from https://www.forbes.com/sites/duncanmadden/2018/02/28/saudi-arabia-signals-tourism-intent-with-release-of-leisure-tourist-visas/#6b3ed8b32065.

Makhzoumi, J. (2016). From urban beautification to a holistic approach:Tthe discourses of 'landscape' in the Arab Middle East. *Landscape Research, 41*(4), 461–470.

Malik, A., & Awadallah, B. (2013). The economics of the Arab Spring. *World Development, 45*, 296–313.

Malmvig, H. (2014). Power, identity and securitization in Middle East: Regional order after the Arab uprisings. *Mediterranean Politics, 19*(1), 145–148.

Mansfeld, Y. (1999). Cycles of war, terror, and peace: Determinants and management of crisis and recovery of the Israeli tourism industry. *Journal of Travel Research, 38*(1), 30–36.

Mills, A. (2012). Critical place studies and Middle East histories: Power, politics, and social change. *History Compass*, *10*(10), 778–788.
Ministry of Economy and Finance (2016). *Economie creative : Panorama et potential* [Creative economy: Overview and potential]. Retrieved from https://www.racines.ma/sites/default/files/Economie%20creative-%20panorama%20et%20potentiel.pdf.
Ministry of Tourism, Air Transport, Handicrafts and Social Economy (2018). Vision 2020. Retrieved from https://www.tourisme.gov.ma/en/actualites/tourism-sector-governments-agenda-0.
Minvielle, J. P., & Minvielle, N. (2010). Le tourisme au Sahara : pratiques et responsabilités des acteurs [Tourism in the Sahara: practices and responsibilities of stakeholders], *Management Avenir*, *3*, 187–203.
Morakabati, Y. (2013). Tourism in the Middle East: Conflicts, crises and economic diversification, some critical issues. *International Journal of Tourism Research*, *15*(4), 375–387.
Morakabati, Y. (2011). Deterrents to tourism development in Iran. *International Journal of Tourism Research*, *13*(2), 103–123.
Moudoud, B., & Ezaïdi, A. (2005). Le tourisme national au Maroc : opportunités et limites de développement [National tourism in Morocco: Opportunities and limits of development], *Téoros. Revue de recherche en tourisme*, *24-1*, 25–30.
Moustafa, L. H. (2016). Cultural heritage and preservation: Lessons from World War II and the contemporary conflict in the Middle East. *The American Archivist*, *79*(2), 320–338.
Munawar, N. A. (2019). Competing heritage: Curating the post-conflict heritage of Roman Syria. *Bulletin of the Institute of Classical Studies*, *62*(1), 142–165.
Naccache, A. F. H. (1998). Beirut's memorycide: Hear no evil, see no evil. In L. Meskell (ed.), *Archaeology Under Fire: Nationalism, politics and heritage in the Eastern Mediterranean and Middle East* (pp. 140–158). London: Routledge.
Noyes, J. (2013). *The politics of iconoclasm: Religion, violence and the culture of image-breaking in Christianity and Islam*. New York: I.B. Taurus.
Observatoire du tourisme Maroc (2014). Étude portant sur le suivi de la demande touristique 2014 [Tourism Demand Tracking Study 2014]. Retrieved from http://www.observatoiredutourisme.ma/wp-content/uploads/2015/10/Etude-sur-la-demande-touristique-2014.pdf.
Okada, M. (2012). The preservation and exhibition of Christian church sites in Israel. *Orient*, *47*, 147–168.
Organisation of Islamic Cooperation (OIC) (2017). *International tourism in the OIC countries: Prospects and challenges 2017*. Ankara: The Statistical, Economic and Social Research and Training Centre for Islamic Countries (SESRIC).
O'Sullivan, A., Rey, M. E., & Mendez, J. G. (2011). Opportunities and challenges in the MENA region. In OECD, *Arab world competitiveness report, 2012* (pp. 42–67). Paris: OECD. Retrieved from http://www.oecd.org/mena/49036903.pdf.
Özkan, H. (2018). Remembering Zingal: State, citizens, and forests in Turkey. *International Journal of Middle East Studies*, *50*(3), 493–511.
Ram, Y., & Hall, C.M. (2020). The camp not taken: Analysis of preferences and barriers among frequent, occasional and non-campers. *Leisure Sciences*. Retrieved from https://doi.org/10.1080/01490400.2020.1731885.
Rashed, D. (2019). Geography, resources and the geopolitics of Middle East conflicts. *E-International Relations*. Retrieved from https://www.e-ir.info/pdf/78744.

Rashed, H., Short, D., & Docker, J. (2014). Nakba memoricide: Genocide studies and the Zionist/Israeli genocide of Palestine. *Holy Land Studies, 13*(1), 1–23.

Rego, N. (2012). Israel, 1948 and memoricide: The 1948 Al-'Araqib/Negev massacre and its legacy. *Holy Land Studies, 11*(2), 205–215.

Reuters (2017). Qatar tourism sector starts to feel squeeze of blockade. *Middle East Eye*, 27 June. Retrieved from https://www.middleeasteye.net/news/qatar-tourism-sector-starts-feel-squeeze-blockade.

Richards, G. (2018). Cultural tourism: A review of recent research and trends. *Journal of Hospitality and Tourism Management, 36*, 12–21.

Rowbotham, J. (2010). 'Sand and Foam': The changing identity of Lebanese tourism. *Journal of Tourism History, 2*(1), 39–53.

Salloukh, B. F. (2013). The Arab uprisings and the geopolitics of the Middle East. *The International Spectator, 48*(2), 32–46.

Samuels, K. L. (2009). Trajectories of development: International heritage management of archaeology in the Middle East and North Africa. *Archaeologies, 5*(1), 68–91.

Sandes, C. A. (2013). Urban cultural heritage and armed conflict: The case of Beirut Central District. In J. Kila & J. Zeidler (eds), *Cultural heritage in the crosshairs: Protecting cultural property during conflict* (pp. 287–313). Leiden: Brill.

Saudi Commission for Tourism and National Heritage (SCTH) (2018a). *National tourism development project in the Kingdom of Saudi Arabia*. Retrieved from https://scth.gov.sa/en/AboutSCTA/Documents/GENERALSTRATEGY.pdf.

Saudi Commission for Tourism and National Heritage (SCTH) (2018b). *Tourism investment in Saudi Arabia*. Retrieved from https://scth.gov.sa/en/TourismInvestment/SupportTourismInvestment/Documents/Touristic_investment_eng.pdf.

Selmi, R., & Bouoiyour, J. (2019). Arab geopolitics in turmoil: Implications of Qatar-Gulf crisis for business. *International Economics*. Retrieved from https://doi.org/10.1016/j.inteco.2019.11.007.

Seyfi, S., & Hall, C. M. (eds) (2018). *Tourism in Iran: Challenges, development and issues*. Abingdon: Routledge.

Seyfi, S., & Hall, C. M. (2019). Deciphering Islamic theocracy and tourism: Conceptualization, context, and complexities. *International Journal of Tourism Research, 21*(6), 735–746.

Seyfi, S., & Hall, C. M. (2020a). Political transition, transition events, and regime change in a tourism destination. *International Journal of Tourism Research*, in press.

Seyfi, S., & Hall, C. M. (2020b). *Tourism, sanctions and boycotts*. Abingdon: Routledge.

Shackley, M. (1998). A golden calf in sacred space? The future of St Katherine's monastery, Mount Sinai (Egypt). *International Journal of Heritage Studies, 4*(3–4), 124–134.

Sidaway, J. D. (1994). Geopolitics, geography, and 'terrorism' in the Middle East. *Environment and Planning D: Society and Space, 12*(3), 357–372.

Steiner, C. (2010). From heritage to hyper-reality? Tourism destination development in the Middle East between Petra and the Palm. *Journal of Tourism and Cultural Change, 8*(4), 240–253.

Stephenson, M. L., & Al-Hamarneh, A. (eds) (2017). *International tourism development and the Gulf Cooperation Council States: Challenges and opportunities*. London: Taylor & Francis.

Tang, C. F., & Abosedra, S. (2014). The impacts of tourism, energy consumption and political instability on economic growth in the MENA countries. *Energy Policy, 68*, 458–464.

Timothy, D. (2019a). *Routledge handbook on tourism in the Middle East and North Africa*. Abingdon: Routledge.

Timothy, D. (2019b). Understanding the Middle East and North Africa. In D. J. Timothy (ed.), *Routledge handbook on tourism in the Middle East and North Africa*. Abingdon: Routledge.

Timothy, D. J., & Boyd, S. W. (2015). *Tourism and trails: Cultural, ecological and management issues*. Bristol: Channel View Publications.

Tomazos, K. (2017). Egypt's tourism industry and the Arab Spring. In R. Butler & W. Suntikul (eds), *Tourism and political change* (pp. 214–229). Oxford: Goodfellow.

United Nations Development Programme (UNDP) (2019). *Human Development Report 2019. Beyond income, beyond averages, beyond today: Inequalities in human development in the 21st century*. New York: UNDP.

UNESCO (2013). Syria's six World Heritage Sites placed on list of World Heritage in danger. Retrieved from https://en.unesco.org/news/syria%E2%80%99s-six-world-heritage-sites-placed-list-world-heritage-danger.

UNESCO (2015). *Practices and know-how concerning the argan tree*. Retrieved from https://ich.unesco.org/fr/RL/largan-pratiques-et-savoir-faire-lies-a-larganier-00955.

UNESCO (2019). *Morocco*. Retrieved from https://whc.unesco.org/en/statesparties/ma.

UNESCO (2020). *World Heritage List*. Retrieved from https://whc.unesco.org/en/list/.

United Nations Institute for Training and Research (UNITAR). (2014). *Satellite-based damage assessment to cultural heritage sites in Syria*. Geneva: Author.

UN World Population (2019). *World population prospects 2019*. UN Department of Economic and Social Affairs Population Dynamics. Retrieved from https://population.un.org/wpp/.

UNWTO (2019a). *Tourism in the MENA region*. Retrieved from https://www.e-unwto.org/doi/pdf/10.18111/9789284420896.

UNWTO (2019b). *International Tourism Highlights 2019 Edition*. Retrieved from https://www.e-unwto.org/doi/pdf/10.18111/9789284421152.

World Bank (2020). *World Bank national accounts data, and OECD National Accounts data files*. Retrieved from https://databank.worldbank.org/home.aspx.

World Economic Forum (2019). *The Travel & Tourism Competitiveness Report 2019*. Retrieved from http://www3.weforum.org/docs/WEF_TTCR_2019.pdf.

World Travel & Tourism Council (WTTC) (2019). *Travel & tourism economic impact 2018 Morocco*. Retrieved from https://www.wttc.org/Morocco.

Wright, W. C., & Eppink, F. V. (2016). Drivers of heritage value: a meta-analysis of monetary valuation studies of cultural heritage. *Ecological Economics, 130*, 277–284.

Youngstedt, S. (2003). Tourism in Morocco: opportunities, challenges, and threats. *Africa Insight, 33*(1/2), 61–68.

Zamani-Farahani, H., & Eid, R. (2016). Muslim world: a study of tourism & pilgrimage among OIC Member States. *Tourism Management Perspectives, 19*, 144–149.

Zandieh, M., & Seifpour, Z. (2020). Preserving traditional marketplaces as places of intangible heritage for tourism. *Journal of Heritage Tourism, 15*(1), 111–121.

2 Tourism and the multi-faith heritage of the Middle East and North Africa

A resource perspective

Dallen J. Timothy

Introduction

The Middle East is the cradle of the three major Abrahamic religions – Islam, Judaism, and Christianity – and the cultural hearth for several other faiths, and esoteric sects and denominations. As a result, the Middle East and North Africa (MENA) abounds in tangible features of the religious landscape, including mosques, churches, temples, synagogues, shrines, battlefields, tombs, and various other manifestations of religious heritage. Intangible culture is equally pervasive, including daily prayers, scripture recitations, pilgrimages, rituals and ceremonies, music, scents and tastes, and poetry. Religion itself is a salient manifestation of culture and everything associated with it forms the foundations of much heritage tourism.

The buildings and structures, beliefs, rites and rituals, gardens and vineyards, celebrations and festivities, sacred spaces, traditions and folklore, food and drink, pilgrimage routes, and veneration of the divine are core elements of the cultural heritage of religion and play a crucial role in attracting people to MENA and stimulating intra-regional travel. Perhaps more than anywhere else in the world, these tangible and intangible manifestations of faith underscore much of the region's heritage tourism product. This chapter examines these elements in the context of heritage tourism in MENA. It looks at different faith traditions, describes various types of religious tourism, and assesses the relationships between tourism and many aspects of religious heritage from a largely supply perspective by providing a typology of religious assets that dominate the heritagescapes of the region.

The religions of MENA

Although some religions are older than the Abrahamic faiths, Judaism, Christianity, and Islam have ancient origins and were born from the harsh physical realities and complex ethno-faith systems of the Middle East. Perhaps more than anywhere else on earth, religion is a key indicator of social identity, individual character, and heritage maintenance throughout MENA (Timothy, 2019a).

Judaism derives from the Bronze Age (3300–1200 BC) in the broader polytheistic religious landscape of Canaan and Babylon. Later, during the early Iron Age (ca. 1200–550 BC), certain factions of the Canaanite religions began to worship a single god (Yahweh), which separated their beliefs and practices from the predominant polytheistic norms that surrounded them (Anderson, 2015). During this period, many of the biblical accounts occurred, which were influential on the development of Judaism and Jewish identity. During the sixth and fifth centuries BC, many of the beliefs of the ancient Israelites were consolidated, becoming the doctrines and practices associated with Judaism today (Davies, 2014). In Israel, most Jews are either Orthodox or secular/non-religious. In other parts of the world, there are more divisions, which include, among others, Orthodox, Reform, Hasidic, Reconstructionist, and Conservative Jews, with some of these overlapping. These various denominations differ in their level of observance, in the languages used in liturgy, their national origins or ethnic identities, and the ways in which holy writ is interpreted (Stern, 2011). Nearly 18 million Jews live in more than 100 countries, with the largest concentrations being in Israel, the United States, and France. Judaism does not encourage or discourage pilgrimage. However, devout Jews are under certain levels of obligation to participate in religious festivals, events, and rituals, which often manifest in pilgrimage-like travel (Cohen Ioannides & Ioannides, 2006).

Christianity is based on the divine nature and teachings of Jesus. The faith essentially began as a branch of Judaism, which remained small during Jesus's life but flourished after his death as his missionary apostles travelled throughout the Mediterranean to spread the declaration that Jesus was the son of God and saviour of the world. His representatives found considerable success, especially when Roman Emperor Constantine the Great converted to Christianity, which enabled and encouraged the religion to spread throughout the Roman Empire. Through time, divisions and reforms occurred based on differing interpretations of the Bible, successions in leadership, and national orientations. Today, Christianity is the world's largest religion, with approximately 2.4 billion adherents, and includes numerous denominations, sub-denominations and non-denominational sects that practise different rites and rituals and adhere to varying interpretations of the Bible (Ron & Timothy, 2019). Although pilgrimage is not an official doctrine or requirement in most Christian churches, many of the Christian faithful visit sites associated with the life of Christ or other sacrosanct places.

Though many Islamic scholars believe that Islam was the faith practiced by early prophets, such as Moses and Abraham, Islam as a religion began in the early seventh century AD in the area of Medina and Mecca in today's Saudi Arabia. To counter the pagan rituals and practices of the area at the time, Muhammad was chosen to be the last prophet through whom God's word would be revealed (Karsh, 2006). Between AD 609 and 632, the will and words of God were revealed to the prophet as contained in the Quran, the revered holy book of the world's 1.9 billion Muslims. The Hadith is also considered sacred writ and is a record of the actions, words, and thoughts of Muhammad. These two sets of writings are the foundations of Islamic beliefs, practices, laws, and cultures (Moufakkir, Reisinger, & AlSaleh, 2019), one of which is the requirement to undertake the pilgrimage (*hajj*) to Mecca at least once in a lifetime. Within Islam, there are various sects and sub-sects that have differing views of Muhammad's successors, interpretations of scripture, and historical cultural practices, or they venerate specific imams. Examples of major sects and sub-sects include Alevis, Alawites, Ishikis, Ishmailis, Shabaks, Shiites, Sufis, Sunnis, and Zaidis.

During the seventh and eighth centuries, Islam spread throughout the Arabian Peninsula, North Africa, the Iberian Peninsula, and parts of Central and South Asia, largely through military conquests. Between the eighth and sixteen centuries, conversions along land and sea trade routes extended the religion into Central Asia, western China, eastern Africa, South Asia, and Southeast Asia. Today, Islam has spread through migration to every corner of the globe. Although most countries of the world now have Islamic populations, Muslims are overwhelmingly concentrated in the Middle East and North Africa, East Africa, Central Asia, South Asia, and Southeast Asia. Indonesia is the largest Muslim-majority country in the world with some 229 million adherents, followed by Pakistan (200 million) and India (195 million).

In addition to Judaism, Christianity, and Islam, the Middle East is the hearth of several other faiths and religious sects (Table 2.1). Some of these have expanded their reach throughout the world through proselytising efforts (e.g. the Baha'i faith) or migration (e.g. Druze), while others have remained concentrated in the Middle East (e.g. Samaritanism). Many denominations and religious traditions intermingle belief systems, overlap in some of their practices and sacred spaces, and share a number of common traditions (e.g. Judaism and Samaritanism; Islam and Shabakism). Yet, many of them also have their own sacrosanct spaces that create unique heritages and pilgrimage traditions that are distinct from other denominations.

The faith-based heritage of MENA

In almost every corner of the world, religious architecture, sacred spaces, and celebrations of faith lie at the heart of heritage tourism (Henderson, 2011; Kessler, 2015; Shackley, 2006). Nearly every package tour of Europe, Asia, and Latin America includes visits to religious heritage sites and extols the virtues of spiritual landscapes (Ron & Timothy, 2019). Religion is one of the factors that coalesces the Middle East and North Africa into a single geographic realm. Religion has left an indelible mark on the forms, functions, and landscapes of MENA's cities and towns (Orbaşli, 2019; Khirfan, 2014).

Outside a few locations in India associated with the Kumbh Mela, the Middle East is the most visited region in the world for pilgrimage and other

Table 2.1 A sample of faith traditions and religions originating in the Middle East

Religion	Period of origination	General location(s) of origination	Approximate number of current adherents
Bábism	1844	Iran	a few thousand
Baha'i Faith	1863	Iran, Syria	6–8 million
Christianity	1st century AD	Israel/Palestine	2.4 billion
Druze	ca. AD 1016	Syria/Lebanon	1–2 million
Islam	ca. AD 610	Saudi Arabia	1.9 billion
Judaism	ca. 1200 BC	Israel/Palestine	15–18 million
Mandaenism	ca. 3rd century AD	Iraq/Syria	70,000
Manichaeism	3rd century AD	Iran	a few hundred
Samaritanism	720 BC	Israel/Palestine	less than 1,000
Yarsanism	14th century AD	Iran	2.5–3.5 million
Yazidism	early 12th century AD	Iraq/Syria	800,000–1 million
Zoroastrianism	1st or 2nd millennium BC	Iran	200,000

Source: Compiled by author from various sources.

forms of religious tourism, and is home to some of the world's best-known faith-derived heritage (Poria, Butler, & Airey, 2003). In fact, most historic sites in the region are religious in nature (Cernea, 2001; Timothy, 2019b). The following sections describe and examine a range of religious heritage assets that comprise much of the tourism resource base in the Middle East and North Africa (Figure 2.1).

Buildings for worship

Historic buildings are among the most sought-after attractions in MENA. Given the wide range of faiths originating from the Middle East or with a modern-day strong presence there, it is little wonder that sacred buildings are the most visited type of religious attraction. Throughout the entire region, mosques, churches, synagogues, and temples are among the most pervasive and imposing structures in community landscapes, and they are often the centrepieces of social life and urban identity.

Thousands of mosques dot the landscapes of MENA; many of these are of recent vintage, whereas others are believed to have been built at the time of Muhammad or soon thereafter. Most mosques are of local acclaim and serve the spiritual needs of resident populations. However, many famous mosques throughout the region also serve as 'anchor' attractions (Huang & Chu, 2019; Kessler, 2015). They tend to be older and are world-famous destinations for Muslims and non-Muslims. Inasmuch as possible, all believers should visit Al-Masjid al-Haram in Mecca during their lifetimes. Other mosques of great consequence include the Al-Masjid an-Nabawi in Medina; the Umayyad Mosque in Damascus; and the Al-Aqsa Mosque in Jerusalem. These and many others serve as significant pilgrimage destinations, as well as cultural attractions for ordinary tourists.

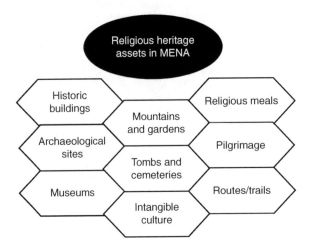

Figure 2.1 Types of religious heritage attractions in MENA.

Several mosques have become salient attractions owing to their distinctive architectural styles or their physical settings. The Masjid Al Rahma (the Floating Mosque) in Jeddah, Saudi Arabia, was built on pylons over the Red Sea, thus appearing to float. It is one of the most visited attractions in Jeddah. The Blue Mosque is one of the best-known mosques in the world and is visited by nearly everyone who visits Istanbul, Turkey (Sahin & Baloglu, 2011). Several earthen mosques in North Africa were constructed in a unique Saharan conical dome style. Atiq Mosque in Awjila, Libya, and the Grand Mosque of Mopti in Timbuktu, Mali, are two prime examples (Poissonnier, 2018).

Because Christianity began in the Middle East and continues to have a strong presence there, churches are another pervasive part of the faith landscapes of the region. Today, several Middle Eastern countries have sizable Christian populations: Egypt, Lebanon, Syria, Iran, Jordan, Israel, Palestine, Iraq, and Turkey in particular. In most cases, these are long-established Christian communities that are home to churches, monasteries, and shrines. Not all of these structures are located in places frequented by tourists, as they serve a primarily local Christian population. However, like mosques, there are some well-known historic churches, particularly in the Holy Land (primarily in Egypt, Israel, and Palestine) that attract Christian pilgrims from around the world. The Church of the Nativity in Bethlehem (built over the traditional birthplace of Jesus) and the Church of the Holy Sepulchre in Jerusalem (built over the traditional tomb of Jesus) are among the most important Christian edifices in the entire region. Several Coptic and Orthodox churches in Egypt are important pilgrimage attractions, and most of the sites in Palestine, Jordan, and Israel associated with the life of Jesus are adorned with churches or shrines, all of which are important attractions for Christian tourists. There are Christian monasteries and churches in other MENA countries (e.g. Syria, Lebanon, and Iran) that are sacred pilgrimage sites for local groups but do not necessarily attract large numbers of international tourists. Some of these are listed as UNESCO World Heritage Sites, such as the Armenian churches of north-western Iran.

The most pervasive Jewish buildings throughout MENA are synagogues, or houses of worship, where groups meet to pray, conduct meetings, or socialise. Most countries of MENA once had large Jewish populations. However, with the establishment of Israel in 1948, and owing to their persecution in many Arab states, the majority of Middle Eastern Jews moved to Israel. In addition to plentiful synagogues in Israel, there are numerous well-known and local synagogues in many MENA countries, where large Jewish populations once lived. Morocco is home to many synagogues, some of which have become significant tourist attractions in Fes, Casablanca, and Marrakesh. There are dozens of synagogues remaining in Tehran, Shiraz, Isfahan, and several other cities in Iran, although the remaining Jewish population in Iran numbers only 8,000–9,000. The Djerba Synagogue in Tunisia continues to serve the community's remaining Jewish population. Many synagogues continue to be maintained as heritage sites in several countries where the Jewish population has diminished or disappeared (e.g. Iran, Iraq, Yemen, Turkey, Lebanon, and Syria). Israeli citizens are not permitted to visit the majority of these countries, although Jews from other countries may be permitted.

Ruins and archaeological sites

MENA is home to some of the most spectacular archaeological sites on earth, many in ruins, but some intact. The region's archaeological record tells stories of indigenous nomadic pasts, the domination of European empires, and even more recently, colonialism. For instance, the Temples of Bacchus and Jupiter in Baalbek, Lebanon, were built by the Romans as places of deity veneration, and remnants of churches and shrines from Late Antiquity and Early Middle Ages abound in Lebanon, Syria, Israel, Palestine, and Jordan (de Vries, 1988; Farra-Haddad, 2020). Some of the region's archaeological sites pre-date Christianity, Judaism, and Islam but nonetheless have a spiritual or religious foundation. For example, Göbekli Tepe, Turkey, built more than 12,000 years ago, is believed to have been a site of worship and sacrifice for the region's nomadic peoples. Likewise, the Karnak Temple Complex (Egypt) pre-dates all three monotheistic faiths and was dedicated to pagan gods. Later, once pagan worship was outlawed in the Roman Empire, many of the original structures at Karnak were incorporated into Christian churches.

Much of MENA's archaeological record is directly connected to religion. Many archaeological sites visited by the general public have religious origins, but there are also faith-specific sites, which, while in a ruinous state, continue to be venerated (Koren-Lawrence & Collins-Kreiner, 2019). For example, ruins of mosques, synagogues, and churches abound, as well as wells, monasteries, shrines, ritual baths (miqvehs/wudu fountains), and other tangible objects. While many of these archaeological remains have become important general tourist attractions, some also remain important religious sites, venerated for their historical importance or their continued presence as *terra sancta*, where once they are sanctified, they continue to be in a state of ruin (Farra-Haddad, 2020). Given their prominence and stature as universally important heritage, many such religious archaeological settings have been inscribed on UNESCO's World Heritage List (Table 2.2).

Museums

Many religious archaeological sites and historic houses of worship are categorised as museums. However, there is another classification of museums that runs throughout the Middle East and North Africa – those that were built to protect artefacts and interpret certain elements of the religious past. While many small-scale, religion-oriented museums can be found in

Table 2.2 Religion-associated archaeological UNESCO World Heritage Sites in MENA

World Heritage Site name	Country	Religious heritage context
Al Qal'a of Beni Hammad	Algeria	Ruins of a great mosque and early Islamic community
Abu Mena	Egypt	Ruins of 3rd century basilica and monastery
Takht-e Soleyman	Iran	Ruins of ancient Zoroastrian sanctuary
Samarra Archaeological City	Iraq	Ruins of 9th century Great Mosque and earthen spiral minaret
Baptism Site Al-Maghtas	Jordan	Jordan River site of Jesus's baptism with ancient church and monastery ruins
Necropolis of Bet She'arim	Israel	3rd century Jewish burial place. Important site for Judaism.
Ephesus	Turkey	Early center of Christianity with ruins of churches
Old City of Sana'a	Yemen	Ancient center of Islam and remains of one of the earliest mosques
Biblical Tels – Megiddo, Hazor, Beer Sheba	Israel	Ruins of important cities in biblical accounts of the Holy Land
Saint Catherine Area	Egypt	Sacred to the Abrahamic religions, Mount Horeb is home to the Orthodox Monastery of St Catherine and ruins of ancient churches and monasteries.

Source: Compiled from UNESCO (2019).

most MENA states, some stand out as important tourist attractions of international renown.

Table 2.3 provides some examples of religion-oriented, purpose-built museums in a few MENA countries. Jerusalem's Bible Lands Museum displays artefacts and interprets the history of the Ancient Near East through various civilisations with biblical and scientific perspectives. In Palestine, the Bethlehem Museum emphasises the city's role in the development of the Christian Holy Land through artefacts, displays, and interpretive media. The Two Holy Mosques Architecture Exhibition in Mecca instructs visitors about the construction of the mosques and their architectural components. The Coptic Museum and the Museum of Moroccan Judaism aim to protect relics, stories, and cultures of religious minorities in North Africa. This is only a small sampling of religious-oriented museums, but as this list and other faith-focused museums in MENA indicate, these institutions can be classified in several ways: art galleries or exhibitions; museums of ancient civilisations and archaeology; establishments that promote religious nationalism; biblical nature museums; and foundations dedicated to recognising religious minority populations.

Mountains and gardens

Mountains and hills are frequently considered hallowed ground, owing to their ascending reach toward heaven and the preponderance of miracles that happen on mountaintops. Caves are also an important element of mountainscapes, many of which served as hiding places or homes for prophets, imams, or other holy people and where they received heavenly guidance. Some of the weightiest events to have occurred in religious history took place on mountains and in caves, and many are therefore venerated in MENA (Table 2.4). The Bible, the Quran, and the Tanakh all revere mountains as important places of godly presence.

The Mount of Olives, a hill overlooking Jerusalem and esteemed by Christians, played an extremely important role in the ministry of Jesus and is home to several churches, tombs, and the Garden of Gethsemane. The Mount of Transfiguration, where Jesus was glorified by God and affirmed to be his son, is believed by contemporary Christians to be either Mount Tabor or Mount Hermon; both are commemorated as potential locations of this sacred event. Mount Sinai, Egypt, is sacred to several faiths, including the three main Abrahamic religions (Grainger & Gilbert, 2008; Shackley, 1998). This is where Moses met the deity and received the Ten Commandments around 1300 BC. Mount Sinai is mentioned frequently in the Bible and the Quran. Saint Catherine's Monastery was built in the sixth century on the mount and is one of the world's oldest functioning monasteries, operated by the Greek Orthodox Church of Sinai. Mount Gerizim is the most sacred place for the remaining 800 Samaritans in Israel and Palestine (Urien-Lefranc, 2016). The remains of their ancient temple and the

Table 2.3 Sample of religious history-oriented museums in MENA

Name of museum	Location	Main emphasis or context
Biblical Museum of Natural History	Beit Shemesh, Israel	Displays natural history, taking a biblical and scientific perspective.
Bible Lands Museum	Jerusalem, Israel/Palestine	Emphasises the rise and fall of civilisations of the ancient Near East.
Bethlehem Museum	Bethlehem, Palestine	Promotes an understanding of Palestine's history, culture and role in the Christian Holy Land.
Imam Ali Religious Arts Museum	Tehran, Iran	Fosters knowledge about Islamic arts, including painting and calligraphy.
Museum of Islamic Art	Doha, Qatar	Features Islamic architecture, ceramics, metal- and woodwork, textiles and jewellery.
The Two Holy Mosques Architecture Exhibition	Mecca, Saudi Arabia	Displays artefacts from the historic mosques in Mecca and Medina and provides information about the unique architecture of mosques.
Coptic Museum	Cairo, Egypt	Houses the largest collection of Coptic Christian artefacts in the world, including manuscripts, artwork, and textiles.
Museum of Moroccan Judaism	Casablanca, Morocco	Tells the story of Morocco's Jewish population and displays many religious and cultural artefacts.
Museé de Religions	Hammamet, Tunisia	Houses objects from all three Abrahamic religions and promotes religious tolerance and dialogue.
Hagia Sophia Museum	Istanbul, Turkey	Served as a church for nine centuries, and a mosque for 482 years. Now a museum.
The Quincentennial Foundation Museum of Turkish Jews	Istanbul, Turkey	Housed in a former synagogue, it commemorates the Turkish Jews from the 4th century BC until modern times.
Sharjah Museum of Islamic Civilization	Sharjah, UAE	Houses artefacts and displays about Islamic art, culture, and scientific innovations. Its faith gallery tells about Islam and its holy writings.
Imam Hussain Museum	Karbala, Iraq	Dedicated to Imam Hussein and houses Islamic artefacts from around the world, including icons associated directly with Muhammad and his family.

Source: Author's compilation from multiple sources.

mountain itself are worshipped as the actual location chosen by God to house his holy temple. Likewise, Mount Hira is honoured by Muslims as the location where Muhammad began receiving revelations from God and where the new religion began.

Table 2.4 Examples of sacred hills and mountains in MENA

Sacred mountain	Location	Reason for veneration
Mount Sinai	Egypt	Moses met God and received the Ten Commandments. Revered by Jews, Christians, and Muslims.
Mount of Olives	Palestine/Israel	Hill outside Jerusalem mentioned frequently in the Bible. Home to ancient Jewish cemeteries and sites of Christian miracles.
Temple Mount	Palestine/Israel	Precipice in Jerusalem holy to all Abrahamic religions. Traditional site of the ancient Jewish temple, and the place from which Muhammad undertook his Night Journey.
Mount of Calvary (Golgotha)	Palestine/Israel	Outside Jerusalem's ancient walls, the site of Jesus's crucifixion. Two possible locations in the modern-day city.
Mount Gerizim	Palestine	Samaritans esteem this as the true location of God's temple. Samaritans visit frequently and celebrate many rituals and holidays here.
Mount of Temptation	Palestine	Near Jericho where Satan tempted Jesus but where Jesus withstood the temptations.
Mount of Transfiguration	Israel	Where Jesus was glorified and affirmed to be the Son of God. Disputed location between Mt Hermon and Mt Tabor.
Mount Carmel	Israel	According to tradition, Mt Carmel is where the prophet Elijah dwelt and performed miracles to show the power of God. Carmel is also sacred for the Bahá'í Faith and is the location of its world headquarters.
Mount of Beatitudes	Israel	On the shore of the Sea of Galilee believed to be the location where Jesus often preached and delivered the Sermon on the Mount.
Mount Ararat	Turkey	Ostensibly the resting place of Noah's Ark. Venerated by Armenian Christians.
Mount Nebo	Jordan	Peak from which Moses saw the Promised Land and where he is believed to be buried.
Mount Hira/Jabal an-Nour	Saudi Arabia	In a cave on Mt Hira, Muhammad received his first revelation from God.
Mount Bull/Jabal Thawr	Saudi Arabia	A mountain in Mecca where Muhammad took shelter from his foes.
Safa and Marwa	Saudi Arabia	Two small hills in Mecca play an important role in the *hajj* rituals. Both are now enclosed within the Al-Masjid al-Haram.

Source: Author's compilation.

Like mountains, gardens are cherished locations of pilgrimage and cultural tourism in the Middle East. The Hanging Gardens of Babylon were one of the Seven Wonders of the Ancient World, although their exact location has not been verified, if they existed at all. Historians and archaeologists believe that the gardens might have been located in Babylon or Nineveh in modern-day Iraq (Dalley, 2013). The existence of other gardens is more verifiable. The Garden of Gethsemane at the base of the Mount of Olives in Jerusalem is a sacred locale for Christians. There, Jesus prayed and suffered for the sins of the world. It is an important part of most Christian tours in Jerusalem, and some of the remaining olive trees have been dated almost to the time of Christ (Ron & Timothy, 2019). The Baha'i World Centre and Shrine of the Báb are located within and against the backdrop of the magnificent Baha'i Gardens in Haifa. In addition to being a major pilgrimage centre for Baha'is, it is a World Heritage Site and one of Israel's most popular tourist attractions (Collins-Kreiner & Gatrell, 2006; Gatrell & Collins-Kreiner, 2006).

Tombs and cemeteries

Tombs, graves, and cemeteries are prominent heritage assets. Many Jews regularly visit the tombs of famous rabbis in Israel and Morocco (Collins-Kreiner, 2007, 2010a; Kosansky, 2002). Graves of influential rabbis abound throughout MENA, but many of them are inaccessible for Jews to visit. Likewise, there are many tombs of famous Old Testament heroes and prophets in Iran, Jordan, Syria, and Iraq. Rachel's Tomb inside the walled area between Jerusalem and Bethlehem, the Tomb of the Prophets in Jerusalem, Joseph's Tomb in Nablus, and the Tomb of the Patriarchs in Hebron all have extreme importance for the Abrahamic faiths, but all of these sites have different levels of accessibility for people of different faiths, owing to Israel's occupation of the West Bank and the general security climate in the region.

Tombs of influential imams and descendants of Muhammad are revered in Islam and are regular pilgrimage attractions (Neveu, 2010). Most countries of MENA are home to imams' tombs that are of local and regional significance. Some of them are transregional in their appeal, however. The resting place of Muhammad and other early Muslim leaders are located inside the Mosque of the Prophet in Medina and is a prominent pilgrimage attraction. One of the main attractions of the Umayyad Mosque in Damascus is the long-held belief that it is the burial place of John the Baptist's head.

The most important tombs in MENA for Christian tourists are the Garden Tomb and the tombs enclosed within the Church of the Holy Sepulchre. The latter is believed by most Catholic and Orthodox denominations to be the burial place of Jesus, while the Garden Tomb is considered the more likely resting place and site of Jesus's resurrection among many Protestant sects (Ron & Timothy, 2019).

Intangible culture

Intangible religious heritage in MENA generally refers to faith traditions, music, calls to prayer, dance, and artistic expressions. These create an unmistakable faith-based ambience, but intangible heritage also refers to living adherents. For Christians, this is especially important. Many group tours in the Holy Land, for example, include visits to Palestinian Christians who have been alienated by Israel and restricted from visiting their sacred spaces in Jerusalem or other occupied lands (Ron & Timothy, 2019). In acts of solidarity, certain Protestant groups from Europe and North America regularly visit Christian Palestinians for purposes of fellowship and 'bringing the gospel' beyond the Israeli partition wall.

Intangible religious heritage also affects other forms of non-heritage tourism. For example, while we generally do not associate cruises, beachfront development, and shopping tourism with religious heritage, these tourisms are indirectly and tangentially connected to religious heritage. For example, religious beliefs have influenced beachfront development in certain ways, such as gender-segregated beaches and swimming pools, or the types of food and drink that can be served in restaurants (Hall & Prayag, 2020). Muslim-friendly family cruises are now offered, and the ubiquitous shopping centres in many MENA countries are increasingly cognisant of their social contexts, providing a mix of traditional shops with Islamic attire and food, as well as non-traditional retailers that cater more to broader market bases. Likewise, certain behaviours are prohibited in shopping contexts, such as public displays of affection, immodest dress, and alcohol consumption.

Related to this is the phenomenon of religious needs in tourism (Timothy & Ron, 2016). Many Jews select their destinations based on the availability of kosher meals. Many Muslim travellers choose their holiday packages based on the level of halal services offered, such as gender-divided spaces, restaurants that do not serve pork products or alcohol, posted prayer times, and qiblats (Mecca directional markers) provided in hotel rooms and lobbies (Hall & Prayag, 2020; Mohsin & Ryan, 2019). Even some Christian sects have prohibitions against certain foods and drinks that may affect the hospitality sector (Timothy & Ron, 2016). All of these recent ways of seeing adherent-friendly destinations, attractions, and services are based on religious heritage beliefs and behaviours.

Religious meals

The Bible is full of references to food, drink, and meals, which arouses a deep interest in the topic among service providers and religious tourists in the Holy Land. There is a growing interest among Christian tourists in Palestine and Israel to learn about the ordinary lives of people, including Jesus, in New Testament times. One manifestation of this is the desire to learn about biblical food and to partake of Bible-era meals (Ron &

Timothy, 2013, 2019). Ron and Timothy (2013) identified five categories of Bible-based food landscapes and experiences related to Christian travel in the Holy Land. These include obedience to the word and will of God, the Holy Land as the Promised Land, the ministry and miracles of Jesus, the crucifixion of Jesus, and the spirit of the Holy Land. Examples include celebratory foods, food-centred branding (e.g. the Land of Milk and Honey), food-related miracles (e.g. turning water to wine), 'last supper' re-enactments, and traditional Jewish cuisine and food souvenirs.

Tourism has contributed to the development of sacred foodscapes throughout MENA, but this is particularly evident in Palestine and Israel. There are several biblical meal providers in the Holy Land, and tour leaders are increasingly requesting biblical meals and Bible food-presentations to be included on their tour itineraries. Biblical food contributes to an unambiguous heritage landscape that underlies much tourism branding and contributes to the religious heritage experience (Ron & Timothy, 2013).

Pilgrimages

Pilgrimage, a specialised form of heritage tourism, utilises both tangible and intangible inheritance to create a unique living heritage with ancient roots and modern expressions (Collins-Kreiner, 2010b; Olsen, 2003; Timothy, 2011). The very act of religious pilgrimage is a manifestation of heritage, as it represents a corporeal journey to physical places and sacrosanct spaces; is motivated by divine obligation, self-purification, intragroup solidarity, altruism, and ultimately spiritual growth; and employs beliefs, utterances, rituals, and ceremonies, which are all manifestations of cultural heritage.

Pilgrimage in the Middle East ranges from a small-scale local activity where the faithful visit shrines or graves of revered imams, rabbis, or saints, to similar national expressions, or it may be done en masse to world-famous shrines, buildings, and miraculous sites (Ron & Timothy, 2019). Localities associated with profound miracles and events, famous leaders, or otherwise deeply revered sacred spaces, draw millions of mass pilgrim-tourists each year. While all of the religious groups noted in Table 2.1 practice some form of pilgrimage, this section focuses on the pilgrim mobilities in Islam, Christianity, and Judaism.

Muslims are required to undertake the pilgrimage to Mecca (*hajj*) at least once in their lifetime, unless they face physical or other challenges that prevent it. Each year, approximately 2.5 million Muslims from across the world gather in Mecca at the Al-Masjid al-Haram and other localities in the city during the month of Dhu al-Hijjah to participate in sacred rites and rituals that purify them and draw them closer to God. In addition to the *hajj*, many Muslims participate in lesser pilgrimages (*umrah*) which, while important, do not replace the required *hajj* (Timothy & Iverson, 2006; Zamani-Farahani, Carboni, Perelli, & Farsani, 2019). Recently, the pilgrimage landscape of Mecca has quickly developed into a pilgrimage–tourism landscape, with the growth of international brand mega-hotels and resorts, luxury transportation, and other lavish services that have in some ways priced out poorer pilgrims but increased the 'leisure' component for the pilgrims who can afford to visit (Qurashi, 2017). Qurashi (2017) raises important questions about the overly ambitious touristic development of Mecca's pilgrimagescape as regards how such developments will affect pilgrims' experiences and behaviours and its incongruence with the teachings of Muhammad: simplicity, equality, and modesty. Despite the over-commercialisation of the *hajj*, it is still an important event, although many Muslim observers have argued that Mecca's overdevelopment may have lessened the spiritual significance of the pilgrimage (Henderson, 2011). In Qurashi's (2017, p. 89) words, the *hajj* has become a 'branded commercial experience'.

Among Shiite Muslims, Iraq is a particularly important pilgrimage destination, as it is home to many tombs and mosques associated with several important Shia imams. In addition to the sacred mosques and burial sites that all Muslims venerate in Saudi Arabia and Jerusalem, Shiite Muslims from around the world regularly gather at the mosques and tombs of famous Shia imams in Iraq and Iran. Iran is home to many famous religious sites, which stimulates much domestic tourism and cross-border travel from Iraq and other countries with large Shiite populations (Seyfi & Hall, 2019). Iran and Syria have considerable potential for the growth of religious tourism among Sunni Muslims, Christians, and Jews, but most of that potential remains untapped (Olsen, 2019; Seyfi & Hall, 2019) owing largely to regional political instability, poor international relations (e.g. international boycotts against Iran), war, and terrorism.

Palestine and the greater Holy Land has an ancient history as a Christian pilgrimage destination (Isaac, Hall, & Higgins-Desbiolles, 2016). Even in modern times, innovators such as Thomas Cook began bringing pilgrimage tour groups to Egypt and Palestine in the 1860s to see places associated with the Bible. Today, the Holy Land (i.e. Egypt, Palestine, Israel, and Jordan) is the most popular religious destination among Christians worldwide (Collins-Kreiner & Kliot, 2000; Isaac, 2010; Ron & Timothy, 2019). Although most Christians view the Holy Land as the ultimate pilgrimage destination, there are places within the region that are more sacred than others to different denominations. Thus, there is a unique geography of religious tourism that sees Roman Catholics, Eastern Orthodox, Southern Baptists, Methodists, Lutherans, or members of the Church of Jesus Christ of Latter-day Saints visiting core Christian sites but also special localities that are unique to their own denominations.

Although Christian pilgrimage destinations in Europe have become over-commercialised, it is less the case in the Middle East. One major critique of much Christian tourism in the Holy Land is its overwhelming religio-political focus on its support for Israel. Some Protestant groups, however, adopt an anti-Israel stance in their support for the Palestinian cause (Ron & Timothy, 2019).

Although pilgrimage was an ancient Jewish requirement (Collins-Kreiner, 2019; Luz & Collins-Kreiner, 2015), today most Jews do not participate in formal pilgrimage as it is conceived in Islam and Christianity, yet devotees regularly visit sacrosanct places. Although Jews revere Jerusalem and its Western Wall (the last remains of the Second Temple) as sacrosanct places and undertake pilgrimage travel there from around the world, beyond the city, Judaism places little spiritual significance on sacred sites the way Christianity and Islam do (Cohen Ioannides & Ioannides, 2006).

Unlike churches and mosques, synagogues are not considered sacred spaces and prayers recited within them are no more effectual or blessed than those offered elsewhere. Nonetheless, as noted above, Jews actively visit tombs of rabbis for social purposes, to celebrate holidays, or to pray. At these localities, 'religion, folk beliefs and customs mix freely' (Collins-Kreiner, 2019, p. 141). Since Jews settled in places throughout the world, the locations where their ancestors lived and where esteemed rabbis lived and died are also revered and are important sites to visit (Cohen Ioannides & Ioannides, 2006). These are especially popular in Israel, Tunisia, and Morocco. Other sites in Iran, Iraq, Lebanon, and Yemen are currently out of reach for most Jewish heritage-seekers, even though these countries' Jewish heritage remains largely intact. Jews visit the ruins of ancient synagogues for various heritage purposes, including education or to feel connected with their own past (Ioannides & Cohen Ioannides, 2002; Koren-Lawrence & Collins-Kreiner, 2019; Krakover, 2017). These latter behaviours are sometimes referred to as 'mitzvahs of nostalgia', one of the most salient manifestations of modern Jewish pilgrimage that has a more secular, folkloristic, or cultural focus (Collins-Kreiner, 1999).

Trails and routes

There are many cultural routes and trails throughout MENA, but the relatively recent phenomenon of faith-oriented heritage trails is receiving considerable attention in the Holy Land (Olsen & Trono, 2018). Timothy and Boyd (2015) outline two main types of heritage trails: organic and purposive. Organic tourist trails are those that developed naturally based on existing trade routes, migrant routes, railways, national borders, and other linear phenomena that were not originally meant to be tourist trails. Purposive routes are planned and designed themed corridors for touristic reasons that link together specific nodes or sites.

The Jesus Trail and the Gospel Trail are two prominent examples. The Jesus Trail, established in 2007, is designed, marked, and maintained by a non-profit organisation that promotes cooperation between Jewish and Palestinian Israelis. The Gospel Trail (established 2011) is managed by the Israeli Ministry of Tourism and other government bodies. Both trails pass through the Galilee region, where Jesus spent most of his life. These have become very popular attractions, but especially among Christian adventure tourists (Timothy & Boyd, 2015). The Nativity Trail is a hiking path through the West Bank to Bethlehem. It roughly parallels the route Joseph and the pregnant Mary might have taken to Bethlehem (Kutulus & Awad, 2016). Finally, the Abraham Path (established 2007) officially extends more than 1,000km through several Middle Eastern countries, but only 400km have been demarcated in Turkey, Syria, Jordan, Palestine, and Israel. The trail connects many places where Abraham possibly lived or worked (Isaac, 2018). Most of the trail is inaccessible to tourists because of the region's volatile security situation but has considerable potential in Palestine, Israel, Jordan, and Turkey (Timothy & Ron, 2019).

Conclusions

This chapter argues that religion and its tangible and intangible characteristics are a critical foundation of heritage tourism in MENA. To this end, the chapter has taken an overtly supply-side view of religion-based heritage tourism, for the majority of heritage sites and living culture is directly or indirectly connected to Islam, Judaism, Christianity, or a handful of other religions native to the region. Even secular tourists are exposed daily to elements of Islamic, Christian, or Jewish heritage that manifest in the everyday urban landscapes of the region.

Religious heritage and its associated tourism in MENA face many challenges (Olsen, 2019). These include active geopolitical conflicts that have annihilated much religious patrimony in countries such as Iraq, Syria, and Yemen, both as an intentional target motivated by hate and political expediency, or as an innocent casualty of war. Secondly, the Israeli occupation of Palestinian lands in the West Bank and the separation barrier between Jerusalem and Bethlehem are significant hindrances to the development of religious tourism in Palestine. The West Bank and Jerusalem barriers are salient obstacles to the holistic development of Christian, Jewish, and Muslim tourism (Isaac, 2010). There is considerable potential for religious tourism to sites in the West Bank, but occupation policies prohibit Israelis from visiting certain parts (Area A) of the Palestinian Territories, and for many Muslims, transiting Israel is a very difficult endeavour with added scrutiny and security requirements. Third, the political manipulation of heritage is also prevalent. In this case, governments or prominent religious groups may appropriate religious archaeology or living and built heritage to fuel their chosen national narratives or to promote one faith over others (Neveu, 2010). Fourth, the heritage of religious minorities is often neglected from a maintenance and archaeological perspective, thereby causing rapid deterioration of patrimonies that do not rank highly as national priorities. Fortunately, several countries (e.g. Iran and Morocco) work closely with religious minority groups to protect and interpret their inheritances. Fifth, over-tourism is partly to blame for the deterioration of Jerusalem and its placement on UNESCO's List of World Heritage in Danger. There are several other overvisited heritage sites in the region, and the rapid development of tourism in certain countries has marginalised the traditional heritage, including mosques and other sacred spaces. Finally, there is no place on earth that is more hotly contested between religious groups than the Middle East. Jerusalem is the best example of religious contestation, which often results in armed skirmishes, vandalism, and other manifestations of malcontent.

Despite these problems, religious heritage underlies the cultural tourism sector of MENA. It remains one of the most visited regions in the world for heritage tourism, and religion influences every aspect of daily life (living heritage), intangible culture, and built environment. Even with regard to historical resources and localities that are seemingly unrelated to faith, religion plays some role in its development, preservation, and consumption in one way or another. Every form of heritage tourism and every type of cultural asset known in the heritage tourism sector is exemplified in the religious patrimony of the Middle East and North Africa.

References

Anderson, J. S. (2015). *Monotheism and Yahweh's appropriation of Baal*. London: Bloomsbury.
Cernea, M. M. (2001). *Cultural heritage and development: A framework for action in the Middle East and North Africa*. Washington, DC: World Bank.
Cohen Ioannides, M. W., & Ioannides, D. (2006). Global Jewish tourism: Pilgrimages and remembrance. In D. J. Timothy & D. H. Olsen (eds), *Tourism, religion and spiritual journeys* (pp. 156–171). London: Routledge.
Collins-Kreiner, N. (1999) Pilgrimage holy sites: A classification of Jewish holy sites in Israel. *Journal of Cultural Geography*, *18*(2), 57–78.
Collins-Kreiner, N. (2007) Graves as attractions: Pilgrimage-tourism to Jewish holy graves in Israel. *Journal of Cultural Geography*, *24*(1), 67–89.
Collins-Kreiner, N. (2010a) Current Jewish pilgrimage tourism: Modes and models of development. *Turizam*, *58*(3): 259–270.
Collins-Kreiner, N. (2010b) Researching pilgrimage: Continuity and transformations. *Annals of Tourism Research*, *37*(2), 440–456.
Collins-Kreiner, N. (2019) Contemporary Jewish tourism: Pilgrimage, religious heritage and educational tourism. In D. J. Timothy (ed.), *Routledge handbook on tourism in the Middle East and North Africa* (pp. 137–146). London: Routledge.
Collins-Kreiner, N., & Gatrell, J. D. (2006). Tourism, heritage and pilgrimage: The case of Haifa's Bahá'í Gardens. *Journal of Heritage Tourism*, *1*(1), 32–50.
Collins-Kreiner, N., & Kliot, N. (2000). Pilgrimage tourism in the Holy Land: The behavioural characteristics of Christian pilgrims. *GeoJournal*, *50*(1), 55–67.
Dalley, S. (2013). *The mystery of the Hanging Garden of Babylon: An elusive world wonder traced*. Oxford: Oxford University Press.
Davies, P. R. (2014). *The origins of Judaism*. London: Routledge.
de Vries, B. (1988). Jordan's churches: Their urban context in Late *Antiquity*. *The Biblical Archaeologist*, *51*(4), 222–226.
Farra-Haddad, N. (2020) Archaeology and religious tourism: Sacred sites, rituals, sharing the *baraka*, and tourism development. In D. J. Timothy & L. Tahan

(eds), *Touring the past: Archaeology and tourism*. Bristol: Channel View Publications.

Gatrell, J. D., & Collins-Kreiner, N. (2006). Negotiated space: Tourists, pilgrims, and the Bahá'í terraced gardens in Haifa. *Geoforum, 37*(5), 765–778.

Grainger, J., & Gilbert, J. (2008). Around the sacred mountain: The St Katherine Protectorate in South Sinai, Egypt. In J.-M. Mallarach (ed.), *Protected landscapes and cultural and spiritual values* (pp. 21–37). Gland: IUCN.

Hall, C. M., & Prayag, G. (eds.). (2020). *The Routledge handbook of halal hospitality and Islamic tourism*. Abingdon: Routledge.

Henderson, J. C. (2011). Religious tourism and its management: The *hajj* in Saudi Arabia. *International Journal of Tourism Research, 13*(6), 541–552.

Huang, J., & Chu, J. (2019). Tourist experience at religious sites: A case study of the Chinese visiting the Sheikh Zayed Grand Mosque. *Journal of China Tourism Research*, DOI: 10.1080/19388160.2019.1658678.

Ioannides, D., & Cohen Ioannides, M. W. (2002). Pilgrimages of nostalgia: Patterns of Jewish travel in the United States. *Tourism Recreation Research, 27*(2), 17–26.

Isaac, R. K. (2010) Palestinian tourism in transition: Hope, aspiration or reality? *Journal of Tourism and Peace Research, 1*(1): 16–26.

Isaac, R. K. (2018). Taking you home: The Masar Ibrahim Al-Khalil in Palestine. In C. M. Hall, Y. Ram, & N. Shoval (eds), *The Routledge international handbook of walking* (pp. 712–183). London: Routledge.

Isaac, R. K., Hall, C. M., & Higgins-Desbiolles, F. (2016). Palestine as a tourism destination. In R. K. Isaac, C. M. Hall, & F. Higgins-Desbiolles (eds), *The politics and power of tourism in Palestine* (pp. 15–34). London: Routledge.

Karsh, E. (2006). *Islamic imperialism: A history*. New Haven: Yale University Press.

Kessler, K. (2015). Conceptualizing mosque tourism: A central feature of Islamic and religious tourism. *International Journal of Religious Tourism and Pilgrimage, 3*(2), 11–32.

Khirfan, L. (2014). *World heritage, urban design and tourism: Three cities in the Middle East*. London: Routledge.

Koren-Lawrence, N., & Collins-Kreiner, N. (2019). Visitors with their 'backs to the archaeology': Religious tourism and archaeology. *Journal of Heritage Tourism, 14*(2), 138–149.

Kosansky, O. (2002). Tourism, charity, and profit: The movement of money in Moroccan Jewish pilgrimage. *Cultural Anthropology, 17*(3), 359–400.

Krakover, S. (2017). A heritage site development model: Jewish heritage product formation in south-central Europe. *Journal of Heritage Tourism, 12*(1), 81–101.

Kutulus, Y., & Awad, M. (2016). Bike and hike in Palestine. In R. K. Isaac, C. M. Hall, & F. Higgins-Desbiolles (eds), *The politics and power of tourism in Palestine* (pp. 53–62). London: Routledge.

Luz, N., & Collins-Kreiner, N. (2015). Exploring Jewish pilgrimage in Israel. In J. Eade & A. Dionigi (eds), *International perspectives on pilgrimage studies: Itineraries, gaps and obstacles* (pp. 134–151). London: Routledge.

Mohsin, A., & Ryan, C. (2019). Halal tourism: A growing market on a global state. In D. J. Timothy (ed.), *Routledge handbook on tourism in the Middle East and North Africa* (pp. 309–318). London: Routledge.

Moufakkir, O., Reisinger, Y., & AlSaleh, D. (2019). Much ado about halal tourism: Religion, religiosity or none of the above? In D. J. Timothy (ed.), *Routledge* handbook on tourism in the Middle East and North Africa (pp. 319–329). London: Routledge.

Neveu, N. (2010). Islamic tourism as an ideological construction: A Jordan study case. *Journal of Tourism and Cultural Change*, 8(4), 327–337.

Olsen, D. H. (2003). Heritage, tourism, and the commodification of religion. *Tourism Recreation Research*, 28(3), 99–104.

Olsen, D. H. (2019). Religion, pilgrimage and tourism in the Middle East. In D. J. Timothy (ed.), *Routledge handbook on tourism in the Middle East and North Africa* (pp. 109–124). London: Routledge.

Olsen, D. H., & Trono, A. (eds) (2018). *Religious pilgrimage routes and trails: Sustainable development and management*. Wallingford: CABI.

Orbaşli, A. (2019). Urban heritage in the Middle East: Heritage, tourism and the shaping of new identities. In D. J. Timothy (ed.), *Routledge handbook on tourism in the Middle East and North Africa* (pp. 95–106). London: Routledge.

Poissonnier, B. (2018). The great mosque of Timbuktu: Seven centuries of earthen architecture. In S. Pradines (ed.), *Earthen architecture in Muslim cultures: Historical and anthropological perspectives* (pp. 22–36). Leiden: Brill.

Poria, Y., Butler, R., & Airey, D. (2003). Tourism, religion and religiosity: A holy mess. *Current Issues in Tourism*, 6(4), 340–363.

Qurashi, J. (2017). Commodification of Islamic religious tourism: From spiritual to touristic experience. *International Journal of Religious Tourism and Pilgrimage*, 5(1), 89–104.

Ron, A. S., & Timothy, D. J. (2013). The land of milk and honey: Biblical foods, heritage and Holy Land tourism, *Journal of Heritage Tourism*, 8(2/3), 234–247.

Ron, A. S., & Timothy, D. J. (2019). *Contemporary Christian travel: Pilgrimage, practice, and place*. Bristol: Channel View Publications.

Sahin, S., & Baloglu, S. (2011). Brand personality and destination image of Istanbul, *Anatolia*, 22(1), 69–88.

Seyfi, S., & Hall, C. M. (eds) (2019). *Tourism in Iran: Challenges, development and issues*. London: Routledge.

Shackley, M. (1998). A golden calf in sacred space? The future of St Katherine's monastery, Mount Sinai (Egypt). *International Journal of Heritage Studies*, 4(3/4), 124–134.

Shackley, M. (2006). Costs and benefits: The impact of cathedral tourism in England. *Journal of Heritage Tourism*, 1(2), 133–141.

Stern, S. (ed.) (2011). *Sects and sectarianism in Jewish history*. Leiden: Brill.

Timothy, D. J. (2011). *Cultural heritage and tourism: An introduction*. Bristol: Channel View Publications.

Timothy, D. J. (2019a). The Middle East and North Africa: A dynamic cultural realm. In D. J. Timothy (ed.), *Routledge handbook on tourism in the Middle East and North Africa* (pp. 24–35). London: Routledge.

Timothy, D. J. (2019b). Tourism trends and patterns in MENA: A resource perspective. In D. J. Timothy (ed.), *Routledge handbook on tourism in the Middle East and North Africa* (pp. 36–54). London: Routledge.

Timothy, D. J., & Boyd, S. W. (2015). *Tourism and trails: Cultural, ecological and management issues*. Bristol: Channel View Publications.

Timothy, D. J., & Iverson, T. (2006). Tourism and Islam: Considerations of culture and duty. In D. J. Timothy & D. H. Olsen (eds), *Tourism, religion and spiritual journeys* (pp. 186–205). London: Routledge.

Timothy, D. J., & Ron, A. S. (2016). Religious heritage, spiritual aliment and food for the soul. In D. J. Timothy (ed.), *Heritage cuisines: Traditions, identities and tourism* (pp. 104–118). London: Routledge.

Timothy, D. J., & Ron, A. S. (2019). Christian tourism in the Middle East: Holy Land and Mediterranean perspectives. In D. J. Timothy (ed.), *Routledge handbook on tourism in the Middle East and North Africa* (pp. 147–159). London: Routledge.

UNESCO (2019) *World Heritage List*. Retrieved from https://whc.unesco.org/en/list/.

Urien-Lefranc, F. (2016) Mount Gerizim, a new 'Geneva for Peace': Capital without a territory? *Ethnologie française*, 4(164), 669–680.

Zamani-Farahani, H., Carboni, M., Perelli, C., & Farsani, N. T. (2019). Islamic tourism in the Middle East. In D. J. Timothy (ed.), *Routledge handbook on tourism in the Middle East and North Africa* (pp. 125–136). London: Routledge.

3 Contesting religious heritage in the Middle East

Daniel H. Olsen and Chad F. Emmett

Introduction

Pilgrimage – a 'journey to a distant sacred goal' (Barber, 1991, p. 1) – has long been a defining practice for most major religions. Indeed, pilgrimage has long been used by religious groups to create and maintain individual and group religious solidarity and identity (Olsen, 2019, 2020). Pilgrimage has also been used to promote control over and to maintain sacred sites and homelands. Such is the case in the MENA region, and particularly in the Middle East, where for centuries Christians, Jews, and Muslims have used pilgrimage to control and contest sacred sites and, in the case of the Israeli–Palestinian conflict, homelands. This has been done through establishing and encouraging pilgrimage to holy sites by religious adherents to sanctifying and legitimising their religious ownership and interpretation.

The MENA region has long attracted pilgrims from the abovementioned and other faiths for centuries because of the abundance of religious and cultural supply in the region. In recent decades pilgrims have been joined by religious tourists who combine religious and touristic motivations in their travels. Indeed, many of the millions of international and domestic visitors that circulate through the MENA region are interested in the tangible and intangible elements of religious cultural heritage. Because of this, many of the countries in the MENA region, such as Turkey and Iran, have begun to use religious tourism as an economic strategy, while Israel and Palestine also promote religious tourism but for more political purposes (Hazbun, 2004; Olsen, 2019).

At the same time, this religious heritage has long been highly contested between and within cultural and religious groups because of their role in national, cultural, and religious identity. The most notable of these contestations is the Israeli–Palestinian conflict and related issues pertaining to the ownership of the location of the al-Aqsa Mosque (Kelman, 1987; Burgess, 2004; Tessler, 2009; de Vries, Kligler-Vilenchik, Alyan, Ma'oz, & Maoz, 2017; Durante & Zhuravskaya, 2018), in part because these regional conflicts have been 'rescaled' (Swyngedouw, 1997) to involve external stakeholders in attempts to re-empower cultural positions. These conflicts have led to the politicisation of religious tourism and pilgrimage to and within the region, with Israelis and Palestinians using tourism as a platform to promote their own views of the contested heritage (e.g., Bajc, 2006; Brin, 2006; Belhaussen & Ebel, 2009; Hercbergs, 2012; Isaac & Ashworth, 2011).

However, there are several other, lesser-known or low-profile heritage conflicts that affect the development and sustainability of pilgrimage and religious tourism in the region. The purpose of this chapter is to discuss some of these lesser-known ways heritage sites are contested (c.f. Timothy & Emmett, 2014), including questions and disagreements related to interpretation, authenticity, designation, encroachment, and visibility. Case studies from the MENA region are used to highlight these types of contestation, including competing claims of authenticity of two Christian baptismal sites on the Jordan River, contention over whether the Hagia Sofia should remain a museum or be re-designated as a mosque, the sharing and interpreting of sacred space in Nazareth, nationalist encroachments at the Tomb of the Patriarchs, and the building of the BYU Jerusalem Centre in Jerusalem and the Baha'i Gardens in Haifa.

Contested religious heritage

Heritage has long been an impetus for travel. Defined as the inheritance of aspects of the past that have been preserved for present and future generations (Lowenthal, 1996; Tunbridge & Ashworth, 1996), heritage can take various forms, whether based on natural history, industrial practices, military events and installations, cultural festivals and pageants, art, architecture, archaeology, music, museums, towns and townscapes, and monuments and statutes (Timothy & Boyd, 2003; Timothy, 2011). These types of heritage also range from global types of heritage (e.g., World Heritage Sites) down to national (e.g., national historic monuments), local (e.g., cultural festivals), and personal types of heritage (e.g., a pocket watch handed down through many family generations) (Timothy, 1997). People travel to these and other types of heritage attractions for many reasons, including nostalgia, education, and curiosity (Timothy & Boyd, 2003; Timothy, 2011).

Heritage is also viewed as inherently political (e.g., Ashworth, 1994; Graham, Ashworth, & Tunbridge, 2000; Harrison & Hitchcock, 2005; Breglia, 2006; Weiss, 2007; Di Giovine, 2008). Not all aspects of the past are preserved and transmitted to the present generation. While natural disasters, accidents, weathering, war, and time have destroyed ancient buildings, writings, belief systems, natural phenomena, and ways of life, governments, historians, archivists, and others in positions of authority and power purposefully choose which cultural and physical artefacts and traditions they deem worthy to be passed down to future generations (Hardy, 1998; Brace, Bailey, & Harvey, 2006). As Tunbridge and Ashworth (1996, p. 6) note, 'history is what a historian regards as worth recording and heritage is what contemporary society chooses to inherit and to pass on'. Since all elements of the past are not present, heritage is therefore a selective attempt to re-create or re-interpret the past (Olsen & Timothy, 2002).

The mediated nature of heritage is problematic from two perspectives. First, this re-creation and re-interpretation of the past makes heritage prone to biases, allowing groups and individuals to 'legitimate contemporary personal, social, and political circumstances' (Norkunas, 1993, p. 6). Heritage can therefore be manipulated and used by groups for their own political purposes. This leads to the second issue, where if heritage is considered an inheritance (Lowenthal, 1996; Tunbridge & Ashworth, 1996), outside of some mutually agreeable arrangement someone will be disinherited. Tunbridge and Ashworth (1996) use the term 'dissonant heritage' to describe situations where competing groups and individuals argue over the questions 'what heritage do we share?' and 'whose heritage do we share?' Absent any cooperation between stakeholders, heritage can be seen as a 'zero-sum' game, where any attempts to negotiate between competing parties are constrained by views that 'an advantage to one stakeholder is simultaneously seen to disadvantage another' (Olsen & Guelke, 2004, p. 503). Heritage, in both intangible and tangible forms, is therefore extremely political in nature.

In addition to disagreements regarding what aspects of the tangible and intangible religious heritage should be preserved and whether this heritage should be used as a basis of commodification (Olsen, 2003; Timothy, 2011), there are several other ways in which religious heritage is contested. First, religious heritage is contested through *interpretation*. According to Timothy and Boyd (2003, p. 195), interpretation is defined as the 'process of communication or explaining to visitors the significance of the place they are visiting'. While interpretation is an important facet of the visitor experience at religious sites (Voase, 2007; Hughes, Bond, & Ballantyne, 2013), it amounts to a 'planned effort' to tell a particular story to visitors 'grounded in relations of power' (Morgan & Pritchard, 1998, p. 6). At religious sites, for example, managers are responsible for presenting a particular version of history and heritage that meets the management and theological goals of religious leaders, and therefore will not include competing discourses regarding the meaning and significance of the site in their interpretive efforts (c.f. Philip & Mercer, 1999; Olsen, 2012). Since interpretation 'justifies and validates the version of history as seen by those in power' (Poria, Biran, & Reichel, 2009, p. 93) and tends to privilege dominant, hegemonic discourses over less-empowered groups, interpretation of religious heritage can be 'indefinitely extended' depending on those who have the power to represent and interpret religious sites and histories (Chidester & Linenthal, 1995, p. 18).

This leads into the second way in which religious heritage is contested, which is through questions related to *authenticity*. If the interpretation of religious history and ownership is negotiable, then so too is authenticity.

Authenticity generally refers to something that is original or historically accurate. This 'objective authenticity' (Wang, 1999) is what gives an object or site value (Tunbridge & Ashworth, 1996). However, with the rise of alternative philosophical viewpoints regarding what constitutes truth, such as constructivism and postmodernism, what is considered authentic or inauthentic has become more subjective and based upon personal perspectives, tastes, and judgements (Reisinger & Steiner, 2006). From this perspective, there are 'degrees of authenticity' (Timothy, 2011) that range from 'objective authenticity' to 'constructive authenticity' (i.e., where stakeholders and producers create 'authentic' places) to 'existential authenticity' (i.e., where visitors determine what places and objects are authentic) (Wang, 1999). As Timothy and Boyd (2003, p. 245) note, this malleable view of authenticity can lead to 'distorted pasts', where stakeholders – intentionally or unintentionally – present a view of the past that is not authentic.

Another way in which heritage can be contested is through *designation*. The act of designation implies the identification of attributes or qualities of a place or a thing that are worthy of being recognised, preserved, and promoted. The World Heritage Site programme by the United Nations Educational, Scientific and Cultural Organization (UNESCO), for example, searches for natural and cultural heritage that is deemed as having outstanding universal value and therefore in need of preservation and conservation for future generations. While many countries are anxious to reap the developmental benefits of a World Heritage designation through increased international investment and tourism (Bandarin, 2005), many issues can arise, including the erasure of other heritage aspects of a destination, the loss of autonomy over the management, representation, interpretation of heritage sites to external stakeholders, and the destruction of urban landscapes due to the need to modernise tourism infrastructure (Orland & Bellafiore, 1990; Dearborn & Stallmeyer, 2009; Poria, Reichel, & Cohen, 2011). These issues are particularly acute for religious heritage sites, where the religious goals of site managers may be subsumed by the wider concerns of outside stakeholders (Shackley, 2001; Olsen, 2003). Also, the secularisation of urban spaces can lead to changes to the remaking of the status and function of religious heritage sites, such as when churches are bought and redeveloped as housing (Mian, 2008; Lynch, 2014). As such, Poria et al. (2013) argue that religious heritage sites should not receive external designation by UNESCO as World Heritage Sites unless they are considered significant to multiple religious groups.

Two additional ways in which religious heritage is contested is through *encroachment* and *visibility*. These two cases revolve around several issues (c.f. Olsen & Guelke, 2004; Collins-Kreiner, 2008) related to the physical aspects of a religious heritage site (i.e., size, scale), the importance of the location where religious heritage is situated, the distance that religious heritage sites are from each other, the timing of the creation of new religious heritage, and the visibility of religious heritage on cultural landscapes. In the case of encroachment, new religious heritage sites can be contested when they are built too close to the heritage sites of other religious stakeholders, while visibility concerns cases where religious heritage sites, as the physical manifestations of ideology and power, are highly visible within a cultural landscape and therefore viewed as threatening or out of place to other religious stakeholders (Olsen & Guelke, 2004). The more conspicuous a religious heritage site or landscape is, the more likely it will be contested.

Case studies

Competing Jordan River baptismal sites

The authenticity of sacred sites in the Holy Land is frequently the source of many questions posed by Christian tourists, who may wonder where Jesus was really born or fed his 5,000 followers; if Mount Hermon or Mount Tabor is the real site of the transfiguration; or whether the Garden Tomb or the Church of the Holy Sepulchre is the place where Jesus was entombed and resurrected. Another question related to religious authenticity stems from concerns regarding the true location of the baptismal site of Jesus. While biblical texts give clues as to the location where Jesus was baptised, early Christian leaders believed that the baptismal site was somewhere on the Perea side (East Bank) of the Jordan River along the river's southern stretch near the City of Jericho. During the Byzantine era, Christian leaders built several Churches along the east bank of the Jordan (which no longer exist), and during the early twentieth century built several churches on the West Bank east of Jericho.

Historically, concerns over the authenticity of Jesus's baptismal site were minimal, as this region has traditionally been part of the same region controlled by one political entity, and from 1948 to 1967 the country of Jordan controlled both sides of the lower Jordan valley. As such, religious pilgrims typically approached the Jordan River baptismal site through the West Bank. However, after the Six-Day War in 1967 the Jordan River became a militarised international border, accessibility to the baptismal area was heavily restricted and the churches on the West Bank were mostly abandoned.

In the wake of this geopolitical turmoil, the Israeli government decided to create and develop an alternative baptismal site 200 kilometres north, and in 1981 opened a baptismal site just a few metres south from where the Jordan River flows out of the Sea of Galilee where the Israeli government controls both sides of the river. The Yardenit Baptismal Site quickly emerged as a top religious tourism destination. In addition to easier access to the Jordan River itself, managers of the site installed ramps and rails to facilitate easy entry to the water for baptism, and changing rooms, pay toilets, and rentable robes were made available to pilgrims. In addition, the biblical account of Jesus's baptism was displayed in many different languages on tiles along the approach to the river, suggesting to visitors an air of authenticity surrounding the site. A restaurant, snack bar, and large souvenir shop were also built by enterprising Israeli Jews.

After the 1994 Jordan–Israel historic peace agreement and the demilitarisation of the Jordan River border, Jordan began to expand its tourist offerings, including the al-Maghtas ('baptism' in Arabic) site, where centuries of neglect had covered most of the evidence of what was once an important pilgrimage site for Christians. Archaeological work at the site uncovered mosaics, the ruins of several churches, and pottery around Elijah's Hill, which contains a cave where John the Baptist lived and where Jesus came to visit. Further excavations in this area revealed three large pools from the Roman era, an extensive water system, and a large Byzantine monastery, and, closer to the Jordan River, the remains of five churches were uncovered, and excavations at the Church of John the Baptist built during the reign of Emperor Anastasius (491–518) revealed marble steps leading down to Jordan River waters. Based on these discoveries, and combined with traveller accounts from Byzantine times detailing visits to the early churches in the area, Jordan moved forward to develop the site which it marketed as the authentic baptismal site of Jesus (Haddad, Waheeb, & Fakhory, 2009). This baptismal site was legitimated by Pope John Paul II, who dedicated the baptismal site during his 2000 trip to the Holy Land (Katz, 2003).

With the development and interest in the Jordanian baptismal site, Israel began to develop another baptismal site directly opposite the Jordanian site (Qasr al-Yahud). The development of the site, however, was slowed by the need to remove landmines that had been installed during the initial tensions between the two countries after the Six-Day War (Sudilovsky, 2011). Once the mines were removed, a terrace much larger than the terrace at the Jordanian site was built with steps to facilitate access to the river. This move to build a competing baptismal site by the Israeli government led to the development of contested discourses between the two countries regarding which site was the most authentic. As Sudilovsky (2011, p. 19) notes 'while the Israelis maintain that the baptism [of Jesus] took place on their side of the river, the Jordanians insist it occurred a few meters across the river on theirs'. As such, the 'baptismal sites function as ciphers for national self-assertion' (Havrelock, 2011, p. 281), with each site proudly flying their national flags above the competing sacred sites. In addition, the Jordanian officials have been successful in having the al-Maghtas baptismal site (also referred to colloquially by Christians as the Bethany-Beyond-the-Jordan baptismal site) recognised as a World Heritage Site, which lends greater credence to their claims of authenticity. However, the Yardnit baptismal site is still the most visited site by pilgrims, in part because the site is more easily accessible to pilgrims because and the downstream baptismal sites are challenged with muddy and polluted water (Peppard, 2013).

The Hagia Sophia

Not all religious sites commemorate a sacred event. Some are revered for their beauty, distinct architecture, historic longevity, or symbolic relevance to a nation. Istanbul's Hagia Sophia, a UNESCO World Heritage Site, was not built on sacred space, but its beautiful dome and piercing minarets represent the multiple, evolving, and contested identities of the peoples and entities who have controlled Constantinople/Istanbul for the past 1,500 years. The Hagia Sophia (Greek for 'divine wisdom') Basilica was competed in 537 CE during the reign of the Byzantine emperor Justinian. Its massive dome dominated the skyline of the capital of the first Christian empire. However, when the Ottoman Turks conquered Constantinople in 1453, Sultan Mehmet II declared the Hagia Sophia his imperial mosque. Four minarets were added to the outside of the structure, while inside the Christian iconography, mosaics, and altar were replaced with Islamic calligraphy, a mihrab (prayer niche) and mimbar (pulpit).

When the modern-day state of Turkey was founded, nationalist leader Kamal Ataturk sought to modernise and secularise the country. In 1935, Ataturk transformed the church-turned-mosque into a national museum and declared it open to 'all nations and religions'. This designation as a national museum, where restored images and decorations from the church and existing decorations from the mosque were displayed, was a symbolic representation of Turkey's desire to forge a new direction that was not shackled to the symbols and world views of the collapsed Ottoman Empire (Nelson, 2004).

The designation of the Hagia Sophia as a museum lasted for decades. However, in recent years there has been a shift towards a more Islamic society, and with this shift has come the call to change the designation of the Hagia Sophia from a museum back to a mosque. In May 2012, thousands of Muslims gathered outside Hagia Sophia to protest the 1934 law that bars religious services of any kind in the former church/mosque. Before praying outside of the Hagia Sophia, protestors chanted: 'Break the chains, let Hagia Sophia Mosque open' (Yackley, 2012). Around the same time, a Muslim cleric recited verses from the Quran at the opening of an exhibit in the Hagia Sophia showing calligraphy devoted to the prophet Mohammed. Also, the call to prayer began to be loudly broadcast five times a day from a small Islamic sanctuary on the grounds of the museum (Matthews, 2015). During Ramadan 2016, in addition to the call to prayer, religious readings were broadcast daily from the Hagia Sophia. These provocative acts compelled the Greek Orthodox Archdiocese of America to express 'its deepest regret' at 'the unexpected and continuing daily reading of the Koran in Hagia Sophia' and then strongly encouraged 'Turkey to preserve Hagia Sophia in a way that respects its tradition and also its complex history' (Greek Orthodox Metropolis of Chicago, 2016).

Controversy erupted again in 2018 when President Recep Tayyip Erdogan recited the first verse from the Quran at the opening of an arts festival at the museum. He dedicated that prayer, in a direct bid to his nationalist base, to the 'souls of all who left us this work as inheritance, especially Istanbul's conqueror' (Bilginsoy, 2018). Even though the Turkish courts turned down the move to designate the Hagia Sophia a mosque (Vågen, 2018), Erdogan has continued to argue that the designation, status, and function of the Hagia Sophia should be changed from a museum back to a mosque (Rudaw, 2019). These statements from Erdogan have prompted responses from both the Greek government and The United States Commission on International Religious Freedom (USCIRF). The USCRIF released a statement, stating that the:

> Hagia Sophia bears profound historical and spiritual significance to Muslims and Christians alike, and its status as a museum must be maintained. President Erdoğan's comments are needlessly provocative and hurtful to Turkey's minority religious communities. Additionally, the implications of such an action are compounded by the deteriorating landscape for religious freedom, democracy, and human rights in Turkey (USCIRF, 2019).

Greek Foreign Minister George Katrougalos also noted that the Hagia Sophia:

> is not only a great temple of Christendom – the largest for many centuries – it also belongs to humanity. It has been recognized by UNESCO as part of our global cultural heritage ... Questioning of this status is not just an insult to the sentiments of Christians, it is an insult to the international community and international law (Hayward, 2019).

UNESCO also was critical of the proposal noting that since the Hagia Sophia was a World Heritage Site (designated such in 1985) any change to its status would require UNESCO approval (The National Herald, 2019).

Sharing space in Nazareth

Nazareth is intimately tied to the early childhood of Jesus. It was in this small and obscure Galilean village of Nazareth that the angel Gabriel came to announce to Mary that she would bear a son to be named Jesus. It was also in this town where Jesus grew 'in wisdom and stature' and where his ministry began with his prophetic synagogue sermon and subsequent rejection by the hometown crowd. The visit of the angel Gabriel to Mary is of great importance to both the Greek Orthodox and Roman Catholic religious communities, with each group believing that the event took place in different parts of Nazareth. According to the Greek Orthodox community, Gabriel first visited Mary at the village spring on the north end of town and then later visited Mary in her home, while the Roman Catholic community believes that Gabriel's announcement happened only in Mary's home. Nazareth therefore has two churches at the sites of the annunciation. While there is disagreement between the two groups regarding location of the event, there is no contention over shared sacred space (Emmett, 1995).

Since the 1960s Nazareth has been a morning or afternoon stop for Christian pilgrims and tourists as a part of their itineraries. However, because of the congestion caused by these pilgrims, the Israeli government has promoted and more heavily invested in Tiberius (an Israeli Jewish town) on the western shore of the Sea of Galilee in terms of tourism infrastructure, as Tiberius had more space to add new hotels and restaurants and was much easier to navigate than Nazareth. However, in the 1990s the Oslo Peace Accords gave the Palestinian Authority limited self-governing status over Bethlehem and other cities in the West Bank. With the Palestinian Authority promoting the birthplace of Jesus to Christian pilgrims, Israel's Ministry of Tourism took a more vested interest in the pilgrimage tourism development of Nazareth. Further incentive to improve the pilgrimage tourism infrastructure of Nazareth came from interest in the year 2000, which marked 2000 years since the birth of Jesus. This event and the accompanying heightened interest in all things Jesus and the announced visit to the city by Pope John Paul II in March 2000 during the Feast of the Annunciation were also factors leading to increased attention on Nazareth.

The Nazareth 2000 project was a joint project of the Nazareth Municipality and the Ministry of Tourism to make Nazareth more tourist-friendly. The plan included upgrading the central market, planting gardens, building museums and new hotels, creating pedestrian paths connecting the two churches of the annunciation, restoring historic Ottoman-era homes, reconfiguring traffic patterns, and installing a new central plaza where groups of pilgrims could gather before setting out to explore the city (Cohen-Hattab & Shoval, 2007). Of these projects, the new central plaza turned out to be the most problematic. Concerns regarding the plaza came from divergent views of what Nazareth was and how the city should be displayed to the rest of the world. Over time the ethnic composition of the city had shifted from a Christian majority (74 per cent in 1912) to a Muslim majority (70 per cent in 2000) (Khamaisi, 2012), and while Muslims in Nazareth are proud of the fact that they live in the city where the prophet Isa (Jesus) and Mary also once lived, many Muslims resented the still-prevalent political and economic dominance in the city by the Christians (Emmett, 1995).

The site of the proposed plaza was at the junction of Pope Paul Street (the main thoroughfare through town) and Casa Nova Street, which leads up to the Basilica of the Annunciation. The land for the proposed plaza was comprised of several parcels—the largest being the empty lot where an Ottoman era elementary school had recently stood. This school had been an Islamic *waqf* (religious endowment), but with the establishment of the State of Israel, jurisdiction over its control had fallen to the Israel Lands Authority. Located adjacent to the proposed plaza and between the Basilica and the plaza was a *maqam* (Muslim burial shrine) for Shahhab al-Din, the nephew of the famed Saladin who defeated the Crusaders. The Shihab al-Din shrine also functioned as a small mosque. For Muslims, the area designated for the plaza had strong links to their historical presence in the city, and therefore, when the Nazareth 2000 project plans were unveiled, political and religious leaders of the Muslim community, who had not been consulted in the development of the plan, saw the plaza as an opportunity to stand up for greater visibility and representation. On 21 December 1997, activists from the Islamic Movement and the local waqf committee pitched a large tent mosque where the plaza was soon to be installed and argued that a mosque should be installed there instead. A billboard posted by the tent mosque showed an artist's rendition of the mosque with towering minarets that challenged the pre-eminence of the basilica.

After contested municipal elections, riots between Christians and Muslims, and various local, national, and international government negotiations (Tsimhoni, 2010; Khamaisi, 2012), in 2001 the State of Israel intervened and removed the foundation for the intended mosque allowing for the plaza to be completed. The plaza now is jointly enjoyed as a gathering point for groups of Christian tourists and pilgrims and as a place of prayer for Muslims on Fridays.

The Tomb of the Patriarchs

One of the most sacred sites in the Holy Land is the Cave or Tomb of the Patriarchs in the city of Hebron in the West Bank. Known as the Cave of Machpelah to Jews and the Sanctuary of Abraham or al-Haram al-Ibrahimi to Muslims, this site is where it is believed Abraham and Sarah, Isaac and Rebekah, and Jacob and Leah are buried. The site is considered second in holiness after the Western Wall and Temple Mount in Jerusalem for Jews, while for Muslims, the site is often considered to be their fourth most holy site. Christians also consider this site holy. Over the past three millennia, the site has gone through several phases of control and transformation, with different groups remaking and at times limiting access to the site to other religious groups.

At the site is a rectangular stone structure from the Herodian era that controls access to the caves. During Byzantine times, both Christians and Jews prayed at the site, with the Christians transforming the structure into a basilica. Following the Muslim conquest of 638 the basilica was converted into a mosque, which was returned to a basilica during the Crusader period, and then again turned into a mosque when Saladin took over the region (Estrin, 2015; Alshweiky & Gül Ünal, 2016). From that time until 1967 non-Muslims were not allowed to enter the structure, and Jews living in and visiting Hebron were relegated to praying on the first seven steps leading up to the southwest corner of the building.

The sanctity of Hebron and this site to both Jews and Muslims has meant that both groups have had to coexist in the city throughout centuries of turmoil. Indeed, Hebron is one of only four cities in Palestine that maintained a Jewish presence throughout the long rule of the Arabs and Turks. Competing nationalisms changed this coexistence, when in 1929 contention over access to and the status of the Wailing Wall in Jerusalem resulted in violence between the two groups, which spread into Hebron where 67 Jews were massacred by Arabs, after which the Jewish community of Hebron was expelled. Israel's occupation of the West Bank in 1967 led to the Jewish community returning to Hebron, and with this Israeli occupation came changes in the status of the Tomb of the Patriarchs. In 1968, Jews were allowed to enter the sanctuary to pray, and in 1971 an ark for Torah scrolls was placed in the Hall of Abraham which then could function as a synagogue. Further encroachment occurred in 1975 when Jews were permitted to pray in the Hall of Jacob and the interior courtyard, and in 1979 when Jewish settlers forcibly entered the large Hall of Isaac hoping to gain more territory for prayers – which request was granted in part of the hall after months of heated deliberations (Emmett, 2000). These moves led to violent conflict with the majority Muslim community in Hebron, culminating in the 1994 Hebron massacre when 29 Muslims were killed by an Israeli settler as they were praying at the site. This massacre led to the Israeli government dividing the building into two sections – a synagogue for the Jews, and a mosque for the Muslims – each with separate entrances.

Every year, both religious communities are allocated ten days (usually holidays) when all of the building is opened up solely to that religious community for prayers. On these days the lack of trust between the communities necessitates rolling up prayer rugs on the Muslim side or having the Torah ark on wheels so it can be hidden away. To prevent further attacks within the synagogue/mosque, each entrance has multiple security checkpoints, and there is also a bulletproof glass dividing the Jewish and Muslim sides of the shrine (Estrin, 2015). Also, contestation takes place in terms of the management of the site, as the sanctuary itself is owned by the Islamic Waqf Department but controlled by the State of Israel, which makes logistical and maintenance support for the structure problematic at best (Alshweiky & Gül Ünal, 2016).

In recent years, Palestinians have sought to strengthen their claims to the holy site by solidifying international recognition. In July 2017, UNESCO voted to recognise Hebron's Old City and Tomb of the Patriarchs as Palestinian heritage sites. During the contentious balloting in the World Heritage Committee, the vote was 12–3 in favour of the measure, with the committee going against strong pressure from Israel and the United States to defeat the proposal. Part of the proposed Palestinian resolution included designating both Hebron and the Tomb of the Patriarchs site as being in danger, which meant that they would be subject to annual review by UNESCO's World Heritage Committee. In speaking of the designation, the Palestinian Ministry of Foreign Affairs argued that:

Hebron is a city in the heart of the State of Palestine that hosts a site invaluable to world heritage and holy to billions of people around the world of the three monotheistic religions. Hebron's Old City and holy site is under threat due to the irresponsible, illegal, and highly damaging actions of Israel, the occupying Power, which maintains a regime of separation and discrimination in the city base on their background and religion (Eglash, 2017).

This statement and the designation of the Tomb of the Patriarchs as an endangered heritage site, much to the chagrin of Israeli authorities, can be viewed as efforts by the Palestinians to draw attention to the encroachment of Jewish settlers in Hebron and to facilitate ongoing monitoring to ensure that more sacred space is not lost.

The Baha'i Gardens and the BYU Jerusalem Center

In addition to major Christian faiths (i.e., Roman Catholics and Protestants) claiming a vested interest in the region called the Holy Land, other religious groups who are not considered 'traditional' or 'historic' religious faiths because of their lack of physical presence in Israel prior to 1967 (Dumper, 2002) have also staked religious claims to this region. Two of the more prominent groups are the Baha'i and The Church of Jesus Christ of Latter-day Saints (also referred to as Mormons). These groups have built large and very visible buildings within the modern state of Israel in attempts to be viewed as legitimate within the regional and global religious community.

The Baha'i World Centre is located in Haifa, Israel, and serves as the administrative and spiritual headquarters for the Baha'i faith. The Baha'i had a presence in the region for over 150 years, when its founder Bahá'u'lláh was exiled from Iran to the region. While in Acre, Bahá'u'lláh was the focus of pilgrimage veneration by his adherence. Upon Bahá'u'lláh's death in 1892, his son, `Abdu'l-Bahá, marked the location of a shrine to his father, the Shrine of the Báb, on Mount Carmel, which mount was believed by Bahá'u'lláh to be sacred space and the centre of the Baha'i faith. The Shrine of the Báb was completed in 1909, and in 1953 the Shrine was enlarged, surrounded by gardens, and capped with a golden dome. By 1983 the faith's Archives and Universal House of Justice had been built. In the mid-1980s a major reconstruction project took place, and presently the World Centre stretches one kilometre in length up the side of Mount Carmel with several terraced gardens, making it one of the most visible religious buildings in the city (Collins-Kreiner & Gatrell, 2006; Gatrell & Collins-Kreiner, 2006). During this time the Baha'i faith was officially recognised by the Israeli government as a religious community in Israel. Although the centre of the faith, presently there are very few Baha'i adherents living in the region (Collins-Kreiner, 2008).

The Brigham Young University (BYU) Jerusalem Center was built in 1988 on the south-west side of Mount Scopus overlooking the Kidron

Valley. Close by is the Mount of Olives where Church Apostle Orson Hyde, during a visit to Palestine in 1841, dedicated the land for the return of the Jews, the building up of Jerusalem, and the rearing of a temple. Between 1980 and 1984, Church leaders negotiated with the Israeli government for the building of a centre that would meet the religious needs of the few Church members in the area and also facilitate the study abroad programmes of Brigham Young University, a Church-sponsored university, in the region. The land in East Jerusalem upon which the Jerusalem Center was eventually built was leased from the Israeli government. Because of its position overlooking the Old City of Jerusalem, the BYU Jerusalem Center is a very visible religious landmark in Jerusalem (Olsen & Guelke, 2004).

From its inception, the building of the BYU Jerusalem Center was fraught with controversy. A small but vocal group of ultra-Orthodox Jews began to contest the Center once the building became more visible on the landscape of East Jerusalem. They argued that because the Church was an active proselytising faith, the location and size of the Center would attract curious Jews, leading to a 'spiritual Holocaust' (Olsen & Guelke, 2004). This group also contested the secularisation and Americanisation of the Jerusalem landscape (Olsen & Guelke, 2004). In addition to being demonified in local and international newspapers, Church leaders were also subjected to bomb and death threats. The displeasure of the ultra-Orthodox community grew to the point where protests were staged at city hall and a vote of no-confidence was brought against the ruling national Labour Party. To alleviate some of the fears of the ultra-Orthodox protesters, Church leaders signed an official document promising not to engage in proselytising efforts in Israel (Olsen & Guelke, 2004).

In contrast, the development of the Baha'i World Centre on Mount Carmel was fully supported by the people and government of Haifa, in part because Haifa is viewed as a multicultural city and open to other religious influences (Gatrell & Collins-Kreiner, 2006). Also, the Baha'i had a long-established presence in Haifa, whereas The Church of Jesus Christ of Latter-day Saints was seen as an American newcomer to Jerusalem's religious scene. While both religious groups built very visible buildings in the cultural landscape of the region, timing, location, local and regional politics, contextualisation, community stakeholders, and other factors led to the contestation of one building project but not the other (see also Collins-Kreiner, Shmueli, & Ben-Gal, 2013a, 2013b, 2015).

Conclusion

The case studies highlighted briefly in this chapter revolve around a number of shared issues. For example, in each instance the stakeholders involved were engaged in struggle for religious prestige (Cohen-Hattab & Shoval, 2007), whether in terms of ownership, interpretation, or determining who is in-place and who is out of place (Cresswell, 1996). Each case also revolved around 'conflict of identities' (Tsimhoni, 2010), or how concerned stakeholders were to be represented and how this representation affected their group identities. Also, what could have been considered local matters were 'rescaled' or scaled up to include or enjoin broader and more powerful political stakeholders to try to temporarily disempower dominant stakeholders (Swyngedouw, 1997). Indeed, failure to gain authority or control over certain religious heritage sites can lead less powerful stakeholders to resort to the use of religious intolerance to justify extreme measures such as sabotage, encroachment, and violence to gain or re-gain power (Reiter & Kobrin, 2013).

Conflict is always an element of 'space' because it is always an element of social relations. However, the degree, nature, extent, issues, and circumstances of each conflict are place-specific and historically situated. As such, considerations of contested religious heritage between one or multiple religious groups need to incorporate not just the larger, more well-known conflicts but also the smaller, lesser-known conflicts to truly understand the stakes when it comes to contested religious heritage.

References

Alshweiky, R., & Gül Ünal, Z. (2016). An approach to risk management and preservation of cultural heritage in multi identity and multi managed sites: Al-Haram Al-Ibrahimi/Abraham's Tombs of the Patriarchs in Al-Khalil/Hebron. *Journal of Cultural Heritage*, 20, 709–714.
Ashworth, G. J. (1994). From history to heritage – from heritage to identity. In G. J. Ashworth & P. J. Larkham (eds), *Building a new heritage: Tourism, culture and identity in the new Europe* (pp. 13–30). London and New York: Routledge.
Bajc, V. (2006). Christian pilgrimage groups in Jerusalem: Framing the experience through linear meta-narrative. *Journeys*, 7(2), 101–128.
Bandarin, F. (2005). Foreword. In D. Harrison & M. Hitchcock (eds), *The politics of world heritage: Negotiating tourism and conservation* (pp. v–iv). Clevedon, UK: Channel View Publications.
Barber, R. (1991). *Pilgrimages*. Woodbridge, UK: Boydell & Brewer Ltd.
Belhassen, Y., & Ebel, J. (2009). Tourism, faith and politics in the Holy Land: An ideological analysis of evangelical pilgrimage. *Current Issues in Tourism*, 12(4), 359–378.
Bilginsoy, Z, (2018). Turkish President recites Muslim prayer at the Hagia Sophia in Constantinople. *The National Herald*, 1 April. Retrieved from https://www.thenationalherald.com/195736/turkish-president-recites-muslim-prayer-at-the-hagia-sophia/.
Brace, C., Bailey, A. R., & Harvey, D. C. (2006). Religion, place and space: A framework for investigating historical geographies of religious identities and communities. *Progress in Human Geography*, 30(1), 28–43.
Breglia, L. (2006). *Monumental ambivalence: The politics of heritage*. Austin, TX: University of Texas Press.
Brin, E. (2006). Politically-oriented tourism in Jerusalem. *Tourist Studies*, 6(3), 215–243.
Burgess, P. J. (2004). The sacred site in civil space: Meaning and status of the temple mount/al-Haram al-Sharif. *Social Identities*, 10(3), 311–323.

Chidester, D., & Linenthal, E. T. (1995). Introduction. In D. Chidester & E. T. Linenthal (eds), *American Sacred Space* (pp. 1–42). Bloomington, IN: Indiana University Press.

Cohen-Hattab, K., & Shoval, N. (2007). Tourism development and cultural conflict: The case of 'Nazareth 2000'. *Social & Cultural Geography*, *8*(5), 701–717.

Collins-Kreiner, N. (2008). Religion and politics: New religious sites and spatial transgression in Israel. *Geographical Review*, *98*(2), 197–213.

Collins-Kreiner, N., & Gatrell, J. D. (2006). Tourism, heritage and pilgrimage: The case of the Haifa's Baha'i Gardens. *Journal of Heritage Tourism*, *1*(1), 32–50.

Collins-Kreiner, N., Shmueli, D. F., & Ben Gal, M. (2013a). Spatial transgression of new religious sites in Israel. *Applied Geography*, *40*, 103–114.

Collins-Kreiner, N., Shmueli, D. & Ben-Gal, M. (2013b). Pilgrimage sites in the Holy Land: Pathways to harmony and understanding or sources of confrontation? In A. M. Pazon (ed.), *Pilgrims and pilgrimages as peacemakers in Christianity, Judaism and Islam* (pp. 177–201). Surrey: Ashgate.

Collins-Kreiner, N., Shmueli, D. F., & Ben Gal, M. (2015). Understanding conflicts at religious-tourism sites: The Baha'i World Center, Israel. *Tourism Management Perspectives*, *16*, 228–236.

Cresswell, T. (1996). *In place/out of place: Geography, ideology, and transgression*. Minneapolis, MN: University of Minnesota Press.

Dearborn, L. M., & Stallmeyer, J. C. (2009). Re-visiting Luang Prabang: Transformations under the influence of world heritage designation. *Journal of Tourism and Cultural Change*, *7*(4), 247–269.

de Vries, M., Kligler-Vilenchik, N., Alyan, E., Ma'oz, M. & Maoz, I. (2017). Digital contestation in protracted conflict: The online struggle over al-Aqsa Mosque. *The Communication Review*, *20*(3), 189–211.

Di Giovine, M. A. (2008). *The heritage-scape: UNESCO, world heritage, and tourism*. Landham, MD: Lexington Books.

Dumper, M. (2002). The Christian churches in the post-Oslo period. *Journal of Palestine Studies*, *31*(2), 51–65.

Durante, R., & Zhuravskaya, E. (2018). Attack when the world is not watching? US news and the Israeli-Palestinian conflict. *Journal of Political Economy*, *126*(3), 1085–1133.

Eglash, R. (2017). Israeli diplomat says UNESCO resolution is less important than fixing his toilet. *The Washington Post*, 9 July. Retrieved from https://www.washingtonpost.com/news/worldviews/wp/2017/07/09/israeli-diplomat-says-unesco-resolution-is-less-important-than-fixing-his-toilet/?utm_term=.51b0057bf3b7.

Emmett, C. (1995). *Beyond the basilica: Christians and Muslims in Nazareth*. Chicago, IL: The University of Chicago Press.

Emmett, C. (2000). Sharing sacred space in the Holy Land. In A. B. Murphy & D. J. Johnson (eds), *Cultural encounters with the environment: Enduring and evolving geographic themes* (pp. 261–282). Lanham, MD: Rowman & Littlefield Publishers.

Estrin, D. (2015). In Hebron, Israelis and Palestinians share a holy site... begrudgingly. *PRI*, 10 November. Retrieved from https://www.pri.org/stories/2015-11-10/hebron-jews-and-palestinians-share-holy-site-begrudgingly.

Gatrell, J. D., & Collins-Kreiner, N. (2006). Negotiated space: Tourists, pilgrims, and the Bahá'í terraced gardens in Haifa. *Geoforum, 37*(5), 765–778.

Graham, B., Ashworth, G., & Tunbridge, J. (2000). *A geography of heritage: Power, culture and economy.* London and New York: Routledge.

Greek Orthodox Metropolis of Chicago. (2016). Greek Orthodox archdiocese protests the reading of Koran in Hagia Sophia. 13 June. Retrieved from http://chicago.goarch.org/news/2016/6/13/greek-orthodox-archdiocese-protests-the-reading-of-koran-in-hagia-sophia.

Haddad, N., Waheeb, M., & Fakhory, L. (2009). The baptism archaeological site of Bethany beyond Jordan: Towards an assessment for a management plan. *Tourism Panning & Development, 6*(3), 173–190.

Hardy, D. (1998). Historical geography and heritage studies. *Area, 20*(4), 333–338.

Harrison, D., & Hitchcock, M. (eds). (2005). *The politics of world heritage: Negotiating tourism and conservation.* Clevedon, UK: Channel View Publications.

Havrelock, R. (2011). *The River Jordan: Mythology of a dividing line.* Chicago, IL: The University of Chicago Press.

Hayward, J. (2019). Greece angered by Erdogan's proposal to turn the Hagia Sophia into a mosque. *Breitbart*, 26 March. Retrieved from https://www.breitbart.com/national-security/2019/03/26/greece-angered-by-erdogans-proposal-to-turn-the-hagia-sophia-into-a-mosque/.

Hazbun, W. (2004). Globalisation, reterritorialisation and the political economy of tourism development in the Middle East. *Geopolitics, 9*(2), 310–341.

Hercbergs, D. (2012). Narrating instability: Political detouring in Jerusalem. *Mobilities, 7*(3), 415–438.

Hughes, K., Bond, N., & Ballantyne, R. (2013). Designing and managing interpretive experiences at religious sites: Visitors' perceptions of Canterbury Cathedral. *Tourism Management, 36*, 210–220.

Isaac, R. K., & Ashworth, G. J. (2011). Moving from pilgrimage to 'dark' tourism: Leveraging tourism in Palestine. *Tourism Culture & Communication, 11*(3), 149–164.

Katz, K. (2003). Legitimizing Jordan as the Holy Land: Papal Pilgrimages – 1964, 2000. *Comparative Studies of South Asia, Africa and the Middle East, 23*(1), 181–189.

Kelman, H. C. (1987). The political psychology of the Israeli–Palestinian conflict: How can we overcome the barriers to a negotiated solution? *Political Psychology, 8*(3), 347–363.

Khamaisi, R. (2012). The impact of conflicts over Holy Sites on city images and landscapes: The case of Nazareth. In E. Barkan & K. Barkey (eds), *Choreographies of shared sacred sites: Religion and conflict resolution* (pp. 270–296). New York: Columbia University Press.

Lowenthal, D. (1996). *Possessed by the past.* New York: The Free Press.

Lynch, N. (2014). Divine living: Marketing and selling churches as lofts in Toronto, Canada. *Housing, Theory and Society, 31*(2), 192–212.

Matthews, O. (2015). Islamists and secularists battle over Turkey's Hagia Sophia museum. *Newsweek*, 2 June. Retrieved from https://www.newsweek.com/2015/06/12/battle-over-hagia-sophia-338091.html. Accessed 13 December 2019.

Mian, N. A. (2008). 'Prophets-for-profits': Redevelopment and the altering urban religious landscape. *Urban Studies, 45*(10), 2143–2161.

Morgan, N., & Pritchard, A. (1998). *Tourism promotion and power: Creating images, creating identities*. New York. John Wiley.

Nelson, R. S. (2004). *Hagia Sophia, 1850–1950: Holy wisdom modern monument*. Chicago, IL: The University of Chicago Press.

Norkunas, M. K. (1993). *The politics of public memory: Tourism, history, and ethnicity in Monterey, California*. Albany, NY: State University of New York Press.

Olsen, D. H. (2003). Heritage, tourism, and the commodification of religion. *Tourism Recreation Research*, 28(3), 99–104.

Olsen, D. H. (2012). Teaching truth in 'third space': The use of religious history as a pedagogical instrument at Temple Square in Salt Lake City, Utah. *Tourism Recreation Research*, 37(3), 227–237.

Olsen, D. H. (2019). Religion, pilgrimage, and tourism in the MENA region. In D. J. Timothy (ed.), *Routledge handbook on tourism in the Middle East and North Africa* (pp. 109–124). London and New York: Routledge.

Olsen, D. H. (2020). Religion, spirituality, and pilgrimage in a globalizing world. In D. J. Timothy (ed.), *The handbook on globalization and tourism*. London: Edward Elgar.

Olsen, D. H., & Guelke, J. K. (2004). Spatial transgression and the BYU Jerusalem Center controversy. *The Professional Geographer*, 56(4), 503–515.

Olsen, D. H., & Timothy, D. J. (2002). Contested religious heritage: Differing views of Mormon heritage. *Tourism Recreation Research*, 27(2), 7–15.

Orland, B., & Bellafiore, V. J. (1990). Development directions for a sacred site in India. *Landscape and Urban Planning*, 19(2), 181–196.

Peppard, C. Z. (2013). Troubling waters: The Jordan River between religious imagination and environmental degradation. *Journal of Environmental Studies and Sciences*, 3(2), 109–119.

Philp, J., & Mercer, D. (1999). Commodification of Buddhism in contemporary Burma. *Annals of Tourism Research*, 26(1), 21–54.

Poria, Y., Biran, A., & Reichel, A. (2009). Visitors' preferences for interpretation at heritage sites. *Journal of Travel Research*, 48(1), 92–105.

Poria, Y., Reichel, A. & Cohen, R. (2011). World Heritage Site – is it an effective brand name? A case study of a religious heritage site. *Journal of Travel Research*, 50(5), 482–495.

Poria, Y., Reichel, A. & Cohen, R. (2013). Tourists perceptions of World Heritage Site and its designation. *Tourism Management*, 35, 272–274.

Reisinger, Y., & Steiner, C. J. (2006). Reconceptualizing object authenticity. *Annals of Tourism Research*, 33(1), 65–86.

Reiter, Y., & Kobrin, N. (2013). Violence on inter-religious background in three Israeli cities: Safed, Nazareth, and Beit Shemesh. *The Romanian Journal of Society and Politics*, 8(1), 55–78.

Rudaw. (2019) 'Erdogan encourages Hagia Sophia to be designated a mosque'. *Rudaw.net*, 28 March. Retrieved from https://www.rudaw.net/english/middleeast/turkey/280320191. Accessed 13 December 2019.

Shackley, M. (2001). *Managing sacred sites: Service provision and visitor experience*. London: Continuum.

Sudilovsky, J. (2011). Israel removes landmines from Jesus baptism site. *The Christian Century*, 14 June. Retrieved from http://www.christiancentury.org/article/2011-05/pilgrims-return-jesus-baptismal-site-israel-removeslandmines.

Swyngedouw, E. (1997). Excluding the other: The production of scale and scaled politics. In R. Lee & J. Wills (eds). *Geographies of economies* (pp. 167–176). London: Arnold.

Tessler, M. (2009). *A history of the Israeli-Palestinian conflict*. Bloomington, IN: Indiana University Press.

The National Herald. (2019). UNESCO Stakes Aghia Sophia Claim, Erdogan says 'no Constantinople'. *The National Herald*, 29 March. Retrieved from https://www.thenationalherald.com/237036/unesco-stakes-aghia-sophia-claim-erdogan-says-no-constantinople/.

Timothy, D. J. (1997). Tourism and the personal heritage experience. *Annals of Tourism Research*, *24*(3), 751–754.

Timothy, D. J. (2011). *Cultural heritage and tourism: An introduction*. Bristol, UK: Channel View Publications.

Timothy, D. J., & Boyd, S. W. (2003). *Heritage tourism*. Essex, UK: Prentice Hall.

Timothy, D. J., & Emmett, C. F. (2014). Jerusalem, tourism, and the politics of heritage. In M. Adelman & M. F. Elman (eds). *Jerusalem: Conflict & cooperation in a contested city* (pp. 276–290). Syracuse, NY: Syracuse University Press.

Tsimhoni, D. (2010). The Shihab Al-Din Mosque affair in Nazareth: A case study of Muslim–Christian–Jewish relations in the state of Israel. In M. J. Berger & L. Hammer (eds), *Holy places in the Israeli-Palestinian conflict: Confrontation and coexistence* (pp. 192–230). London: Routledge.

Tunbridge, J. E., & Ashworth, G. J. (1996). *Dissonant heritage: The management of the past as a resource in conflict*. Chichester, UK: John Wiley & Sons.

United States Commission on International Religious Freedom (USCIRF). (2019). USCIRF condemns Erdogan's threats to change status of Hagia Sophia. *USCIRF*, 28 March. Retrieved from https://www.uscirf.gov/news-room/press-releases-statements/uscirf-condemns-erdogan-s-threats-change-status-hagia-sophia.

Vågen, A. (2018). Turkish courts reject converting Hagia Sophia into a Mosque. *The Heritage Daily*, 14 September. Retrieved from https://www.heritagedaily.com/2018/09/turkish-courts-reject-converting-hagia-sophia-into-a-mosque/121656.

Voase, R. (2007). Visiting a cathedral: The consumer psychology of a 'rich experience'. *International Journal of Heritage Studies*, *13*(1), 41–55.

Wang, N. (1999). Rethinking authenticity in tourism experience. *Annals of Tourism Research*, *26*(2), 349–370.

Weiss, L. (2007). Heritage-making and political identity. *Journal of Social Archaeology*, *7*(3), 413–431.

Yackley, A. J. (2012). Hagia Sofia: Thousands pray for Istanbul landmark to become mosque. *HuffPost*, 26 May. Retrieved from https://www.huffpost.com/entry/hagia-sofia_n_1548019.

4 Making a sense of place for Safranbolu World Heritage Site
An analysis of *Safranbolu: Reflections of Time*

Enis Tataroglu

Introduction

One of the subjects emphasised by scholars is how heritage is used to construct and negotiate a range of identities, social and cultural values, and meanings in the present. Heritage, which includes various practices, such as visitation, management, interpretation, and conservation, concretises various social and cultural acts while constructing a sense of place and belonging in the present. It is not only about the meaning of the past and the cultural, social, and political needs of the present, but also about negotiating new ways of expressing identity using the past and collective or individual memories.

The negotiation of new ways of identifying and making sense of place is socially constructed, and discourses function as a power, forming many practices of heritage. This study is concerned with how the meaning of heritage and a sense of place is constructed in Safranbolu, one of the first sites inscribed as a World Heritage Site in Turkey. Through analysis of a documentary that substantially contributed to the construction of a heritage discourse and conservation process that led to Safranbolu becoming a World Heritage Site, an attempt will be made to address the social and cultural factors that led to the making of an official heritage discourse. In addition, the ideological implications of the elements constituting the official heritage discourse of Safranbolu will be discussed.

Sense of place and heritage discourse

Sense of place has been discussed by different perspectives drawing on different theoretical approaches, although it is usually primarily addressed in two different ways, through either the concept of local distinctiveness (*genius loci*) or the ways of experiencing and understanding of places (Convery, Corsane, & Davis, 2014). Accordingly, 'sense of place' refers to the unique features that give an area its character and the manner in which people relate to this feature. In other words, 'sense of place is inevitably dual in nature, involving both an interpretive perspective on environment and an emotional reaction to the environment' (Hummon, 1992, p. 262). Therefore, the concept comprises very subjective attributions to places (Agnew, 1987) and is based on symbolic meanings attributed to the setting (Hummon, 1992; Greider & Garkovich, 1994; Williams & Stewart, 1988).

Like sense of place, heritage is also a meaning-based concept. This meaning, however, is primarily socially constructed and indicative of the significance of language in the formation of people–place relationships, Tuan highlights the fact that speech and the written word construct place and by imparting emotion and personality make it visible (Tuan, 1991). Tuan (1980) also argues that people 'make' or 'unmake' places by talking about them. Drawing upon the idea that the social construction process is rooted in language, it is argued that the lived experience and the meanings people attribute to the world are also created by linguistic practices (Di Masso, Dixon, & Durrheim, 2014). Hence, referring to the arguments of constructionist approaches, it may be claimed that sense of place is an interpretative process dependent on making meaning through linguistic practices. Moving from this point, it may be claimed that sense of place is a discursive process practised by certain agents aiming to produce heritage by imparting sense-making to places in order to persuade people to take action or to provide them with an idea of heritage.

Defined as 'a system of statements which constructs an object' (Parker, 1992, p. 5), discourses are practices not just for representing the world, but of signifying the world, and constituting and constructing the world in meaning (Fairclough, 2013). Discourse is not only 'used' to do things by actors but also do things to actors and is productive independent of actors (Bourdieu & Wacquant, 2001). Discourse therefore not only reflects social meanings and relations but also constitutes and governs them (Smith, 2006). It contributes to the making of dimensions of the social, which shapes and constrains it, and is socially constitutive and socially shaped. Discourse constitutes objects of knowledge, social identities, and relationships between people and place. Discourses are inherent in social contexts, and these social contexts are the socio-cultural environments that foster ideologies, just as Wallwork and Dixon (2004) demonstrated how producing a particular version of the countryside reproduced nationalist ideology. Ideology and discourse activate the identification of places, making and unmaking certain senses and attitudes of people toward the past and heritage.

The significance of Safranbolu World Heritage Site

Turkey has a multi-layered history, and its heritage assets inscribed by UNESCO belong to different civilisations that settled in Anatolia, such as the Roman, Greek, Byzantine, Seljuk, and Ottoman. The official discourse heritage of the Republic of Turkey, however, called 'Anotolism', has emerged as an imagination based on the land, not an ethnic identity. This has produced an official discourse that embraces all cultures in the Anatolian geography, including classical Greek and Byzantine, and considers the past as a whole

(Özdoğan, 1998). Nevertheless, since Turkey has been depicted as a place where East and West meet and as the melting points of different cultures, the issues concerned with identity, belonging, and lifestyle have always become the subject of controversial discussions. This has led to a divergence between individuals in terms of establishing a bond of belonging with past cultures, depending on the differences between various cultural and social groups regarding the symbolic and cultural meanings of past civilisations. In other words, though the World Heritage assets of the country are scientifically or aesthetically significant at the national or universal level, the bond of belonging with heritage develops under various effects, including the cultural and ideological.

Safranbolu, a town in the Turkish province of Karabük, was designated a UNESCO World Heritage Site in 1994. Turkey's World Heritage Sites have been generally designated as such because of their scientific, aesthetic, and universal importance; among 18 UNESCO World Heritage assets of the country, there are only a few places signified and constructed by discourses related to social and cultural identity. What makes Safranbolu special is that the city has become a heritage site represented and identified by the cultural and heritage assets remaining from the Ottoman past and lifestyle. In other words, unlike in many other UNESCO World Heritage Sites of Turkey, Safranbolu has not become a heritage place for aesthetic, scientific, or universal concerns. During the process of designating Safranbolu a heritage site and the subsequent social practices surrounding it, the dynamics resulting from a series of social and cultural changes from below have been decisive. Hence, the heritage practices of Safranbolu have been shaped and constructed by distinctive discourses, depending on the ideas and attributions regarding modernity, tradition, and identity. Significantly, this process was completed by marking and experiencing Safranbolu as a heritage site showing the past as belonging to a specific cultural or ideological orientation.

In the process of making sense of place and constructing a heritage discourse for Safranbolu, the role played by a documentary is remarkable, especially in its transformation of the relationships between people and the town. *Safranbolu'da Zaman* [*Safranbolu: Reflections of Time*] (Arın, 1976), played a significant role in raising awareness for the first time of the conservation of heritage. As a constitutive and persuasive source of power, the documentary developed a language of heritage, place, and identity to mobilise individuals to practise heritage conservation. In this study, to understand how Safranbolu and heritage is sensed, the documentary *Safranbolu: Reflections of Time* was taken as a text (Feighery, 2006; Shurmer-Smith, 2002) and analysed using discourse analysis. The documentary was assumed as a 'fabric' of identity, signifying how meanings of place and people are crafted and constructed. In doing so, the text of the documentary has been translated from Turkish to English by the author.

Why *Safranbolu: Reflections of Time*?

It cannot be said that the language and expressions of *Safranbolu: Reflections of Time* reflect all the elements of the official heritage discourse of Turkey. Since its production in 1976, however, the film has continued as a means of exchanging the idea and meaning of heritage. In other words, from its production to today, this documentary has become an 'everyday linguistic practice' (Di Masso et al., 2014, p. 83) through which the meaning of heritage and person–place relationships are created and produced.

Expressed as a 'Lament for Safranbolu' by its director Suha Arın, *Safranbolu: Reflections of Time* has become a cultural text that mediates the many negotiated meanings related to cultural heritage conservation and collective memory in the city. When the film was released, it immediately attracted the interest of the country's leading political figures, who participated in the premiere, was the subject of numerous articles in the national press, received awards at festivals, and aired twice on the country's only TV channel, TRT. The film raised the profile of Safranbolu until 1994, when Safronbolu was inscribed in the UNESCO World Heritage List. Safranbolu, which had no hotels in the years of the documentary's production, began to attract the interest of the tourism industry, and its mansions that were being destroyed began to be converted into hotels. In addition, the term *Safranbolu: Reflections of Time* has become an idiom used on various platforms. Moreover, since 2000, a festival showing only documentary films has been organised each year on a theme designated as cultural heritage and protectionism in Safranbolu. It has been made explicit that heritage, Safranbolu, and the art of documentary are now interconnected thanks to the film and its director, Suha Arın. The importance attributed to the film and its director in the construction of the meaning of heritage, sense of place, and the formation of various cultural and tourism practices has continued until recently. In 2015, a culture and art centre was opened on behalf of Suha Arın, whose name was given to one of the district's main squares. The speeches at the ceremony held in 2015 are remarkable in terms of showing the film's continuing role in reproducing the identity of the city and its sense of place (Yenişafak Gazetesi, 2015):

> Suha Arın means the beginning of the tourism movement for Safranbolu (Mayor Necdet Aksoy).
> *Safranbolu: Reflections of Time* is the cornerstone for us. Suha Arın made Safranbolu to be known by everyone (District Governor Murat Bulacak).
> When my brother directed *Safranbolu: Reflections of Time*, he would not have predicted that the film would still be on the agenda even after so many years (Reha Arın).

Since 1976, *Safranbolu: Reflections of Time* has continued to be a narrative used by the tourism industry to incorporate the town into the production and consumption processes of tourism. A travel agency's description of Safranbolu illustrates this:

> An Ottoman town that defies centuries and whose fate changed with a documentary. Safranbolu, which has been revived and brought to tourism with Suha Arın's documentary *Safranbolu: Reflections of Time* and inscribed in the UNESCO world heritage list, invites you with its authentic streets and Ottoman mansions (Biletiniz Turları, 2019).

The above quotations from various figures related to Safranbolu indicate that the documentary, which produces meanings about many social practices for the conservation of cultural heritage, still has an effect and has been constantly consumed, negotiated, and reproduced. As a cultural text that constitutes ideological dilemmas and constructs the discourse of heritage, the documentary is also embraced by the mayor, governor, and ruling elites and has become one of the texts of authorised heritage discourse (Smith, 2006).

Discourse analysis of *Safranbolu: Reflections of Time*

Discourse analysis focuses on the role of discourse in producing and reproducing social reality and seeks to explain the processes by which power is legitimised and enacted in the rhetoric of dominant groups or institutions (Feighery, 2012). From a Foucauldian perspective, the idea of heritage in Safranbolu is constituted by certain discourses that cause people to act and think in accordance with its inscribed meanings. Hence, the discursive practice of *Safranbolu: Reflections of Time* has emerged as a power that creates identity and the meaning of heritage. In other words, the places and heritage crafted in *Safranbolu: Reflections of Time* become part of the language for the people who imagine and talk about the city. The language of the documentary is performative and functional, constructing a heritage identity of how people think, feel, and act in their relationships with heritage and place.

The Foucauldian method of analysis, however, concerns neglecting the material, economic, and structural factors in the way power and knowledge are deployed (Smith, 2006; Hannam & Knox, 2005). According to Feighery (2006), discourse analysis revolves around finding the structure between the micro-structures of the text and the social and cultural phenomena in which the discourse is embedded. The methodological approach of analysis is based on providing a description and explanation by creating discourses about the social and cultural phenomenon taken into consideration and eliminating the barriers between discourse and practice (Smith, 2006).

In this study, the three-dimensional approach of Fairclough (2013) – textual analysis, discursive practice, and socio-cultural practice – will be used to analyse the documentary. In the study, the first dimension is taken depending on the rhetoric and semantics of the film and the determination of words and phrases that produce meaning in different story patterns. As the discursive practice is concerned with how text is produced and consumed, the aim in the second stage is to describe and explain the orientation of the producers. In other words, the question is: to whom is film speaking and what kind of sense of place do the filmmakers aim to construct? The third stage of the analysis discusses the interpretation of the ideology, supporting the discursive practice of the film. In other words, the question of this dimension is simply what kind of ideological orientation is adapted in the documentary in making sense of place for Safranbolu as a world heritage place.

The socio-economic and cultural context in the 1970s

In discursive/constructionist approaches to the sense of place, the macro-structural context within which the text is embedded (Feighery, 2006) needs close examination, and general key concepts of analysis are applied to a social problem with a focus on understanding how language figures into that problem because the processes that create a sense of place are determined by the social, cultural, and economic context in which they occur (Ennen & van Maanen, 2013), making the connections between socio-cultural context and discourse appear to be the significant factor of the analysis (Hannam & Knox, 2005).

The following summarises well the socio-economic environment of the period in which the document was produced and the text flourished:

> Safranbolu had an introverted social life in the 1970s, which was in constant economic decline. In those years, the most important field of business and the place to work was to enter Karabük Iron and Steel Factory as a worker. Being a worker was like winning a lottery because of social rights and was identical to winning social status. The desire of craftsmen to become workers in iron and steel factories by closing their workplace that began in the 1950s and continued to increase led to the end of commercial life in Safranbolu to a great extent in the 1970s (Kuş & Kızıltan, 2015, p. 335).

From this, it would not be wrong to connect many practices of heritage conservation with the problems that the city was faced with, namely the economic and social decadence of the city. The discourses created by these macro-structural conditions are crafted in the documentary around some themes and narratives.

Making sense of place from sadness and sorrow

Safranbolu: Reflections of Time is mainly a narrative, making sense of place in terms of heritage and time. Based on the comparison of past and present, the documentary depicts and expresses the aesthetic characteristics of Safranbolu houses, the past social life in these houses, intergenerational relations, nature–human interactions, and forgotten professions. Most of the 40-minute documentary film is devoted to detailed views or scenes of Safranbolu houses, and the film depicts the destruction of time in these houses. Numerous phrases allude to time, such as 'the time that leave us alone', 'hard time', 'the time that is wearing down', 'the time that has rigid heart', 'time that takes away the most beautiful days', 'the houses fall prey to time', 'the time that bends joy', 'the time that leaves', 'the time that stole the most beautiful days', 'the time that destroys man', 'the time that takes everything away', and 'the time that takes many things that were created and produced with pride'. Expressions like 'surrendered by time', 'fallen by time', and 'the overwhelming superiority of time' are frequently repeated in the film. An image of a Safranbolu succumbing to time is presented to the viewer. The narrated or imagined time is not only the present time but also past times. The filmmaker uses the concept of time in terms of change involving a two-way process, both good and bad; good times are identified with the glorification of heritage and culture, and bad times are associated with the processes that spoil and demolish heritage. In other words, Safranbolu, which has succumbed to time, is the one place that cannot stand the destructive effects of modernisation.

In crafting the discourse for heritage, language is used in a variety of ways as a persuasive power to sense place in a certain way. Choosing autumn for the season of production is tied with the intention to reinforce feelings of sadness and sorrow in the audience and make people sense the place with these emotions. The sad form of traditional Turkish music, whose origins are in Ottoman palace music, is heard throughout the film. *Safranbolu: Reflections of Time* conveys sadness and regret in its songs, words, images, and content. In order to build the practices of protecting heritage, the filmmakers fundamentally aim to manage the senses of individuals by arousing emotions, such as pain, sadness, and fear, which Spinoza defines as bad emotions. This strategy is manifested mainly in four major narratives.

Narrative 1: The discourse of heritage against modernity

While making sense of Safranbolu, the main route followed by the producers is based on provoking the audience to think and imagine the city through various dichotomies. Indeed, the general ideological scheme continues on a basic dichotomy indicated by emphasising positive things about 'us' and emphasising negative things about 'them' (Van Dijk, 2000). Based on this perspective, the discourse of heritage is made by comparing and constructing two main social and cultural conditions: i.e., tradition and modernity. The 'us' and 'them' duality is interpreted as 'ideas', a 'way of signifying' or a 'way of life' attributed to different cultural realms, rather than identifying two different concrete groups. That is, in the analysis of the discursive construction of heritage, the dimension of 'emphasising positive things about us' has been assumed to be a positive narrative of heritage. The following are some of the clauses of the rhetoric that presents the positive 'us' or self. The meaning of the phrase is indicated in parentheses.

'The priceless gift of time is the houses with the pool' (pricelessness); 'harmonious sound that has not changed over time' (eternity); 'the rooms with a pool are as nice and expressive as a poem' (lyricism); 'houses and neighbourhoods that never cover each other's field of vision' (respectfulness); 'skilfully made decorations' (mastery); 'lines and colours are the products of a fine art' (fine art); 'a set of old Turkish words that have an aesthetic meaning' (aesthetic), 'smiling old houses with their unique faces, habits, personalities, and things to tell' (authenticity and individuality); 'time has left a separate trial in every corner of Safranbolu; those wandering in the narrow streets feel that each structure has a story to tell' (subjectivity); 'elegance and elaborateness in the subtle arrangements of the rooms' (elegance); 'timeless walnut base' (timelessness). In the dimension of the positive narratives of heritage discourse, features such as pricelessness, harmony, mastery, fine art, aesthetic meaning, authenticity, individuality, subjectivity, elegance, and timelessness are pointed out. As a result of a number of factors, however, it is stated that these unique qualities have undergone some transformations, and the current state of the heritage houses is indicated as follows: 'houses defeated by time' (defeat); 'disappearing professions, craftsmen surrendering to time' (annihilation), 'derelict houses, houses in pain, forgotten houses, houses where the sense of being lost is felt, sad stories' (dereliction, being lost, pain, sadness).

Moreover, the text does not fail to show the cause of these negatives or the social factors that are destructive to heritage; they are presented as modernity and change. The dimension of 'emphasising negative things about them' of the general ideological schema emerges in relation to the destructive effects of modernity. The clauses are: 'the pain of a cruel change and degeneration' (degenerating change); 'the pain of old windows pushed aside with their subtle elegant looks and chocolate-coloured shutters' (change leading to pain in elaborateness and elegance); 'today's windows, the pain of injury of a Safranbolu house' (change that causes pain); 'some of the houses with smiling faces are now meaningless, surly, and confused' (change causing meaninglessness and confusion); 'houses that lost their resistance to earthquakes with the change in their traditional structure' (change that disrupts technical harmony with nature); 'modernised life consumes blacksmithing as well as many other things' (modernity that consumes).

Safranbolu: Reflections of Time constructs heritage discourses in the face of modernity. A sense of heritage that cannot resist time and change is emphasised, and all these negativities experienced by the heritage are passed on to the audience through passive sentence structures. In this context, heritage and tradition are presented through the words of aesthetics, supremacy, uniqueness, harmony, art, beauty, functionality, delicacy, personality, nature, and colour. Also, modernity and change are signified with words of pain, sadness, forgiveness, disappearance, corruption, and defeat. In the positive self, there is the glorification of heritage, culture, and tradition, and in the presenting of the negative other, the sadness, abandonment, forgottenness, rootlessness, and fragmentation arising from change and modernity are expressed. Illustrating the contrast between the old and the new and the effect of economic and social change on heritage, the narrator also describes the old as having 'personality', 'subjectivity', 'originality', and suggests that the modern houses have no unique character. Safranbolu's new type of multi-story apartment buildings developed as workers' houses next to the town is described in the following sentences:

> With the overwhelming support of time, the change is leaping from home to home as an *infectious disease*, and a new Safranbolu is formed in and around the old Safranbolu. The old faces have their own *distinctive features, their personalities, and their character*, and the apartments that are different from those smiling houses.

The contradiction between the new and old houses depends on some well-known themes of modernity critiques, such as standardisation, loss of subjectivity, and the rising of objective culture, found in the Simmelian way of understanding modern city life. The documentary shows all these processes as the source and cause of pain, sadness, and grief. Modernity is portrayed as a disruptive process leading to the disappearance of subjective culture and the rise of objective culture (Simmel, 2013). Therefore, the film's relationship with modernity is painful and presented as a 'dark' experience (Wang, 2000) leading to a social formation that erodes solid structures. The real effect created by modernity in Safranbolu, however, is that houses are not only shown for their aesthetic ugliness, loss of distinctiveness, and perhaps technical weakness because of losing their resistance to earthquakes but also it is associated with the cultural sphere, and this critique manifests itself most clearly in the idea of home and family.

Narrative 2: The discourse of home and uprootedness

In terms of the identity levels of heritage (Howard, 2003), *Safranbolu: Reflections of Time* constructs heritage identity at the levels of home, neighbourhood, and locality. More than half of the 40-minute film features functional, artistic, and aesthetic values and paintings and narratives of houses and mansions. Houses, however, are not only subject to sublimation strategies due to their aesthetic, artistic, and functional features, but also considered a social space where issues related to belonging are discussed:

> Old houses that live in oblivion. Grandparents, fathers, and grandchildren lived together in these houses. They once respected the tradition of not extinguishing the elaborately protected father's house as an heirloom. The pain of the lost and forgotten is felt in the houses.

In traditional social formations, it is a common experience that when people are uprooted and cut off from family and communities, they lose the social connections that define them. One of the target groups of the documentary is the social group that experiences these feelings: that is, those who have lost ties with their old houses due to social and cultural transformations. A paternalist discourse is used by affirming the lifestyles and family structure of the past, and social change is marked as the 'negative other' of heritage that leads to destruction. The social phenomenon behind this discourse of uprootedness is connected with the individualisation and loosening of traditional informal relations stemming from the experience of industrialisation of Safranbolu. As argued by Ashworth, Graham, and Turnbridge (2007), in the process of heritage production, the selected heritage assets mark the imagined future of the society. Therefore, it might be suggested that film imagines a social order based on the close, warm, and informal relationships of the past, which disappear because of urbanisation and modernisation. In this context, heritage is seen as a haven in response to the sense of uprootedness and displacement. Social dissolution and integration are dialectically interconnected. The fact that the film's discourse has survived for so long and that the creators' efforts continue to be commemorated with gratitude shows that the city and its social life have a relationship with the process of modernity in all its contradictions. Taking into consideration that heritage is present-centred and created in response to the demands of the present (Ashworth et al., 2007), it can be argued that a discourse of home in this way is shaped in opposition to the perceived painful experience of the ongoing practices of urbanisation and modernisation.

Narrative 3: Making sense of place from the discourse of nature–culture harmony

The documentary also develops a language for nature–human relationships, signifying nature as the source of life. The past is imagined as a life where the city and nature are intertwined. Rather than aesthetic consumerism, the principles of pragmatism are seen in the presentation of nature, and the general themes of romantic discourse, such as 'reconstruction of the unity between nature and culture', 'emotion and intuition against reason', and 'naturalisation' are implied in this way of imaging place. Nevertheless, a frightening myth is used as a persuasive power in the construction of discourse that will maintain this meaning of nature:

> It is believed that the 'Father of Deer' lovingly cared for the deer and looked after them. Once the villagers started overhunting them, the 'Father of Deer', who wanted to prevent them, was unsuccessful in this effort and said that six houses should not be seven. Since then, Göveren Village cannot exceed six households.

Here, the myth of the 'Father of Deer' is used as a form of speech (Barthes, 1972) and used to strengthen the people's bond to place (Tuan, 1991). The myth of the 'Father of Deer' makes a connection between the falling population of the Göveren village of Safranbolu and the disappearance of the deer population due to excessive hunting. Here, it is seen from the Spinozist point of view that the director aims to construct the discourse of heritage conservation by creating a sense of fear, saying that if nature is not protected, the population of Safranbolu cannot grow. Therefore, the discourse of natural heritage protection is built by cultivating an emotion of sadness as well as fear. The myth of the 'Father of Deer' serves the function of a management tool for pushing people to take action to protect nature and heritage.

Narrative 4: The discourse of craftsmen

The craftsman is the primary victim of the labour process of capitalist modernisation, and what happened to the crafts in Safranbolu is not very different from any other social formations. The scale advantages of mass production result in the closure of workshops and proletarianisation as a result of the decrease in the production power and market share of these segments. In the narrative of discontent caused by this social transformation, the producers want to leave an impact reminiscent of the old reputation of the craftsmanship by emphasising the value of the profession. As a matter of fact, the only subjects of the 39-minute film who speak and are introduced by their names are a few male artisans. These sentences express the spirit of the age: 'Modernised life consumes blacksmithing as well as many other things. Watchmaker Rıfat Usta, who fused his life in time and struggled for the flow of time. Yakup Usta, another person who tries to stop time with his forty-year-old machine.'

In the craftsmanship narrative of the documentary, there is not only regret for the loss of professions and the closure of workshops. In order to create a sense of place from a myth, the following quotation is remarkable in terms of implying the relationship between the craftsman's labour process and heritage:

> One day when the key of a lock with a history of approximately 350 years was forgotten inside the inn, all the craftsmen in Demirciler Bazaar were mobilised, but none of them could open it. The walls were opened with a thousand difficulties, the key was found, and it was only then possible to open the inn. The lock maintains its authenticity and functions even if time passes.

Here, craft products are marked by durability and longevity, and the latent meaning of this expression lies in the signification that the products of the modern era are standardised and non-durable. The craftsmen narrative of the documentary indicates that modernity is a process that destroys not only the assets of tangible heritage but also the intangible ones, such as skills and values. A craftsman who sets up and maintains the clock in the clock tower is shown as a person who connects the past with the present and protects the past of the city, and this action is shown and affirmed as one of the few rituals through which the city stays in touch with the past. The craftsman narrative is presented as a sad story, suggesting that nothing can be the same as before, while the few craftsmen who have been able to continue their profession are praised as those who have not lost their past. The discourse emerges as a sublimation of subjectivity against developing an objective, standardised labour culture. The emergence of this discourse is also associated with the homogenisation of labour processes in the most important iron and steel factory of the country, established next to Safranbolu. The language of *Safranbolu: Reflections of Time* is based on certain themes of romantic ideology with respect to both nature and the labour process.

Cultural conservatism: The official heritage discourse of Safranbolu

Attributing existential importance to the preservation of old cultural heritage, the choice of wood in architecture, the avoidance of the geometric, the defence of traditional architecture against standardised modern architecture, nostalgia, and melancholy for the harmonious world of Ottoman high culture as well as neighbourhood life and artisan culture are some main themes of Turkish cultural conservatism (Bora, 2016). In this context, it is seen that the documentary has a language that matches the romantic thought that values intuition and emotion, individuality and subjectivity, against materialism. The originality and subjectivity of the heritage saying that each building has a story to be told is affirmed against the developing standardised modern housing types, highlighting craftsman labour, old neighbourhood life, and nostalgia for informal relations. The language aimed at protecting nature and re-establishing this relationship in the face of the nature–human relationship transformed by modernisation, with emphasis on traditional aesthetics and creativity through the emphasis on wooden house decorations, are some discourses used by conservative ideologies in general. In addition, urbanisation, anomie, and the erosion of common values have been the general concerns of Turkish conservatism (Bora, 2016), which has led them to a line of modernisation that has been reconciled with tradition and history while preserving the sustained characteristics of cultural identity. It has been claimed that conservatism in Turkey has emerged as a way of thinking and acting based on a non-political cultural reactionism rather than a political ideology (Çiğdem, 1997). In this context, the sublimation of cultural values and heritage, and associating the destruction of heritage with the process of modernisation has moved the discourse of film closer to the general characteristics of romantic discourses with an ideology of cultural conservatism.

Summary and conclusion

The documentary *Safranbolu: Reflections of Time* is an important cultural text that allows the formation of a heritage gaze in a society that has not developed symbolic connection with the past and whose relationship with the present is painful. By disciplining how to gaze at the place, heritage, and society, it allows people to make sense of heritage and Safranbolu and build some discourses about it. A series of economic and social factors with which the town has been living for a long time have been decisive in the construction of these discourse orders and the structuring of meaning as an official heritage discourse over time. The documentary, which treats these transformations well, shows that the main factors in becoming a World Heritage Site are social dynamics rather than aesthetic, universal, or scientific concerns. The discourse of heritage in Safranbolu is not decreed from above but built from below.

The extinction of traditional professions, immigration, breaks of intergenerational ties, weakening of primary social relations, and displacement and sense of rootlessness created by the transition from a culture based on collectivism to an individualistic one are the social and cultural elements with which the discourse of heritage is built. The sense of social disintegration and collapse resulting from the factors associated with the transition from a traditional society to a modern one is significant in this process of sense-making. Thus, an aim of the documentary is to create a collective memory for the re-establishment of community ties with the past. To attain this goal, the power of discourse is reinforced through provoking emotions like sadness, grief, and pain. Every discourse is opposed to something and intended to distort its meaning. In the case of Safranbolu, discourse structures are built on the sublimating heritage and the critique of modernity and change. In this context, subjectivity, nature–culture harmony, aesthetics, and authenticity are inclusive in the construction of discourse structures, while modernity, change, and objective culture are excluded. Indeed, it is possible to see these themes in many points in the film's critique of modernity based on Romantic discourse. In making sense of heritage, the common rhetoric of a Romantic discourse is shared by many Turkish cultural conservatives, and the ideology that the documentary is embedded in may be claimed to be 'Romantic conservatism'.

References

Agnew, J. A. (1987). *Place and politics: The geographical mediation of state and society*. London: Allen and Unwin.

Arın, S. (1976). *Safranbolu: Reflections of time* [video file, uploaded 14 September 2014]. Retrieved from https://www.youtube.com/watch?v=2SY17O_ZlB0.

Ashworth, G. J., Graham, B., & Tunbridge, J. E. (2007). *Pluralising pasts: Heritage, identity, and place in multicultural societies*. London: Pluto Press.

Barthes, R. (1972). *Mythologies*. (A. Lavers Trans.). New York: Hill and Wang.

Biletiniz Turları (2019). Safranbolu-Yenice Turu. Retrieved from http://turlar.biletiniz.com/turlar/safranbolu-yenice-turu/.

Bora, T. (2016). *Cereyanlar: Türkiye'de siyasi ideolojiler* [Currents: political ideologies in Turkey]. Istanbul: İletişim Yayınları.

Bourdieu, P., & Wacquant, L. (2001). Neoliberal newspeak: Notes on the new planetary vulgate. *Radical Philosophy*, *105*, 1–6.
Çiğdem, A. (1997). Muhafazakârlık Üzerine [On conservatism]. *Toplum ve Bilim Dergisi* [Society and Science], *74*, 32–50.
Convery, I., Corsane, G., & Davis, P. (eds). (2014). *Making sense of place: Multidisciplinary perspectives.* UK: Boydell & Brewer Ltd.
Di Masso, A., Dixon, J., & Durrheim, K. (2014). Place attachment as discursive practice. In L. C. Manzo & P. Devine-Wright (eds), *Place attachment: Advances in theory, methods and applications* (pp. 75–86). Abingdon: Routledge.
Ennen, E., & van Maanen, E. G. O. M. (2013). Telling the truth or selling an image? Communicating heritage as an instrument in place marketing. In J. Kaminski, A. M. Benson, & D. Arnold (eds). *Contemporary issues in cultural heritage tourism* (pp. 45–56). Abingdon: Routledge.
Fairclough, N. (2013). *Critical discourse analysis: The critical study of language* (2nd edn). London: Routledge.
Feighery, W. (2006). Reading tourism texts in context: A critical discourse analysis. *Tourism Analysis*, *11*(1), 1–11.
Feighery, W. G. (2012). Tourism and self-orientalism in Oman: A critical discourse analysis. *Critical Discourse Studies*, *9*(3), 269–284.
Greider, T., & Garkovich, L. (1994). Landscapes: The social construction of nature and the environment. *Rural Sociology*, *59*(1), 1–24.
Hannam, K., & Knox, D. (2005). Discourse analysis in tourism research a critical perspective. *Tourism Recreation Research*, *30*(2), 23–30.
Howard, P. (2003). *Heritage: Management, interpretation, identity.* London: Continuum.
Hummon, D. M. (1992). Community attachment. In I. Altman & S. M. Low (eds). *Place attachment. Human behavior and environment* (pp. 253–278). Boston, MA: Springer.
Kuş, A., & Kızıltan, U. (2015). *Safranbolu Korumada 40.yıl (1975–2015) 40 Söyleşi (1975 öncesi ve sonrası)* [40th Anniversary of Conserving Safranbolu (1975–2015) 40 Interviews (Before and After 1975)]. Istanbul: Safranbolu Kültür ve Turizm Vakfı.
Özdoğan, M. (1998). Ideology and archaeology in Turkey. In L. Meskell (ed.), *Archaeology under fire: Nationalism, politics and heritage in the Eastern Mediterranean and Middle East* (pp. 111–123). London: Routledge.
Parker, I. (1992). *Discourse dynamics: Critical analysis for social and individual psychology.* London: Routledge.
Shurmer-Smith, P. (2002). Reading texts. In P. Shurmer-Smith (ed.), *Doing cultural geography*, (pp. 123–136). London: Sage.
Simmel, G. (2013). The metropolis and mental life. In J. Lin & C. Mele (eds), *The urban sociology reader* (2nd edn, pp. 37–45). Abingdon: Routledge.
Smith, L. (2006). *Uses of heritage.* London: Routledge.
Spinoza, B. (2015). *Ethics: Demonstrated in geometrical order* (R. H. M. Elwes Trans.). Scotts Valley, CA: CreateSpace Independent Publishing Platform.
Tuan, Y. F. (1980). Rootedness versus sense of place. *Landscape*, *24*, 3–8.
Tuan, Y. F. (1991). Language and the making of place: A narrative-descriptive approach. *Annals of the Association of American Geographers*, *81*(4), 684–696.

Van Dijk, T. A. (2000). *Ideology and discourse. A multidisciplinary introduction.* Pompeu Fabra University, Barcelona [pdf]. Retrieved from http://www.discourses.org/OldBooks/Teun%20A%20van%20Dijk%20-%20Ideology%20and%20Discourse.pdf.

Wallwork, J., & Dixon, J. A. (2004). Foxes, green fields and Britishness: On the rhetorical construction of place and national identity. *British Journal of Social Psychology, 43*(1), 21–39.

Wang, N. (2000). *Tourism and modernity: A sociological analysis.* Oxford: Pergamon.

Williams, D. R., & Stewart, S. I. (1998). Sense of place: An elusive concept that is finding a home in ecosystem management. *Journal of Forestry, 96*(5), 18–23.

Yenişafak Gazetesi (2015). Süha Arın Kültür ve Sanat Merkezi' açıldı. [Süha Arın Culture and Art Centre opened]. Retrieved from https://www.yenisafak.com/hayat/suha-arin-kultur-ve-sanat-merkezi-acildi-2129427?p=1.

5 Cultural heritage and tourism in Tunisia

Evolution, challenges, and perspectives

Najem Dhaher, Siamak Seyfi, and C. Michael Hall

Introduction

Tunisia has long been a communication channel between Europe and Africa and between the East and the Arab Maghreb (Poirier, 1995). It has inherited an exceptional heritage legacy that is among the richest in the Mediterranean, including archaeological sites of all eras (ancient, medieval, Arab–Muslim), monuments (baths, temples, amphitheatres, mosques, museums), as well as popular arts and artisanal traditions (mosaics, statues, costumes, and jewellery) (Rey, 2019). Tunisia is home to many ancient remains and buildings of international heritage interest such as the cities of Carthage, Utica, the amphitheatre of El Jem, Bulla Regia, and Oudhna. Arab and Ottoman buildings and cities dominate the historic centres of several cities including mosques, ribats, ksours, zaouias, and souks. The rural areas include agricultural landscapes (oases, olive groves, vineyards) and traditional practices that illustrate the legacy of different historical periods. The country's rich intangible heritage has survived despite attempts of acculturation throughout its history (Nozha, 2010), although it is currently endangered by modernist and tourist hegemony, with many heritage sites being exploited for touristic purposes and losing their authenticity, although tourism has also contributed to the material preservation of these sites.

This chapter provides an overview of the historical evolution of heritage tourism development in Tunisia and the challenges it faces. It also provides perspectives on the future of cultural heritage and tourism development in Tunisia given the recent political transitions in the country.

Tourism development in Tunisia

Following its independence from France in 1956 and the abolition of the monarchy in 1957, the Tunisian government showed a special interest in tourism as a lynchpin of the post-decolonisation development strategy to ensure the economic independence of the country. The mass arrival of European tourists in the 1960s had a considerable influence on the geopolitical and geoeconomic axes favoured by the authorities. In the Saharan cities of south-west Tunisia, recognised for their culture, traditions, and architecture, cultural and heritage tourism have become integral to the wider tourist offering and to the promotion of local economic development. In these fragile and vulnerable desert areas tourism and heritage have become two realities that deeply mark contemporary landscapes, economic and cultural activities, and population movements. These processes, which have become one of the concerns of both public and private actors, have also contributed to changes in the representation and use of places. For example, the traditional Saharan city and its oasis, which was a territorial commons par excellence that nourished the place attachment of individuals and their identity and culture, is now being reinvented for the commercial demands of tourism and place marketing (Dhaher, 2017).

Tunisia was one of the first Muslim countries that attempted to explore the potential of tourism and has been more moderate in its approach toward Western-style tourism development given its economic value (Seyfi & Hall, 2019; Gan & Smith, 1992; Hall & Prayag, 2020; Hazbun, 2008). The development of tourism in Tunisia was directed from a central state planning strategy during the different administrations of the Bourguiba (1957–1987) and Ben Ali presidencies (1987–2011), as well as the post-revolution era (2011 onwards) (Miossec, 1999; Weigert, 2012). According to Perelli and Sistu (2013), tourism has been one of the pillars of Tunisia's economy under all these regimes. Therefore, the contemporary transition towards a 'new Tunisia' offers an opportunity to describe how tourism strategies have been central to Tunisian development and the links between heritage sites and mass tourism development.

A generally 'Eurocentric' approach has been taken toward tourism development in the Tunisian moderate Islamic context (Poirier, 1995; Hazbun, 2008), with the majority of visitation to the country traditionally coming from European countries (mainly France, Germany, Italy, and the UK) through all-inclusive packages in seaside resorts (Carboni & Perelli, 2020; Carboni, Perelli, & Sistu, 2014; Jeffrey & Bleasdale, 2017). Nevertheless, it has been argued that the over-reliance on 3S tourism (sun, sea, and sand) has paralysed the diversification of tourism products and negatively affected the competitiveness of the tourism sector (Souissi, 2010). However, given the relatively unique offering of Tunisia among other Maghrebian countries, there has been some interregional visitation to the country, mainly from Libya, Algeria, Morocco, and Mauritania. Prior to the 2011 revolution, it was estimated that the country attracted 6,902,749 international tourists, of which 55.3 per cent were from Europe (ONTT, 2012), while the rest were from neighbouring countries who do not usually use all-inclusive packages and rarely stay in hotels (19 per cent in 2010, ONTT, 2012). While Europeans travel to Tunisia for leisure tourism and to stay in hotels and resorts, Maghrebians mainly visit Tunisia for shopping, medical tourism, or a more liberal environment where they can experience a wider range of tourism practices (Carboni et al., 2014, 2017; Souissi, 2010). According to Carboni et al. (2014), although Tunisia has become a mature tourism destination, it still suffers from issues of product quality, seasonality, and hotel sector attractiveness. In addition, events such as the terrorist attack in Djerba in 2002 and successive terrorist attacks in 2015 (the Bardo National Museum attack, Sousse attacks, and the Tunis bombing) and the 2018 shooting have threatened perceptions of the country's relative political stability in the region and, as a result, have negatively affected the country's image as a tourism destination (Porter, 2015; Morris, 2019). For example, in 2014, 427,000 UK citizens visited the country, while in 2016 the number fell to less than 50,000 (Morris, 2019), with the figure being influenced by a combination of safety perceptions, government travel advisories, insurance premiums, and reduced numbers of charter flights (Belaid, 2018). All these events have been a cause for the country to partially lose its international reputation as a safe destination.

The economic significance of changes in perception of the country cannot be overestimated. In 2014 tourism accounted for 14 per cent of the country's GDP and employed almost half a million people in a population of 11 million (Belaid, 2018). However, a state of emergency has been in effect since 2015 and tourism has partially bounced back as government increased security around popular destinations (Morris, 2019). According to the World Travel & Tourism Council (WTTC) (2019), in 2017 the direct contribution of the tourism industry to the country's GDP was TND6,631.7mn (USD2,740.4mn), 6.9 per cent of total GDP, and is forecast to rise by 3.0 per cent per annum in 2018–2028, to TND9,246.6mn (USD3,820.9mn) or 6.6 per cent of total GDP in 2028.

The heritage and tourism interface in Tunisia

In the Tunisian context, national heritage strategies, heritage site selection, conservation practices, and the discourses around national identity have been shaped by the country's development approach (Perelli & Sistu, 2013). From the 1950s to the early 2000s tourism development was essentially monocultural and concentrated on seaside hotel tourism. In such a context, heritage was narrowly defined and commodified (Dhaher, 2016). However, since the 1990s, an increase in tourist visitation to monuments and historic sites and the growing public attachment of Tunisian people to heritage as part of their identity have contributed to government interest in heritage tourism.

In Tunisian cities renowned for their culture, traditions, and architectural heritage, tourism has encouraged greater reflexivity on the concept of heritage given its use within the tourism offering and the promotion of local development. This has meant that in Tunisia, as in many developing countries, the potential to commoditise heritage has become an economic issue, although, ideally, the cultural and tourist valuation of heritage go hand in hand. Indeed, the growing interest of local authorities in the provision of cultural amenities, which results in conservation and enhancement schemes at the municipal or regional level, demonstrates the potential of heritage for local development.

Tourism has seemingly come to be regarded as the only economic path for places that have been left out of other development strategies (Jeffrey & Bleasdale, 2017). Tourism and heritage have therefore become closely entwined. The reference to heritage is increasingly used in a number of contexts, whether in terms of urban projects, sustainable local development, tourism strategy, job creation, or strengthening of social ties, and serves to broaden socio-economic practices (Lazzarotti, 2000). Tangible and intangible heritage have become an economic issue in many Tunisian cities. Nevertheless, the current situation is marked by a sort of antagonism between awareness of the economic importance of heritage that has emerged in recent years and the purely mercantile behaviour that followed without sufficient consideration of the wider values of heritage. Such a situation raises significant questions as to whether local authorities and local populations have managed to reconcile conservation and the economic use of heritage.

Cultural heritage development in Tunisia

In Tunisia and the Arab world, the development of the concept of heritage (*Turâth* in Arabic) has followed a tortuous route. The notion of heritage emerged gradually in Tunisia and the Arab countries since the end of the nineteenth century as part of broader processes of cultural and national identity formation and change (Picton, 2010; Rabbat, 2016). After independence in 1956, the concept has become a part of various discourses and fields being framed in terms of ideology, Westernisation, colonialism, totalitarianism, globalism, and even terrorism (Leïla, 2013). Indeed, the relative valuation and/or depreciation of a heritage is inherent to the broader processes of the politics of public memory in the region.

In Tunisia, the concept of heritage has long been linked to European and especially French cultural inheritance from the colonial period. The French Protectorate, through the service of the antiquities and arts, was the first to recognise heritage in terms of markers of colonial culture, along with the ruins and the vestiges of the antiquity. However, during the first decade of the twentieth century, European builders began to draw on local heritage and imitate it in the design of new architectural projects. Indeed, colonial intervention has often been stigmatising. The movement to utilise local architectural and built forms was not limited to the use of elements of the architectural decoration of local Muslim buildings, but continued in the form of an authentic reinterpretation of local architectures, in terms of their arrangements and their spatial organisations until the early 1930s. These processes have continued to the present day. For example, several old souks, schools (madrassa), and palaces have undergone conversion work to enable new functions (Ammar, 2017). Nevertheless, following such actions and the emerging practices of tourism, exoticism, and the search for authenticity, heritage conservation has become more widely concerned with the Muslim heritage, local building traditions, crafts, and lifestyles.

The architectural and cultural transformations that have been introduced since the 1910s and especially in the 1920s continue to affect heritage policy. Nevertheless, over the past 30 years cultural heritage conservation has entered a new stage characterised by citizen action and a substantial emphasis on urban historic and archaeological sites, together with the protection and conservation of local heritage through the development of Maghreb tourism. Outcomes of such shifts include the establishment of protection zones around the monuments of antiquity, such as El Jem and Carthage, and the use of expropriation decrees in the development of archaeological sites, such as Dougga and Bulla Regia (Bacha, 2008). Such changes in public attitudes towards heritage also proved significant in resisting attempts by the country's post-independence leaders to endow Tunisia with the built attributes of modernity. For example, in 1957, the draft plan of Tunis proposed the development of a broad boulevard to enter the Medina in order to connect it to the neighbourhood of the Casbah at the Porte de France and to make the medina the heart of a modern urban agglomeration, with tall buildings and car parking. A decade after the approval of this planning document, the state held an international design competition to develop the boulevard project, but it was never developed following strong negative reactions from civil society. Importantly, public mobilisation against planned changes to the medina also led to the creation of the Safeguarding Association of the Medina of Tunis in 1967 (Leïla, 2013), which began to work in the field of preservation, safeguarding, and rehabilitation of the historic city.

The development of new urban plans that served as a symbol of Tunisia's modern status was not the only policy shift to influence the country's heritage. Among the first political decisions of the new independent regime to impact heritage in Tunisia was the abolition of Habous foundations and the creation of an Institute of Archaeology and Art in 1973. The abolition of Habous (religious foundations, *waqf* outside North Africa) and their incorporation into public lands was catastrophic for a significant number of historic buildings that have since remained without guardianship, status, and financial resources. In addition, the changed status has allowed the demolition of many of them. For example, between 1962 and 1970 the city of Tunis lost more than three-quarters of its oratories, mausoleums, and madrasas (Ammar, 2017).

The 1990s were fundamental with the overhaul of cultural institutions and the recognition of heritage by the state, through its integration into urbanism, ecology, the economy, tourism, and place marketing (Bacha, 2008; Gravari-Barbas & Violier, 2003). A national agency for the development and exploitation of archaeological and historical heritage has been created and:

> charged with ensuring the cultural, touristic and commercial purposes the realization and the management of the program of enhancement and exploitation of the archaeological, historical and museum heritage as well as natural sites of a historical nature; promote and develop cultural tourism and promote the creation and development of cultural industries in relation to heritage and cultural property (Ministére des affaires culturelles, 1988, Article 2, p. 1247 (our translation)).

Nevertheless, the 'museographic' conception of heritage that has prevailed for a long time has limited the possibilities of highlighting a wider understanding and portrayal of heritage (Rey, 2019). Tourism development has historically been limited in the scope of its heritage offerings; however, while Carthaginian and Roman heritage remains significant, tourism is also implicated in the development and promotion of other forms of heritage and culture.

The complexities of heritage tourism development in Tunisia

In a country with limited natural resources, tourism and heritage have become extremely important economically. The current development logic is that they serve to create new places and products that increase place attractiveness and activities that can be undertaken and thereby create wealth and jobs. Heritage, as a symbolic resource, has also become an economic resource. In addition, the highlighting of a rewarding past, the care taken to revive it, and the enhancement of the living environment are all amenities sought by the local population, the users, and the consumers of services, which public officials and developers seek to attract. Nevertheless, while the country offers an exceptionally rich urban heritage and several sites such as the Medina of Tunis, the archaeological site of Carthage, the amphitheatre of El Jem and Kairouan are inscribed on the World Heritage List (UNESCO, 2019) (Table 5.1), heritage and culture remain insufficiently presented and still relatively little exploited as tourism attractions (Hall, 2006b).

Table 5.1 Historical and archaeological sites in Tunisia

Protected historical and archaeological sites	Monuments of the Islamic era	Ancient monuments	UNESCO World Heritage Sites	Sites on the UNESCO Tentative World Heritage list
943	15	9	8	13

Source: National Institute of Heritage (INP) and personal surveys, 2018.

Despite its economic significance, Tunisian tourism has not fundamentally enhanced or transformed cultural resources with the exception of some coastal resort areas although changes are definitely occurring. This has meant that the very rich and varied cultural potential of some less visited parts of the country, nested for the most part in the cultural sites of the inland and Saharan regions, are not yet commoditised. The focus on coastal development, which had reached a very high level at the beginning of the 2000s (Hall, 2006a), is marked by a preponderance of seaside resorts and contrasts sharply with the tourist voids of the hinterland (Weigert, 2012) and the Gafsa-Tozeur area, which the authorities previously attempted to develop in the 1980s with a view to boosting Saharan tourism. The north is dotted with pre-Islamic archaeological sites (Dougga, Bulla Regia, and Sbeitla), while the south is home to an important Berber heritage (The Ksours (castles) of Matmata and Tataouine).

Although endowed with important cultural and natural assets, the hinterland is considered a marginal area for tourism. Most of these regions have never been connected to the seaside tourism system with the possible exception of Kairouan, Mahdia, and Sidi Bou Said. However, the present cultural offering of the coastline, whether museums, archaeological sites, or urban neighbourhoods, is not very popular with international tourists (Souissi, 2010). This has meant that issues of heritage rehabilitation, conservation, and protection have only recently become a concern for policy actors. Indeed, it is recognition of the limitations of a tourism industry based on a mass beach product that has encouraged the wider promotion of heritage and local cultural development, particularly in non-urban areas. As a result, the growing interest of the various public and private actors in heritage has started to lead to the restoration and enhancement of heritage sites and is testimony to the growth potential that cultural heritage can represent for local development (El Gaied & Meyer, 2014). This situation has meant that tangible and intangible heritage, with the latter often being marginalised, has gradually become an economic issue and is opening up new horizons, putting an end to a 'museographic' conception of heritage that has prevailed for a long time. However, the current situation is also marked by a kind of antagonism between the phenomenon of awareness of the economic importance of heritage and the purely mercantile behaviour that has followed. Something that is reminiscent of Viard's (2000, p. 33) description of this problem as 'the economy of reuse'.

Heritage valorisation through tourism in Tunisia

As the search for new economic resources grows, the economic interest in heritage is increasingly growing, especially in countries with few natural resources (Ashley, Osmani, Emmitt, Mallinson, & Mallinson, 2015; Throsby, 2016). This renewed interest in heritage is often oriented towards a tourism development perspective. In Tunisia, public and private investment in cultural heritage tourism projects is a recent practice. This has led to restoration operations with a view to attracting tourist flows as is the case in Tunis, Kairouan, Djerba, Tozeur, and Nefta. The choice to encourage heritage tourism development is a Tunisian government policy that is both strategic and emblematic and is the result of seeking ways to diversify Tunisian tourism in response to competitive pressure. Yet, many monuments and archaeological sites, particularly in the north-western region, are not always integrated into cultural tourism circuits despite their potential; examples include the Paleolithic site of Sidi Zin, the basilica and ancient Roman ramparts, the mausoleum of Sidi Bou Makhlouf, the Al-Qadriya Mosque, Dougga, Makthar, Zama, Bulla Regia, and Kesra.

In recent years, intangible cultural heritage has gained increasing recognition and its safeguarding has become one of the priorities of international cooperation as a result of the adoption of the UNESCO convention in 2003. Cultural festivals in several Tunisian cities in turn provide a very favourable field of observation for studying the processes of conserving and building the intangible heritage value of local populations, especially from the community perspective. The events that take place every year in southern Tunisia at the start of the winter tourist season present various dimensions of the life of the Saharan populations and the craft and artistic skills that attract mainly North African and European tourists. These cultural expressions appear to play an increasingly important role not only in safeguarding cultural traditions but also in the local economy. However, such tourism development can create tensions between the desire for local appropriation that reinforces the sense of belonging and a desire to commodify and instrumentalise it to attract tourists with the support of activities that are not always the expression of intangible culture (Dhaher, 2012).

Admittedly, the promotion by tourism of local heritage specificities has generated relative growth and mostly temporary jobs. The tourist industry has even had an effect of 'fixing' some features of the traditional local culture (Puig, 2004) especially in the Saharan cities. Often conflicts and externalities emerge as a result of the staging of cultural and natural amenities for sale to tourists. For example, the folklorisation of local cultures that appears in commercial representations in recent years is often misguided. In historic urban and village centres, the structures and textures of the old buildings that have been modified by the effects of time and abandonment are often refurbished for tourism purposes in a manner that is insensitive to the values of historic buildings. In the medinas of Tunis, Sousse, and Tozeur, and under the pretext of facilitating the reception of a growing number of tourists, some developments are poorly adapted to local conditions and devoid of any cultural reference. The focus on economic benefits have led to the inadequate recognition of the importance of many traditional buildings and the gradual loss of their cultural identity. Similarly, the oasis has also become transformed into a space of leisure and 'marketing'. The referent landscape has become that of the traditional oasis which is maintained and recreated in a decorative gardening logic, where the aesthetic dimension is sometimes sterile and imported (Carpenter & Gana, 2012).

In 2007, the National Heritage Institute organised the first international meetings of intangible cultural heritage following which Tunisia ratified, on 15 February 2007, the 2005 *Convention on the Protection and Promotion of the Diversity of Cultural Expressions*. However, the institutionalisation of this heritage is problematic given the logics of the different actors involved. Local authorities are becoming more active in heritage conservation, identification, and management. This has meant that awareness of the technical, cultural, and social values of heritage and their integration into contemporary urban contexts has become an issue for the development and identity of some ancient Tunisian cities. However, it is to be feared that tourism, which seemed to be in these areas a vehicle for raising awareness of the value of heritage as a founding element of local cultural identity, is no more than another form of 'cultural consumption'. Despite the emergence of new, citizen-oriented heritage enhancement initiatives at several sites, overly focusing on the commercial consumption of heritage could result in a rapid trivialisation of heritage that could undermine the memory of places and historic urbanisation and the loss of identity and local heritage landscapes.

Emergence of new safeguarding and heritage promotion practices

The 2011 revolution, which revealed the failings of an overconcentration on the seaside tourism model, encouraged people in some cities to revive Saharan tourism. There is currently an emergence of new tourism practices based on different heritage values of Saharan and oasis resources characterised by the orientation of demand towards more 'authentic' and 'meaningful' consumption. Local cultural heritage in these regions is meant to be an everyday experience and not an object of contemplation that is exhibited in museums and often transformed into folklore. Examples of such tourism include the redevelopment of the Nefta (an oasis town in the Tozeur Governorate) ecological tourism circuit '*Ras al-Ain*' (head of the spring) and the development of agritourism in the oasis of Tozeur via model farms that demonstrate traditional agricultural practices. The protection and enhancement of the few ancient oases that still use traditional irrigation systems and attempts by local authorities to develop old palm groves as tourist attractions also meet the expectations of tourists. Similarly, the traditional brick of Tozeur, an oasis and a city in south-west Tunisia, which is particularly characteristic of the local architecture and which was the object of a municipal decree to ensure its conservation and use, has become one of the pillars of the visitor economy of the city.

The growing interest in heritage has also resulted in its spatial and temporal expansion as a regulatory object. Rather than isolated monument, public policies are now being focused on protecting entire urban centres by taking into account the significance of some historical sites. However, the symbolic and legal characterisation of ancient spaces can lead to a change in their status. For example, deprived areas become attractive places as a result of their reconversion. Initially, the focus was on the ancient nuclei of cities such as Tunis, Tozeur, Djerba, and Kairouan. More recently, Berber villages have experienced changes in heritage status. For example, the town of Douiret in the Tataouine district of southern Tunisia is now considered a jewel of the architectural and urban heritage of Tunisia after seemingly being caught in a process of irreversible degradation. The local population, who feared before the recent revolution that local decline would be insurmountable, is now hoping that intangible heritage, which constitutes an immense cultural wealth for the area, represents an opportunity for local social and economic development.

Examples from both Tunis and smaller towns and cities indicate that local people want to profit economically from the presence of a tourist activity while developing mechanisms that can simultaneously ensure the preservation of this heritage, including the use of real or virtual presentations in festivals and events where the cultural heritage of the villages is highlighted. Cultural festivals are often designed to bring together inhabitants, especially those of the desert, around their common interests and values. Nevertheless, despite the positive local territorial dynamics in terms of heritage tourism and the promotion of appropriate tourist activities that are respectful of the local ecosystem and which generate local income, domestic tourism including Saharan and oasis does not yet seem to be able to ensure the sustainability of these ecosystems (occupancy rates remain low and the average length of stay is limited to 1.5 days). Given the absence of a public strategy for these new tourist dynamics, tourism in these areas is still a form of transit tourism that does not yet have a significant impact on the local economy. It may be that governments and NGOs provide further incentives for appropriate tourism development and build regulatory goals and tools that are adapted to the local context. The private sector must also be encouraged to pursue the opportunities available to develop appropriate heritage tourism. However, the implementation of management or other plans by local authorities for the conservation of heritage is not enough to protect cultural sites against the damage caused by mass tourism, as evidenced by the current state of the Kairouan World Heritage Site and coastal city of Monastir. Even though conservation is often perceived as an expensive public choice, such examples illustrate that large-scale tourism development must be controlled and well managed in order to sustainably preserve cultural heritage.

Conclusion

The ambiguity that currently colours the values of cultural heritage in Tunisia can be related to that which affects sustainable tourism development. It is increasingly feared that tourism, which seemed to be an excellent vehicle for raising awareness of the value of heritage as an element of cultural identity, is no more than another form of 'cultural consumption' that leads to a rapid trivialisation of heritage. The few citizen actions that connect tourism to Saharan cultural heritage are still evolving and need further support, accompaniment, and encouragement. The need for empowerment or capacity building through training and funding as part of a broader sustainable tourism strategy where social, economic, environmental, and spatial factors are considered is clear. The means by which to actually do this is still emerging in Tunisia, as in many other destinations, and the articulation of appropriate local actions and public policies remains problematic (Hall & McArthur, 2000) – although this remains one of the major responsibilities of the various territorial actors which have the moral obligation to bequeath the heritage inheritance to future generations.

In the 2020s, after the limitations of the coastal mass tourism development have been recognised and faced with forms of heritage tourism which are leading to the commodification of culture and heritage, new citizen practices are emerging as well as initiatives by some organisations and NGOs to design and implement actions that try to reconcile tourism, heritage, and sustainable development. Part of this includes the invention of a 'citizen tourism' in support of local ecologically and socially sensitive development strategies and the fight against poverty as a basis for genuine intercultural dialogue and sustainable tourism (Hall, 2019). Given the current political transitions in the country and the wider region, tourism public policies are also being developed that attempt to create improved synergies between tourism, crafts, local products, and heritage through experiences that support the enhancement of local cultural identity, develop new integrated products, and market destinations away from the traditional tourist routes. Importantly, the various experiments being implemented in Tunisia around the value of local products, craft creation, and alternative tourism are a promising starting point for developing a national approach towards the creation of inclusive tourist spaces and terroirs.

References

Aissa, S. B., & Goaied, M. (2016). Determinants of Tunisian hotel profitability: The role of managerial efficiency. *Tourism Management*, *52*, 478–487.

Ammar, L. (2017). Les enjeux du patrimoine ancien et récent à Tunis aux XIXe et XXe siècles, entre volontés de sauvegarde et périls [The challenges of ancient and contemporary heritage in Tunis in the 19th and 20th centuries, between desires to safeguard and perils], *Al-Sabîl: Revue d'Histoire, d'Archéologie et d'Architecture Maghrébines*, retrieved from https://www.al-sabil.tn/?p=2877.

Ashford, D. E. (1967). *National development and local reform: Political participation in Morocco, Pakistan and Tunisia*. Princeton: Princeton University Press.

Ashley, K. S., Osmani, M., Emmitt, S., Mallinson, M., & Mallinson, H. (2015). Assessing stakeholders' perspectives towards the conservation of the built heritage of Suakin, Sudan. *International Journal of Heritage Studies, 21*(7), 674–697.

Bacha, M. (2008). La construction patrimoniale tunisienne à travers la législation et le journal officiel, 1881–2003: de la complexité des rapports entre le politique et le scientifique [The construction of Tunisian heritage through legislation and the official gazette, 1881–2003: the complexity of the relationship between the politicians and the scientists]. *L'année du Maghreb, 4,* 99–122.

Belaid, F. (2018). Tunisia moves to reassure tourists after suicide attacks. *France 24,* retrieved from https://www.france24.com/en/20190628-tunisia-tourism-suicide-blasts-tunis.

Berriane, Mohamed (2010). Suivi de la stratégie méditerranéenne pour le développement durable. Promouvoir un tourisme durable au Maroc, Étude nationale du Maroc [Monitoring Mediterranean strategy for sustainable development. Promoting sustainable tourism in Morocco, national study of Morocco]. *Sophia Antipoli.*

Berriane, M., & Moizo, B. (2014). Initiatives locales, politiques publiques et développement du tourisme en milieu rural au Maroc: bilan de quinze années de tourisme dans l'arrière-pays [Local initiatives, public policies and the tourism development in rural areas in Morocco: assessment of fifteen years of tourism in the hinterland]. In M. Berriane (ed.), *Le tourisme dans les arrière-pays méditerranéens: des dynamiques territoriales locales en marge des politiques publiques* [Tourism in the Mediterranean hinterlands: local territorial dynamics on the fringes of public policies] (pp. 21–42). Rabat: Université Mohammed V Agdal.

Bleasdale, S., & Tapsell, S. (1999). Social and cultural impacts of tourism policy in Tunisia. In M. Robinson & P. Boniface (eds), *Tourism and cultural conflicts* (pp. 181–204). Wallingford: CABI.

Caffyn, A., & Jobbins, G. (2003). Governance capacity and stakeholder interactions in the development and management of coastal tourism: Examples from Morocco and Tunisia. *Journal of Sustainable Tourism, 11*(2–3), 224–245.

Carboni, M., & Perelli, C. (2020). The Muslim-friendly option: Tunisia's (mass) tourism in times of crisis. In C. M. Hall & G. Prayag (Eds.), *The Routledge handbook of halal hospitality and Islamic tourism* (pp. 169–179). Abingdon: Routledge.

Carboni, M., Perelli, C., & Sistu, G. (2014). Is Islamic tourism a viable option for Tunisian tourism? Insights from Djerba. *Tourism Management Perspectives, 11,* 1–9.

Carboni, M., Perelli, C., & Sistu, G. (2017). Developing tourism products in line with Islamic beliefs: Some insights from Nabeul–Hammamet. *The Journal of North African Studies, 22*(1), 87–108.

Carpenter, I., & Gana, A. (2012). Les oasis du sud Tunisien, le patrimoine comme levier du développement territorial? [The oases of southern Tunisia, heritage as a lever for territorial development?] *Revue des Régions Arides, 28,* 225–237.

Chaabeni, R. (2004). *Écotourisme et tourisme culturel durable en Tunisie. Situation actuelle et perspectives* [Ecotourism and sustainable cultural tourism in Tunisia. Current situation and prospects]. *Rapport du Programme des Nations Unies pour le Développement,* retrieved from https://www.academia.edu/5329253/ECOTOURISME_ET_TOURISME_CULTUREL_DURABLE_EN_TUNISIE_Situation_actuelle_et_perspectives.

Cortes-Jimenez, I., Nowak, J. J., & Sahli, M. (2011). Mass beach tourism and economic growth: Lessons from Tunisia. *Tourism Economics*, *17*(3), 531–547.

Dhaher, N. (2012). Les ambivalences de la mise en tourisme du patrimoine. Le cas du centre ancien de Tozeur (Tunisie) [The ambivalence of heritage tourism. The case of the ancient centre of Tozeur (Tunisia)], *Mondes du tourisme*, *6*, 23–33.

Dhaher, N. (2016). Mise en tourisme du patrimoine saharien Tunisien: construction problématique d'une dynamique de développement [Tourism development of Tunisian Saharan heritage: problematic construction of a dynamic development]. 5th Sino-European Tourism Colloquium 'Tourism, Heritage and Memories in the 21st Century', Ningbo, University of Ningbo.

Dhaher, N. (2017). Le patrimoine saharien tunisien au défi d'un tourisme durable: le cas de Tozeur et Nefta [Tunisian Saharan heritage and the challenges of sustainable tourism: the case of Tozeur and Nefta]. *Arbor*, *193*(785), 398.

El Gaied, M., & Meyer, V. (2014). Communication, tourisme et développement territorial: l'exemple des Gsours du sud-est tunisien [Communication, tourism and territorial development: the case of the Gsours in south-eastern Tunisia]. *Les Enjeux de l'information et de la communication*, *1*, 5–15.

Gan, R., & Smith, J. (1992). Tourism and national development planning in Tunisia. *Tourism Management*, *13*(3), 331–336.

Gravari-Barbas, M., & Violier, P. (2003). *Lieux de Culture-Culture des lieux. Production (s) culturelle (s) locale (s) et émergence des lieux: dynamiques, acteurs, enjeux* [Places of culture-culture of places. Local cultural production(s) and the emergence of places: dynamics, actors, issues]. Rennes: Presses Universitaires de Rennes.

Halioui, S., & Schmidt, M. (2017). Participatory decision-making for sustainable tourism development in Tunisia. In V. Katsoni, A. Upadhya, & A. Stratigea (eds), *Tourism, culture and heritage in a smart economy*. Cham: Springer.

Hall, C. M. (2006a). Tourism urbanisation and global environmental change. In S. Gössling & C. M. Hall (eds), *Tourism and global environmental change: Ecological, economic, social and political interrelationships* (pp. 142–156). London: Routledge.

Hall, C. M. (2006b). Implementing the World Heritage Convention: What happens after listing? In A. Leask & A. Fyall (eds), *Managing World Heritage Sites* (pp. 20–34). Oxford: Elsevier.

Hall, C. M. (2019). Constructing sustainable tourism development: The 2030 agenda and the managerial ecology of sustainable tourism. *Journal of Sustainable Tourism*, *27*(7), 1044–1060.

Hall, C. M., & McArthur, S. (2000). *Integrated heritage management*. London: HMSO.

Hall, C. M., & Prayag, G. (eds) (2020). *The Routledge handbook of halal hospitality and Islamic tourism*. Abingdon: Routledge.

Hazbun, W. (2008). *Beaches, ruins, resorts: The politics of tourism in the Arab world*. Minneapolis: University of Minnesota Press.

Jeffrey, H., & Bleasdale, S. (2017). Tunisia: Mass tourism in crisis? In D. Harrison & R. Sharpley (eds), *Mass tourism in a small world* (pp. 191–199). Wallingford: CABI.

Lazzarotti, O. (2000). Patrimoine et tourisme: un couple de la mondialisation [Heritage and tourism: a couple of globalization]. *Mappemonde*, *57*(1), 12–16.

Leïla, A. (2013). L'architecture tunisienne des premières années de l'indépendance. Modernité et défis 1956–1970 [Tunisian architecture from the first years of independence. Modernity and challenges between 1956–1970], *Revue Archibat*, *30*, 24–27.

Ministére des affaires culturelles. (1988). Décret no. 88-1591 du 24/8/1988 Portant organisation administrative et financière de l'agence nationale de mise en valeur et d'exploitation du partimoine archéologique et historique [Decree number 88-1591 dated 24/8/1988 on the administrative and financial organisation of the national agency for the development and exploitation of archaeological and historical heritage], *Journal Officiel de la République Tunisienne, 131*(90), 1247–1249.

Miossec, J. M. (1999). Les acteurs de l'aménagement tunisien: les leçon d'une performance [The actors of Tunisian planning: the lessons of a performance]. In M. Berriane & H. Popp (eds), *le Tourisme au Maghreb: diversification du produit et développement local et régional* (pp. 65–85). Rabat: Faculté des Lettres et Sciences Humaines de Rabat.

Morris, H. (2019). Is it safe to book a holiday to Tunisia? *The Telegraph*, retrieved from https://www.telegraph.co.uk/travel/destinations/africa/tunisia/articles/thomas-cook-tunisia-cheap-holidays-is-it-safe/.

National Heritage Institute (2018). List of protected and classified historical and archaeological monuments in Tunisia. Retrieved from http://www.inp.rnrt.tn/Monuments_classees/monuments_classes.pdf.

Nozha, S. (2010). À propos du patrimoine immatériel: réflexion autour des savoir-faire des femmes en Tunisie [About intangible heritage: reflections on the skills of women in Tunisia]. *Quaderns de la Mediterrània, 14*, 125–131.

Office National du Tourisme Tunisien (ONTT) (2012). *Le Tourisme Tunisien en chiffres 2011* [Tunisian tourism in figures 2011]. Tunis: Office National du Tourisme Tunisien.

Ouerfelli, C. (2008). Co-integration analysis of quarterly European tourism demand in Tunisia. *Tourism Management, 29*(1), 127–137.

Perelli, C., & Sistu, G. (2013). Jasmines for tourists: heritage policies in Tunisia. In D. Arnold, A. Benson, & J. Kaminsky (eds), *Contemporary issues in cultural heritage Tourism* (pp. 99–115). London: Routledge.

Picton, O. J. (2010). Usage of the concept of culture and heritage in the United Arab Emirates – an analysis of Sharjah heritage area. *Journal of Heritage Tourism, 5*(1), 69–84.

Poirier, R. A. (1995). Tourism and development in Tunisia. *Annals of Tourism Research, 22*(1), 157–171.

Poirier, R. A., & Wright, S. (1993). The political economy of tourism in Tunisia. *The Journal of Modern African Studies, 31*(1), 149–162.

Porter, L. (2015). Images of 7/7 bombings used to promote Tunisia tourism. *The Telegraph*, retrieved from https://www.telegraph.co.uk/travel/destinations/africa/tunisia/articles/Images-of-77-bombings-used-to-promote-Tunisia-tourism/.

Puig, N. (2004). *Bédouins sédentarisés et société citadine à Tozeur (Sud-Ouest tunisien)* [Sedentary Bedouins and urban society in Tozeur (South-West Tunisia)]. Edition IRMC-Khartala. Tunis–Paris.

Rabbat, N. (2016). Heritage as a right: Heritage and the Arab Spring. *International Journal of Islamic Architecture, 5*(2), 267–278.

Rey, V. (2019). *Mediating museums: Exhibiting material culture in Tunisia (1881–2016)*. London: Brill.

Seyfi, S., & Hall, C. M. (2019). Deciphering Islamic theocracy and tourism: Conceptualization, context, and complexities. *International Journal of Tourism Research, 21*(6), 735–746.

Souissi, M. (2010). Le tourisme international en Tunisie: vers de nouvelles formes et la réorganisation de l'espace touristique [International tourism in Tunisia: towards new forms and the reorganization of the tourist space]. *Carnets de géographes* (online), retrieved from http://journals.openedition.org/cdg/2310.

Throsby, D. (2016). Investment in urban heritage conservation in developing countries: Concepts, methods and data. *City, Culture and Society*, 7(2), 81–86.

UNESCO (2019). *Tunisian properties inscribed on the World Heritage List*, retrieved from http://whc.unesco.org/en/statesparties/TN.

Viard, J. (2000). *Court traité sur les vacances, les voyages et l'hospitalité des lieux* [Short treatise on vacation, travel and hospitality of the places]. Paris: éditions de l'Aube.

Weigert, M. (2012). *Le tourisme Tunisien: les défis à l'heure de la transition démocratique* [Tourism in Tunisia: challenges in the age of democratic transition], retrieved from http://www.ipemed.coop/fr/publications-r17/les-notes-ipemed-c48/le-tourisme-en-tunisie-les-defis-a-lheure-de-la-transition-democratique-a1143.html.

World Travel & Tourism Council (WTTC) (2019). Travel & tourism economic impact 2018 Tunisia, retrieved from https://www.wttc.org/economic-impact/country-analysis/country-reports/.

6 Touring 'our' past
World Heritage tourism and post-colonialism in Morocco

Bailey Ashton Adie

Introduction

While many post-colonial societies distance themselves from their colonial past, this is often undertaken via the creation of a new, unified identity built on their existing heritage, which in many cases is the same heritage that has been preserved by the colonisers (Sinamai, 2019). This is clearly visible in Morocco where colonial heritage protection policies are still maintained. The emphasis on colonially dictated heritage narratives becomes increasingly problematic when heritage and culture are important aspects of the post-colonial state's tourism policy. World Heritage amplifies these issues through its inherent international focus, presenting a heritage, which may, in certain instances, be disconnected not only from post-colonial citizens' identities but also what they deem to be culturally significant. To this end, this chapter presents the concepts of Orientalism in relation to the development of post-colonial national identities and how these, in turn, influence national heritage tourism policies. This then turns into a discussion of these concepts in relation to the Moroccan post-colonial heritage tourism context, specifically discussing the archaeological site of Volubilis (a World Heritage Site).

Tourism, Orientalism, and the post-colonial state

Orientalism, according to Said (2003, p. 57), is where 'Europe ... articulates the Orient; this articulation is the prerogative, not of a puppet master, but of a genuine creator, whose life-giving power represents, animates, constitutes the otherwise silent and dangerous space beyond familiar boundaries'. Thus, the imagery of the Orient in the West can be derived from what Europe has already written about it, which then informs the Westerner in regards to what is and is not 'Oriental'. Furthermore, 'the heritage of the people that is handed down to the next generation is that of the colonizers', making it very difficult for the local people to develop an independent heritage of their own' (Said, 2003, p. 57). This is in part due to the impact that colonial powers had on local identities. According to Sinamai (2019, p. 157), 'colonialism not only changed and emphasised certain identities, it also gave people new identities'. Given that a community's identity plays a significant role in what heritage is and is not protected (Sinamai, 2019), the discourse around heritage, as an internalised part of the identity of the touring culture, perpetuates this colonial-era Western cultural construct. This is clearly visible in the case of Malaysia where the development of a defined Malay identity was heavily supported by the colonisers and then co-opted by Malay nationalists in the 1920s and 1930s which eventually fed into the development of a national cultural narrative driven by Malay identity (Worden, 2010). According to Worden (2010, p. 140), this is why the Malay elements of Melaka are prioritised over its 'cosmopolitan character'.

The Orientalist attitude is so pervasive within the general understanding of non-Western countries that it becomes the mode by which identity is displayed to the world, particularly in relation to national marketing campaigns and outward-facing tourism initiatives (Echtner & Prasad, 2003; Feighery, 2012; Palmer, 1994). For example, in their analysis of an Omani destination marketing video, Feighery (2012, p. 279) noted that the film's 'narrative embraces aspects of the Arabist tradition of travel writing in portraying Omani cultural heritage through representations of the desert and the Bedouin people'. This is, according to Feighery (2012), a process of self-orientalisation which is designed not only to create a politically expedient unified identity but also assist in the economic goals of the country with regard to tourism development. However, by internalising and projecting this 'Orientalist' discourse, campaigns similar to the Omani example merely reinforce pre-conceived perceptions of non-Western cultures. The imagery used in tourism is often riddled with Orientalist undertones, especially in countries with a history of colonial interference. This is due, in part, to a long history of Orientalist travel literature throughout which, as Said (2003) noted, the authors superimposed themselves and their world views on the countries, which they visited while simultaneously placing themselves as opposite the 'other-ness' of the 'Oriental'.

This 'othering' or exoticising of the non-Western world has become integrated not only into Western discourses but also into those of the non-Western countries as well. These discourses are what, in turn, lead to distorted tourism imagery, often originating from the non-Western country itself. Returning to the example of Oman, Causevic and Neal (2019) note that, in some instances, this self-Orientalisation is actually a result of de-historification of sites in order to represent a unified and unproblematic past. The Orientalist narrative is pushed at a national level in order to counter negative perceptions and problematic histories that may otherwise deter visitors. While the Omani example exhibits a less common reason for the utilisation of Orientalist narratives, in many cases, self-Orientalist tourism narratives are driven, in major part, by the desire to increase foreign tourist-driven economic benefits within a country. For example, in the case of India, the 'Incredible India' tourism marketing campaign has been highly successful with a noted increase in foreign arrivals after its debut (Kerrigan, Shivanandan, & Hede, 2012). However, according to Kerrigan et al. (2012), this campaign utilises a romanticised image of India which harkens back to colonial representations of the exotic 'other' while also failing to convey the contemporary lived experience of the average Indian.

This national-level Orientalisation of the tourism landscape poses particular issues for the local population, especially when they are, by essence of their local environment, driven to act out a part in the Orientalist narrative. While the Orientalist and non-Orientalist narratives can exist concurrently, as evidenced by Gutberlet's (2019) German-speaking cruise tourists in the frankincense shop whose experience was sequestered from the actual commerce occurring between the shop owner and both local and regional customers. This is predominantly due to the fact that these tourist groups are guided through the Orientalist *souq* by a local tour guide, who serves as a narrator of an imagined, Orientalist reality, reinforcing the marketing materials the tourists were given prior to disembarking. Gutberlet (2019, p. 131) highlights that, as the space is shared by both local shoppers and these tourist groups, 'locals adjust themselves within traditional and Oriental identities', which, in essence, imposes the false narrative onto the local population wherein 'local communities may find themselves trapped in an ancient Oriental setting'.

This is especially problematic as Orientalist-driven tourism tends to focus on luxury, exoticism, and historical consistency. It emphasises the richness of the past, supported by the Orientalist understanding of history within that country. Namely, 'their great moments were in the past; they are used in the modern world only because the powerful and up-to-date empires have effectively brought them out of the wretchedness of their decline' (Said, 2003, p. 35). Therefore, cultural alterations that adapt the tourist offering to this ideology result in the presentation of a culture frozen in time wherein the only accessible aspects of modernity are those associated with the colonisers. Echtner and Prasad (2003, p. 669) note that this results in the neo-colonial tourist

> expect[ing] to find legendary lands—to uncover their mystical secrets, to marvel at their exotic people, and to wonder at their opulence. These representations are strongly reminiscent of the colonial eras of exploration, trade and conquest. In many ways, modern day tourists are encouraged to relive the journeys and experiences of colonial explorers, traders, treasure hunters, archeologists, etc.

This becomes even more problematic given the common reliance on former coloniser nations as source countries for the post-colonial destinations, as this perpetuates the colonial power dynamic, albeit with a new façade of political, if not wholly economic, independence (Palmer, 1994).

The Moroccan colonial context

This Orientalist imagery is especially clear in the case of Morocco, which can in part be attributed to its French colonial history as well as the manner in which its national identity was developed following the departure of the French. The contemporary Moroccan state can trace its roots back to AD 788 with the establishment of the Idrisid dynasty as a result of almost a century of Arab conquest, which also led to the introduction of Islam to the region. The next almost 900 years were marked by several different dynasties, both Arab and Berber, and fluctuating geographical boundaries. The current royal family, the Alaouites, have been in power since 1666, thus providing a sense of historical continuity reaching back to the pre-colonial period. Interestingly, Morocco had managed predominantly to escape early 'direct military intervention' from European powers due to 'diplomatic tensions' (Wyrtzen, 2015, p. 16). However, as a result of several different events and directly following a revolt against the sultan, Morocco's independence, in essence, came to an end on 30 March 1912 with the signing of the Treaty of Fez, under which most of Morocco became a French Protectorate, with the remaining areas, the far south Saharan region and north coastline, falling under a Spanish Protectorate.

Spain and France remained in place as protectors, albeit not outright colonial rulers, until 1956 when Morocco was made independent once more. What is interesting to note is that, during the Protectorate period, Morocco was technically a sovereign state, and the sultan continued to have dominion over the country. However, French control over the Protectorate was significant, and, as a result, there was visible resistance to their control from the inception of the Protectorate period. Although there were multiple opposition movements throughout the entirety of the Protectorate period, of particular note is the nationalist movement of the 1930s. Led by urban elites, the nationalists mobilised under an Arab-Islamic identity which was placed in opposition to the French colonisers and occurred as a result to the Protectorate's decision to separate the Berber and Islamic legal systems (Wyrtzen, 2015). The nationalists opposed the legal distinction between these two groups as they advocated for a unified Moroccan identity, which was not only Arab and Muslim but also relied on the importance of the sultan. It is this unified identity that would be utilised following independence to develop a new national narrative (Wyrtzen, 2015).

While unified national identity narratives are common features of postcolonial states, the reliance on this specific dichotomy can be traced directly to French colonial policy in Morocco, which relied on the separation of the traditional (Moroccan) and the modern (French) (Wyrtzen, 2015). This separation was driven by the new French colonial strategy, association, which replaced the previous, assimilation (Wright, 1987; Minca, 2006). Perhaps the most rapid and visible implementation of the association strategy occurred under the auspices of French Résident Général, Hubert Lyautey, who was highly active in the preservation of Morocco's heritage during his residency from 1912 to 1925, particularly in respect to the introduction of conservation methods for built heritage and urban environments (Alami, 2001). His influence is especially evident in Protectorate-era city planning, which created a 'dual city' wherein the medina was preserved and protected while the *ville nouvelle*, which was designed for the French minority and those in the local population who chose to assimilate, was built to highlight colonial urban modernity, while also incorporating certain distinct local design elements (Wright, 1987). Lyautey's cities, then, represent the physical reinforcement of these distinctions wherein Moroccan heritage and identity are representative of the past while the French represent the future.

In contrast to previous French colonial policy that focused on assimilation, colonialism in Morocco was driven in part by the need to place the indigenous culture firmly within the sphere of 'primitive' and 'traditional' in order to justify the continued presence of the French Protectorate. According to Minca (2006, p. 159), 'Lyautey believed that by preserving local ways of life, *association* could sponsor the renewal of indigenous culture and the creation of a modern, prosperous colonial state'. However, this focus on preservation, particularly in the urban medinas, was often to the detriment of the local residents and shop owners who wished to modernise their environment. For example, in Fez, a law was passed in 1923 which

> established a list of 'architectural elements' permitted for use in the medina's houses. The French regulated a house's external molding, chimneys, windows, awnings, doors, and grillwork. They also set rules for decorative aspects of a house acquired through use of painted wood, sculpted plaster, varnished tiles, and wrought iron. To ensure that houses met the criteria of this 'Fassi style,' the colonial government required all residents to apply for building permits (Holden, 2006, p. 308).

As can be observed in Fez, colonial preservationist policies were especially restrictive, and colonial officials were willing to actively control and alter the urban fabric in order to conform to 'a romanticized image of a traditional medieval city in North Africa' (Holden, 2006, p. 313).

Tourism and heritage in Morocco

In tandem with the French policy of association within Moroccan urban planning and heritage preservation, colonial-era tourism similarly reinforced this binary of tradition and modernity, and official tourist guiding materials from this period emphasise this, stressing the historicity of places. For example, Holden (2006) draws attention to one official's narration of a tourist visit to Fez, starting in the modern *ville nouvelle*, and slowly making their way back in time as they worked their way through the medina. In another example from Fez from 1916, 'a geographer working for the Protectorate, insisted that sixteenth-century descriptions of these suqs could still guide modern tourists' (Holden, 2006, p. 306). The colonial tourist, then, is a time traveller, uncovering the past in the present. The importance of this romanticised Morocco as a tourist attractor was not lost on Résident Général Lyautey. In 1914, during a speech in Paris, he stated:

> Since the recent, intense development of large-scale tourism, the presentation of a country's beauty has taken on an economic importance of the first order. To attract a large tourist population is to gain everything for both the public and the private budgets (Lyautey, cited in Wright, 1987, p. 304).

Therefore, he was well aware of the influence that an 'exotic' and 'traditional' environment, underpinned by both tangible and intangible heritage, would be particularly attractive to Western tourists, who would, in turn, provide an economic boost to the local economy.

Today, tourism still plays an important role in the Moroccan economy. It is the 12th largest contributor to the nation's GDP as well as the 12th largest source of employment. The industry's direct impact has been estimated by the Ministry of Tourism as being approximately 11 per cent of GDP and accounting for 548,000 direct jobs, 5 per cent of the total number of employed workers (Ministère du Tourisme du Maroc, n.d.b). In fact, according to the goal of the Moroccan Vision 2020 plan, 'in 2020 Morocco will be among the top 20 global destinations and emerge as a Mediterranean example of sustainable development' (Author translation, Ministère du Tourisme du Maroc, n.d.c). Additionally, one of their objectives is to double tourist arrivals, which would include doubling the arrivals from the already key traditional European market while simultaneously attracting one million new visitors from emerging markets. Furthermore, they hope 'to triple the number of domestic trips in order to democratize tourism within the country' (Author translation, Ministère du Tourisme du Maroc, n.d.c). Based on these goals and objectives, it can be seen that tourism development is and will be a high priority for the Moroccan government in the future.

Unsurprisingly, given the ministerial focus on tourism, the industry in Morocco has grown exponentially over the last 20 years. Between 2016 and 2017, total arrivals rose from 10,331,731 to 11,349,344, an increase of approximately 10 per cent (Ministère du Tourisme du Maroc, n.d.a). In 2018, this increased again to approximately 12.3 million arrivals, a growth of 8 per cent (Ministère du Tourisme du Maroc, n.d.b). It is interesting to note, particularly for this chapter, that the number of arrivals from foreign tourists is marginally larger, at 52 per cent of total foreign arrivals, than that of Moroccans Resident Abroad (MREs) (Ministère du Tourisme du Maroc, n.d.b). While the total number of arrivals is fairly evenly distributed between foreign tourists and MREs, the disparity between foreign and domestic tourists in relation to hotel nights is significantly more pronounced. Domestic tourists in 2017 saw a growth in overall hotel nights of 7 per cent but account for only 32 per cent of total hotel nights. In comparison, foreign tourists saw a growth of 18 per cent in total hotel nights, more than double domestic tourists. What is notable about these statistics is that there is no change in the share of hotel nights between residents and non-residents over a period of two years, with the 2015 statistics also showing residents accounting for 32 per cent of total hotel nights (Observatoire du Tourisme, Maroc, 2017). However, it needs to be noted that this disparity could be attributable to the fact that domestic tourists may frequent non-monitored lodgings such as unregistered hotels and the homes of family and friends. Thus, for the formalised tourism industry, foreign tourists are still the main source of income, but overall domestic tourism estimates may be artificially lower due to the focus on official hotel nights.

While foreign tourists may be the dominant tourist group, at least on paper, it would incorrect to assume that visitors from abroad are geographically diverse. According to Moroccan data, the vast majority of tourists are European. In fact, seven of the top nine source countries are located in Europe and account for 71 per cent of all foreign tourist arrivals in 2015 (Observatoire du Tourisme, Maroc, 2017). In acknowledgement of this European market dominance, the 2020 plan focuses specifically on targeted marketing to this group, with this already occurring in France and Spain. However, they do indicate that this dependence on their 'traditional markets' can be viewed as a limitation (Ministère du Tourisme du Maroc, n.d.e). Of these traditional markets, the largest, by far, are the French, both as a result of the country's status as a former protectorate as well as its geographic proximity (Haut-Commissariat au Plan du Maroc, 2011). This is visible in the foreign arrivals from 2017 where France was the largest tourist-generating country for Morocco, with 1,614,011 arrivals, equating to 27.5 per cent of all non-MRE foreign visitation. In comparison, the Spanish, the second largest group of foreign tourists, only accounted for 710,729 arrivals, or 12.1 per cent, less than half the number of French (Ministère du Tourisme du Maroc, n.d.a). With over a quarter of all foreign tourist income received from one nation and, taking into consideration the complex history that Morocco and France have, activities designed to attract tourists may potentially be considered problematic.

Heritage tourism, then, given colonial policies around preservation and conservation, could be especially difficult to promote. Notwithstanding these complications, heritage is one of Morocco's key tourism offerings, and, as such, is one of the foci of the 2020 tourism plan. This plan places particular emphasis on the creation of 'interpretation circuits running through the medinas of the Kingdom's major imperial cities' which, when combined thematically, should allow tourists to understand the 'fundamentals of Moroccan culture' (Ministère du Tourisme du Maroc, n.d.d). This prioritisation of Morocco's cultural offering has not changed much in the last 20 years. Youngstedt (2003, p. 65) found that tourism marketers at the turn of the century were highlighting that not only was Morocco a cultural destination but one which was 'traditional, authentic, rustic, nostalgic ... where tourists can safely indulge their curiosities and fantasies'. This is highly similar to the colonial rhetoric used to justify the concept of dual cities and is explained by Porter (2003, pp. 125–126), who notes that 'through the heritage preservation project and its reliance on French colonial sources, colonial definitions of Morocco are reemerging as authentic and legitimate definitions of the post-colonial Moroccan nation'. In fact, in 2000, Morocco actually reinstated the Protectorate-era medina preservation programme due to the perceived economic potential driven by tourism (Lee, 2008). Therefore, the modern heritage movement in Morocco is merely recycling colonial conceptions of what is 'Moroccan'.

Nowhere is this more visible than at Jamaa el Fna in Marrakech, where multiple authors have highlighted the manner in which the square functions as an Orientalist landscape consumed by tourists (Borghi, 2005; Minca, 2006, 2007; Schmitt, 2005). The importance of this space traces its roots back, again, to Lyautey who was the first to demarcate specific boundaries to the space as well as to stress its importance as 'a representative site of Moroccan heritage and culture' (Minca, 2006, p. 167). This led Minca (2007, p. 446) to conclude that

> colonial legacies thus 'prepared' Morocco in both tourist and local imaginations and today's Moroccan tourist geographies exemplify a 'colonial' re-enactment in place, where diverse (contemporary) performances and identity strategies intersect with traces of the colonial project and local re-interpretations of the very concepts of 'heritage' and 'cultural identity'.

Thus, not only is Morocco drawing from the colonial heritage preservation movement, but it is also, by internalising the colonial discourse around its cultural heritage, reinforcing Orientalist conceptualisations of space, particularly urban, in post-colonial Morocco.

Given this focus on colonial heritage preservation traditions, the composition of Morocco's World Heritage List is unsurprising. Currently, Morocco has nine listed sites, all of which are cultural, as well as 13 on their tentative list, of which nine are cultural. The sites which comprise Morocco's World Heritage offering are as follows:

- Medina of Fez
- Medina of Marrakesh
- Ksar of Ait-Ben-Haddou
- Historic City of Meknes
- Medina of Tétouan
- Archaeological Site of Volubilis
- Medina of Essaouira

- Portuguese City of Mazagan (El Jadida)
- Rabat, Modern Capital and Historic City: A Shared Heritage.

The Moroccan government considers these 'must-see' tourist sites, which are the 'cultural showcase of Morocco' (Author's translation, Haut-Commissariat au Plan du Maroc, 2011, p. 28). What is interesting to note is that, of these nine sites, many were of significant interest to the French Protectorate, who, as has been mentioned, had a penchant for medinas in particular.

The Archaeological Site of Volubilis

The Archaeological Site of Volubilis is located three kilometres west of Moulay Idriss Zerhoun, the holiest city in Morocco, in the province of Meknès El Menzeh. The site was most likely inhabited from the Neolithic Period (UNESCO, 1997). Volubilis, historically, functioned as the capital of Mauritania though it is rarely mentioned in ancient literature due to use of Iol, later called Caesarea under Juba II (48 BC–AD 23/24), as an official royal city (Roller, 2003). However, upon the rise of Juba II, Volubilis was treated only as a secondary royal city due, in part, to Juba II's political ties to Rome, and thus the logical choice for a political centre was Caesarea as it was located on the Western Mediterranean (Roller, 2003). After the execution of Ptolemaios, the heirless son of Juba II, Mauritania, including Volubilis, fell under the direct control of the Roman Empire in AD 40 (Roller, 2003). It was given the title of municipium after Roman annexation of the kingdom as a result of Juba II's loyalty to Rome (International Council on Monuments and Sites (ICOMOS), 1997; Raven, 1993).

In gratitude for their having favoured Rome in the small rebellion that followed the death of Ptolemaios, the citizens of Volubilis were given a dispensation lasting a decade regarding tax payments as well as the benefits of Roman citizenship (MacKendrick, 1980). However, the Romans quickly abandoned the region in 285 for reasons unknown, leaving the town to the inhabitants who were predominantly Berber by this period. After the Roman desertion, the population shifted to the west of the triumphal arch, and evidence found in this community's graveyard indicates that they were Christians (UNESCO, 1997). However, at some point prior to the arrival of Moulay Idris, who was assassinated in 791, the residents had already converted to Islam (ICOMOS, 1997). It experienced a very brief period as the Idrisid capital, but lost this status when the capital was moved to Fes under Idris II (Jodin, 1987; ICOMOS, 1997). The town remained inhabited until approximately the eleventh century when it is believed that the Almoravid raids ended any remaining settlement on the site (ICOMOS, 1997).

A French archaeologist, De la Martinière, undertook initial excavation of the site from 1887 to 1892. Additional excavations occurred under the French Protectorate, beginning in 1915 under the insistence of Résident

Général Lyautey, and not ending until 1941, with their recommencement after the end of the Second World War. Reconstruction of certain elements of the town occurred both before and after the Protectorate period, and work continues to this day on the site (ICOMOS, 1997). While Morocco ratified the *World Heritage Convention* on 28 October 1975, the Archaeological Site of Volubilis was not inscribed until 1997. The criteria under which it received its inscription are II, III, IV, and VI, emphasising the site's long history as town tracing its roots back to high antiquity and illustrating multiple sociocultural changes in the region. In order to visit the site today, visitors can stay at Moulay Idriss Zerhoun, the nearest town, but many tourists arrive at the site on day excursions from either Meknes, 45 minutes away by car, or Fes, an even further hour and a half from the site. Entrance to the site is not free, and foreign tourists pay a higher entry fee, approximately 70 dirhams for an adult, in comparison with 10 dirhams for Moroccans. Additionally, Moroccan visitors receive free entry every Friday and on the first day of all religious and national holidays (Volubilis, 2019).

Whose heritage is Volubilis?

The archaeological site of Volubilis is an interesting case to consider when discussing the internalisation of colonial heritage ideals. While much of the focus in previous research and, indeed, in colonial policy has focused on urban spaces and heritage, Volubilis would appear to fall outside of that sphere, being uninhabited and located in the countryside. However, as has already been noted, it was predominantly the French who displayed an interest in the site, with excavations occurring throughout much of the Protectorate period. The key as to why this is may be in the name of the site itself, 'Volubilis'. The first line in the site's statement of Outstanding Universal Value states that 'Volubilis contains essentially Roman vestiges of a fortified municipium built on a commanding site at the foot of the Jebel Zerhoun' (UNESCO, n.d.). In fact, much of the Outstanding Universal Value statement focuses on the site's Roman attributes. It could be argued that, in contrast to the medinas and souks of the Moroccan urban spaces, Volubilis was, and still is, viewed as a European heritage site. Thus, it is interesting to analyse who actually visits the site, which in turn may perhaps indicate who deems it to be an important tourist site.

Based on the recent findings from a study by Adie and Hall (2017), 52.6 per cent of all visitors to Volubilis during the study period were Europeans, with the largest proportion coming from France (34.8 per cent). In fact, only 13.3 per cent of all visitors were domestic, which is of particular note given the site's vicinity to Moulay Idriss Zerhoun, Morocco's holiest site. Moulay Idriss Zerhoun houses the remains of the founder of Morocco, and, according to UNESCO (n.d.), 'is the subject of an annual pilgrimage'. Additionally, Moulay Idriss Zerhoun has been on the Moroccan World Heritage Tentative List since 1995 and would appear to be, given its spiritual importance to Moroccans, of greater cultural significance than Volubilis. While Volubilis was, briefly, Moulay Idriss's capital, it seems that, potentially due to the official discourse about the site which stresses its Roman connections, Volubilis is of greater interest for European, and particularly French, tourists. However, by putting Volubilis forward as a World Heritage Site, Morocco has in essence nationally promoted a site which, until the French colonial period, was used as a source of cut stones used to build Moulay Idriss Zerhoun, an arguably much more significant location both spiritually and from the perspective of national identity. However, the fact that this site is still on the tentative list after almost 25 years is potentially indicative of the Moroccan self-Orientalisation process, wherein only those sites which were important for the colonial powers are strongly promoted at the international level, as is clearly visible in the nine listed World Heritage Sites mentioned previously.

Conclusion

Colonial policies and discourses still continue to pervade post-colonial national narratives, which often leads to the internalisation of the very identities from which the now independent nations are trying to distance themselves. This internalised Orientalism can then express itself through the post-colonial state's tourist offering, particularly when the targeted audience is the former colonising nation. This is clearly visible in Morocco, where the national tourism policy has been driven by a continuation of colonial conceptualisations of heritage and culture. Their World Heritage Sites are an emblematic example of the reiteration of the French colonial narrative, particularly with the emphasis on medinas. However, while most of the listed sites display attributes which align with the colonial definition of Moroccan identity, Volubilis is different due to the stress on its connection to ancient Rome. This chapter has argued that Morocco has internalised the colonial identity dictated by the French which in turn has impacted upon the heritage tourism industry, focusing on World Heritage in particular. Yet, as Morocco has promoted heritage that was deemed important by the Protectorate, Volubilis has been promoted as a World Heritage Site with a European-dominant narrative which does not resonate with the Moroccan population. This begs the question – if the prioritisation of heritage is driven by internalised colonial identities and former colonial tourism markets, whose heritage is being protected?

References

Adie, B. A., & Hall, C. M. (2017). Who visits world heritage? A comparative study of three cultural sites. *Journal of Heritage Tourism*, *12*(1), 67–80.
Alami, M. H. (2001). The fiction of architectural identity in contemporary Morocco. *ISIM Newsletter*, *1*(8), 27.

Borghi, R. (2005). Riflessioni sul Senso del Luogo: il Caso della Piazza Jamaa Al Fna di Marrakech. *Bolletino della Società Geografica Italiana*, 1–17.

Causevic, S., & Neal, M. (2019). The exotic veil: Managing tourist perceptions of national history and statehood in Oman. *Tourism Management*, *71*, 504–517.

Echtner, C. M., & Prasad, P. (2003). The context of third world tourism marketing. *Annals of Tourism Research*, *30*(3), 660–682.

Feighery, W. G. (2012). Tourism and self-Orientalism in Oman: A critical discourse analysis. *Critical Discourse Studies*, *9*(3), 269–284.

Gutberlet, M. (2019). Staging the Oriental other: Imaginaries and performances of German-speaking cruise tourists. *Tourist Studies*, *19*(1), 110–137.

Haut-Commissariat au Plan du Maroc (2011). *Prospective Maroc 2030: Tourisme 2030, Quelles ambitions pour le Maroc?* Retrieved from https://www.hcp.ma/downloads/Maroc-2030_t11885.html.

Holden, S. E. (2006). When it pays to be medieval: Historic preservation as a colonial policy in the Medina of Fez, 1912–1932. *The Journal of the Historical Society*, *6*(2), 297–316.

International Council on Monuments and Sites (ICOMOS) (1997). World Heritage List. Volubilis (Morocco). No. 836. *Advisory Body Evaluation, ICOMOS*. Retrieved from http://whc.unesco.org/en/list/836/documents/.

Jodin, A. (1987). *Volubilis Regia Ivbae: Contribution á l'étude des Civilasations du Maroc Antique Préclaudien*. Diffusion de Boccard: Paris.

Kerrigan, F., Shivanandan, J., & Hede, A.-M. (2012). Nation branding: A critical appraisal of Incredible India. *Journal of Macromarketing*, *32*(3), 319–327.

Lee, J. M. (2008). Riad fever: Heritage tourism, urban renewal and the medina property boom in old cities of Morocco. *E Review of Tourism Research*, *6*(4), 66–78.

MacKendrick, P. (1980). *The North African stones speak*. London: The University of North Carolina Press.

Minca, C. (2006). Re-inventing the 'square': Postcolonial geographies and tourist narratives in Jamaa el Fna, Marrakech. In C. Minca & T. Oakes (eds). *Travels in paradox: Remapping tourism* (pp. 155–184). Oxford, UK: Rowman & Littlefield.

Minca, C. (2007). The tourist landscape paradox. *Social & Cultural Geography*, *8*(3), 433–453.

Ministère du Tourisme du Maroc (n.d.a). *Arrivées des touristes*. Retrieved from https://www.tourisme.gov.ma/fr/tourisme-en-chiffres/arrivees-des-touristes.

Ministère du Tourisme du Maroc (n.d.b). *Chiffres Clés*. retrieved from https://www.tourisme.gov.ma/fr/tourisme-en-chiffres/chiffres-cl%C3%A9s.

Ministère du Tourisme du Maroc (n.d.c). *Vision 2020: Engagement & objectifs*. Retrieved from https://www.tourisme.gov.ma/fr/vision-2020/presentation/engagement-objectifs.

Ministère du Tourisme du Maroc (n.d.d). *Vision 2020: Patrimoine & héritage*. Retrieved from https://www.tourisme.gov.ma/fr/vision-2020/promotion-et-transport-aerien.

Ministère du Tourisme du Maroc (n.d.e). *Vision 2020: Promotion et transport aérien*. Retrieved from https://www.tourisme.gov.ma/fr/vision-2020/promotion-et-transport-aerien.

Observatoire du Tourisme, Maroc (2017). *Annuaire Statistique du Tourisme: Panorama des Performances Touristiques au Titre de l'Année 2015*. [pdf]. Retrieved from http://www.observatoiredutourisme.ma/wp-content/uploads/2017/03/Annuaire-Statistique-du-Tourisme-2015.pdf.

Palmer, C. A. (1994). Tourism and colonialism: The experience of the Bahamas. *Annals of Tourism Research*, *21*(4), 792–811.

Porter, G. D. (2003). Unwitting actors: The preservation of Fez's cultural heritage. *Radical History Review*, *86*, 123–148.

Raven, S. (1993). *Rome in Africa* (3rd edn). Abingdon, UK: Routledge.

Roller, D. W. (2003). *The world of Juba II and Kleopatra Selene: Royal Scholarship on Rome's African Frontier*. Abingdon, UK: Routledge.

Said, E. W. (2003). *Orientalism*. London: Penguin Classics (Original work published 1978).

Schmitt, T. (2005). Jemaa el Fna Square in Marrakech: Changes to a social space and to a UNESCO Masterpiece of the Oral and Intangible Heritage of Humanity as a result of global influences. *The Arab World Geographer*, *8*(4), 173–195.

Sinamai, S. (2019). *Memory and cultural landscape at the Khami World Heritage Site, Zimbabwe: An un-inherited past*. Abingdon, UK: Routledge.

UNESCO (n.d.). *Archaeological Site of Volubilis*. Retrieved from http://whc.unesco.org/en/list/836/.

UNESCO (1997). *Decision: CONF 208 VIII.C. Inscription: The Archaeological Site of Volubilis (Morocco)*. Retrieved from http://whc.unesco.org/en/list/836/documents/.

Volubilis (2019). *Volubilis: Un site archeologique fascinant en Afrique du Nord*. Retrieved from http://volubilis.ma/fr/accueil/.

Worden, N. (2010). National identity and heritage tourism in Melaka. In M. Hitchcock, V. T. King, & M. Parnwell (eds). *Heritage tourism in Southeast Asia* (pp. 130–146). Copenhagen: NIAS Press.

Wright, G. (1987). Tradition in the service of modernity: Architecture and urbanism in French colonial policy, 1900–1930. *The Journal of Modern History*, *59*(2), 291–316.

Wyrtzen, J. (2015). *Making Morocco: Colonial intervention and the politics of identity*. London: Cornell University Press.

Youngstedt, S. (2003). Tourism in Morocco: Opportunities, challenges, and threats. *Africa Insight*, *33*(1–2), 61–68.

7 National park or urban green space
The case of [Tel] Ashkelon

Yael Ram

Introduction

Ashkelon is a city in the Southern District of Israel on the Mediterranean coast, 50 kilometres south of Tel Aviv. The municipal area of Ashkelon contains the remains of an ancient seaport city, with origins in the late Chalcolithic Period. In the course of its history, ancient Ashkelon was conquered by the Egyptians, Canaanites, Philistines, Assyrians, Babylonians, Greeks, Phoenicians, Hasmoneans, Romans, Persians, Arabs, and Crusaders, until it was destroyed by the Mamluks in 1270 (Municipality of Ashkelon, 2017; Central Bureau of Statistics (CBS), 2019).

The Arab Village of Majdal had been established a few kilometres from the ancient seaport by the late fifteenth century. In early 1948, Majdal had about 10,000 Arab inhabitants. In November 1948 the Israeli Defense Forces conquered the Majdal village and the remains of the ancient city of Ashkelon nearby. The first neighbourhood of the modern city of Ashkelon was built in the early 1950s between the area of Majdal and the ancient remains, populated primarily by new immigrants from South Africa. From this location, the modern Ashkelon grew, and has now included the former Arab village and approached the ancient remains. Today, about 140,000 people live in the 3,000 km^2 of Ashkelon, almost all of whom are Jewish (Municipality of Ashkelon, 2017; CBS, 2019; Sasson, 2018; A. Sasson, personal communication, 9 April 2019).

The ancient part of Ashkelon has attracted archaeologists' attention since the nineteenth century. In 1965 the area was declared as the first heritage protected area in Israel. However, the area itself was left under the authority of the municipality of Ashkelon, who used it as a public green space (Committee of the National Parks, 2016; Mitrani, 2020). During the 1980s, Harvard University began to conduct annual excavations at the ancient seaport city of Ashkelon (Leon Levy Expedition to Ashkelon, n.d.), even though the area was not managed as a national or protected area. The first step in changing the situation was taken in 2000, when the National Parks Authority (NPA) of Israel decided to take back control of the ancient city of Ashkelon, thereby enforcing the protected area law.

Since then, the area that used to be a green space for locals and a national park *de jure* gradually turned into a National Park *de facto* (Committee of the National Parks, 2016). The process of promoting the protected area laws was reinforced further from 2011 when the NPA enforced the regulation that prohibits playing loud music in the area of the park (O. Bouhnik, personal communication, 1 April 2019).

This chapter follows the process of changing the focus of the National Park of Ashkelon from recreation to heritage, with evidence provided from on-site survey, data on visitation patterns and interviews with stakeholders. The chapter explores how the expectations of visitors were shaped by the different characteristics of the park and examine how the policies of the NPA were accepted by the visitors. The chapter also portrays how residents respond to cultural heritage assets and values that do not exactly conjoin their own heritage, a situation that is common across the MENA region (see Chapter 1, this volume). The present-day population in MENA are often asked to protect and preserve such sites, even when it clashes with their priorities and needs. This situation creates conflicts between authorities and the population and generates dilemmas among stakeholders.

Cultural heritage and archaeology

Cultural heritage is defined as tangible and intangible expressions of the ways of living, developed by a community and passed on from generation to generation, including customs, practices, places, objects, artistic expressions, and values (International Cultural Tourism Committee (ICOMOS), 2002). The notions of community values and identity are also incorporated in the concept and are considered as core elements in creating a meaningful heritage for society (Loulanski, 2006; Vecco, 2010) and promoting a wide range of economic, environmental, social, and community development objectives (Loulanski, 2006).

Archaeology is one of the main pillars of tangible cultural heritage. It includes objects such as paintings and sculpture alongside immovable monuments and sites (UNESCO, 2017). Britt and Chen (2005) indicated that archaeology *in* and *of* places is important to historic cities for two main reasons: First, they may raise income for management authorities; and second, they can 'provide the authenticity needed for historic preservation and renewal projects to take shape and succeed' (Britt & Chen, 2005, p. 26). However, alongside the positive impacts of archaeology, Walker and Carr (2013, p. 14) noted that archaeology can also be perceived as a 'destructive process', which has long-term impacts on the local community and the environment. Their perspective implies that although archaeology is considered to be a part of the heritage, it is not always clear whose heritage it is. In other words, the archaeological site and artefacts may be a part of heritage and cultural tourism but are not necessarily a part of the heritage and culture of the local community (Hall & McArthur, 1999).

Urban parks – between nature and heritage

Natural areas in urban settings are becoming increasingly important for the quality of societies and human life as well as the sustainability of cities (Chiesura, 2004). Oguz (2000, p. 170) indicated that one of the important functions of urban parks is to enable all groups of society to enjoy nature: 'Therefore, for lower- and middle-income group users the most convenient and economic way to make contact with nature and enjoy leisure is to go and visit public parks'.

Previous academic literature tends to link urban parks to natural assets (Chiesura, 2004; Wolch, Byrne, & Newell, 2014) and to associate urban conservation with heritage (Nasser, 2003). However, Bonn, Joseph-Mathews, Dai, Hayes, and Cave (2007) pointed out that this categorisation is overly simplistic. According to their observations, there are many types of sites: 'From natural parks to archaeological sites, each type of attraction has its own unique combination of benefits and advantages; some focus more on the historical aspect, some on the cultural, and others mix geographic and heritage elements' (Bonn et al., 2007, p. 346). The unique positioning of each site is important in creating a special appeal and an emotional bond with the visitors. Visitors to natural parks look for different advantages than visitors to cultural sites: 'This emotional uniqueness can serve as a form of competitive differentiation for that specific attraction' (Bonn et al., 2007, p. 346).

In this context, it is important to note that not only residents enjoy urban parks, but visitors are also attracted to sites that are on the edge of urban destinations. Dwyer and Edwards (2000) divided the visitors to nature-based sites on the edge of urban settlements to different segments and suggested that not all visitors to natural parks are interested in nature. Their segmentation corresponds well with the idea of positioning and differentiation of Bonn et al. (2007) as well as with the need to develop a special bond between the characteristics of the site and the needs of the visitors to promote a successful marketing offer.

Visitor satisfaction and urban parks

The task of managing heritage sites has traditionally been polarised between the curatorial approach, prioritising the protection of the historic structures and valuable artefacts and the approach that is directed to visitor satisfaction as a priority over authenticity and conservation (Calver & Page, 2013). Nevertheless, the marketing appeal also refers to general aspects in managing urban parks such as cleanliness, order and safety, maintenance, facilities, and crowd control (Arnberger, 2012; Mohamed & Othman, 2012).

The range of different sites (heritage vs. natural) as well as the segmentation of visitors suggest that the visitor experience is a complex concept and cannot be operated according to the 'one size fits all' principle. Cultural sites, for example, are advised by Bonn et al. (2007) to invest in factors such as lighting, colour, signage, spaciousness, and traffic flow rather than facility attractiveness, tour guide availability, music, and merchandise quality. On the other hand, Dwyer and Edwards (2000) suggest that general tourists to nature-based attractions would be satisfied by providing them with high levels of infrastructure and services as well as good accommodation, restaurants, and sightseeing, and other 'city' activities. Learning activities for general tourists would be undertaken only as a part of organised guided tour activities.

Calver and Page (2013) concluded that the understanding of what the visitor requires and how the visitors co-create value in their visitation experiences can be further enriched by a greater dialogue, engagement, and knowledge transfer between the heritage sector and academia. Previous studies focused on this issue, in off-site (Mohamed & Othman, 2012) and on-site (Arnberger, 2012; Calver & Page, 2013; Oguz, 2000) studies. However, these studies do not refer to mixed urban parks that include both heritage and natural assets and attract different visitor segments. The present study focuses on this issue and asks how visitor expectation and satisfaction are influenced by the complex identity of the urban park of Ashkelon, which includes heritage and natural assets. Furthermore, the study examines the situation when the heritage that is expressed by the national park of Ashkelon does not necessarily 'belong' to the locals and visitors but rather to ancient populations and 'conquerors' of the MENA region.

2015 visitors survey

The first part of the study was aimed at learning more about the satisfaction of the visitors to Ashkelon National Park and comparing the visitor experience of locals to those of day tourists. Furthermore, some of these issues were analysed not just in the national park of Ashkelon but also in comparison to other similar national parks in Israel.

A survey was undertaken in Ashkelon National Park for visitors, locals, as well as domestic day tourists. This research tool was developed with the National Park Authority and was composed of items regarding visitor satisfaction (adopted and translated to Hebrew from Calver & Page, 2013), place attachment (adopted and translated to Hebrew from Gross & Brown, 2006 as well as Yuksel, Yuksel & Bilim, 2010), motivation for the visit (picnic, beach, nature, enriching knowledge) socio-demographic questions (gender, party size and profile, subscription to the NPA, place of residence), and three open questions: suggestions for future improvements, general impression (for first-time visitors) and changes from the last visit (to repeat visitors).

The survey was handed by national park staff to visitors. In total, 347 questionnaires were distributed to visitors from April to August of 2015. About half (51 per cent) of the respondents were women and 82 per cent of respondents reported visiting the park with their children. Almost half (45 per cent) of the visitors identified themselves as locals, contributing to a bias distribution of average distance from the national park that ranged between 1 km to 190 km, with a mean of 28.91 km (SD = 33.41 km). Sixty-six per cent of the respondents did not have a subscription to the National Parks of Israel which provides an entry fee for park access.

The findings of the on-site visitor survey are presented in Table 7.1. Enjoyment, satisfaction, and recommendation were given medium to good scores, which ranged between 4 to 6 in a 1–7 Likert scale. The motivation that received higher scores from the respondents was related to having time with the family, followed by the motivation to have outdoor recreation in nature. Additionally, respondents reported on medium scores of place attachment ranging between 3.8 to 5.1 on a 1–7 Likert scale.

To examine how the various motivations, place attachment, and socio-demographic variables influence the visitor experience of Ashkelon National Park, three linear regression models were set, with the recommendation, satisfaction, and enjoyment as dependent variables. All models were found significant (Table 7.2). Place attachment to the Ashkelon National Park was found as a significant predictor in all equations. Surprisingly, living in Ashkelon was also found as a significant predictor in all equations, but in the opposite direction, meaning that local residents have worse visitor experiences in Ashkelon National Park than people who do not live in Ashkelon.

The open questions produced 213 comments that were written by 176 respondents, 116 of them live in Ashkelon (66 per cent). Most of the comments (172 items, 80 per cent) focused on ideas on how to improve the service of the place. Interestingly, the majority (96 items) offered to diminish or trim natural aspects and develop more built attractions and artificial facilities such as options to music, water slides, facilities for children, inflatables for children, swimming pools, and synthetic grass. Other suggestions focused on the improvement of the natural environment, with suggestions including more natural shade, prohibition on BBQs, an accessible path to the beach, and humorous comments such as warming up the sea or decreasing the number of jellyfish at summertime. Only eight suggestions (3.7 per cent) discussed the historical and archaeological aspects of the park.

An additional study was conducted of the visitation patterns of subscribers to NPA. These subscribers have a free pass to almost all national parks after an initial payment that is equivalent to 3–4 visits for a family for a year. Based on internal data of the NPA, the visitation patterns of subscribers of NPA to three national parks that are located near urban centres were compared. While in other national parks, such as Tel Afek and Apolonia, 41–46 per cent of all independent domestic visitors in 2014 and 2015 held a subscription to the NPA, the share of subscribers out of all independent domestic visitors in Tel Ashkelon was low at 10 per cent in 2014 and 14 per cent in 2015.

Table 7.1 Descriptive statistics of the study's variables

Topic	Item	Mean (SD)
Satisfaction	I am satisfied with the visit	5.971 (1.353)
	I am satisfied with the appearance of the place	5.755 (1.464)
	I am satisfied with the cleanliness of the place	4.846 (2.207)
	I am satisfied with the maintenance of the place	5.308 (1.944)
	I am satisfied with the picnic options	5.967 (1.557)
	I felt I discovered something surprising and valuable as a result of my visit	4.191 (2.315)
	I didn't waste time waiting in lines	5.751 (1.806)
	I am satisfied with the various options the place provides	5.325 (1.820)
	The property informed and stimulated my interest in history and nature	4.295 (2.387)
	The service that I received at this property contributed to my enjoyment	5.047 (2.212)
	I am satisfied with the beach service	4.644 (2.621)
	It was easy to find my way around	5.557 (1.751)
Mean satisfaction (Alpha Cronbach = 0.868)		5.246 (1.256)
Place attachment	I get more satisfaction out of visiting Ashkelon National Park than any other National Park	5.11 (1.731)
	I am very attached to Ashkelon National Park	4.579 (2.131)
	Visiting Ashkelon National Park is more important to me than visiting any other National Park	4.528 (2.207)
	Visiting Ashkelon National Park says a lot about who I am	4.048 (2.221)
	I wouldn't substitute any other place for the type of experience I have in the Ashkelon National Park	3.841 (2.156)
	Ashkelon National Park means a lot to me	4.425 (2.174)
Mean Place Attachment (alpha Cronbach = 0.926)		4.423 (1.804)
Recommendation	I would recommend a visit to this park	5.921 (1.583)
Enjoyment	I enjoyed my visit	5.980 (1.354)
Motivations	Outdoor recreation in nature	6.105 (1.362)
	Picnic options	5.977 (1.552)
	Time with the family	6.375 (1.139)
	Enriching my knowledge	4.809 (1.987)
	Sea and Sun	5.360 (2.058)

n = 347.

Table 7.2 Regression coefficient for the study variables

Variable	Enjoyment	Satisfaction	Recommendation
Outdoor recreation in nature	0.096	0.192**	0.135*
Picnic options	0.161**	0.059	0.135*
Time with the family	0.167*	0.097	0.257**
Enriching my knowledge	–0.092	0.063	–0.010
Sea and Sun	–0.074	0.083	0.002
Place attachment	0.471***	0.488**	0.376**
Local (0 – no; 1 – yes)	–0.169**	–0.176**	–0.133*
Subscription of NPA	0.085	0.049	0.137**
Gender (1 – man; 2 – woman)	–0.020	0.001	0.001
With children (0 – no; 1 – yes)	–0.037	–0.043	0.064
R^2	0.333	0.501	0.423
ANOVA model	F = 12.871**	F = 25.882**	F = 18.915**

*$p < 0.05$; **$p < 0.01$

The visitor survey revealed that place attachment to the park was the most significant predictor of a positive appraisal of the visit. Interestingly, residency in the city of Ashkelon decreases rather than increases the positive appraisal of the park. Subscribers of the NPA were found as a significant source for a positive recommendation, but further analysis indicated that they represented a low share of the total number of independent domestic visitors to Ashkelon National Park. The open questionnaire explored confusion among respondents who did not perceive the national park as a heritage site or even as a green space, but rather a place for urban recreation. This confusion between the different aspects of the park is in line with previous academic literature that observes the implications for urban parks of different segments of visitors (Dwyer & Edwards, 2000) and different managerial perspectives and priorities (Arnberger, 2012; Calver & Page, 2013; Mohamed & Othman, 2012).

Following the survey, the NPA decided to prioritise the visitor segments that are interested in nature, cultural heritage, and archaeology, and to enhance further the aspects of nature and history over the recreation perspectives. The name of the national park was officially changed in January 2019 to Tel Ashkelon. The Hebrew word 'Tel' means an ancient place. Additionally, a four-year special budget was assigned to the park (financed mutually by the NPA and the city of Ashkelon) aiming to develop the archaeological remains of the site and to relocate the recreation areas of the park to its margins (E. Mitrani, personal communication, 31 March 2019).

2019 triangulation of perspectives

The second part of the study was designed to estimate the chances of success of the new policy at the Tel Ashkelon National park. A qualitative research method was applied, along with a triangulation technique. Triangulation means looking at a phenomenon or a research question from more than one perspective (Decrop, 1999). According to the triangulation principle, there are more than two observations, and the observations are not made from 'similar' viewpoints (Oppermann, 2000). In the present case, Study 2 compares three different perspectives: the viewpoints of the NPA representatives, the insight of the senior academic advisor of the park, and the opinions of residents of Ashkelon.

Five interviews were held in March and April 2019. Two separate face-to-face interviews were conducted with NPA employees, one face-to-face conversation with two residents of Ashkelon, and one phone call to a senior academic, who has worked with the municipality of Ashkelon and the national park for more than two decades. An additional request was made to the Tourism Department of the Ashkelon Economic Company, but with no response. All interviews were documented and analysed to explore underlined themes, contradictions, and insights. Table 7.3 shows detailed information about the interviewees.

Three main themes were revealed in the interviews – the issue of the ownership of the land, the competition between different heritages (including conflicts and clashes between different heritages), and the unclear identity of the beneficiaries of the national park. Interestingly, the views on the park were so diverse that sometimes the impression was that the interviewees were discussing different sites. The next section will discuss each of these themes and diverse views and will portray the challenges this diversity creates for the managers and the planners of the national park of Tel Ashkelon.

Occupied territories

Omri Bouhnik, the manager of Tel Ashkelon National Park, opened his interview by stating that 'for locals, the national park is the "occupied territories".' When he was asked about the geo-political connotation that the phrase raises, he confirmed that the meaning was 'the same.' Dr Avi Sasson agreed with this observation but did not see it as a negative situation: 'yes, it is true that this is an occupied territory. I think it is a good thing that the place belongs to a national authority.' David S., a resident of Ashkelon, didn't explicitly refer to the place as an occupied territory, but noted the good memories he has there *'until the place was handed* to the national authority' (this author's emphasis). Dr Eyal Mitrani, on the other hand, discussed the place as a 'returned territory' by saying that 'the founding authority was the municipality, and it was its property. The city managed the place as an urban green space. The NPA tried to *turn it back* to a national park, with international and national values of heritage and nature, but the city was complaining.' The interviewees agreed that the place was taken from one entity and was transferred to another; however, they disagreed if this act was negative or positive, and even from whom it was taken.

Table 7.3 Detailed information about the interviewees

Perspective/affiliation	Name	Title/position	Years in position	Comments
NPA	Dr Eyal Mitrani	Head of the department of visitors and community of the Center District of NPA	>10	Wrote a book about the history of all national parks in the NPA 1955–1998 (in Hebrew, in press), and a paper on the national park of Ashkelon (2011, in Hebrew)
NPA	Omri Bouhnik	Manager of Tel Ashkelon national park	Worked in the park since 2008, as manager – since 2011	Left his position a week after the interview. The manager who replaced him, Ronit Rozen, participated in the interview as a part of her training to the new job
A resident of Ashkelon – man	David S.		Has lived in the city since the 1960s (except a few 'bad years' in another city)	
A resident of Ashkelon – a woman	Miri M-Y.		Has lived in the city all her life (since the 1970s)	
Academia	Dr Avi Sasson	A researcher of Israel Studies and History – Ashkelon Academic College	Researching the city and working with the authorities of Ashkelon for more than two decades	The first publication on Ashkelon – 2002

Multiple heritages

The history of the place is not a part of the heritage of the locals, as Dr Avi Sasson noted 'I do not expect that the residents of Ashkelon will be attached to Tel Ashkelon. They feel bonding to the place because of their social memories ... they don't need the national park; they want it because they get used to the BBQ and the music events [an annual music festival which was called "Briza"]'. Omri Bouhnik agreed with Dr Sasson that the historical heritage is less significant to the residents, but noted that 'in Ashkelon, the place [the national park] is not part of the heritage, but the BBQ is definitely part of the heritage of the city'.

The social memories of the place were found as very meaningful for the two residents who were interviewed. David S. mentioned the graduation ceremonies that were conducted in the site before it was handed over to NPA, as well as the 'Briza' music festival. Miri M-Y mentioned that 'I deeply loved the "Briza" music festival in the Amphitheatre. My wedding photos were taken in the place ... we walked to the park with the children on Saturdays, and in Lag BaOmer [a Jewish holiday] were sleeping there.' The story of sleeping in the place was also mentioned by David S. who remembered that 'when I was in high school, we were sleeping there the day before the Independence Day, to reserve our spot there.'

The stories about the 'Briza' music festival, BBQs, sleeping outside experiences, graduation ceremonies, and wedding photos can be defined as intangible expressions of cultural heritage according to the ICOMOS (2002) definition that includes ways of living, customs, and practices. Nevertheless, Dr Mitrani did not address these themes as heritage and stated that 'urban green space is not meaningful for residents. Only when the place will address these [understanding the history] processes and activities, we will get a learning process and a community ... only when people will benefit from the process, in pride, money, and interest – only then people will be connected to the place.'

Cultural heritage was also defined as the link between past and present, or the way the past is still present in present time (Smith, 2006; Zhang & Smith, 2019). Dismissing the heritage of the present (BBQs, music shows) and prioritising of the heritage of the past (archaeology, history) happens in Tel Ashkelon mainly because there is no clear common heritage that links the past to the present. One reason for this situation is the absence of a component of Jewish heritage: 'Tel Ashkelon, one of its disadvantages is that there is no Jewish story, and consequently, the guides face a problem' (Dr Avi Sasson). This missing link between the present Jewish settlement and the past inspires Dr Sasson to re-discover a story: 'about two years ago we [Avi Sasson and Gad Sobol] offered Omri [Bouhnik] to tell how Shimon Ben Shetach [a Jewish religious leader that lived about 2000 years ago] hunted witches in the place. We found a cave from Byzantium time and even made a sign. But the project got stuck; I don't know why.'

The efforts to create a link between past and present led Omri Bouhnik and Dr Avi Sasson to identify water as an appropriate theme. Dr Sasson told that 'Already before 15 years I offered to characterize the place around the water theme and got a fund to restore unique wells in the place, but the process got stuck ... I raised the idea of paddling pools because it corresponds with the unique historical pumping method'. The failure of the paddling water project pushed Omri to quit his job as the park manager: 'I developed a program, but when they canceled the paddling pools, I knew the site would decline. All they want is to take the BBQ out.'

Who are the beneficiaries?

Omri Bouhnik described the visitors of the park as 'repeat customers' and identified the majority of visitors as BBQ lovers. However, he argued that the NPA does not like BBQ lovers: 'this is a low hierarchy of visitors. Tourists are more valuable, and the park does not attract tourists, only 4,000 per year.' However, he also noted that the BBQ lovers of present times are more welcomed than the historical BBQ lovers: 'there is no vacuum when bad visitors leave good visitors to come. We have a good population here; visitors are very nice today.' Interestingly, he concluded the interview with an open question about the profile of the visitors: 'the question is what is wrong if we have BBQ lovers?'

The opposite view was expressed by Dr Eyal Mitrani, who supports the displacement of BBQ lovers: 'we are going to change the profile of the visitors, but this is not happening, yet. We are going to take the BBQ out to the margin of the park.' The view of Dr Mitrani was also echoed by David S., the resident of Ashkelon, who complained: 'today, unfortunately, 85% percent of visitors are coming to BBQ. This is not the purpose of the place!' Between the view that accepts BBQ and the perspective that wants to take it out of the park, Dr Avi Sasson implies that there is no clear dichotomy: 'today the visitors that are coming to travel in the park are also doing BBQ' but concluded that there is a need to change the current situation and 'we need lots of patience'.

Tel Ashkelon National Park hosts more than 400,000 visitors per year, but it seems that nobody is fully satisfied with the present profile, and most parties want to attract new or different visitors: 'nice people', locals and non-locals, preferably tourists, who may or may not like BBQ and are attached to the nature and culture of the place. Even the two locals who were interviewed couldn't remember when they visited the park for the last time. Miri M-Y assessed that it was 'at least four years ago' and David S. said 'for years! More than five.' The desirable profile of visitors represents an autoptic description of beneficiaries. No wonder David S. concluded the interview with the comment 'too bad, too bad, too bad! What a wasted place', and Miri M-Y joined his comment by saying 'Too bad, it is a beautiful place'.

Conclusion – preservation of cultural heritage in the MENA

Tel Ashkelon can be considered as a microcosm of the situation in MENA. Beautiful places, rich with heritage and nature, but controversial: the locals and the authorities hold different perspectives; locals are less satisfied with places that do not represent their heritage and plans are managed in a top-down manner. It is not just the implications of archaeology as a 'destructive process' (Walker & Carr, 2013) but also the tension between recreation and conservation. Nevertheless, the findings of the study show that place attachment contributes to positive appreciation. Consequently, the main question should be – how should authorities enhance the components of place attachment in such divided situations?

The case study of Tel Ashkelon National Park presents three possible solutions for strengthening place attachment in cultural heritage sites. First, a top-down policy of prioritising past culture(s) over the present heritage of the locals, in a process that was coined by the interviewees as the 'occupied territories' situation. Second, a 'two parks to two populations' solution, which is the programme that is now promoted by the NPA and the city of Ashkelon. According to this programme, the BBQ area would be relocated to the margins of the park. The third solution – finding a common theme – was initiated by Dr Avi Sasson and the former manager of the park, Omri Bouhnik. However, their idea about promoting water as past and present heritage did not gain support.

The MENA region hosts multiple heritages and a divided history between 'winners' and 'losers'. Conservation of cultural sites will always set problems such as those described above: the tension between locals and authorities, clashes between past and present heritages, and multiple uses of the same space. The three solutions of Ashkelon – 'occupied territories,' 'two places to two populations', and 'one inclusive place' – may be relevant to many heritage sites as well as many disputed places. In this manner, the case study of Tel Ashkelon is not just an example of conservation of cultural heritage site, but a mirror to the geopolitical situation of the MENA, to the key role of place attachment in this process, and the sad consequences when one heritage is prioritised over others.

Acknowledgement

The author would like to thank the NPA for their cooperation, and Eyal, Omri, Avi David, and Miri for their openness and kindness. Thank you.

References

Arnberger, A. (2012). Urban densification and recreational quality of public urban green spaces—a Viennese case study. *Sustainability*, *4*(4), 703–720.

Bonn, M. A., Joseph-Mathews, S. M., Dai, M., Hayes, S., & Cave, J. (2007). Heritage/cultural attraction atmospherics: Creating the right environment for the heritage/cultural visitor. *Journal of Travel Research*, *45*(3), 345–354.

Britt, K. M., & Chen, C. (2005). The (re-) birth of a nation: Urban archaeology, ethics, and the heritage tourism industry. *The SAA Archaeological Record*, *5*(3), 26–28.

Calver, S. J., & Page, S. J. (2013). Enlightened hedonism: Exploring the relationship of service value, visitor knowledge and interest, to visitor enjoyment at heritage attractions. *Tourism Management*, *39*, 23–36.

Central Bureau of Statistics (CBS) (2019). *Ashkelon*. Retrieved from https://www.cbs.gov.il/he/Settlements/Pages/%D7%99%D7%99%D7%A9%D7%95%D7%91%D7%99%D7%9D/%D7%90%D7%A9%D7%A7%D7%9C%D7%95%D7%9F.aspx%20 (in Hebrew).

Chiesura, A. (2004). The role of urban parks for the sustainable city. *Landscape and Urban Planning*, *68*(1), 129–138.

Committee of the National Parks. (2016). *A protocol of a meeting of the Council of National Parks and Nature Reserves*, Number 158, 25.2.2016. Jerusalem: The Ministry of Environmental Protection.

Decrop, A. (1999). Triangulation in qualitative tourism research. *Tourism Management*, *20*(1), 157–161.

Dwyer, L., & Edwards, D. (2000). Nature-based tourism on the edge of urban development. *Journal of Sustainable Tourism*, *8*(4), 267–287.

Gross, M., & Brown, G. (2006). Tourist experience in a lifestyle destination setting: The roles of involvement and place attachment. *Journal of Business Research*, *59*(6), 696–700.

Hall, C. M., & McArthur, S. (1999). *Integrated heritage management: Principles and practice*. Norwich: HMSO.

International Cultural Tourism Committee (ICOMOS) (2002). *ICOMOS international cultural tourism charter. Principles and guidelines for managing tourism at places of cultural and heritage significance*. Burwood, Victoria: Australian ICOMOS.

Leon Levy Expedition to Ashkelon. (n.d.). *Home page*. Retrieved from http://digashkelon.com/thesite.

Loulanski, T. (2006). Revising the concept for cultural heritage: The argument for a functional approach. *International Journal of Cultural Property*, *13*(2), 207–233.

Mitrani, E. (2020). *National park authority – tourism and recreation sites of Israel 1955–1968* (in Hebrew). Jerusalem: National Park Authorities.

Mohamed, N., & Othman, N. (2012). Push and pull factor: Determining the visitors satisfactions at urban recreational area. *Procedia – Social and Behavioral Sciences*, *49*, 175–182.

Municipality of Ashkelon (2017). *The story of Ashkelon*. Retrieved from http://www.ashkelon.muni.il/English/Pages/The-Story-of-Ashkelon.aspx.

Nasser, N. (2003). Planning for urban heritage places: Reconciling conservation, tourism, and sustainable development. *Journal of Planning Literature*, *17*(4), 467–479.

Oguz, D. (2000). User surveys of Ankara's urban parks. *Landscape and Urban Planning*, *52*(2–3), 165–171.

Oppermann, M. (2000). Triangulation—a methodological discussion. *International Journal of Tourism Research*, *2*(20), 141–145.

Sasson, A. (2018). *Ashkelon as a field of study*. Ashkelon (in Hebrew).

Smith, L. (2006). *Uses of heritage*. Abingdon: Routledge.

UNESCO. (2017). What is meant by 'cultural heritage'? Retrieved from http://www.unesco.org/new/en/culture/themes/illicit-trafficking-of-cultural-property/unesco-database-of-national-cultural-heritage-laws/frequently-asked-questions/definition-of-the-cultural-heritage/.

Vecco, M. (2010). A definition of cultural heritage: From the tangible to the intangible. *Journal of Cultural Heritage, 11*(3), 321–324.

Walker, C., & Carr, N. (eds). (2013). *Tourism and archaeology: Sustainable meeting grounds*. Walnut Creek, California: Left Coast Press.

Wolch, J. R., Byrne, J., & Newell, J. P. (2014). Urban green space, public health, and environmental justice: The challenge of making cities 'just green enough'. *Landscape and Urban Planning, 125*, 234–244.

Yuksel, A., Yuksel, F., & Bilim, Y. (2010). Destination attachment: Effects on customer satisfaction and cognitive, affective and conative loyalty. *Tourism Management, 31*(2), 274–284.

Zhang, R., & Smith, L. (2019). Bonding and dissonance: Rethinking the interrelations among stakeholders in heritage tourism. *Tourism Management, 74*, 212–223.

8 Cultural heritage in Palestine
Challenges and opportunities

Rami K. Isaac

Introduction

Between 1967 and 1993 Israel assumed complete civil administration and military control over the West Bank, Gaza Strip, and East Jerusalem. The archaeological research conducted in Palestine at this time was often devoid of Palestinian participation and, in fact, Palestinians were positioned as silent witnesses to a heritage narrative, generated from their homeland, that did not identify or acknowledge their interpretations of the region's history. The diggings that did proceed in Palestine during this period were almost exclusively focused on 'biblical' sites and typically directed by archaeologists from Europe, Israel, or the United States (Sauders, 2008).

Throughout the era of complete Israeli occupation and civil control in Palestine, at least 1,700 now major sites were kept under the Israeli military's staff Officer for Archaeology, as required by Israeli military order (el-Hafi, 2003). To date, in spite of the Oslo Accords and the creation of the Palestinian National Authority (PNA), the Israeli military still maintains complete custodianship over the archaeological materials from Area C of the West Bank. The signing of the Oslo Accords in 1993, which carved the occupied territories of Palestine into a complex mosaic of areas A, B, and C, have resulted in fractured oversight of heritage sites and objects (Kersel, 2014). In the West Bank, Area A, under direct Palestinian control, includes the major populated cities but constitutes no more than 3 per cent of those areas; Area B encompasses 450 Palestinian towns and villages representing 27 per cent of the West Bank, jointly controlled territory in which the Palestinians would exercise civil authority but Israel would retain security control; and Area C, in which Israel has exclusive control, constitutes the rest of the West Bank (70 per cent), including agricultural land, the Jordan Valley, natural reserves, areas with lower population density, Israeli settlements, and military areas (Hanafi, 2009). The interplay of Israeli occupation and cultural heritage considerations in the West Bank is evident in the establishments of illegal Israeli settlements in the Palestinian territories of Palestine.

Archaeologically, the Oslo Accords were intended as replacements for the existing Israeli military orders in Area C, until such time as the Palestinian government passed relevant legislation regarding the protection and preservation of cultural heritage (Kersel, 2014). In 2003, the PNA introduced draft cultural heritage legislation aimed at protecting both the natural and cultural environment. As a result of a complex legal system including Ottoman, British Mandatory, Egyptian (the Gaza Strip), Jordanian (the West Bank), Israeli military orders, and international accords (Oslo), preservation and protection of cultural heritage in Palestine can be considered broken and inconsistent. According to Bshara (2013, p. 299), 'after over two decades since the Oslo accords, there remains no real legal framework in place to protect cultural heritage and very few government initiatives to preserve and to protect Palestinian resources'.

Legal issues

It is almost impossible to discuss the case of Palestine without talking about the land. At the same time, it is impossible to talk and discuss cultural heritage and management without considering the context in which the work is being undertaken. The international conventions under which Israel, as an occupying power, is bound mean that it has a responsibility to protect the cultural heritage of the occupied territories of Palestine. Many tools have been developed by the international community to protect the cultural heritage during political instability and armed conflict, such as the Hague Convention in 1907, which prohibits an occupying power from the destruction and demolition and theft of cultural property (United Nations, 1949).

The most important instrument of international law is the *Convention for the Protection of Cultural Property in the Event of Armed Conflict* (UNESCO, 1954). Article 4(3) maintains that contracting parties must prohibit, prevent, and if necessary put a stop to any form of theft, pillage, or misappropriation, and any acts of vandalism directed against cultural property and to refrain from requisitioning movable cultural property (UNESCO, 1954). UNESCO's recommendations on international principles applicable to archaeological excavations of 1956, which have been signed by Israel, explicitly require that the occupying power, Israel, must refrain from carrying out archaeological excavations in the occupied territories of Palestine (UNESCO, 1956).

The impact of the Israeli military occupation on conservation of cultural heritage in Palestine

The Hague Convention (UNESCO), though, is an important tool for protecting the heritage of the occupied territories of Palestine; it has a vague definition of 'salvage excavation'. The Israeli authorities have used this ambiguity to serve its illegal actions of building and expanding settlements and roads as well as the destruction of heritage and archaeological sites in the occupied territories of Palestine (Rjoob, 2009). All these activities and actions have been conducted for a wide variety of ambiguous ideological and political purposes (Abu el-Haj, 2001). The openings that made such areas available to 'research' were not unplanned, but the result of deliberate colonial acts. These have included the building of military outposts, illegal settlements, the by-pass roads that connect all illegal settlements in the West Bank, and the construction of the segregation wall on Palestinian land (Chamberlain, 2005). During the occupation and until today, many sites have been irreversibly destroyed by the Israeli military. To mention a few places, there are: the destruction of the Moroccan quarter in the old city of Jerusalem (Abu el-Haj, 2001); the transfer of archaeological finds from the Palestine Archaeological Museum in East Jerusalem to the Israel Museum in West Jerusalem; the blockade of the Church of Nativity in Bethlehem (Isaac, 2010); and the destruction of classified buildings in the old town of Hebron, Nablus particularly in 2003 and 2004 (Rjoob, 2009).

Facts on the ground

According to Rjoob (2009), Israel has violated most international conventions. Israel has chosen not to approve the 1970 UNESCO Convention, which protects cultural heritage resources during peace as well as war times. Israel has endlessly broken international law concerning the protection and preservation of Palestinian cultural heritage property in the occupied territories of Palestine through: illegal archaeological excavations and surveys; deliberate destruction and demolition of cultural heritage; neglecting the protection of cultural heritage places in the occupied territories of Palestine; abuse of Palestinian heritage for Zionists' ideological and political purposes; transferring artefacts out of Palestine and displacing parts of immovable heritage; and illegally encouraging the illegal trade of antiquities.

Israel has used cultural heritage and archaeological excavations and research as an important ideological (Zionist) instrument to justify its own political claim to the occupied territories of Palestine. Carrying our archaeological excavations is not only a violation of international law and conventions, but also denies the right of Palestinian people to explore their past in their own manner and by their own methods, which inevitably vary from Israeli ones (Rjoob, 2009). Archaeology has been an important national cultural practice since the establishment of the state of Israel, whilst ancient biblical tales and sites have inspired Israeli public sentiment. According to Abu el-Haj (2001), archaeology plays a crucial role in the formation and enactment of colonial-national historical imagination and in authenticating Israel's territorial claims. Therefore, many Jewish organisations such as the Jewish National Funds and others have repeatedly used archaeology to support the Zionists' project in Palestine since the nineteenth century and to facilitate Israel's territorial expansion and to justify land expropriation (Rjoob, 2009). Another example is the destruction of Mamluk-era houses on the settlers' road through the old city of Hebron.

After a few years of legal delays and a court-ordered reduction in the number of historic buildings slated for destruction from 22 to 3, Israeli military bulldozers flattened three centuries-old building complexes and damaged five others in Hebron, West Bank, Palestine.

In the same vein, the basis of the Israeli-Palestinian conflict is built upon the confrontation and contradiction between two narratives, the Israeli Zionist and the Arab Palestinian, where each attempts to use the particularity of the place, including its religious, historical, and cultural significance, to justify its own existence and continuation. The Zionist project, since the establishment of the state of Israel, has been concentrating on the religious Jewish narratives that see Palestine as the Promised Land for Jews. Within these narratives, Israel has undertaken two paths. First, destroy, mutilate, and neglect everything that confirms or is a reminder of Palestinian existence, Palestinian rights, or Palestinian history. According to Ibrahim (2013), the millennia-long history of Palestine is portrayed as though it started with the emergence of the Jewish religion, when in fact Palestine and its people existed long before there was ever a Jewish presence. The magnitude of this plan culminated in the destruction of more than 450 Palestinian villages in 1948 after their Palestinian inhabitants were expelled. The stones of these homes were then reused in the construction of Jewish homes as a sign of originality.

After the proclamation of the state of Israel, several steps were undertaken: the theft of archaeological findings such as the Dead Sea Scrolls, pottery, and coins, and the claim of their 'legal' possession; the destruction of several historic buildings that attest to hundreds of years of Palestinian existence; the destruction of the Al-Kasaba Quarter in Nablus; the takeover of Rachel's Tomb in Bethlehem (see Isaac & Platenkamp, 2018) and many other places in the West Bank.

The implementation of Israeli policies has included rebuilding the symbols, names, and culture of specific places in order to confirm and prove the credibility and historicity of the Israeli narrative (Ibrahim, 2013). To achieve this goal, Israel has undertaken several steps, such as taking over historic sites and changing their Arabic names, giving them names that match accounts of the Torah (Ibrahim, 2013).

Illegal Israeli settlements and bypass roads

Many illegal excavations have been carried out in Jerusalem, especially along the southern and south-western wall of the Haram Al-Sharif (The Great Mosque), in association with illegal settlement activity.

These illegal colonies of Israel control more than 900 cultural and archaeological sites and features in Palestine (Department of Antiquities and Cultural Heritage (DACH) Database, 2008). For example, the construction of the largest settlement on occupied Palestine, Ma'ale Adumim, east of Jerusalem during the 1980s, needed significant excavations. Ruins of a

Byzantine monastery were uncovered. According to Dr Magen, 'these excavations in 1993 were one of the largest projects undertaken in Judea and Samaria particularly, and in Israel in general' (Oyediran, 1997, p. 43). Another devastating example as a result of the illegal settlements is ancient Hebron, which is called 'Tell el-Rumeida'. It represents a typical example of violation of international law by Israel and its systematic destruction of Palestinian heritage through military and settler power. Tell-el-Rumeida is one of the largest tells in Palestine, which is believed to have been inhabited continuously from the beginning of the third millennium BC. In 1984 radical Israeli settlers seized part of the site, and turned it into a permanent settlement (Wilder, 2003, cited in Rojoob, 2009).

In addition to the illegal settlement activities, the huge 'bypass' road network built by the Israeli military occupation for Israeli settlers to avoid contact with Palestinians is also significant. There are around 200 colonies of Israel in the West Bank, connected by a network of roads (bypass roads) that separates each Palestinian town from the next and confined their abilities to expand. These bypass roads demanded further salvage heritage and archaeological excavations. These constructions of bypass roads have had an extraordinarily destructive impact on the cultural and natural landscape of Palestine. Furthermore, during the time of the Israeli occupation, looting of natural and archaeological heritage sites has become a constant and accepted socioeconomic phenomenon within Palestinian society, encouraged by the economic deprivation of the villagers and poor law enforcement.

Deliberate destruction of cultural heritage

The Israeli response to the second intifada (Al-Aqsa uprising) in October 2000 has resulted in an unprecedented level of intentional destruction of cultural heritage in two ways: first, the destruction of historic town centres, and second, in the building of the segregation wall on Palestinian land. Several Palestinian heritage centres have been damaged by Israeli military operations during the second intifada. One of the most well-known examples is the siege of the Church of Nativity in Bethlehem in 2002, where a site of international cultural pilgrimage was damaged by the Israeli military. Furthermore, the old town of Nablus has been one of the hardest hit Palestinian cities. The town of Nablus derives from the Roman town of Neapolis built in AD 72 (Ministry of Tourism and Antiquities, 2005). The city has a wide diversity of cultural heritage assets from the Roman era. Following the second uprising, the city was hit by several rockets and shelled by tanks, causing a massive destruction of historical and cultural heritage sites (DACH database, 2008).

In April 2002, the Israeli military decided to construct a segregation wall to separate Israel from Palestine. Several security concerns have been used by Israel to excuse the confiscation of Palestinian water and land.

The segregation wall consists of concrete walls, razor-wire, trenches, sniper tower, military roads, and remote-controlled infantry and a buffer-zone that sometimes stretches over 100 m wide (Isaac, 2009). In 2004, the International Court of Justice ruled that the wall was a violation of international law and human rights and ordered it to be dismantled (Isaac, 2009). The segregation wall was built on Palestinian land, to confiscate more land and swallow it into Israel. The wall cuts deeply through Palestinian towns and villages, separating Palestinian families from each other, swallowing and expropriating lands owned by Palestinian people (see Isaac, 2013). The wall prohibits Palestinians from accessing their agricultural lands to collect crops, and allows for the seizing of more Palestinian land, water resources, and cultural and natural resources (Applied Research Institute – Jerusalem (ARIJ), 2005). The wall has economic and social impacts for thousands of Palestinian families and has a devastating effect on tangible as well as intangible cultural heritage. Many cultural and archaeological sites have been demolished as a result of the segregation wall and hundreds of archaeological sites and places have been annexed within Israel or within the illegal Israeli settlements in the West Bank. Some 2,460 cultural heritage sites have been destroyed and/or cut off from the West Bank (DACH database, 2008). All these annexed areas in Palestine are declared closed military zones, making them virtually impossible for Palestinian individuals and archaeologists to access. In the same way, the proposed wall along the Jordan Valley will annex the entire Jordan Valley to Israel. This means that Israel will have control over all the archaeological and natural heritage sites in the Jordan Valley, other than Jericho city.

Since 1967 the Israeli military occupation has monopolised all aspects of cultural heritage in the occupied territories of Palestine, including exploration, excavation, protection, and preservation. Rjoob (2009) quotes Greenberg's statement on this issue, and is one of the most thought-provoking observations by an Israeli scholar to date:

> An occupying force arrives from outside and makes unilateral decisions, without consulting the local residents. Archaeology has social significance, because you are taking part of the landscape and giving archaeologists a kind of veto power over it. That is why archaeologists must be transparent; we must report to the public on what we are doing. We, as historians, must be sensitive to such matters. We have to know that what is being done in the territories of Palestine is a crime (Greenberg, as cited by Rapoport, 2006) (Rjoob, 2009, p. 233).

This domination by the Israeli military occupation gravely violates the most basic rights of the Palestinian people. They have deprived the Palestinian people of the opportunity to examine sites with appropriate scientific techniques; they have placed thousands of artefacts discovered in archaeological excavations in the custody of the Israeli military and beyond the reach of Palestinian archaeologists; and Palestinians have been alienated and deprived of their cultural heritage through the abuse of the Israeli military occupation using a set of military orders to the domestic antiquities laws, to purse its own (Zionist) national objectives (Rjoob, 2009).

Road map to cultural and archaeological site protection

The Palestinian DACH has now been in existence for more than 25 years since its establishment in 1994 following the Oslo Peace Process between Israel and Palestine. Following the Palestinian-Israeli agreement in 1993, Jericho and Gaza were handed over to Palestinian control. Next, in autumn 1994 and December 1995 the Palestinian National Authority was given control throughout the West Bank and Gaza Strip of several spheres, including archaeology in area A and B (Taha, 2010). In some parts of area C powers and responsibilities over archaeology were to be transferred gradually to Palestinian jurisdiction.

Since its establishment, DACH has carried out over 600 salvage excavations and joint projects with North American and European partners at different sites in the West Bank. DACH routinely issues permits to Palestinian archaeologists from Birzeit University and Al-Quds University to carry out archaeological examinations. At the national level, the PNA and its agents are focused on the acquisitions of World Heritage status for the natural and cultural sites of Palestine, which may be to the detriment of smaller sites not deemed of 'outstanding universal value' (Bshara, 2013; De Cesari, 2010).

Activating Palestine's UNESCO membership

Palestine gained membership of the United Nations Educational, Scientific and Cultural Organization (UNESCO) in 2011 but its representatives have not yet made best use of this status due, in part, to pressure by Israel and the United States. The day after Palestine gained membership of UNESCO, which took place on 30 October 2011, the Israeli Prime Minister accelerated the construction of 2,000 illegal settlement homes and froze Israel's contribution to UNESCO's budget. Followed by the United States, which also cut off funds to UNESCO. Yet even before Palestine gained membership, UNESCO had proved itself an important forum for upholding international law in relation to unlawful Israeli practices in the occupied territories of Palestine (Azarov & Sliman, 2013). For example, UNESCO reaffirmed that Israel's attempt to include the Haram al-Ibrahim/Tomb of the Patriarchs in Hebron and the Mosque of Bilal bin Rabah (Tomb of Rachel) in Bethlehem on Israel's national heritage (see Isaac & Platenkamp, 2018) list was a violation of international law, UNESCO conventions, and UN resolutions.

In 2002, the World Heritage Committee condemned the destruction and damage caused to the cultural heritage of Palestine and emphasised its exceptional value (UNESCO, 2002). In addition, the committee invited the director general of UNESCO in consultation with the chairperson of the World Heritage Committee to assist with the task of establishing an inventory of this cultural and natural heritage, assessing the state of its conservation and the measures undertaken for its preservation and rehabilitation (Sorosh-Wali, 2017). This resulted in an inventory of cultural and natural heritage sites of potential universal value in Palestine and was prepared by the Ministry of Tourism and Antiquities (MOTA) with support of the World Heritage Fund and technical support from UNESCO. A training workshop on the implementation of the World Heritage Convention was undertaken at ICCROM in Rome, in September 2003 (Taha, 2009), with the participation of 16 specialists in cultural and natural heritage from various Palestinian institutions. Almost all trainees were involved in the preparation of the tentative list and associated activities. The inventory of cultural and natural heritage sites covers 20 sites that represent Palestine's rich and diverse heritage. In 2002, most of these sites were included in the Palestinian Tentative List, which contains the properties Palestine intends to consider for future nomination to the World Heritage List (UNESCO, 2012). Some of the sites included in the inventory were located in Area C where, according to the Oslo Accords, Israel exercises full security control and occupation and assumes responsibility for most administrative affairs. These sites include the Old Town of Hebron, Mount Gerizim and the Samaritans, Qumran: Caves of the Monastery of the Dead Sea Scrolls, and Sebastia. These are all in Area C and the lack of access to the Palestinian cultural heritage sites that are located in Area C prevents Palestinian public officials from assuming their full role in the effective conservation and management of these sites. One of the main challenges for Palestinian cultural and heritage management is the lack of a legal framework for the adequate protection and conservation of cultural heritage in Palestine (Sorosh-Wali, 2017). In 2015, the Draft Palestinian Cultural Heritage Law was a major joint project between UNESCO and MOTA. Facilitated by the Ramallah office of UNESCO, Palestinian ministers, civil society organisations, academics, and individual experts drafted a new law comprehensively aligned with national priorities and international conventions, and which is particularly responsive to the needs of the local key stakeholders working in the context of Palestine and cultural heritage conservation and management. The tangible heritage law was prepared and submitted on 30 May 2017 by MOTA to the Palestinian cabinet for endorsement, representing a key step towards a modern Palestinian cultural law.

Despite the gloomy context, there are reasons for hope. For example, the protection and the promotion of Palestinian cultural heritage is included in the national development plans and in the National Policy Agenda 2017–2022. Accordingly, UNESCO has provided technical assistance to the Ministry of Culture and MOTA for the preparation of their (2017–2020) sector strategies towards culture and heritage in line with the UN 2030 Agenda for Sustainable Development.

Palestine has approved all six UNESCO conventions and protocols in the field of culture. Palestine submitted the World Heritage nomination files for 'Birthplace of Jesus: Church of Nativity and the Pilgrimage Route, Bethlehem', and for 'Palestine: Land of Olives and Vines – Cultural Landscape of Southern Jerusalem, Battir' in 2012 and 2014, respectively, with the sites then included in the World Heritage List and the World Heritage List in Danger. Such acknowledgement demands a rigorous approach to mapping and to the assessment and the management of these sites. Therefore, UNESCO supported MOTA financially and technically in the preparation of integrated conservation and management plans to ensure effective protection and conservation of these sites (Sorosh-Wali, 2017). The World Heritage Committee recognised the outstanding universal value of Palestinian heritage and approved US $150,000 for supporting Palestinian cultural and natural heritage in order to assist Palestine in establishing an inventory of potential World Cultural and Natural Heritage places (Taha, 2009).

In the field of preserving and promoting cultural heritage in Palestine, important projects and initiatives have been implemented to complement the role of the government. Funded by the Swedish International Development and Cooperation Agency (SIDA), UNESCO is implementing a project entitled Local Development through the Rehabilitation and Revitalization of the Historic Built Environment in Palestine. They work in cooperation with four Palestinian cultural and heritage organisations. The aim of the project is to enforce local development and enhance the socioeconomic situation through the revitalisation of cultural heritage assets. Recently, 50 cultural and heritage sites have been renovated in historic towns, centres, and rural communities in Palestine, including sites listed on the Tentative List of Palestine, such as the Old Town of Hebron, the Old Town of Nablus, and Tell Balata Archaeological Park in Nablus. These have been achieved through a productive partnership between MOTA; the University of Leiden, the Netherlands; and UNESCO, with financial support from the Kingdom of the Netherlands (Sorosh-Wali, 2017).

In addition, UNESCO has improved a number of cultural heritage sites, such as Al-Khader ancient Monastery and Shrine in Deir Al-Balah and As-Saqaa mansion in Shujahia. UNESCO has also conducted emergency conservation measures at archaeological site Tell Umm Amer/Saint Hilarion Monastery in Nuseirat and it continues to advocate the interrelated protection, conservation, and management of this archaeological resource as a priority for cultural development of the local communities living in Gaza Strip.

Statehood status and accession to international organisations and treaties can afford protection for rights, but they also require obligations on the part of the state (Palestine). Therefore, Palestine is required to adjust its national legal system and relevant institutions in accordance with its obligations under the UNESCO Constitution and conventions. In addition, Palestine should demonstrate its own good faith commitment to UNESCO's protection framework by adopting the necessary legal systems and measures in its national law and seeking their enforcement to the extent possible as long as Israel continues to maintain its control over Palestinian territories. It is in Palestine's best interest to fulfil its international legal obligations that come with reclaiming possession of stolen cultural and natural heritage and properties and further its efforts to regain control over its territory (Azarov & Sliman, 2013).

Conclusion

In recent years, there has been a dramatic increase in attention to the topic of cultural heritage. Heritage is important because it provides symbolic and economic ingredients, meaning, and dignity to human lives. It legitimises territorial and intellectual ownership and is a critical factor in the formation of social identity, in the case of Palestine (Logan, 2007; Smith, 2007).

The fruitful cooperation of various national as well as international organisations noted above will be continued for the benefit of the Palestinian people who deserve to see their culture, identity, and natural heritage safeguarded for future generations. The archaeological and cultural heritage sites of Palestine have tremendous tourism potential that can be leveraged into a powerful economic foundation for the emerging Palestinian state. The cultural and religious significance of heritage sites in Palestine is important not only for Palestinians but also for Muslims and Christians worldwide.

Nevertheless, the occupied territories of Palestine are an arena for the disobedience of international law on cultural and heritage preservation and conservation. Israel denies its responsibilities in aiding the implementation of such protection, as it is bound to by international law. Moreover, it commits illegal acts, which aim at destroying Palestinian cultural heritage and archaeology and are condemned by international organisations such as UNESCO.

References

Abu el-Haj, N. (2001). *Facts on the ground: Archaeological practice and terminal self-fashioning in Israeli society*. Chicago: University of Chicago Press.

Applied Research Institute – Jerusalem (ARIJ) (2005). *Report on the Israeli colonization activities in the West Bank & the Gaza Strip*. Vol. 89, December 2005 Issue. Bethlehem: ARIJ.

Azarov, V., & Sliman, N. (2013). *Activating Palestine's UNESCO membership*. Washington, DC: The Palestinian Policy Network.

Bshara, K. (2013). Heritage in Palestine: Colonial legacy in postcolonial discourse. *Archaeologies, 9*(1), 295–319.

Chamberlain, K. (2005). Stealing Palestinian history. *This week in Palestine,* 9 August. Retrieved from http://archive.thisweekinpalestine.com/details.php?id=1451&ed=107.
De Cesari, C. (2010) Creative heritage: Palestinian heritage NGOs and defiant acts of government. *American Anthropologist, 112*(2), 625–637.
Department of Antiquities and Cultural Heritage (DACH) database (2008). *The database of the Department of Antiquities and Cultural Heritage.* Unpublished.
el-Hafi, N. (2003). Palestine, a despoiled archaeological heritage. Paper presented at the Fifth World Archaeological Congress, Washington, DC, 21–26 June.
Hanafi, S. (2009). Spacio-cide: Colonial politics, invisibility and rezoning in Palestinian territory. *Contemporary Arab Affairs, 2*(1), 106–121.
Ibrahim, N. (2013) *Tourism and heritage in Palestine: A conflict between two narratives.* Alternative Tourism Group (ATG): Beitsahour.
Isaac, R. K. (2009). Alternative tourism: Can the segregation wall in Bethlehem be a tourist attraction? *Tourism, Hospitality, Planning and Development 6*(3), 247–254.
Isaac, R. K. (2010). Alternative tourism: New forms of tourism in Bethlehem. *Current Issues in Tourism, 13*(1), 21–36.
Isaac, R. K. (2013). Palestine: Tourism under occupation. In R. Butler & W. Suntikul (eds), *Tourism and war* (pp. 143–158). London: Routledge.
Isaac, R. K., & Platenkamp, V. (2018). The actualization of the critical impulse in critical theory: Dialogical rationality around Rachel's Tomb in Bethlehem, Palestine. *Tourism Analysis, 24*(1), 101–113.
Kersel, M. M. (2014). Fractured oversight: The ABCs of cultural heritage in Palestine after the Oslo Accords. *Journal of Social Archaeology, 15*(1), 24–44.
Logan, W. (2007). Closing Pandora's box: Human rights conundrums. In H. Silverman & D. F. Ruggles (eds), *Cultural heritage and human rights* (pp. 33–52). New York: Springer.
Ministry of Tourism and Antiquities (2005). *Inventory of cultural and natural heritage sites of potential outstanding universal values in Palestine.* Ramallah: Al-Nashir.
Oyediran, J. (1997). *Plunder, destruction and despoliation: An analysis of Israel's violations of the international law of cultural property in the occupied West Bank and Gaza Strip.* Ramallah: Al-haq.
Rapoport, M. (2006). Buried treasure that's kept in the dark. *Haaretz.* Retrieved from http://www.haaretz.com/hasen/pages/ShArt.jhtml?itemNo=8017929.
Rjoob, A. (2009). The impact of Israeli occupation on the conservation of cultural heritage sites in the occupied Palestinian territories: The case of 'salvage excavations'. *Conservation and Management of Archaeological Sites, 11*(3–4), 214–235.
Sauders, R. R. (2008). Between paralysis and practice: Theorising the political liminality of Palestinian cultural heritage. *Archaeologies, 4*(3), 471.
Smith, L. (2007). Empty gestures? Heritage and politics of recognition. In H. Silverman & D. F. Ruggles (eds), *Cultural heritage and human rights* (pp. 99–114). New York: Springer.
Sorosh-Wali, A. (2017). Cultural heritage in Palestine: Current challenges and future horizons. *This Week in Palestine,* 30 May.
Taha, H. (ed.) (2009). *Inventory of cultural and natural heritage sites of potential outstanding universal value in Palestine.* Ramallah: MOTA.
Taha, H. (2010). The current state of archaeology in Palestine. *Presents Pasts, 2*(1), 16–25.

UNESCO (1954). *Convention for the protection of cultural property in the event of armed conflict with regulations for the execution of the Convention 1954*. The Hague, 14 May. Paris: UNESCO. Retrieved from http://www.icomos.org/hague/.

UNESCO (1956). *Recommendations on international principles applicable to archaeological excavations*. Paris: UNESCO. Retrieved from http://www.icomos.org/unesco/delhi56.html.

UNESCO (2002). *Decisions of the 26th Session of the World Heritage Committee. WHC-02/CONF.202/25*. Paris: UNESCO. Retrieved from http://whc.unesco.org/archive/2002/whc-02-conf202-25e.pdf.

UNESCO (2012). *Tentative lists: Palestine*. Paris: UNESCO. Retrieved from http://whc.unesco.org/en/tentativelists/state=ps.

United Nations (1949). *Geneva Convention IV: Relative to the protection of civilian persons in times of war*. New York: United Nations. Retrieved from http://www.un-documents.net/gc-4.htm.

# 9 Visitors' expectation and experience in a World Heritage Site

Evidence from ancient Göbekli Tepe, Sanliurfa, Turkey

Ali Rıza Manci

Introduction

Cultural and heritage tourism is an increasingly important segment of the tourism industry (Huh & Uysal, 2003; Richards, 2018; Timothy, 2018), as well as a significant area of tourism research (Albayrak et al., 2018; Asmelash & Kumar, 2019; Ung & Vong, 2010), especially in relation to World Heritage (Adie, 2017, 2019; Adie, Hall, & Prayag, 2018; Dans & González, 2019; Ramires, Brandão, & Sousa, 2018). Nevertheless, while consumer behaviour concepts, such as expectation (Muka & Cinaj, 2015), experience (Masilo & Van der Merwe, 2016), satisfaction (Olya, Lee, Lee, & Reisinger, 2019), loyalty (Abuamoud, Amal, & Alrousan, 2018), motivation (Albayrak & Caber, 2018), self-identification (Alrawadieh, Prayag, Alrawadieh, & Alsalameen, 2019), and service quality (Sayareh, Iranshahi, & Golfakhrabadi, 2016) are frequently examined in the broader tourism literature, they only receive relatively limited attention in the context of heritage tourism, and especially visitation at World Heritage Sites (WHS). However, an understanding of tourist demographics and behaviour is an integral element of heritage site marketing, including in cooperation with tourism stakeholders (Adie & Hall, 2017; Kempiak, Hollywood, Bolan, & McMahon-Beattie, 2017; Milman & Tasci, 2018; Yoon & Uysal, 2005), while visitor satisfaction has a vital role in planning and management. Therefore, it is necessary to explore the emotional and cognitive dimensions of the experience for WHS visitors in order to sustain growth, attract tourists, and improve management (Leask, 2016).

This chapter presents the results of research on visitor satisfaction at Göbekli Tepe in south-east Anatolia, Turkey. Göbekli Tepe is a pre-pottery Neolithic archaeological site dating to the tenth millennium BCE, approximately 12 km northeast of the city of Urfa (Şanliurfa, known in ancient times as Edessa) that was designated a UNESCO World Heritage Site (WHS) in 2018. The tell consists of about 20 circular structures with over 200 T-shaped columns and carved stone figures and is internationally significant because it contains some of the world's oldest megaliths and predates sedentary society (UNESCO, 2019).

The level of satisfaction of visitors toward Göbekli Tepe was analysed via a survey of 693 on-site visitors who were interviewed face to face via a structured questionnaire in April 2019. The chapter first provides a brief review of relevant literature and the study site before presenting the results of the survey.

Literature review

In recent years, the number of people who have wanted to experience new and different cultures through their travel experiences has appeared to have increased substantially (Richards, 2018). Historical and cultural sites in the UNESCO World Heritage List are regarded as particularly significant locations for tourism development (Adie, 2019). However, the interplay between heritage conservation and tourism means that it is important to understand tourist consumer behaviour in order to help ensure their sustainability, competitiveness, and effective visitor management. Consumer satisfaction is a particularly important metric in such research as it influences consumption during visit, loyalty, and recommendations (Alrawadieh & Kozak, 2019).

Studies of tourist satisfaction have been undertaken in a wide range of tourism businesses and attractions, including restaurants (Meng & Choi, 2017), hotels (Choi & Kandampully, 2019), theme parks (Milman & Tasci, 2018), festivals (Lee, Lee, Lee, & Babin, 2008), and heritage sites (Poria, Reichel, & Biran, 2006; Trinh & Ryan, 2016). However, there is only limited study of satisfaction of WHS (Adie & Hall, 2017; Herzig, 2017).

The exact definition and nature of satisfaction is a source of considerable debate (Prayag, Hassibi, & Nunkoo, 2019). Oliver (1999) defined satisfaction as a result of the consumption of a product or service to meet consumers' desires, demands, and needs. In a study of service quality at a Malaysian WHS, Guliling and Aziz (2018) suggest that satisfaction is a level of happiness that results from the fulfilment needs of tourists. The level of customer satisfaction or dissatisfaction was defined as the difference between customer expectations and the actual situation resulting from consumption in Oliver's (1999) expectation–disconfirmation model. This model emphasised that the cognitive attitudes of the consumer include post experience evaluation, suggesting that satisfaction is the difference between expectation and the experience of travel. However, Tse and Wilton (1988) argue that pre-visit expectation is not taken sufficiently into consideration when determining visitor satisfaction.

A number of scales have been developed to measure customer satisfaction in different service quality contexts. SERVQUAL (Musa & Thirumoorthi, 2011), HISTOQUAL (Putra, 2016), DINESERV (Stevens, Knutson, & Patton, 1995), HOTELQUAL (Falces, Sierra, Becerra, & Briñol, 1999) are among the most commonly used scales in tourism studies (Moore, Rodger, & Taplin, 2015). HISTOQUAL was developed to understand historical sites' service dimensions (Putra, 2016). HISTOQUAL has 24 items in five dimensions of responsiveness, tangibles, communication, consumables, and empathy. This study used a modified HISTOQUAL of 25 items in four dimensions of facilities and employees, physical appearance and maintenance, accessibility, and interpretation (see Baker & Crompton, 2000).

Hypotheses

Attractions managers and providers need to understand how the elements of their service delivery are evaluated by visitors (Frochot & Hughes, 2000). Successful heritage site management is subject to perceived levels of service quality (Beattie & Schneider, 2018). Quality is also 'one of the elements leading to satisfaction evaluations, which in turn have strong influences on post-purchase behavior' (Frochot, 2004, p. 224). The following hypotheses were adopted from Herzig's (2017) study of visitor satisfaction in Omani WHS:

H1. There is a positive and significant relationship between satisfaction and service quality and its dimensions.

H1a. There is a positive and significant relationship between the dimension of facilities and employees and overall satisfaction.

H1b. There is a positive and significant relationship between the dimension of physical appearance and maintenance and overall satisfaction.

Tverijonaite, Ólafsdóttir, and Thorsteinsson (2018) and Sæþórsdóttir and Hall (2019) showed that site accessibility related to quality of roads, distance from main centres, travel time, infrastructure, and access is related to visitation levels and crowding.

H1c. There is a positive and significant relationship between the dimension of accessibility and overall satisfaction.

The quality of interpretation has long been recognised as an important factor in visitor satisfaction at heritage sites (Hall & McArthur, 1993; Lee, 2009). Beattie and Schneider (2018) also found that satisfaction with interpretation is a significant element of the overall visitor heritage experience.

H1d. There is a positive and significant relationship between the dimension interpretation and overall satisfaction.

H2. There is a positive and significant relationship between satisfaction and behavioural intention.

Some studies have suggested that satisfaction changes according to the visitors' demographic profiles. Milman and Tasci (2018) argued that socio-demographic characteristics of tourists are drivers of satisfaction and it is essential for managers to determine the characteristics of tourists which affect consumer behaviour. Kao, Patterson, Scott, and Li (2008) also showed that heritage visitors differed not only according to their motivations to visit heritage sites but also their demographic profiles.

H3. There is a difference between country/age/education and overall satisfaction.

Adie (2017) and Adie and Hall (2017) note that many tourism and heritage stakeholders suggest that UNESCO World Heritage designation is important for tourists' visitations.

H4. Visitors who have visited other UNESCO sites before were significantly more satisfied with their visit.

Method

A sample of 693 on-site visitors (Yamane, 2006) were interviewed face to face via a structured questionnaire in the tourist-intensive season in April 2019. The first part of the questionnaire covers visitors' personal demographic characteristics in addition to how many days they stayed in the city, who they visited, the sources of information about the site, whether they had visited other UNESCO World Heritage Sites like Göbekli Tepe before, and whether their expectations were met. The second part consists of HISTOQUAL statements using a 5-point Likert scale aimed at measuring the experiences of the visitors. The questionnaire was provided both in Turkish and English and was developed in accordance with the structure of a similar study carried out by Herzig (2017).

Findings

Visitor demographics

Survey respondents were predominantly male (56.4 per cent) (Table 9.1). Most visitors (35.5 per cent) were aged between 25 and 34, and 22.2 per cent of visitors were between 35 and 44. More than half of visitors (56.3 per cent) reported that it was their first visit to the site, 20.2 per cent of them reported visiting twice a year. Surprisingly, 17.7 per cent of respondents visited the site often. A majority of the visitors (50.4 per cent) had obtained master's and PhD degrees and 19.8 per cent of respondents had a bachelor's degree. 65.2 per cent of respondents had previously visited a cultural site on the UNESCO World Heritage List. A quarter of the respondents were international tourists, with the remainder domestic. Respondents reported that their experience had been better (37.7 per cent) and much better (37.7 per cent), neither worse nor better (14.3 per cent), and a small

Table 9.1 Demographic characteristics of the visitor

		Origin of the visitor					
		International		Domestic		Total	
		N	%	N	%	N	%
Gender	Male	69	51.9	322	57.5	391	56.4
	Female	64	48.1	238	42.5	302	43.6
Age	18–24	25	18.8	84	15.0	109	15.7
	25–34	31	23.3	215	38.4	246	35.5
	35–44	25	18.8	129	23.0	154	22.2
	45–54	26	19.5	56	10.0	82	11.8
	55–64	13	9.8	61	10.9	74	10.7
	65 and above	13	9.8	15	2.7	28	4.1
Employment	Public servant	22	16.5	198	35.3	220	31.8
	Student	31	23.3	86	15.3	117	16.5
	Artisan	4	3.0	14	2.5	18	2.6
	Worker	13	9.7	31	5.5	44	6.4
	Retired	13	9.7	46	8.2	59	8.6
	Businessperson	10	7.5	41	7.3	51	7.4
	Unemployed	4	3.0	9.0	1.6	13	1.9
	Other	36	27	135	24.1	171	24.8
Frequency of visitation	First visit	105	78.9	288	51.2	393	56.5
	Two times per year	19	14.3	121	21.7	140	20.3
	Three times per year	2	1.5	15	2.7	17	2.5
	Four times per year	2	1.5	18	3.2	20	2.9
	Often (more than four times a year)	5	3.8	118	21.2	123	17.8
Highest level of education	Primary school	1	0.7	21	3.7	22	3.1
	Middle school	24	18.0	54	9.6	78	11.2
	College	30	22.5	76	13.5	106	15.2
	University	37	27.8	141	25.1	178	25.6
	Master/PhD	41	30.8	268	47.8	309	44.5
Number of days of accommodation	Less than one full day	10	7.5	145	26.0	155	22.5
	One day	36	27.1	110	20	146	21.3
	Two days	28	21.1	112	20	140	20.2
	Three days	10	7.5	60	10.7	70	10.1
	Four days	10	7.5	19	3.4	29	4.2
	Five days and more	39	29.3	111	19.9	150	21.6
Had previously visited a UNESCO World Heritage Site	Yes	103	77.4	349	62.3	452	65.2
	No	30	22.5	211	37.6	241	34.7

(Continued)

Table 9.1 Continued

		Origin of the visitor					
		International		Domestic		Total	
		N	%	N	%	N	%
Experience of visit compared to expectation	Much worse	3	2.25	14	2.5	17	2.4
	Worse	8	6.01	25	4.4	33	4.7
	Neither worse nor better	30	22.5	69	12.3	99	14.2
	Better	27	20.3	236	42.1	263	37.9
	Much better	62	46.6	199	35.5	261	37.6
	Don't know	3	2.25	17	3.0	20	2.8
Number of respondents		133	100.0	560	100.0	693	100.0

portion of respondents said worse (4.8 per cent) and much worse (2.5 per cent) than expected.

Cronbach's alpha values obtained from reliability analysis were 0.948 for HISTOQUAL, 0.807 for facilities and employees, 0.742 for physical appearance and maintenance, 0.605 for accessibility, 0.869 for interpretation, and 0.866 for satisfaction. All dimensions had a Cronbach's alpha higher than 0.600. For visitor satisfaction purposes, statements with a mean between 1 and 2.99 were considered unsatisfactory, 3 and 3.49 indifferent, and 3.5 and 5 satisfactory (Table 9.2). In this framework, out of the 34 statements, 26 were found to be satisfactory, seven to be indifferent and one as indicating visitor dissatisfaction. Means of the dimensions are all higher than 3.66. The element of the visit with which visitors were dissatisfied was the entrance fee. However, this depended on the nature of the market, as while domestic visitors of Göbekli Tepe were dissatisfied with the entrance fee (mean = 2.75), international visitors were satisfied (mean = 3.84). The statements which were evaluated as 'indifferent' by the visitors point to certain site improvements that could be undertaken. In this framework, shortcomings included shopping opportunities, information tools, souvenir shops, rest areas, indoor spaces, and the quality of presentations.

As dimensions have a different number of statements, the means of the dimensions with respect to the statements they cover were calculated and then rounded to integer values ranging from 1 to 5. In the ordered probit models, the means of the dimensions which were defined as new variables were taken as the dependent variables and independent variables. The probit model also included socio-demographic characteristics of the visitors. Male, single, domestic, and satisfied dummy variables were defined as dummy (0 and 1); age and education were defined as categorical; revisit, facilities,

Table 9.2 Statements of the modified HISTOQUAL scale – dimensions and descriptive statistics

	Origin of the visitor								
	International			*Domestic*			*Total*		
	Mean	SD	N	Mean	SD	N	Mean	SD	N
Facilities and employees	3.83	0.72	133	3.51	0.81	560	3.57	0.81	693
Toilets were clean and properly marked on site	3.74	1.14	133	3.61	1.27	560	3.63	1.25	693
Shopping mall facilities were enough	3.75	1.18	133	3.15	1.25	560	3.27	1.26	693
Employees were helpful, knowledgeable and available when needed	4.02	0.97	133	3.61	1.30	560	3.69	1.25	693
Tea–coffee needs and other services were available	4.12	1.08	133	3.76	1.17	560	3.83	1.16	693
I had the chance to engage with members of the local community	3.59	1.25	133	4.00	1.06	560	3.92	1.11	693
Phyical appearance and maintenance	4.11	0.68	133	3.96	0.72	560	3.99	0.72	693
The visitor center was informative	3.73	1.19	133	3.29	1.36	560	3.38	1.33	693
The sovenirs shop offered good quality arts and crafts of Sanliurfa	3.76	1.18	133	3.26	1.28	560	3.36	1.28	693
There were sufficient rest areas available on site	3.89	1.16	133	3.38	1.24	560	3.48	1.24	693
This site was clean and litter free	4.49	0.80	133	4.16	0.96	560	4.23	0.94	693
This site had good safety measures	4.29	0.87	133	4.27	0.86	560	4.27	0.86	693
It has enough infrastructure	4.08	1.01	133	3.75	1.21	560	3.82	1.18	693
This site had enough indoor space	3.95	1.11	133	3.28	1.28	560	3.41	1.27	693
The architecture of this site was impressive	4.03	1.16	133	4.09	1.08	560	4.08	1.10	693
Weather condition was suitable for visit	3.83	1.34	133	4.19	1.03	560	4.13	1.11	693
Accessibility	4.12	0.76	133	3.71	0.95	560	3.78	0.93	693
Roads leading to the site were in good condition	4.07	1.07	133	3.58	1.31	560	3.67	1.28	693
It was easy to reach this site	4.23	0.96	133	3.82	1.26	560	3.90	1.22	693
I would visit easily because of uncrowded	4.06	1.09	133	3.71	1.24	560	3.78	1.22	693

(*Continued*)

Table 9.2 Continued

	Origin of the visitor								
	International			Domestic			Total		
	Mean	SD	N	Mean	SD	N	Mean	SD	N
Interpretation	4.01	0.88	133	3.83	0.85	560	3.86	0.86	693
Information panels were well placed, easy and interesting to read	4.08	1.07	133	3.71	1.18	560	3.78	1.17	693
The visitor centre was informative	3.73	1.19	133	3.29	1.36	560	3.38	1.33	693
The tourist guides were enough; presentation quality was good	3.70	1.24	133	3.32	1.32	560	3.39	1.31	693
Visiting Göbekli Tepe was quite impressive	4.19	1.12	133	4.13	1.04	560	4.14	1.06	693
Visiting Göbekli Tepe was exciting	4.16	1.14	133	4.17	1.02	560	4.17	1.04	693
This visit was opportunity to learn new things	4.13	1.22	133	4.18	0.99	560	4.17	1.03	693
Visiting Göbekli Tepe is like making a trip in history	4.16	1.19	133	4.06	1.15	560	4.08	1.16	693
I was informed about the universal and cultural value of this UNESCO site	4.13	1.22	133	3.56	1.34	560	3.67	1.33	693
Behavioural intention	3.92	.99	133	3.79	0.94	560	3.81	0.95	693
Based on my visit here I will visit other UNESCO sites in Turkey	4.11	1.13	133	4.11	1.06	560	4.11	1.07	693
I would recommend other people to visit this UNESCO site	4.11	1.22	133	4.10	1.07	560	4.10	1.10	693
I would be willing to pay more to enter this UNESCO site	3.52	1.29	133	3.08	1.43	560	3.16	1.41	693
I would like to visit this place again	3.96	1.28	133	3.85	1.27	560	3.87	1.27	693
Overall satisfaction	4.09	0.97	133	3.77	0.99	560	3.83	0.99	693
I am satisfied overall with the visit to this UNESCO site	4.17	1.08	133	4.04	1.03	560	4.06	1.04	693
I was satisfied with the management's effort to make this place worthwhile	4.15	1.04	133	3.87	1.20	560	3.92	1.17	693
I was satisfied with the services I received at this UNESCO site	4.00	1.19	133	3.61	1.21	560	3.69	1.21	693

(Continued)

	Origin of the visitor								
	International			Domestic			Total		
	Mean	SD	N	Mean	SD	N	Mean	SD	N
I was satisfied with the information provided at this UNESCO site	4.03	1.27	133	3.55	1.23	560	3.64	1.25	693
Entrance fee was suitable for me	3.84	1.19	133	2.75	1.47	560	2.96	1.49	693

and employees (FAC), physical appearance and maintenance (PAM), accessibility (ACC), interpretation (INT), overall satisfaction (OS), and service quality (SQ) were defined as Likert (1 = Exactly disagree, 5 = Exactly agree); behavioural intention (BI) was defined as Likert (1 = Exactly disagree, 5 = exactly agree). Ordered probit models (statistically significant at $\alpha = 0.10$) were estimated in four different models, each analysing the hypotheses of this chapter. Model 1, Model 2, and Model 3 examined the relationships between overall satisfaction and socio-demographic variables and dimensions of the HISTOQUAL. Model 4 was an ordered model to probe what variables affected the revisit of the visitors.

Model 1: Overall satisfaction = −0.0127626 Male + 0.0891458 Age* + 0.134942 Education* − 0.185230 + Alone − 0.489499 Domestic* − 0.0483155 Visited other UNESCO sites
Log-likelihood = −891.0386*, Correctly predicted = 39.8%

Model 2: Overall satisfaction = 0.524126 FAC* + 0.156837 PAM* + 0.123458 + ACC* + 0.798103INT* + 0.904951 BI*
Log-likelihood = −540.9317*, Correctly predicted = 67.1%

Model 3: Overall satisfaction = 0.186211 PAM* + 0.230395 ACC* + 0.537298 INT* + 0.637607 BI* + 1.16417 SQ
Log-likelihood = −814.4989*, Correctly predicted = 50.3%

Model 4: Revisit = 0.0582994 Male − 0.0530815 Age* + 0.0803591 Education* + 0.0254316 Alone − 0.0348827 Domestic + 0.754157 OS*
Log-likelihood = −368.5592*, Correctly predicted = 81.4%

Satisfaction

In order to test the hypotheses of this chapter, four different ordered probit models were estimated. All the models were found statistically significant at 0.10. In model 1, overall satisfaction is a function of socio-demographic variables. Male and female visitors have the same overall satisfaction. The age of visitors positively affects the overall level of satisfaction. This means that elder visitors find more overall satisfactory than younger visitors. As the education level of the visitors increases, overall satisfaction increases. Visitors travelling alone or in groups have the same overall satisfaction. Domestic visitors are less satisfied overall while international visitors are more satisfied.

In model 2, overall satisfaction is a function of four dimensions of model. Each of the dimensions has a statistically significant positive effect on the overall satisfaction. As any of the dimensions increases, overall satisfaction increases as well.

In model 3, overall satisfaction is a function of four dimensions of HISTOQUAL and service quality. Each of the four dimensions has a statistically significant positive affect on the overall satisfaction. As any of the four dimensions included increases, overall satisfaction increases as well. The higher the service quality, the higher the satisfaction level.

In model 4, the tendency of the visitors to revisit Göbekli Tepe is a function of socio-demographic variables. Both genders have the same tendency to come back to the site for one more visit. The age of the visitors negatively affects the tendency to revisit. Younger visitors tend to revisit Göbekli Tepe more than elderly visitors. The education level of the visitors affects the tendency for revisit positively. More educated visitors tend to revisit more than less educated visitors. Travelling singly or in a group appears to have no influence on site revisitation. Domestic and international visitors have the same tendency to revisit. The higher the service quality, the higher the tendency to revisit.

Length of stay in Sanliurfa

The length of stay of visitors in Sanliurfa was examined in terms of socio-demographic variables by means of a probit model. All the variables included in the probit model to understand what affects length of stay were found statistically significant. Visitors who stay in Sanliurfa up to three days are coded as 0 and stays longer than three days are coded as 1. The probit model predicts 64.8 per cent of cases correctly.

Stay days = 0.446268* + 0.376013 Male* − 0.0714111 Age* − 0.102114 Education* + 0.47503Alone* − 0.239790 Domestic* − 0.270694 Satisfied Dummy*
Log-likelihood = −428.1009*, Correctly predicted = 64.8% (*Statistically significant at $\alpha = 0.10$)

Male visitors tend to stay longer than female with the probability of males staying longer than three days being 13.7 per cent more than females. The older a visitor is, the shorter the stay in Sanliurfa. Also, the more educated the visitor is, the shorter the stay in Sanliurfa. Visitors travelling alone tend to stay longer than those travelling in groups. Single visitors are 18.5 per cent more likely to stay longer than three days when compared to visitors travelling in groups. Domestic visitors tend to stay shorter than international visitors, with domestic visitors 9.1 per cent less likely to stay longer than three days when compared to an international visitor. Satisfied visitors tend to stay in Sanliurfa no longer than three days. A satisfied visitor is 10.3 per cent less likely to stay longer than three days when compared to an unsatisfied visitor.

Table 9.3 presents the test results of the hypotheses. All the hypotheses except H4 have been supported.

Discussion and conclusion

Consumer satisfaction is a major concern in tourism research (Prayag et al., 2019). However, there are only a limited number of studies that have examined visitor satisfaction in the context of WHS (Alrawadieh et al., 2019; Bec et al., 2019; Phaswana-Mafuya & Haydam, 2005; Wan & Cheng, 2011). The present chapter's goal was to investigate the relationships between service quality and its dimensions and visitor satisfaction at the Göbekli Tepe WHS. As expected, service quality has a considerable effect on satisfaction on visitors. The conclusion that emerges from this chapter is similar to that of Wan and Cheng (2011) at Macao's WHS and confirms Guliling and Aziz's (2018) results from their study of a Malaysian WHS, which found that the higher the service quality perceived by tourists in the heritage destination, the more satisfied they will be.

Contrary to previous research (Zhao, Nyaupane, & Andereck, 2011), this study identifies a significant difference between the perceptions, the sociodemographic characteristics, and the travel patterns of tourists visiting heritage sites for variables such as age, education, travelling alone or in a group, or being domestic or international visitors. The overall satisfaction of visitors regarding the Göbekli Tepe site was found to be positively related with all the dimensions of HISTOQUAL scale, such as facilities and employees, physical appearance and maintenance, accessibility, interpretation, and behavioural intention, although the response of visitors did suggest that improvements could be made with respect to shopping, informative tools, souvenirs, rest areas, indoor spaces, and presentation quality.

The research findings also correspond with those of Beattie and Schneider (2018), who found that interpretation plays a significant role in satisfaction, as well as that of Tverijonaite et al. (2018) who found that ease of site access could increase the level of satisfaction. Satisfaction has a positive impact on intention to revisit. Similar to the results of Milman and Tasci (2018) and Kao et al. (2008), overall satisfaction is also affected by the socio-demographic characteristics of the visitors, such as country, age, and education.

Domestic visitors are less satisfied than international tourists. It is possible that domestic visitors do receive sufficient information about the site and its

Table 9.3 Test results of the hypotheses

Hypothesis	Coefficient	Decision
H1: There is a positive and significant relationship between satisfaction and service quality	1.16417*	Confirmed
H1a: There is a positive and significant relationship between the dimension 'Facilities and employees' and overall 'Satisfaction'	0.524126*	Confirmed
H1b: There is a positive and significant relationship between the dimension Physical appearance and maintenance and overall Satisfaction	0.156837*	Confirmed
H1c: There is a positive and significant relationship between the dimension accessibility and overall satisfaction	0.123458*	Confirmed
H1d: There is a positive and significant relationship between the dimension interpretation and overall satisfaction	0.798103*	Confirmed
H2: There is a positive and significant relationship between 'Overall Satisfaction' and Behavioural Intention	0.904951*	Confirmed
H3: There is a difference between origin of visitors/age/ education and overall satisfaction	−0.489499* 0.0891458* 0.134942*	All confirmed
H4: Visitors who have visited other UNESCO sites before were significantly more satisfied with their visit	−0.0483155	Rejected

Note
*Statistically significant at $\alpha = 0.10$.

historical importance. Nevertheless, there is no difference in the overall satisfaction of visitors who have visited other WHS before and those who have not. Younger visitors tend to revisit more than older tourists, while those with higher levels of education are also more likely to revisit (see also Abuamoud et al., 2018).

As of 2019 the entrance fees to the site are approximately between $15 and $20 per international visitor and $5 for domestic visitors, which is quite affordable when compared to other historical sites. For instance, entrance to Petra in Jordan is approximately $70, Stonehenge about $30, the Pyramids of Egypt about $20, and the archaeological site of Troy $20. Manci (2016) suggested that the willingness to pay (WTP) for Göbekli Tepe, using stated preferences of the visitors when there was no entrance fee, was $22. However, even though this may be affordable for international visitors, domestic visitors who were not satisfied with the current much lower entrance fee would definitely not be happy with this level of entrance fee. Therefore, it is highly likely that differential entrance fees will continue to be charged between domestic and international visitors in order to meet the needs of the domestic market.

For the accommodation sector in Sanliurfa, demographic differences in length of stay may be significant. Male visitors tend to stay longer than females, the older and more educated the visitor is the shorter the length of stay, and visitors travelling alone tend to stay longer than those travelling with others. Although domestic and international visitors have the same tendency to revisit, international visitors are willing to stay longer, which may have significant implications for tourism marketing and management, including the relationship of Göbekli Tepe to other cultural and heritage sites in the region.

References

Abuamoud, I., Amal, I., & Alrousan, R. M. (2018). Measuring tourists' satisfaction and loyalty: A perception approach. *Quality Management Journal*, 25(2), 101–107.

Adie, B. A. (2017). Franchising our heritage: The UNESCO World Heritage brand. *Tourism Management Perspectives*, 24, 48–53.

Adie, B. A. (2019). *World Heritage and tourism: Marketing and management*. Abingdon: Routledge.

Adie, B. A., & Hall, C. M. (2017). Who visits World Heritage? A comparative analysis of three cultural sites. *Journal of Heritage Tourism*, 12(1), 67–80.

Adie, B. A., Hall, C. M., & Prayag, G. (2018). World Heritage as a placebo brand: A comparative analysis of three sites and marketing implications. *Journal of Sustainable Tourism*, 26(3), 399–415.

Albayrak, T., & Caber, M. (2018). Examining the relationship between tourist motivation and satisfaction by two competing methods. *Tourism Management*, 69, 201–213.

Albayrak, T., Herstein, R., Caber, M., Drori, N., Bideci, M., & Berger, R. (2018). Exploring religious tourist experiences in Jerusalem: The intersection of Abrahamic religions. *Tourism Management*, 69, 285–296.

Alrawadieh, Z., & Kozak, M. (2019). Exploring the impact of tourist harassment on destination image, tourist expenditure, and destination loyalty. *Tourism Management*, 73, 13–20.

Alrawadieh, Z., Prayag, G., Alrawadieh, Z., & Alsalameen, M. (2019). Self-identification with a heritage tourism site, visitors' engagement and destination loyalty: The mediating effects of overall satisfaction. *The Service Industries Journal*, 39(7–8), 541–558.

Asmelash, A. G., & Kumar, S. (2019). The structural relationship between tourist satisfaction and sustainable heritage tourism development in Tigrai, Ethiopia. *Heliyon, 5*(3), e01335.

Baker, D. A., & Crompton, J. L. (2000). Quality, satisfaction and behavioral intentions. *Annals of Tourism Research, 27*(3), 785–804.

Beattie, J. M., & Schneider, I. E. (2018). Does service type influence satisfaction? A case study of Edinburgh Castle. *Tourism Management, 67*, 89–97.

Bec, A., Moyle, B., Timms, K., Schaffer, V., Skavronskaya, L., & Little, C. (2019). Management of immersive heritage tourism experiences: A conceptual model. *Tourism Management, 72*, 117–120.

Choi, H., & Kandampully, J. (2019). The effect of atmosphere on customer engagement in upscale hotels: An application of S-O-R paradigm. *International Journal of Hospitality Management, 77*, 40–50.

Dans, E. P., & González, P. A. (2019). Sustainable tourism and social value at World Heritage Sites: Towards a conservation plan for Altamira, Spain. *Annals of Tourism Research, 74*, 68–80.

Falces, D., Sierra, D., Becerra, G., & Briñol, T. (1999). HOTELQUAL: A scale for measuring perceived quality in lodging services. *Estudios Turísticos, 139*, 95–110.

Frochot, I. (2004). An investigation into the influence of the benefits sought by visitors on their quality evaluation of historic houses' service provision. *Journal of Vacation Marketing, 10*(3), 223–237.

Frochot, I., & Hughes, H. (2000). HISTOQUAL: The development of a historic houses assessment scale. *Tourism Management, 21*(2), 157–167.

Guliling, H. H., & Aziz, Y. A. (2018). Historical service quality assessment of Malaysia's World Heritage Site. *Journal of International Business, Economics and Entrepreneurship, 3*(2), 12–22.

Hall, C. M., & McArthur, S. (eds) (1993). *Heritage management in New Zealand and Australia: Visitor management, interpretation and marketing*. Auckland: Oxford University Press.

Herzig, P. J. C. (2017). *Visitor satisfaction at UNESCO World Heritage Sites: The case of the Oasis of Bahla and Land of Frankincense in the Sultanate of Oman*. (Unpublished master's thesis). University of Ljubljana and the German University of Technology, Faculty of Humanities.

Huh, J., & Uysal, M. (2003). Satisfaction with cultural/heritage sites: Virginia historic triangle. In J. A. Williams & M. Uysal (eds), *Current Issues and Development in Hospitality and Tourism Satisfaction* (177–194). New York: The Haworth Hospitality Press.

Kao, M. C., Patterson, I., Scott, N., & Li, C. K. (2008). Motivations and satisfactions of Taiwanese tourists who visit Australia: An exploratory study. *Journal of Travel & Tourism Marketing, 24*(1), 17–33.

Kempiak, J., Hollywood, L., Bolan, P., & McMahon-Beattie, U. (2017). The heritage tourist: An understanding of the visitor experience at heritage attractions. *International Journal of Heritage Studies, 23*(4), 375–392.

Leask, A. (2016). Visitor attraction management: A critical review of research 2009–2014. *Tourism Management, 57*, 334–361.

Lee, T. H. (2009). A structural model for examining how destination image and interpretation services affect future visitation behavior: A case study of Taiwan's Taomi eco-village. *Journal of Sustainable Tourism, 17*(6), 727–745.

Lee, Y. K., Lee, C. K., Lee, S. K., & Babin, B. J. (2008). Festivalscapes and patrons' emotions, satisfaction, and loyalty. *Journal of Business Research*, *61*(1), 56–64.

Manci, A. R. (2016). Evaluating foreign tourists' willingness to pay for ancient Gobeklitepe-Sanliurfa, Turkey. *International Journal of Health Management and Tourism*, *2*(3), 14–26.

Masilo, H., & Van der Merwe, C. D. (2016). Heritage tourists' experiences of 'struggle heritage' at Liliesleaf Farm Museum and the Hector Pieterson Memorial & Museum South Africa. *African Journal of Hospitality, Tourism and Leisure*, *5*(3), 1–20.

Meng, B., & Choi, K. (2017). Theme restaurants' servicescape in developing quality of life: The moderating effect of perceived authenticity. *International Journal of Hospitality Management*, *65*, 89–99.

Milman, A., & Tasci, A. D. A. (2018). Exploring the experiential and socio-demographic drivers of satisfaction and loyalty in the theme park context. *Journal of Destination Marketing and Management*, *8*, 385–395.

Moore, S. A., Rodger, K., & Taplin, R. (2015). Moving beyond visitor satisfaction to loyalty in nature-based tourism: A review and research agenda. *Current Issues in Tourism*, *18*(7), 667–683.

Muka, M., & Cinaj, N. (2015). Motivation, perception and expectation of visitors in heritage sites, case: Bunk'Art. *Academic Journal of Interdisciplinary Studies*, *4*(3), 697–705.

Musa, G., & Thirumoorthi, T. (2011). Red Palm: Exploring service quality and servicescape of the best backpacker hostel in Asia. *Current Issues in Tourism*, *14*(2), 103–120.

Oliver, R. L. (1999). Whence consumer loyalty? *Journal of Marketing*, *63*(4), 33–44.

Olya, H. G. T., Lee, C.-K., Lee, Y.-K. & Reisinger, Y. (2019). What are the triggers of Asian visitor satisfaction and loyalty in the Korean heritage site? *Journal of Retailing and Consumer Services*, *47*, 195–205.

Phaswana-Mafuya, N., & Haydam, N. (2005). Tourists' expectations and perceptions of the Robben Island Museum—a World Heritage Site. *Museum Management and Curatorship*, *20*(2), 149–169.

Poria, Y., Reichel, A., & Biran, A. (2006). Heritage site management: Motivations and expectations. *Annals of Tourism Research*, *33*(1), 162–178.

Prayag, G., Hassibi, S., & Nunkoo, R. (2019). A systematic review of consumer satisfaction studies in hospitality journals: Conceptual development, research approaches and future prospects. *Journal of Hospitality Marketing and Management*, *28*(1), 51–80.

Putra, F. K. K. (2016). Implementation of HISTOQUAL model to measure visitors' expectations and perceptions in Museum Geology Bandung. In *Asia Tourism Forum 2016 – the 12th Biennial Conference of Hospitality and Tourism Industry in Asia*: Atlantis Press, 322–327.

Ramires, A., Brandão, F., & Sousa, A. C. (2018). Motivation-based cluster analysis of international tourists visiting a World Heritage city: The case of Porto, Portugal. *Journal of Destination Marketing and Management*, *8*, 49–60.

Richards, G. (2018). Cultural tourism: A review of recent research and trends. *Journal of Hospitality and Tourism Management*, *36*, 12–21.

Sæþórsdóttir, A. D., & Hall, C. M. (2019). Contested development paths and rural communities: Sustainable energy or sustainable tourism in Iceland? *Sustainability*, *11*(13), 3642.

Sayareh, J., Iranshahi, S., & Golfakhrabadi, N. (2016). Service quality evaluation and ranking of container terminal operators. *Asian Journal of Shipping and Logistics, 32*(4), 203–212.

Stevens, P., Knutson, B., & Patton, M. (1995). DINESERV: A tool for measuring service quality in restaurants. *The Cornell Hotel and Restaurant Administration Quarterly, 36*(2), 5–60.

Timothy, D. J. (2018). Making sense of heritage tourism: Research trends in a maturing field of study. *Tourism Management Perspectives, 25*, 177–180.

Trinh, T. T., & Ryan, C. (2016). Visitors to heritage sites: Motives and involvement—a model and textual analysis. *Journal of Travel Research, 56*(1), 67–80.

Tse, D. K., & Wilton, P. C. (1988). Models of consumer satisfaction formation: An extension. *Journal of Marketing Research, 25*(2), 204–212.

Tverijonaite, E., Ólafsdóttir, R., & Thorsteinsson, T. (2018). Accessibility of protected areas and visitor behaviour: A case study from Iceland. *Journal of Outdoor Recreation and Tourism, 24*, 1–10.

UNESCO, World Heritage Centre (2019). Göbekli Tepe. Available at https://whc.unesco.org/en/list/1572.

Ung, A., & Vong, T. N. (2010). Tourist experience of heritage tourism in Macau SAR, China. *Journal of Heritage Tourism, 5*(2), 157–168.

Wan, P. Y. K., & Cheng, E. I. M. (2011). Service quality of Macao's World Heritage Site. *International Journal of Culture, Tourism and Hospitality Research, 5*(1), 57–68.

Yamane, T. (2006). *Elementary sampling theory*. New Jersey: Prentice Hall.

Yoon, Y., & Uysal, M. (2005). An examination of the effects of motivation and satisfaction on destination loyalty: A structural model. *Tourism Management, 26*(1), 45–56.

Zhao, S., Nyaupane, G. P., & Andereck, K. (2011). Exploring the differences between tourists visiting heritage sites and those visiting cultural events: A cognitive perspective. Paper presented at *TTRA2011, Travel and Tourism Research Association: Advancing Tourism Research Globally, 54*. Available at https://scholarworks.umass.edu/ttra/2011/Oral/54.

10 Theme park Arabism

Disneyfying the UAE's heritage for Western tourist consumption

Salma Thani and Tom Heenan

Introduction

In the mid-2000s, a watershed moment occurred in the United Arab Emirates (UAE). The Arab heritages of the major sheikdoms, Dubai and Abu Dhabi, were rediscovered. For over three decades the power-elites of these emirates pursued modernisation agendas that transformed once sleepy pearling ports into global cities. Fuelled by oil revenues, Abu Dhabi and Dubai became iconic, Disneyfied cityscapes and major global aviation hubs. Whether it be the excessive grandeur of the self-proclaimed seven-star Burj Al-Arab Jumeirah Hotel or the world's tallest building, the Burj Khalifa, Dubai morphed into a hyper-modern city where only the biggest and the best would do; while the more conservative but oil-rich Abu Dhabi invested petrodollars on theme parks, high-culture 'name' museums and globally eye-catching special events.

The cities symbolised a modern Arab excess that was not threatening to Western tourists in the post-9/11 world. Indeed, it proved extremely appealing with both cities – though most notably Dubai – developing into global aviation, tourism, and retail consumption centres. The cities were marketed as hyper-modern, semi-Disneyfied theme parks, welcoming Western tourists, middle-management workers, and investors. As this chapter shows, the emphasis began to shift after 9/11 with the need to allay Western tourists' fears of the Arab world; as well as a re-packaging of the UAE for a growing intra-Arab tourist trade; and the solidification of the UAE's national identity amid emerging movements for democratic reform across the Middle East. Co-existing with the modern was an emerging interest in the nation's heritage which has since become a growing area in the UAE's tourism market. More conservative emirates, such as Sharjah, led the way with investments in heritage restoration projects, and the promotion of traditional handicrafts and cultural practices. This rediscovery has extended throughout the UAE, but it has resulted in mainly sanitised and Disneyfied representations of the region's past, carefully crafted for Westerners' consumption. This strategy involved attracting high-end, Western, and globally recognisable brands to the region, while marketing Dubai and Abu Dhabi centres of Disneyfied spectacle and consumeristic excess.

As this chapter emphasises, the strategy has succeeded, though at the expense of the UAE's diverse tribal heritage. In developing their tourism markets, Dubai and Abu Dhabi have tapped into a growing economic sector which contributed US$7.6 trillion, or over 10% per cent, to global GDP in 2016 (World Economic Forum, 2017). Globally, international arrivals have increased from 954 million in 2015 to 1.4 billion in 2018 (UNWTO, 2019). A contributing factor is growth in the Middle Eastern and Asian tourism markets. As Sharpley (2009) notes, leisure tourism was considered culturally and economically undesirable in the Middle East, but attitudes have shifted with the region experiencing 5 per cent growth in 2017 (UNWTO, 2018). According to the World Economic Forum (2017), the UAE has the highest growth rate in the Middle Eastern tourism market, increasing by 1.4 per cent annually since 2015. However, the predominant share of the UAE market remains leisure-seeking Western tourists, attracted by sun, beaches, and theme parks, as well as high-end accommodation and shopping. This market was secured at the expense of the UAE's diverse cultural heritage which has been sanitised, commodified, and Disneyfied to align with Western tourists' expectations.

Sanitising the past

Under the International Charter of Venice (1964) (International Council of Monuments and Sites (ICOMOS), 1964), heritage is defined as 'works of the past which have acquired cultural significance with the passing of time'. The concept encompasses both tangible materials of human creation, such as artworks and visual expressions of culture, but it also includes intangible aspects, such as landscapes, historic sites, artefacts, and cultural practices and lived experiences (Jugmohan, Spencer, & Steyn, 2016). Hence, heritage tourism centres on lived and constructed aspects of culture, encompassing tangible and intangible representations of the past packaged as tourism products (Timothy & Nyaupane, 2009). The quality of the tourist experience depends on the interpretation of a heritage site or event and, most importantly, its perceived authenticity as a cultural artefact or representation of the past (Chhabra, 2001). Authenticity is an underlying determinant of heritage tourism (Silver, 1993). Tourists expect heritage sites and experiences to be authentic, though this is not always the case in the UAE. In order to sell heritage to tourists, UAE tourism authorities have either reinvented or selectively constructed the past, or simply imported heritage artefacts from elsewhere to meet with tourist expectations.

Since the mid-2000s, the UAE has placed increasing emphasis on protecting its national heritage and promoting heritage tourism. A major factor was the large heritage tourism markets in Egypt, Jordan, Syria, Saudi Arabia, and Oman which have all remained buoyant tourist destinations after 9/11, especially with the growth of the intra-Arab tourism market. Realising this market's importance, the UAE became an active international player through the United Nations Educational, Scientific and Cultural

Organization (UNESCO) in the protection of heritage sites. Internally, emirates established statutory authorities to preserve their sites, undertook heritage projects, and promoted heritage tourism. In 2008 Dubai's Culture and Arts Authority (DCAA) was founded to promote the emirate's cultural achievements through the development of museums and heritage sites and districts, and the organisation of festivals and art fairs (DCAA, 2019). The DCAA sought to add a cultural dimension to the architectural excess, spectacle, and hyper-consumerism associated with Dubai's global brand. In 2011, the Abu Dhabi Tourism and Culture Authority was established, which later became the Abu Dhabi Department of Culture and Tourism (ADDCT) (2019) after it was merged with the Abu Dhabi Authority for Culture and Heritage in 2012. By integrating the emirate's culture with tourism, the ADDCT attempted to counter the widely held contention that UAE cities were excessively sterile and devoid of cultural heritage and history. Instead, they were cultural centres in their own rights (Ajana, 2015). But there was another dimension to this rediscovery of Abu Dhabi and Dubai's pasts. Heritage and cultural sites are also economic assets and generators of income through the tourism industry (Ajana, 2015). The UAE's sites have been sanitised and commodified to meet the demands of a predominantly Western tourism market. Preservation of key heritage sites centred on their economic viability as major tourist attractions and contributors to the UAE's tourism economy.

Arguably, the most authentic centre of UAE heritage tourism was, and remains, Sharjah. Unlike its nearby neighbour, Dubai, Sharjah has remained culturally conservative and sought to preserve or reconstruct old quarters of the city as heritage districts. This has been achieved through three government bodies: the Institute for Heritage, the Museums Department, and the Art Foundation. Unlike Abu Dhabi and Dubai, these bodies are primarily responsible for the preservation and promotion of heritage within the emirate, and not the revival of heritage to diversify predominantly Western-oriented UAE tourism markets. With the growth of intra-Arab tourism post-9/11, and the resultant increase of Sharia hotels, Sharjah is better equipped to attract the more conservative Arab or Islamic tourist than Abu Dhabi or Dubai. As detailed in their long-term strategies – *Abu Dhabi 2030 Economic Vision* and Dubai's *Tourism Vision 2020* – cultural heritage protection is an important aspect of the cities' tourism agendas and is considered a vital economic asset (The Government of Abu Dhabi, 2019; The First Group LLC, 2019). In contrast, Sharjah's heritage is perceived as representative of 'real' Arab culture, although the perception is misleading. Despite traditional appearances, Sharjah also offers a sanitised version of the region's culture and heritage, though under a more authentic guise. As will be shown, this is evident in contrasting the UAE's themed cultural districts, such as Saadiyat Island and the Heart of Sharjah, which have been selectively packaged and commodified to represent idealised constructs of their regions' pasts.

However, there is another aspect to this sanitised rediscovery of heritage that cannot be ignored. Museums, heritage villages, and districts, as well as festivals and traditional sports like falconry and camel racing, have been used by authorities to bolster a distinct cultural identity and boost national pride. According to Durmaz, Platt, and Yigitcanlar (2010), cultural heritage is the only tourism product that gives cities and countries a cultural identity which differentiates them from their competitors. This is evident in the UAE's case.

Cultural heritage sites and activities form part of a threefold UAE government strategy. Firstly, in preserving and re-imaging the region's heritage, they emphasise a progressive nationalist narrative about the transformation of poor pearling ports and nomadic Bedouin tribespeople into a modern, wealthy, and progressive Arab state. For a nation comprising seven diverse tribal sheikdoms, heritage has become an important unifying factor in the construction of the UAE's cultural identity; but it has also provided a means for differentiating the UAE's heritage tourism product from those of its competitors. Secondly, heritage both diversifies and softens the UAE tourism product from the predominant focus on modernist excess, spectacle, and hyper-consumerism. Thirdly, the emphasis on heritage also softens the image of the UAE and Arab world in the wake of 9/11, and in the face of modernity and the global mobility of people. A particular concern of the UAE federal government is people movement. Because of labour shortages, the UAE imports foreign workers to service all sectors of the economy. Consequently, non-nationals or foreigners comprise over 89 per cent of the UAE's total population, prompting fears that Emiratis are foreigners in their own country (De Bel-Air, 2018). To both protect and bolster Emirati identity, and to differentiate it from those of neighbouring countries, the UAE government guards the traditional culture, setting policies to revive, protect, and promote local heritage and a progressive nationalistic narrative (Khalaf, 2002).

As Lawson and Al-Naboodah (2008) suggest, there has been a rapid growth in cultural heritage projects since the mid-2000s which has seen a significant shift in the cultural nationalism of the UAE. Langham and Barker (2014) contend that the UAE is at a similar stage of cultural re-emergence as nineteenth century Europe which saw the revival of traditional cultures, folklore, and localised sports, and a surge in the development of museums. Falconry and camel racing, as well as folk festivals and handicrafts, have been revitalised in the UAE, and museums and heritage villages established. This cultural renaissance not only enabled the UAE to diversify its tourism base (Ursache, 2015), but also to rebrand the nation as the region's cultural capital. As Anderson (1991) states, nations are constructed imagined communities and the UAE is a notable example. The ruling elites have reconfigured the region's cultural heritage to construct a progressive nationalist narrative about the formation and evolution of the federated UAE state with its unified national identity. In doing so, they diversified the tourism market based on a unified cultural heritage. But this has come at a cost. The melding of the contemporary UAE with traditional tribal cultures has not provided the ruling elites with a buffer against modernity or global forces. Like Dubai's iconic cityscape, heritage has been modernised and thematised into 'must-see' tourist attractions, akin to Disneyfied theme parks.

Disneyfying the past

Disneyfication is a term used to define societies or cities that have assumed the character of Disney Corporation theme parks. Established in 1923, Walt Disney expanded his business from animation features to an entertainment network with a band of theme parks spread across the USA, Europe, and Asia. The success of these parks lay in their appeal to a mass tourism market through the incorporation of a diverse range of entertainment activities. The term Disneyfication was coined by Zukin (1995) to explain the influence of the Disney theme park on suburban developments, and was popularised by Bryman (1999, 2004) in *The Disneyization of Society*. Bryman (1999), Matusitz and Palermo (2014), and Wasko, Phillips, and Meehan (2001) have used the term to explain the universality of American mass culture, while Ferrell (2002) and Sorkin (1992) have employed it to exemplify the theme park characteristics of urban developments and the transformation of public spaces in US cities. Ritzer (2007) drew on the concept to analyse how nations and multinational corporations extend their global reaches and maximise their profit-making capacities by delocalising indigenous cultures and introducing a process of cultural and economic imperialism centred on mass consumption.

Abu Dhabi and Dubai exemplify Ritzer's (2007) notion of Disneyfication. They are theme park cities based on excess, abundance, and mass consumption. Tribal cultures have been delocalised, colonised, and commodified, while themed cultural heritage areas have been developed for mass tourism consumption. Abu Dhabi's Saadiyat Island, the Heart of Sharjah, and Dubai's heritage villages are prime examples of Disneyesque theme parks that have packaged the region's heritage and culture for the mass tourism market. Local heritages and cultures have been colonised and homogenised into Disneyesque entertainments or products to attract tourists. This sanitised commodification of diverse tribal cultural heritages has produced Disneyesque theme parks where manufactured Easts meet consumer-driven Wests at a cost to the region's diverse cultural heritages (Langton, 2017).

As Bryman (2004) suggests, Disneyfication involves theming, consumption, merchandising, or branding, and performative labour. He contends that theming, or the application of a narrative or an identity to a place, numbers among the most prominent aspects of Disneyfication. Narrative or identity usually exist external to a place, but shape its character and image, and add symbolism to objects consumed within that place. Theming produces unified identities or narratives that inform how symbols are to be employed (Kolb, 2008), evident in the UAE. Diverse tribal cultures and heritages have been reconstructed into a unified whole and set alongside the consumerism and hyper-modernisation of Dubai and Abu Dhabi. Traditional heritages have been stripped of their complexity and reinvented for a Westernised consumer culture to diversify the tourism market, as well as engendering a progressive nationalist narrative that reinforces the prevailing political hegemony. Designated spaces within UAE cities have been themed on a perceived past period and culture. But such perceptions are selectively framed, commencing with the precursor to the contemporary UAE federation, the Trucial States, and sanitised for the international tourist market, and to reinforce the nationalist narrative.

Abu Dhabi's Saadiyat Island is an example of a themed cultural district. It houses branches of the leading international museums, the Louvre and Guggenheim, as well as institutions celebrating the UAE's history and culture, such as the Zayed National Museum, the Performing Arts Centre and the Maritime Museum. The symbolism behind this fusion of global and local heritages reinforces the progressive nationalist narrative. The Maritime Museum details the region's pearling past, while the Louvre and Guggenheim reinforce oil-fuelled splendour and excess and the UAE's position as a leading Arab and global cultural centre. The aim as detailed on the Abu Dhabi Department of Culture and Tourism website is to present the emirate as an international cultural destination (ADDCT, 2019). Reinforcing this perception are the buildings themselves. They are art forms, designed by Western celebrity architects, and representing a Disneyesque fusion of Eastern and Western cultures. Saadiyat signals that Abu Dhabi and the UAE are global cultural centres on a par with New York, Paris, and London, and on the 'bucket lists' of culturally refined Western and Middle Eastern tourists.

With its fusion of art and culture, Saadiyat symbolises cultural equivalence between East and West. The designs of the Guggenheim and Louvre museums incorporate symbols of the UAE's heritage and identity. The Louvre museum, for example, is cast as a floating dome structure on water. The sun's rays pass through the dome's webs, symbolising sunlight passing through palm trees in a desert oasis. This visual representation of Arab culture, combined with the location of the Louvre in the Gulf, reinforces the progressive nationalist narrative, but also signifies a shift in cultural power. Western and Arab art forms and heritages share cultural equivalency on Saadiyat, but they mask the UAE's tribal diversity. The tribal heritage has been emptied of its complexity to present a themed and homogenised Arab culture that does not complicate the nationalist narrative. Heritage has been Disneyfied for Western and Arab tourist consumption and to reinforce the ruling power-elite.

But there is another side to Saadiyat. It undoubtedly holds great cultural capital, but it also generates revenue for other sectors of Abu Dhabi's economy through the commodification of both culture and heritage (Ajana, 2015). The fusion of local heritage with international high-cultural brands promotes the island and Abu Dhabi globally. But Saadiyat also houses high-end tourism resorts, property developments, and entertainment and retail centres. As the Abu Dhabi Tourism Authority boasts, Saadiyat is a world-class leisure, residential, and business centre, as well as a cultural hub, accommodating the world's largest single concentration of premier cultural assets (Visit Abu Dhabi, 2019b). Heritage and culture are part of the Saadiyat package; commodities used to promote the island and Abu Dhabi as a global cultural centre, but also as themed spaces for leisure, consumption, and spectacle in the mass tourism market. As Melotti (2014) notes, heritage sites in the UAE are used to strike a balance between modernisation, urban regeneration, and cultural conservation. The balance is achieved on Saadiyat through the melding of themed spaces and iconic structures which is intended to turn tourist stopovers into prolonged stays (Winfree, Rosentraub, & Mills, 2011; Rosentraub, 2014), thereby increasing consumer consumption while place-marketing Abu Dhabi internationally. The local heritage has been sanitised and commodified to brand Abu Dhabi, serve the tourism market, and enhance consumption.

Though more traditionally based, Heart of Sharjah provides another example of a Disneyfied heritage district sanitised for tourist consumption. As the name signifies, the district with its Islamic-Arabic roots, is the traditional cultural core of Sharjah and its identity. However, Heart is merely another themed heritage space that is still very much under construction. According to Heart's web page, when completed the district will reflect Sharjah's history and heritage (Heart of Sharjah, 2019). Indeed, it is the largest historical preservation and restoration project in the region. A recent visit to Heart revealed that the project involves the restoration of historical buildings and the construction of new 'traditional' structures, fashioned in Islamic style to promote Islamic-Arab identity. In contrast to the modernist excess and spectacle of neighbouring Dubai, Heart celebrates its Islamic heritage.

Unlike liberal Dubai, Sharjah adheres to the stricter and more conservative Saudi Wahhabism. Sharjah's ruler, Sheikh Sultan, has decreed that all of the sheikhdom's official edifices will be built in an Islamic style. Khalaf (2006) argues that by incorporating symbols from the emirate's heritage, Sharjah is seeking to preserve its culture in the face of both globalisation and modernisation. Radoine (2013), however, contends that Heart's Islamic featurism is extravagant and eclectic, and themed on the UAE's abundance and excess mantra. Rather than reinforcing Sharjah's Arabic heritage, the designs are intended to attract international visitors, and promote the Emirate as *the* UAE cultural and heritage destination. Heart's cultural heritage and symbolism constitutes little more than a modernist interpretation of a new traditionalism that attempts to reinvent the district as representative of an authentic Islamic-Arab identity. Heart is essentially a themed heritage space, fashioned on a perceived Islamic past. Heritage is being employed to rebrand Sharjah as the UAE's cultural capital in opposition to Abu Dhabi. The result is a Disneyfied heritage space in which Islamic symbolism melds with traditional handicrafts, cuisine, and entertainments to theme Sharjah as the 'real' UAE for both the Arab and Western tourist markets.

Sharjah's success has not been lost on neighbouring Dubai. To counter the drift of heritage tourists to Sharjah, Sheikh Mohammed Al Maktoum, Dubai's ruler, approved plans in 2015 to develop what is left of his city's historic district into the leading cultural and heritage centre in the region (Gulf News, 2015). As with Sharjah and Abu Dhabi, Dubai recognises the importance of the heritage tourism market. For a city that has destroyed many of its old quarters, and markets itself on modernist excess, heritage is being Disneyfied to suit the city's established tourism market. Situated on Dubai Creek, Old Dubai is little more than a themed Disneyfied consumer space that sits uneasily alongside the architectural excess and hyperconsumerism of the contemporary city.

Al Ain is another heritage city with Disney-like appeal. Situated in the eastern region of Abu Dhabi, the city has rich heritage credentials. Archaeologists have uncovered evidence of human settlement dating from the Bronze Age. The 'digs' were included on UNESCO's World Heritage List in June 2011. There is no doubting the historical significance of these sites. However, like other UAE heritage sites, Al Ain has been commercialised, commodified, and branded. The Al Ain web page 'invites [tourists] … to journey into the past and experience traditional UAE life' (Visit Abu Dhabi, 2019a). Like Disney's theme parks, Al Ain offers a diverse range of activities and entertainments, all with an emphasis on capturing the traditional UAE experience. They include camel racing and falconry, a local market selling handicrafts, and cafés serving traditional cuisine, as well as two theatres featuring folk entertainments. These activities overshadow the authenticity of the archaeological 'digs' and their Bronze Age artefacts. They do not fit snugly into the UAE's contemporary progressive nationalist narrative. The narrative is a more recent invention than the Bronze Age relics, encompassing the transformation of a pearling backwater into an oil-rich, global aviation, tourism, and cultural centre. Theme park Al-Ain reinforces this narrative which is disseminated nationally and internationally through the tourism market. Tourism is a business and heritage is an important selling point. Therefore, more authentic heritage places such as Al Ain have been sanitised and repackaged to engender the nationalist narrative and bolster Western tourist consumption.

There is a performative aspect in the presentation of Al Ain and other UAE heritage sites which reinforce their Disneyesque appeal. As Bryman (2004) notes, Disneyfication encompasses the theming of physical space and human activities. Performance, role playing, and even sporting activities are important parts of the Disneyfication process. Traditional sports, such as camel racing and falconry, are expressions of indigenous cultures and performative acts. Falconry is very much part of the region's cultural heritage, with the falcon being the UAE's national symbol. Camel racing, too, is synonymous with the region's heritage, though it has had a troubled recent past with the exploitation and abuse of child jockeys. Both sports are performative acts. Khalaf (2002, p. 249) sees camel racing as 'a large stage upon which culture is played out, reconstituted and invested'. The reconstitution of culture is evident in the impact of tourism on the sport. The local authorities promote camel racing as a 'must-see' tourist attraction (Melotti, 2014). The sport is no longer purely an expression of the UAE's cultural heritage or identity, but also a performative activity for tourists' consumption. Consequently, a significant heritage activity has been partly sanitised, colonised, and commodified. Wakefield (2012) contends that commodification either destroys the cultural meaning of the sport, or results in the emergence of new meanings that are presented as authentic heritage. Tourism's impact has reconstituted these sports as performative acts for both Western and local consumption. Once sports become performative and part of the tourist experience, however, they lose their traditional cultural meanings and must be reconfigured to meet the demands of a more diverse consumer base.

A similar scenario is being acted out in the hospitality sector of heritage areas. Bryman (2004) argues that there is a growing trend in the service sector for labour to morph into theatre-like performances. Workspaces become quasi-theatres where workers act out roles in costumes. This is evident in Sharjah's Heart district where waiters in restaurants dress in national costumes – head-cloths for men and long thobes for women.

In wearing symbols of the UAE's national heritage, the costumes are part of a performative act meant to add authenticity to the tourist experience. In actuality, both the costumes and acts are Disneyfied constructs, modelled on similar heritage re-creations found in Disney theme parks. They are not authentic representations of the past, but reinventions designed to reaffirm Western preconceptions of the Arab world and promote consumption through a staged, tourist-packaged and mock-authentic performative act.

Ritzer (2007) suggests that Disney theme parks are 'cathedrals of consumption'. The same could be said of the heritage-themed spaces of Abu Dhabi, Dubai, Sharjah, and Al Ain. They contain themed urban spaces in which consumption and entertainment options are confined within designated areas (Rosentraub, 2014; Winfree et al., 2011), all controlled by tourism or cultural authorities, and under the overall authority of the UAE's ruling families. Consequently, theming and consumption are tightly controlled by the ruling power-elite and are used to disseminate the nationalist narrative locally and globally.

This is evident in the luxury hotel accommodation market. A major factor in the region's tourism development was transforming stopovers into prolonged stays. As Matusitz and Palermo (2014, p. 98) contend, 'the more needs are fulfilled, the longer people will stay'. A contributing factor in meeting the tourists' needs was substantial investment in tourism infrastructure, especially at the luxury end of the accommodation market. Financed from oil revenues, luxury hotels were constructed in themed districts, such as Saadiyat and Dubai's Jumeirah. Traditional Islamic laws were waived to lure high-end Western tourists. No expense was spared as Dubai, in particular, transformed its cityscape with globally iconic structures, one of the most notable being the self-proclaimed 'seven-star' Burg Al-Arab Hotel. Situated off-shore, the dhow-shaped Al-Arab stands as a symbol of both Arab excess and success, while reinforcing the progressive nationalist narrative. Maritime symbolism has been used to emphasise Dubai's transformation into a modern, luxurious global city.

As Melotti (2014) contends, cultural heritage plays an important role in theming hotels and resorts. The use of heritage images and symbols in luxury hotels has mushroomed throughout the UAE. Representations are more reflective of a pan-Arab potpourri than the individual tribal heritages of specific UAE emirates. The luxury Al Bait Sharjah Hotel in the Heart of Sharjah merges Gulf Arab, Moroccan, and Egyptian architecture and designs in its interior. Dubai's One & Only Royal Mirage and Abu Dhabi's Emirates Palace are more specifically styled as Arab palaces, though the overall effect is the stylisation of heritage to meet the expectations of the luxury tourism market. As Steiner (2010) asserts, the use of fantasy images in hotels is an attempt to exploit the exotic and orientalist perceptions that have hindered Western understanding of the Arab World. Melotti (2014) agrees, stating that themed Arabian architecture conjures a by-gone 'Grand Tour' atmosphere for tourists' consumption. Heritage is themed to remove tourists from the realities of daily Emirates' life and to mask authentic local cultures. The tourist 'authentic' exists as a Disneyfied, pan-Arab potpourri, or luxury orientalist fantasy, conjured for Western consumption.

Conclusion – relocating a lost past

The Heart of Sharjah's Al Shanasiyah and Dubai's Shindagha *souks* offer glimpses of an alternative, more fluid heritage. A walk through the *souks* reveals Persian rugs, Kashmiri pashmina, spices, and arts and crafts which are not indigenous to the UAE. What passes for locally produced Emirati goods are more reflective of items that have been traditionally traded across the Middle East and South Asia for centuries (Picton, 2010). The Gulf and Trucial States were part of a broad regional trading network that offers a more complex glimpse of an alternative heritage based on trade, people mobility, and intercultural exchanges.

The 1971 federation of seven disparate emirates to form the UAE necessitated that their heritages be reconstructed and homogenised to bolster nationalism. The diversification of the economy away from its dependence on oil heralded the reinvention of Dubai and Abu Dhabi as modern global aviation, tourism, and consumer consumption hubs. In Dubai, especially, the old city was cleared for the construction of an iconic and modern cityscape, though Sharjah and the more traditionally conservative emirates protected their pasts. The rediscovery of heritage after 9/11 coincided with the growth of intra-Arab tourism. But the UAE's heritage was now problematic, structured to support a nationalist narrative and 'cash in' on growing intra-Arab and Western tourist markets. The result has seen the rise of Disneyfied heritage parks and districts, constructed to reaffirm Western tourists' orientalist fantasies of the Arab world. Though these themed areas contrast with Dubai's modern cityscape, they share a progressive nationalist narrative about the transformation of one-time pearling backwaters into global cities that now rival Paris, New York, and London. But this is only one of the region's narratives. Another is found in the stalls of the *souks* and beyond Dubai and Abu Dhabi's Disneyfied heritage and cultural theme parks. This heritage is based on trade, people movement, and cultural exchange, and is far more reflective of the region's past, the UAE's present, and the contemporary globalised world.

References

Abu Dhabi Department of Culture and Tourism (ADDCT). (2019). *Who we are*. Retrieved from https://tcaabudhabi.ae/en/who.we.are/the.authority.in.a.glance.aspx.
Ajana, B. (2015). Branding legitimation and the power of museums: The case of the Louvre Abu Dhabi. *Museum & Society*, *13*(3), 316–335.
Anderson, B. (1991). *Imagined communities*. London: Verso.
Bryman, A. (1999). The Disneyization of society. *The Sociological Review*, *47*(1), 25–47.
Bryman, A. (2004). *The Disneyization of society*. London: Sage.
Chhabra, D. (2001). *Heritage tourism: An analysis of perceived authenticity and economic impact of the Scottish Highland Games in North Carolina* (unpublished doctoral dissertation). North Carolina State University.
Dubai's Culture and Arts Authority (DCAA). (2019). *Home page*. Retrieved from https://dubaiculture.gov.ae/en/Pages/default.aspx.
De Bel-Air, F. (2018). *Demography, migration, and the labour market in the UAE* [pdf]. Retrieved from http://cadmus.eui.eu/bitstream/handle/1814/36375/GLMM_ExpNote_07_2015.pdf.
Durmaz, B., Platt, S., & Yigitcanlar, T. (2010). Creativity, culture tourism and place-making: Istanbul and London Film Industries. *International Journal of Culture, Tourism and Hospitality Research*, *4*(3), 198–213.
Ferrell, J. (2002). *Tearing down the streets: Adventures in urban anarchy*. New York: Hill and Wang.
Gulf News (2015). *Shindagha, Bur Dubai, Deira and Al Fahidi to get a facelift*, 3 February. Retrieved from https://gulfnews.com/uae/shindagha-bur-dubai-deira-and-al-fahidi-to-get-a-facelift-1.1451044.
Heart of Sharjah (2019). *Welcome to the heart of Sharjah*. Retrieved from https://www.heartofsharjah.ae/.

International Council of Monuments and Sites (ICOMOS) (1964). *International charter for the conservation and restoration of monuments and sites (The Venice Charter 1964)* [pdf]. Retrieved from https://www.icomos.org/charters/venice_e.pdf.

Jugmohan, S., Spencer, J. P., & Steyn, J. N. (2016). Local natural and cultural heritage assets and community based tourism: Challenges and opportunities. *African Journal of Physical and Health Sciences, 22*(12), 306–317.

Khalaf, S. (2002). Globalisation and heritage revival in the gulf: An anthropological look at Dubai Heritage Village. *Journal of Social Affairs, 18*(75), 13–42.

Khalaf, S. (2006). The evolution of the Gulf city type, oil and globalization. In J. Fox, N. Sabbah, & M. al-Mutawa (eds), *Globalization and the Gulf*, (pp. 244–265). Oxford: Routledge.

Kolb, D. (2008) *Sprawling places*. Atlanta: University of Georgia Press.

Langham, E., & Barker, D. (2014). Spectacle and participation: A new heritage model from the UAE. In K. Excell & T. Rico (eds), *Cultural heritage in the Arabian Peninsula: Debates, discourses and practices* (pp. 85–98). Surrey: Ashgate Publishing.

Langton, J. (2017). Louvre Abu Dhabi: Museum where 'East meets West' opens to the world. *The National*, 8 November. Retrieved from https://www.thenational.ae/uae/louvre-abu-dhabi-museum-where-east-meets-west-opens-to-the-world-1.674207.

Lawson, F., & Al-Naboodah, H. (2008). Heritage and cultural nationalism in the United Arab Emirates. In A. Alsharekh & R. Spingborg (eds), *Popular culture and political identity in the Arab Gulf States* (pp. 15–31). London: Saqi Books.

Matusitz, J., & Palermo, L. (2014). The Disneyfication of the world: A grobalisation perspective. *Journal of Organisation Transformation & Social Change, 11*(2), 91–107.

Melotti, M. (2014). Heritage and tourism. Global society and shifting values in the United Arab Emirates. *Middle East Topics & Arguments, 3*, 71–91.

Picton, O. J. (2010). Usage of the concept of culture and heritage in the United Arab Emirates – an analysis of Sharjah heritage area. *Journal of Heritage Tourism, 5*(1), 69–84.

Radoine, H. (2013). Cultural resilience in contemporary urbanism: The Case of Sharjah, UAE. *International Development Planning Review, 35*(3), 241–260.

Ritzer, G. (2007). *The globalization of nothing 2*. Thousand Oaks, CA: Pine Forge Press.

Rosentraub, M. S. (2014). *Reversing urban decline: Why and how sports, entertainment, and culture turn cities into major league winners*. Boca Raton, FL: CRC Press.

Sharpley, R. (2009) *Tourism development and the environment: Beyond sustainability?* London: Earthscan.

Silver, I. (1993). Marketing authenticity in third world countries. *Annals of Tourism Research, 20*(2), 302–318.

Sorkin, M. (1992). *Variations on a theme park: The New American city and the end of public space*. New York: Macmillan.

Steiner, C. (2010). From heritage to hyper-reality? Tourism destination development in the Middle East between Petra and the Palm. *Journal of Tourism and Cultural Change, 8*(4), 240–253.

The First Group LLC (2019). *Dubai unveils latest cultural tourism attraction*, 13 April. Retrieved from https://www.thefirstgroup.com/en/news/2019/4/dubai-unveils-latest-cultural-tourism-attraction/.

The Government of Abu Dhabi (2019). *The Abu Dhabi economic vision 2030*. Abu Dhabi: General Secretariat of the Executive Council, Department of Planning and Economy, Abu Dhabi Council for Economic Development [pdf]. Retrieved from https://www.ecouncil.ae/PublicationsEn/economic-vision-2030-full-versionEn.pdf.
Timothy, D. J., & Nyaupane, G. P. (2009). *Cultural heritage and tourism in the developing world: A regional perspective*. New York: Routledge.
UNWTO. (2018). *UNWTO tourism highlights 2018 edition*. Retrieved from https://www.e-unwto.org/doi/pdf/10.18111/9789284419876.
UNWTO. (2019). *UNWTO world tourism barometer, Volume 17, Issue 1, January 2019, EXCERPT* [pdf]. Retrieved from http://cf.cdn.unwto.org/sites/all/files/pdf/unwto_barom19_01_january_excerpt.pdf.
Ursache, M. (2015). Tourism – significant driver shaping a destination heritage. *Procedia – Social and Behavioural Sciences, 188*, 130–137.
Visit Abu Dhabi (2019a). *Heritage theme park*. Retrieved from https://visitabudhabi.ae/en/see.and.do/attractions.and.landmarks/cultural.attractions/heritage.theme.park.aspx.
Visit Abu Dhabi (2019b). *Saadiyat Island*. Retrieved from https://visitabudhabi.ae/en/explore/islands/saadiyat.island.aspx.
Wakefield, S. (2012). Falconry as heritage in the United Arab Emirates. *World Archaeology, 44*(2), 280–290.
Wasko, J., Phillips, M., & Meehan, E. R. (eds). (2001). *Dazzled by Disney? The global Disney audiences project*. London: Leicester University Press.
Winfree, J. A., Rosentraub, M. S., & Mills M. B. (2011). *Sports finance and management: Real estate, entertainment, and the remaking of the business*. Boca Raton, FL: CRC Press.
World Economic Forum. (2017). *The travel & tourism competitiveness report 2017* [pdf]. Retrieved from http://www.sela.org/media/2756841/the-travel-and-tourism-compettiveness-report-2017.pdf.
Zukin, S. (1995). *The cultures of cities*. Oxford: Blackwell.

11 Integrated cultural heritage planning in Egypt
A catalyst for tourism after the Arab Spring?

Eman M. Helmy

Introduction

Egypt has a remarkably distinctive number of heritage sites that are scattered in different regions across the country and which reflect the various civilisations and eras of its over 4,000-year history (Osman, 2018). Such rich cultural heritage had left numerous monumental artefacts and remains, many of which have not been excavated, in addition to the renowned World Heritage Sites. Such heritage has long been at the forefront of tourism in Egypt. Thomas Cook organised his remarkable trip to the Egyptian archaeological sites in 1869, paving the way for cultural tourism in Egypt where culture, heritage, and crafts are key attractions for visitors (Helmy, 2014). Almost one century later, Egypt has realised the interrelationship between heritage and tourism as collaborative industries, with heritage converting locations into destinations and tourism making them economically viable, and managed to position its heritage sites as leading cultural tourism destinations in the world (Smith, 2003; Cassel & Pashkevich, 2014; Mbaiwa, 2011). Although Egypt had managed to develop internationally popular recreational destinations in the Red Sea and Sinai by the 1980s, such as Hurghada and Sham El-sheikh, the Egyptian tourism sector is still uniquely dependent on cultural heritage (Helmy, 2014).

By the first decade of the third millennium, the Egyptian cultural heritage sector came to realise the crucial importance of having a comprehensive vision for cultural heritage tourism management. Such consciousness coincided with the increased inclusion of sustainable development practices within cultural heritage management and conservation (Barre, 2002; Ozer Sari & Nazli, 2018). Accordingly, the Egyptian Supreme Council of Antiquities has begun to think and act more broadly than the frame of its traditional tasks of monument excavation and restoration to consider other management, conservation, and sustainable development actions. For example, at the site level some management techniques had to be implemented and actions taken regarding issues such as site carrying capacity, visitor management in general, and visitor centres in particular, evaluating admission fee mechanisms, tourist facilities and amenities, marketing programmes to augment site revenues, the integration of technology and digitalisation into heritage resources, managing community engagement, making operations more environmentally friendly, and outreach programmes. The need to develop management and conservation capacities, modest articulation and liaison with relevant authorities, and limited funds are also among the challenges facing cultural heritage management planning.

However, the adverse impacts of the 2011 Arab Spring revolution on the Egyptian tourism sector in general and on tangible cultural heritage in particular were dramatic, as the number of international tourists dropped to 9.4 million from over 14 million the previous year. The economic impacts were also substantial, with a decrease in tourist receipts from US $12.5 billion in 2010 to US $8.7 billion in 2011 (UNWTO, 2012). Heritage sites and museums suffered incidents of violence, looting, and vandalism which were evident in all Arab nations that experienced the Arab Spring across the Middle East and North Africa (MENA) region (Parcak, 2017). The turmoil lasted for almost four years in Egypt, with the impact on international tourism reaching its nadir in 2016 when number of international tourists in 2016 fell to 5.3 million and only US $2.6 billion in tourism receipts were recorded (UNWTO, 2017). The collapse in tourist numbers and income also affected the revenues obtained by the Antiquities Authority from tourism and site entrance fees, which consequently negatively impacted its budget and led to the suspension of most of the conservation projects. On the positive side, however, the crisis revealed shortcomings in the cultural heritage management system, such as inefficient security systems for museums and sites and lack of comprehensive documentation for the monumental artefacts.

As Egypt is currently witnessing a shift in its economic reform and community development programs, it is targeting the transformation of many sectors which can lead to a diversification of its economic revenues and improved socio-cultural sustainability. Such vision has recently influenced the cultural heritage conservation and management sector, resulting in an active movement towards the integration of sustainability into operational schemes and the inauguration of a distinctive set of cultural heritage tourism projects.

This chapter focuses on elements of the value chain as a means to trace changes which the Egyptian cultural heritage tourism sector has experienced before, during, and after the 2011 revolution. It diagnoses the weaknesses in the cultural heritage management mechanism before 2011, indicates the deterioration of heritage sites and the adverse impacts that occurred during the turmoil, and discusses the ongoing evolution in cultural heritage sustainability. The chapter concludes by noting the mega integrated planning project of developing a tourist capital for Egypt that will take place in the west of Greater Cairo, relying on the Grand Egyptian Museum (GEM) which will be inaugurated in 2020, the rejuvenation of the Pyramids region, and the construction of Sphinx International Airport.

Cultural heritage tourism in Egypt in the face of value chain analysis

Value chain analysis seeks to identify the key activities that are required to craft a competent and competitive cultural heritage tourism sector and their adequacy and effectiveness (Song, Liu, & Chen, 2013). Ten determinants of the performance of the Egyptian cultural heritage tourism sector are identified and discussed below: governance and stewardship; a comprehensive integrated planning approach; enforcing a strict regulatory framework for heritage region land use; site management programmes; local community engagement; adequate conservation budgets; artefact recording and documentation; proactive strategies to combat looting; cultural heritage tourism marketing; and visitor management, education, and satisfaction programmes.

Governance and stewardship

In 1994, the Supreme Council of Antiquities was established under the umbrella of the Ministry of Culture to set policies and implement programmes for antiquities conservation and restoration as well as museum management. More recently, after the 2011 revolution, a fully fledged Ministry of State for Antiquities was established and later upgraded to Ministry of Antiquities in 2015. The Ministry of Antiquities along with its Supreme Council of Antiquities have launched national mega projects such as the Grand Egyptian Museum to be inaugurated in 2020 and the renovations at the Pyramids region. The major projects have been developed in conjunction with a remarkable increase in the number of excavations, increased collaborative work with foreign financing and technical teams at different archaeological sites, and a growing number of inaugurated museums. Yet the task of sustainably managing cultural heritage tourism sites calls for the collaboration and involvement of other officials as well as non-governmental stakeholders such as the Ministry of Tourism, local authorities of each governorate, the Ministry of Interior Affairs, local community lobbies, media entities, and technology and tourism amenity investors. Although the Antiquities Authority has become fully aware of the importance of such collaboration and is seeking strong ties with the relevant parties, the collaborative approach has yet to be shifted smoothly from the decision-making level to the lower implementation teams.

Comprehensive integrated planning approach

Most of the heritage sites are located in the core of the Egyptian cities in Upper Egypt and the Delta and are surrounded by crowded residential areas, agricultural lands and industrial zones. Arguably, the planning of the heritage site cannot be approached without a comprehensive integrated planning process which considers the region's infrastructure, superstructure, local community, economic activities, and local crafts, among other factors. For example, Abu Mena is a World Heritage Site inscribed in the UNESCO list in 1979 that was added in 2001 to the World Heritage in Danger List. The site has suffered severe subsidence in recent years as a result of ill-conceived agricultural irrigation projects nearby. The site is currently closed to the public while remedial restoration work is carried out (UNESCO, 2019; African World Heritage, 2018).

A 'Cultural Heritage Integrated Management Plan' (CHIMP) is an innovative instrument to effectively manage the sustainable safeguarding and development of historic urban areas and their cultural heritage to attractive, competitive, and multifunctional places. It balances and coordinates the cultural heritage needs with the needs of the (manifold) 'users' of the historic urban area and the responsible governmental bodies (demands of and towards the historic urban area and its cultural heritage). Thus, a cultural heritage integrated management plan determines and establishes the appropriate strategy, objectives, actions, and management structures to safeguard the cultural heritage, to balance the different needs, and to use historic urban areas and their cultural heritage as development assets (Scheffler, Ripp, & Buhler, 2010, p. 4).

Remarkably, the comprehensive development plan that took place in Luxor during the first decade of the third millennium was a good initiative towards integrated planning. The plan was based on a vision of transforming the east bank of Luxor into an open-air museum as a means to regenerate the city. The integrative broad vision entailed the execution of a set of site restoration projects that combined tourism-specific development with urban developments. For example, the restoration of the ancient avenue of the Sphinxes, focusing on Kebash Road, that links the Luxor and Karnak temples, was seen as a major contributing component to the open-air museum to improve the visitors' experience (Kamar, 2014). The establishment of Luxor visitor centre was also part of the cultural tourism plan to offer an improved experience to visitors. As part of the urban development plans, the projects sought to tackle multiple issues such as the expansion of informal urban settlements in heritage areas, the development of a new community in the New Luxor region, the development of the destination resort of El-Toad, the provision of infrastructure services for New Luxor and El-Toad, and the establishment of high-value agriculture (Kamar, 2014). In the West Bank, the revitalisation of a project relocating residents of old Gourna village who lived amid the Theban Necropolis and above the ancient tombs sought to achieve two objectives. The first was to combat the theft of artefacts from the heritage area and the second was to offer appropriate housing conditions to local communities in order to have better access to education, infrastructure, and economic development opportunities (World Monuments Fund (WMF), 2011). To respond to the challenges that faced the project, the World Monuments Fund undertook a study in 2010, in collaboration with UNESCO and the Luxor Governorate, to understand the relationship between the people and place of New Gourna. The study emphasised the crucially important role of sustainable development in local community engagement and participation in the development programmes, local architecture conservation, and social empowerment (WMF, 2011).

While the above-mentioned comprehensive plan was supposed to offer social, economic, and environmental benefits to Luxor and its local communities, the impacts of the revolution that broke out by early 2011 and the unstable political and security circumstances that lasted for almost four years after undermined the outcomes of the projects. In addition, the execution phases of certain projects ceased or were delayed, such as Kebash road linking the Luxor and Karnak temples. The consequences of the political instability on tourist arrivals badly affected Luxor's economy which depends primarily on tourism and put substantial pressures on Luxor's communities for which tourism is the main source of income.

Enforcing a strict regulatory framework for heritage region land use

Practical actions to implement land use law to combat the expansion of unplanned residential areas to the heritage site zones are regarded as an important part of integrated planning. In February 2014, the leader of the National Organization for Urban Harmony, Samir Gharib, said, 'since 2011, we have been living in the time of the great downfall of Egyptian urbanization' (quoted in Osman, 2018, p. 2908). However, Egypt's cultural heritage regions have been in decline some time from before 2011, with the revolution only exacerbating prior issues. For example, Hawas (1998) raised the issue of the growth of adjacent urban villages as one of the challenges facing the conservation plan in the Giza Plateau where the Great Pyramids stand. Undoubtedly, massive population growth in the areas where the archaeological sites exist has only intensified the pressure. For instance, some archaeological sites such as old historic houses and Islamic mosques are located in the heart of residential areas where it is hard to surround such sites with a buffer zone to protect them (Al-Sadaty, 2018). Nazlat El-Semman and Abu Rawash villages in Giza are another two cases exemplifying the threats that result when unplanned residential areas are neighbouring heritage sites.

As the relocation of such overpopulated villages seems to be difficult at present, the development of awareness programmes for enhancing residents' consciousness, fostering respect for national heritage, and helping inhabitants to understand the sustainable development programmes for heritage sites should be undertaken. This will help improve public recognition and understanding and encourage local people to contribute to site preservation rather than damaging it (Fushiya, 2010). This approach is crucial to any sustainable development plan in the cultural heritage regions. The implementation of this scheme in practice might need the collaboration of some other stakeholders with the archaeological authority, such as local authorities, sociologists, media, and political lobbies.

Site management programmes

Site management seeks to explore the ways in which various values of archaeological sites can be successfully preserved or maximised, and to reduce any damage to a site's integrity. Such plans should include consideration of the appropriate level of visitor access and tourism at the site. The site management should include three dimensions: conservation and site plan, land use plans that entails drawing boundary lines and buffer zones, and a community engagement plan. As far as tourism is concerned, it also has to look at a broader set of activities such as transportation to and from the site and at the site; the range of guest services available, including visitor centres; site tours, interpretation, and travel information and signposting; admission tickets; visitor walkways; and sales outlets and souvenirs (Pedersen, 2002).

Until recently, excavation, restoration, and preservation activities were the top priorities of Egyptian archaeological conservation plans. However, the Ministry of Antiquities has become increasingly aware of the benefits of integrating site management and visitor management techniques into their plans. This has clearly been reflected in the installation of the newly inaugurated museums such as the National Museum of Egyptian Civilization in Fustat/Cairo. In some cases, the Archaeological Authority had to rejuvenate museums partially destroyed during the period of unrest (2011–2014) and restore vandalised artefacts such as in the cases of the Malawi Museum in Al-Minya and the Cairo Museum of Islamic Art. The Archaeological Authority captured the opportunity of renovating the museums to deliver an educational message through new exhibition halls as well as installation of a competent security system.

Arguably, site conservation prepared by professional experts with a broad knowledge of site management techniques is able to offer added value to site sustainability and revenues, local community, and destination image. This is particularly the case given that most of the archaeological sites in Egypt still face threats resulting from various causes such as excessive tourism, looting, lack of conservation and management programmes, illegal land use, and expansion of farmland, industrial, and residential areas (Fushiya, 2010). Nevertheless, the task of site and visitor management calls for collaborative efforts between archaeologists, site managers, tourism planners and marketers, technology specialists, local community representatives, and the concerned local authority as well as private sector identities.

Local community engagement

Sustainable heritage planning can only be achieved if developed with the acceptance and participation of local communities and, in the African context, traditional rulers (e.g. tribal leaders) (Fredholm, 2016; Mina, Kalliopi, & Nikolaos, 2018). Arguably, local people in Egypt, in many cases, lack the knowledge of the direct and indirect destructive impacts of their activities in the sites. Accordingly, within the context of sustainable heritage site planning in Egypt, local community engagement issues entail a set of actions that starts with raising public awareness, setting communication networks, and opening dialogues to enable community support and involvement.

Effective capacity building and communication programmes are crucial to empowering local communities and their engagement in sustainable heritage site planning and underpin their active role in project implementation. It should also foster appreciation among local community and help gain their support for the different phases of heritage site planning schemes (Mbaiwa, 2011; Destination BC Corp, 2014). However, in augmenting socioeconomic benefits and improving rural livelihoods, the capacity building programmes struggle to sustain the engagement of personnel from the local community in tourism services and amenities in the heritage tourism areas, i.e. attracting and retaining a mix of economic activities that meet the needs of the local community and visitors (shops, jobs, housing, culture) and respecting the character of the heritage location (Scheffler et al., 2010).

In the same vein, craftsmanship is one tool for local economic development and for generating income to local communities. 'Creative Egypt' is an Industrial Modernisation Centre (IMC)/Ministry of Trade and Industry initiative, established in 2015 as the first integrated cultural hub to enable local craftspeople and artisans to market and sell their products locally as well as globally. In this context, it aims at promoting Egypt's heritage and achieving sustainable development for Egyptian artisans (IMC, 2016).

Conservation budgets

One of the challenges facing the Antiquities Authority is the inadequate funds available to carry out the required conservation and restoration plans. Financial restrictions also affect excavation projects and limit the implementation of sustainable resource and visitor management techniques to rejuvenate the image of the sites to appeal to visitors. Arguably, the delayed action towards conservation and restoration projects may increase the cost of addressing problems (Osman, 2018). The Ministry of Antiquities is mostly a self-financed authority which relies on the revenues of tourist visits to archaeological sites. Although the antiquities income has been insufficient for so many decades, the revenues dropped extensively after the 2011 revolution due to the decline in tourist visits. According to the Minister of Antiquities, in 2010 the Ministry made 1.3 billion Egyptian pounds while in 2015 income was down to 275 million Egyptian pounds and less than 100 million pounds in 2016 (Elkhatib & Aboulenein, 2016; Al-Shuwekhi, 2017).

International aid and loans to undertake heritage projects have been used in Egypt since UNESCO's landmark project of rescuing Nubian monuments and sites affected by the Aswan High Dam in the 1960s–1970s. Nevertheless, heritage excavation, restoration, and conservation require significant financial resources and the willingness of Egyptian political decision-makers to invest in cultural heritage as an instrument of economic rejuvenation has led government to directly fund a range of heritage projects from the state budget. Such financial support has enabled the Authority of Antiquities to resume a number of projects that were suspended for decades. For example, Sohag's National Museum was inaugurated in 2018 after 25 years' delay and the Pyramid of Pharaoh Unas as well as three ancient tombs in Saqqara were reopened in 2016. The Pyramid Complex had been closed since 1998 for fear of overcrowding and high humidity levels that affected its burial chamber (Elkhatib & Aboulenein, 2016; Tawfeek, 2018).

Egypt is also planning to construct its first antique reproduction factory, with a budget estimated at one million Egyptian pounds, in order to cover products to be sold locally and internationally with the Supreme Council of Antiquities' stamp (Tawfeek, 2018). However, the Grand Egyptian Museum (GEM) mega project received the largest amount of public financial support in addition to the foreign loans it has received from partnering countries such as Japan.

Artefact recording and documentation

'Recording is the capture of information which describes the physical configuration, condition and use of monuments, groups of buildings and sites, at points in time, and it is an essential part of the conservation process' (International Council on Monuments and Sites (ICOMOS), 1996, p. 49). New technological advancements in both hardware and software have created new recording techniques, tools, and approaches (Georgiadis, Patias, & Tsioukas, 2016). According to the Minister of Antiquities, the issue of artefact recording and documentation in Egypt is challenging as artefacts are currently registered but many of them have not yet been documented (El-Aref, 2016). The lack of a professional recording and documentation process for the Egyptian monuments and the urgent need to develop a centralised database system for antiquities are another burden added to the responsibilities of the Antiquities Authority. The issue is challenging due to the abundance of artefacts and monuments to be documented on one hand and the shortage in experienced staff to carry out such a process professionally. Consequently, problems in documentation have undermined the efforts of Egypt retrieving artefacts that were smuggled or patriated to other countries (El-Aref, 2016). The issue has become intensified as the Ministry of Antiquities Recovery and Repatriation Unit investigates many cases each year but does not have potential site provenience data for the thousands of recovered objects in their database from seizures in Egypt or abroad (Parcak, 2017).

Integrative planning, however, implies collaboration between the Ministry of Antiquities and the Centre for Documentation of Cultural and Natural Heritage (CULTNAT) which is one of the research centres of Bibliotheca Alexandrina, stationed in Cairo and supported by the Ministry of Communication and Information Technology. 'The Centre aims to apply the latest technological innovations in documentation and dissemination of Egypt's cultural heritage, tangible and intangible' (CULTNAT, 2019). In this respect, CULTNAT can extend its support in two ways: to carry out the project of the 3D scanning of the archaeological collection and to help build capacity at the Ministry of Antiquities with regard to the digital documentation of monuments.

Proactive strategy to combat looting

For hundreds of years, illegal quarrying and encroachment on monuments have been persistent challenges confronting the sustainability of Egypt's cultural heritage. However, the political upheaval of 2011 resulted in a remarkable increase in antiquities crime. 'This significant increase in looting has been attributed to both the economic downturn and the weak security with regards to guarding the nation's exhibition halls and archaeological sites' (Osman, 2018, p. 2908). The most referred to incident is the looting of the Malawi Museum in Minya, at the beginning of August 2013, when looters broke into the museum and took more than a thousand artefacts (Parcak, 2017). The illegal and unplanned expansion of residential settlements next to heritage sites such as in Nazlat El-Semman, Abu Rawash, Dashur, and Lisht, also gave access to illegal digging and excavation. For example, in the Dahshur and Lisht regions, illegal quarrying increased by 29.7 per cent between 2002 and 2013, and escalated dramatically following the 2011 unrest with hundreds of tombs being partially destroyed (Parcak, 2017). According to the Minister of Antiquities, in July 2016 alone, in collaboration with the Tourism and Antiquities Police and the Giza Governorate, the Ministry succeeded in removing 23 encroachments on archaeological sites in Dahshur (El-Aref, 2016).

Arguably, the looting issue calls for a proactive strategy that tackles all gaps that lead to encroachments on archaeological sites and empowers the Ministry of Antiquities Recovery and Repatriation Unit to track and retrieve stolen artefacts. To respond to the need of such a strategy, in 2016 the Minister of Antiquities took the initiative of reconvening the meetings of the National Committee for the Repatriation of Stolen and Smuggled Antiquities (NCRSSA) that had been suspended after 2010 (El-Aref, 2016). More recently, the Ministry of Antiquities has been working closely with the Ministry of Interior Affairs as well as local authorities to confront the crimes of illegal excavation and looting and to capture smuggled objects at the airports. The Ministry of Foreign Affairs has also supported the Ministry of Antiquities in repatriating artefacts from abroad.

While the upgrade of the security systems is part of a proactive strategy to safeguard heritage sites, museums, and the Ministry of Antiquities stores where the un-exhibited artefacts are kept in each region, a dialogue with local communities to raise awareness is also needed to complement the technological developments. However, outreach programmes are easy to recommend but hard to implement in practice, especially in communities that still struggle with problems of illiteracy, poverty, and over-population.

Cultural heritage tourism marketing

Integrated planning implies the implementation of more efficient marketing campaigns for Egyptian cultural heritage tourism to be developed and carried out collaboratively between the Ministry of Antiquities and Ministry of Tourism. In order to better connect heritage sites to market demands, ICT should be incorporated into marketing campaigns both for pre-visit promotion and during site visits. Digital technology products such as Virtual Reality (VR), Augmented Reality (AR), mobile apps, and advances in 3D modelling offer great opportunities to access heritage tourism market segments and augment site revenues (Kim & Hall, 2019; Yung & Khoo-Lattimore, 2019). Such devices can be used for site promotion and be employed at a site in a manner that fully respects its identity and spirit and sustains the authenticity of its monuments while adding to visitor satisfaction and enjoyment. Critically, the Egyptian CULTNAT can play a vital role in the production of the digital marketing materials due to the sophisticated expertise and advanced technological techniques it employs while documenting the heritage of Egypt. For example, four different methodologies for employing computer graphics have been used in visualising the ancient Egyptian scenes of four projects: the botanical garden in Karnak Temple, the Zodiac of Dendera Temple, the Opet Festival, and Kadesh Battle (Saleh, Badawi, Harb, & Omar, 2014).

The Ministry of Antiquities is also keen to change its traditional image as an authority solely in charge of monuments' excavation and restoration. Accordingly, it is seeking to promote its heritage treasures by taking advantage of every single event it organises. For instance, 150 artefacts of the collection of the young Pharaoh King Tutankh Amun have been hosted in an immersive exhibition, inaugurated on 23 March 2019, at the Grande Halle de La Villette in Paris, 52 years after its last visit in 1967 (El-Aref, 2019; Deyaa', 2019). Consequently, streets, shops, buses, the metro, the façade of buildings, hotels, and restaurants were all plastered with posters of the symbolic golden coffin of the young Pharaoh (El-Aref, 2019). The extraordinary media coverage of the event and the remarkable demand it received are certainly good promotional tools to stimulate demand for Egypt's cultural heritage tourism. To reinforce the impact of the exhibition which lasted for six months in Paris, the exhibition is also stopping in London before returning to Egypt. As part of promotion activities, foreign embassies in Egypt are also invited to all major archaeological excavation and site inauguration events with international media organised to cover such events.

To tackle the drastic decline in international tourist visits and revenues in 2016, the Ministry of Antiquities was also forced to adopt new promotional pricing techniques for site admission tickets. The 'Luxor Pass', issued in October 2016, followed by 'Cairo Pass', first issued in 2017, are two visitor passes that allow tourists to enter museums and archaeological sites for five consecutive days during official visiting hours with an unlimited number of entries during the validity period (Ministry of Antiquities, 2018).

Visitor management, education, and satisfaction

Contemporary cultural and heritage tourists seek a wide range of services and amenities at heritage sites and have high expectations that have to be met by the site management team. Visitor centres arguably play a significant role in the tourism planning process, as they can effectively manage the existing tourism flows and attract more (Karipis, Tsimitakis, & Skoultsos, 2009). A visitor centre distinguishes itself by its historical interpretation, so that visitors can gain an overview of a site and better understand its significance (Ripp, 2016). To deliver the educational and information messages and to provide visitor services, a number of visitor centres have been established at heritage sites such as at Tel Al-Amarna in Minya, the National Museum of Egyptian Civilization and Egyptian Museum in Cairo, El-Karnak Temple in Luxor, and Nubia Museum in Aswan. However, many other sites still lack visitor centres due to challenges such as budgetary constraints and a lack of space in the area that surrounds the site. Meanwhile, some other tourist services remain limited at many of the heritage sites such as information desks, signage, audio guides, dining areas, and souvenir shops.

Proper site zoning is part of an integrated planning scheme that actively responds to the visitor needs and copes with recent changes in heritage tourism market expectations. Although services to special-needs visitors have been initiated at Luxor Temple and Karnak Temple in Luxor in partnership with Helm, a non-governmental organisation (NGO), such services have to be supplied at all sites (El-Aref, 2018). In this context, integrated planning approaches suggest that stronger ties are needed between the NGOs and private sector social responsibility programmes to enable the Ministry of Antiquities to execute such visitor service programmes. In addition, environmentally friendly practices also need to be incorporated into heritage site stewardship along with technological empowerment and a full consideration of the socio-cultural aspects and benefits of heritage conservation practices (Ozer Sari & Nazli, 2018; Heesup, Hossein, Sun-bai, & Wansoo, 2018).

Moving towards integrated planning: The transformation of the Giza tourist region

The Giza tourist region is currently undergoing a comprehensive redevelopment which employs integrated planning to position the region as a landmark city that offers all amenities and services needed by the cultural heritage tourism market. At present, four mega projects are underway in the region:

- The establishment of the Egyptian Grand Museum (GEM) to be inaugurated in 2020
- Tourist service projects and zoning schemes at the Giza Plateau where the Great Pyramids and Sphinx are located

- Infrastructure network projects, including the construction of Sphinx International Airport and the development of accessible highways and roads to link the city with the other regions of Egypt
- The development of 'Sun City' as a tourist capital of Egypt, bordering the newly developed main gate of the Pyramids area, to offer accommodation, and cultural, entertainment, amusement, and recreational activities to tourists.

The execution of the above-mentioned mega projects has involved various governmental authorities as well as private sector entities. These include the Ministry of Antiquities, Ministry of Investment and International Cooperation, Ministry of Tourism, Ministry of Civil Aviation, Ministry of Housing, Ministry of Transportation, Ministry of Interior Affairs, Giza Governorate Authority, as well as Orascom Investment Holding Company, real estate companies, and private sector investors.

The Grand Egyptian Museum

The Grand Egyptian Museum (GEM) is built inside a unique site, overlooking the Great Pyramids at the Giza Plateau. GEM is planned to be one of the largest museums in the world, reflecting Egypt's past from prehistory until the Greek and Roman Periods (Ministry of Investment and International Cooperation (MIIC), 2018). The design of the museum building, which will exhibit more than 100,000 artefacts of Egyptian antiquities, was decided by means of an international architectural competition and its construction encompasses state-of-the-art technology and museum activities. The museum will be inaugurated in 2020 with the attendance of international celebrities. GEM will be a cultural hub that will include a children's museum as well as a centre offering conservation, restoration, storage, research, and museum education facilities (Islam, 2018). GEM is also designed to be an entertaining cultural and touristic destination, offering a wide range of services such as a conference centre, modern cinema theatre, restaurants overlooking the Pyramids, food courts, cafeterias, retail and commercial areas, bookshops, traditional arts and crafts centres, and gardens hosting year-round events and activities overlooking the Giza Plateau (MIIC, 2018). As part of the integrated planning approach, a tunnel is currently under construction to prohibit surface traffic in the area between the museum and the Giza Plateau as the 2-km distance will be developed as a tourist walking passage while environmentally friendly shuttle buses will also be running between the two sites. In addition, a 'metro station' is being developed close to the museum to link GEM with the other parts of Greater Cairo.

Tourist service projects and zoning schemes at the Giza Pyramids

For several decades, the Pyramids region has been suffering shortages in many tourist services and amenities as well as from a lack of sustainable development practices, namely visitor management, zoning, and environmentally friendly operations. The long-awaited rejuvenation projects commenced when the Supreme Council of Antiquities signed a contract with Orascom Investment Holdings in late 2018 to provide and operate high-quality services and facilities in the area surrounding the Pyramids of Giza, while retaining the council's authority over the whole area (Invest-gate, 2018). The contract allocates half of the net profit from the services to the Supreme Council of Antiquities which will receive a specified minimum amount, regardless of the profit gained, while the Supreme Council will continue receiving admission ticket revenue, which includes bus services, inside the Giza Plateau (Egypt Today, 2018; Cairo360, 2018). Furthermore, a promotional and marketing campaign for the Pyramid's region will also be launched by Orascom.

As Orascom will be managing the parking area in front of the new entrance on the Fayoum Road, no vehicles will be allowed to access the archaeological site. A visitor centre will also be managed by Orascom which will offer the educational and orientation services and will include coffee shops, cafeterias, a gift shop, and a photo and painting booth. While the movie theatre, connected to the visitor centre, will be operated by Orascom, the movie material to be screened will be reviewed by the council. Orascom is also tasked with providing technological services such as a free Wi-Fi connection, digital guides, and smartphone applications. Thirty environmentally friendly buses and 20 golf carts will also be operated by Orascom to transport visitors from one site to another inside the Plateau (Egypt Today, 2018).

As zoning was one of the region's main problems, a recreational area will be designated to horse and camel drivers who will be provided a uniform while new horse-drawn vehicles will be bought. Restaurants and coffee shops will also be allowed in certain areas. At the end of their journey, visitors will reach a shopping area which will contain 16 bazaars where they can buy souvenirs and gifts (Invest-gate, 2018; Egypt Today, 2018).

In order to help ensure quality services, Orascom will train craftspeople, vendors, photographers, and horse and camel drivers to improve their customer satisfaction and communication skills. The adoption of the zoning scheme will limit the access of camel and horse drivers, photographers and peddlers to the archaeological sites where they harass visitors to use their services, an issue that has historically caused significant visitor dissatisfaction.

Sphinx International Airport

Major infrastructure projects have been taking place to serve the historic city such as newly developed highways and roads to easily link the west of Greater Cairo, where the Pyramids' region and the Grand Egyptian Museum are located, with the other parts of Cairo and Egypt's governorates. The Sphinx International Airport has been constructed near the Cairo–Alexandria desert road in the west of Cairo, to serve potential tourists coming to visit the Pyramids and the new Grand Egyptian Museum (GEM).

It aims at alleviating pressure on Cairo International Airport, which is located in the east of Greater Cairo, and better serve the expected short trips and one-day tours as well as charter flights targeting visits to the historic city (Alaa El-Din, 2019). It also aims at serving domestic flights to directly connect the western region of Cairo with other tourist destinations in Egypt such as Luxor, Aswan, Sharm El-Sheikh, and Hurghada.

The airport, partially inaugurated in January 2019, currently serves domestic flights as a trial operation at a capacity of 300 passengers per hour. The capacity is planned to reach 1,600 per hour by the opening of the 'GEM' in 2020 to host both domestic and international flights, while the third planned phase will be able to serve 2,600 passengers (Al-Youm, 2019; Alaa El-Din, 2019).

Developing 'Sun City' as a tourist capital of Egypt

Egypt is currently developing its tourist city in a desert area at Cairo–Fayoum highway, bordering the new gate of the Pyramid's region to provide up-to-date tourist services and entertainment activities. The tourist capital will be offering various tourist projects such as a monorail which will end its tour by the main entrance of the Pyramids' region, Sun Piazza, planned to be a 14-acre circular walk surrounded by a range of restaurants, cafés, and shops, the largest outlet mall in Africa and the Middle East, an open air museum, concert hall, and an international medical centre. Although there are a number of hotels at the historic region, where the Giza Plateau and GEM are located, the tourist capital will comprise a wide range of accommodation types such as hotels and apartments. In addition, three hotels will be constructed close to GEM, inspired by the Pharaonic architectural design, replacing EL-Remaya sporting club which will be moved to the new administrative capital city in the extreme east of Cairo.

Conclusion

The Egyptian cultural heritage tourism sector is regarded as a key component in economic development and competitiveness. Critically, an integrated planning approach should be based on a comprehensive vision for the cultural heritage tourism sector, which implies setting an effective strategic management plan and identifying goals and objectives for cultural heritage tourism at the national level and scheduling programmes for reaching such goals at the local and site levels. Having such an approach in mind, the strategy should determine the tasks and duties of the concerned stakeholders with action plans to be executed and monitored at each phase and a continuous evaluation of the articulation and liaison of all parties. A value chain approach reflects the need for a continuous cooperative and integrative effort among stakeholders to foster the economic benefits of the cultural heritage tourism sector in Egypt. This is illustrated in the comprehensive planning projects underway in the development of the west of the Greater Cairo region as a cultural heritage tourism destination. In the future, such an approach has to be transferred and adopted with regard to the other mega projects related to Egypt's cultural heritage, such as the development of religious tourism.

References

African World Heritage (2018). *Abu Mena – Egypt: In danger since 2001*. Retrieved from https://www.africanworldheritagesites.org/cultural-places/egypt-after-the-pharaohs/abu-mena.html.

Alaa El-Din, M. (2019). Egypt's new Sphinx International Airport opens for first run of regular domestic flights. *Ahram Online*, 26 January. Retrieved from http://english.ahram.org.eg/NewsContent/1/64/322437/Egypt/Politics-/Egypts-new-Sphinx-International-Airport-opens-for-.aspx.

Al-Sadaty, A. (2018). Historic houses as pillars of memory: Cases from Cairo, Egypt. *Journal of Open House International, 43*(3), 5–13.

Al-Shuwekhi, A. (2017, 28 May). Ministry of Antiquities offers annual museum tickets at discounted prices. *Daily News Egypt*. Retrieved from https://ww.dailynewsegypt.com/2017/05/28/ministry-antiquities-offers-annual-museum-tickets-discounted-prices/.

Al-Youm, A.-M. (2019). Egypt's Civil Aviation Minister inaugurates Sphinx International Airport. *Egypt Independent*, 26 January. Retrieved from https://www.egyptindependent.com/egypts-civil-aviation-minister-inaugurates-sphinx-international-airport/.

Barre, H. (2002). Cultural tourism and sustainable development. *Journal of Museum International, 54*(1&2), 126–130.

Cairo360 (2018). *Everything you need to know about Orascom's management of the Pyramids of Giza*. 16 December. Retrieved from http://www.cairo360.com/article/sights-travel/everything-you-need-to-know-about-orascoms-management-of-the-pyramids-of-giza/.

Cassel, S. H., & Pashkevich, A. (2014). World Heritage and tourism innovation: Institutional frameworks and local adaptation. *Journal of European Planning Studies, 22*(8), 1625–1640.

Centre for Documentation of Cultural and Natural Heritage (CULTNAT) (2019). *About CULTNAT*. Retrieved from http://www.cultnat.org.

Destination BC Corp (2014). *Cultural and heritage tourism development. The essential guide for BC tourism businesses interested in developing a cultural or heritage tourism operation*. Vancouver, BC: Destination BC Corp.

Deyaa', N. (2019). Paris dresses up for ancient Egypt's young king. *Daily News Egypt*, 18 March. Retrieved from https://dailynewsegypt.com/2019/03/18/paris-dresses-up-for-ancient-egypts-young-king/.

Egypt Today (2018). *Orascom investment holding to provide Giza Pyramids' visitors with services*. 16 December. Retrieved from http://www.egypttoday.com/Article/1/62031/Orascom-Investment-Holding-to-provide-Giza-Pyramids-visitors-with-services.

El-Aref, N. (2016). Egyptian minister talks about challenges for antiquities. *Ahram Online*, 17 July. Retrieved from http://english.ahram.org.eg/NewsContent/9/40/233406/Heritage/AncientEgypt/Interview-Egyptian-minister-talks-about challenges.aspx.

El-Aref, N. (2018). Egypt's archaeological sites to be made more accessible to people with disabilities. *Ahram Online*, 29 January. Retrieved from http://english.ahram.

org.eg/NewsContent/9/40/288996/Heritage/Ancient-Egypt/Egypts-archaeological-sites-to-be-made-more-access.aspx.

El-Aref, N. (2019). 'Paris seized by Egyptomania' as Tutankhamun, the Treasures of the Pharaoh show opens. *Ahram Online*, 29 March. Retrieved from http://english.ahram.org.eg/NewsContent/9/40/329053/Heritage/Ancient-Egypt/Paris-seized-by-Egyptomania-as-Tutankhamun,-the-Tr.aspx.

Elkhatib, S., & Aboulenein, A. (2016). Egypt's economic crisis weighs heavily on heritage: Minister. *Cairo: Reuters*, 25 August. Retrieved from https://uk.reuters.com/article/us-egypt-antiquities/egypts-economic-crisis-weighs-heavily-on-heritage-minister-idUKKCN1101EG.

Fredholm, S. (2016). Assets in the age of tourism: The development of heritage planning in Ghanaian Policy. *Journal of Contemporary African Studies*, *34*(4), 498–518.

Fushiya, T. (2010). Archaeological site management and local involvement: A case study from Abu Rawash, Egypt. *Conservation and Management of Archaeological Sites*, *12*(4), 324–355.

Georgiadis, C., Patias, P., & Tsioukas, V. (2016). Recording and modelling of monuments' interior space using range and optical sensors. *The International Archives of the Photogrammetry, Remote Sensing and Spatial Information Sciences*, *41*(B5), 939–944.

Hawas, Z. (1998). Site management: The response to tourism. *Museum International*, *50*(4) 31–37.

Heesup, H., Hossein, O., Sun-bai, C., & Wansoo, K. (2018). Understanding museum vacationers' eco-friendly decision-making process: Strengthening the VBN framework. *Journal of Sustainable Tourism*, *26*(6), 855–872.

Helmy, E. (2014). Political uncertainty: Challenges to Egyptian tourism policy. In E. Fayos-Solà, M. Alvarez, & C. Cooper (eds), *Tourism as an instrument for development: A theoretical and practical study* (pp. 301–315). Bingley: Emerald.

Industrial Modernisation Centre (IMC) (2016). *Creative Egypt*. Retrieved from http://creative.nextmp.net/?SID=0ld6044u8agfe0j5vd237preb1.

International Council on Monuments and Sites (ICOMOS) (1996). *Principles for the recording of monuments, groups of buildings and sites*. Ratified by the 11th ICOMOS General Assembly in Sofia (pp. 49–52). Rome: ICOMOS.

Invest-gate (2018). *Orascom to provide tourist facilities at Giza Pyramids*. 16 December. Retrieved from https://invest-gate.me/news/orascom-to-provide-tourist-facilities-at-pyramids-of-giza/.

Islam, S. (2018). A new Egyptian museum will bring treasures of the pyramids back to practically where they were buried. *Global Post*, 7 March. Retrieved from https://www.pri.org/stories/2018-03-07/new-egyptian-museum-will-bring-treasures-pyramids-back-practically-where-they.

Kamar, G. (2014). *The development of Luxor Open Air Museum and its social impacts: An assessment using geographic information systems*. Unpublished doctoral dissertation. University of Leicester, UK.

Karipis, K., Tsimitakis, E., & Skoultsos, S. (2009). Contribution of visitor information centres to promoting natural and cultural resources in emerging tourism destinations. *International Journal of Tourism Policy*, *2*(4), 319–336.

Kim, M. J., & Hall, C. M. (2019). A hedonic motivation model in virtual reality tourism: Comparing visitors and non-visitors. *International Journal of Information Management*, *46*, 236–249.

Mbaiwa, J. (2011). Cultural commodification and tourism: The Goo-Moremi Community, Central Botswana. *Tijdschrift voor Economische en Sociale Geografie*, *102*(3), 290–301.

Mina, D., Kalliopi, F., & Nikolaos, G. (2018). Community participation in heritage tourism planning: Is it too much to ask? *Journal of Sustainable Tourism*, *26*(5), 759–781.

Ministry of Antiquities (MoA) (2018, 26 July). *Newsletter of the Ministry of Antiquities*. Retrieved from MoA_Newsletter_26_English.pdf.

Ministry of Investment and International Cooperation (MIIC) (2018). The Grand Egyptian *Museum*. *Arab Republic of Egypt, MIIC*, 6 June. Retrieved from http://www.miic.gov.eg/English/MediaCenter/News/Pages/GEM_ENG.aspx.

Ministry of Tourism (MOT) (2011). *Tourism in Figures for 2010*. Cairo: Ministry of Tourism.

Osman, K. (2018). Heritage conservation management in Egypt. A review of the current and proposed situation to amend it. *Ain Shams Engineering Journal*, *9*(4), 2907–2916.

Ozer Sari, F., & Nazli, M. (2018). Sustaining cultural heritage by means of museums in an ever-changing world. *Gaziantep University Journal of Social Sciences*, *17*(1), 1–14.

Parcak, S. (2017). Moving from space-based to ground-based solutions in remote sensing for archaeological heritage: A case study from Egypt. *Remote Sensing*, *9*(12), 1297. Retrieved from https://doi.org/10.3390/rs9121297.

Pedersen, A. (2002). Managing tourism at World Heritage Sites. A practical manual for World Heritage Site managers. *UNESCO World Heritage Centre*. Retrieved from http://whc.unesco.org/uploads/activities/documents/activity-113-2.pdf.

Ripp, M. (2016). Visitor centres vs. museums. *GoUNESCO*, 31 January. Retrieved from https://www.gounesco.com/visitor-centres-vs-museums/.

Saleh, F., Badawi, M., Harb, M., & Omar, K. (2014). Reviving ancient Egyptian scenes. *International Conference on Virtual Systems & Multimedia (VSMM)*, 9–12 December, Hong Kong, China, pp. 169–174. New Jersey: IEEE.

Scheffler, N., Ripp, M., & Buhler, B. (2010). Cultural heritage integrated management plans. Thematic Report 4. *HerO (Heritage as Opportunity) & European Union*. Retrieved from https://urbact.eu/sites/default/files/import/Projects/HERO/projects_media/Vilnius_Thematic_report04.pdf.

Smith, M. (2003). *Issues in cultural tourism studies*. London: Routledge.

Song, H., Liu, J., & Chen, G. (2013). Tourism value chain governance: Review and prospects. *Journal of Travel Research*, *52*(1), 15–28.

Tawfeek, F. (2018). New discoveries to be announced soon: Antiquities Minister. *Egypt Independent*, 30 June. Retrieved from https://ww.egyptindependent.com/new-discoveries-announced-soon-antiquities-minister/.

UNESCO (2019). *Abu Mena*. Retrieved from https://whc.unesco.org/en/list/90.

UNWTO (2012). *UNWTO tourism highlights 2011 edition*. Retrieved from http://mkt.unwto.org/sites/all/files/docpdf/unwtohighlights11enhr.pdf.

UNWTO (2017). *UNWTO tourism highlights for 2016*. Retrieved from http://UNWTO_Tourism-Highlights_2017.pdf.

World Monuments Fund (WMF) (2011). *New Gourna village: Conservation and community*. New York: WMF.

Yung, R., & Khoo-Lattimore, C. (2019). New realities: A systematic literature review on virtual reality and augmented reality in tourism research. *Current Issues in Tourism*, *22*(17), 2056–2081.

12 UNESCO's World Heritage Sites

The interplay between international and local branding for the Gonbad-e Qābus Brick Tower, Iran

Bardia Shabani, Hazel Tucker, and Amin Nazifi

Introduction

While United Nations Educational, Scientific and Cultural Organization (UNESCO) World Heritage Site (WHS) designation can be beneficial for the tourism industry at the broader destination, it can have its own challenges (Adie, 2019). The strong relationship between identities and community is discussed by Ballesteros and Ramírez (2007), who identified the main role of the symbolic community in heritage tourism development and the influence of tourism on identities. In the case that local authorities and other tourism stakeholders at the destination do not consider the role of local communities in tourism development, those communities surrounding the site may feel excluded from the management of their own heritage. As UNESCO, as an international brand, takes over representation, and to some extent presentation, of the site, the other challenge is to match the demands of tourism to local needs, while making it sustainable and viable. As a multifaceted industry, tourism has significant impacts, not only on the heritage sites themselves, but on the entire community and environment that surrounds the heritage site (Salazar, 2012).

Despite Iran having inscribed 24 properties (22 cultural and 2 natural sites) on the United Nations Educational, Scientific and Cultural Organization (UNESCO) WHS list, in addition to its 57 sites on the tentative list, it plays only a small role as an international tourism destination. (UNESCO, 2019). This small role is the consequence of different factors, including international sanctions against the country (since 1995), lack of a formidable and ongoing long-term strategy for the tourism industry of the country, and insufficient infrastructure for tourism (Seyfi & Hall, 2018; Shabani & Tucker, 2018). Moreover, in the case of each designated site, there is invariably a particular, and often problematic, interplay between the international WHS 'brand' and the local 'brand(s)', or cultural identity/ies (Adie, Hall, & Prayag, 2018).

This chapter offers an empirical examination of this interplay in the context of the Gonbad-e Qābus Brick Tower, in North-East Iran. Registered as a WHS in 2012, this outstanding masterpiece of early Islamic brick architecture is one of the most iconic symbols of the ancient cultural exchange between Central Asian nomads and Iran's ancient civilisation. As such, it can shed light on the different dimensions of cultural exchange, as well as potentially highlight the Turkmen minority's culture and its role in the formation of a new tourism image and presentation of the area surrounding the WHS. The discussion in the chapter will focus on the influence of the heritage site designation brand upon the prior image, or 'brand', of the destination (Turkmen culture). Furthermore, the chapter considers how far both brands can be unified within the destination. Firstly, the mission of UNESCO will be outlined, before discussing the role of the local community and their attitudes toward the Gonbad-e Qābus tower becoming a WHS. The chapter will then focus on the challenges of designating an international brand for the local community at the destination and how and if local people will accept the effect of the newly assigned brand on their own culture.

UNESCO, the mission of a big brand

Every year, the cultural committees of UNESCO in Paris publish the lists of WHS properties and Intangible Cultural Heritage (ICH) elements, in which the exceptional universal value of each site is stated. Inscription is a reminder that all the people of the world are not only the owners but are also responsible for these places or intangible elements. Moreover, the World Heritage lists reinforce the identification, preservation, and transmission to future generations of these valuable places and monuments from the perspective of history and art (Saipradist & Staiff, 2008). While the main purpose of these recognitions by UNESCO is to preserve and conserve those sites, inscription often leads to a significant increase in tourist numbers (Adie, 2019; Adie & Hall, 2017; Adie et al., 2018; Breakey, 2012). Indeed, the notion of heritage sites having a cultural tourism purpose is integral to UNESCO's production of what Di Giovine (2009) calls the global heritage-scape, in that it plays a major role in harnessing 'the global flows of international travellers to interact with the authentic monuments *in situ*' (Di Giovine, 2009, p. 42).

Further to this point, Meskell (2014, p. 237) has argued that the 1972 *World Heritage Convention* 'is not so much about protection anymore, but instead about branding, marketing, and promoting new nominations in an increasingly acquisitive heritage economy'. According to Su and Wall (2011), this trend creates a paradoxical condition; while the basic objective of UNESCO is to promote the protection and preservation of sites, some destinations are prioritising tourist development, especially in new destinations or those that are little known. This sudden increase in the number of visitors can put the survival of the WHS in danger (Abuamoud, Libbin, Green, & Alrousan, 2014; Breakey, 2012; Landorf, 2009). WHS designation plays a 'labelling' (Yang, Lin, & Han, 2010) or 'branding' (Adie et al., 2018; Timothy, 2011) role for the destinations and can be a significant motivator for those tourists who seek culture and heritage experiences (Adie & Hall, 2017; Caust & Vecco, 2017; Correia, Kozak, & Ferradeira, 2013; Poria, Butler, & Airey, 2003; Poria, Reichel, & Cohen, 2013; Timothy & Boyd, 2006).

The three conventions passed by UNESCO in order to protect the world's built and created treasures include: *Convention Concerning the Protection of the World Cultural and Natural Heritage* (1972) (World Heritage Convention), *Convention for the Safeguarding of the Intangible Cultural Heritage* (2003), and *Convention on the Protection and Promotion of the Diversity of Cultural Expression* (2005). As Article 2 of UNESCO's Convention regarding the safeguarding of ICH explains, '"Safeguarding" means measures aimed at ensuring the viability of the intangible cultural heritage, including the identification, documentation, research, preservation, protection, promotion, enhancement, transmission, particularly through formal and non-formal education, as well as the revitalization of the various aspects of such heritage' (UNESCO, 2003). The question then arises as to whether there is a desire locally to 'revitalise' the heritage and make it 'viable'. Accordingly, this could be interpreted as a way of making a site or culture come alive, while trying to maintain its unique characteristics. However, the World Heritage list has been criticised for having a Eurocentric bias with respect to 'monumentality' (Alivizatou, 2012). While there are attempts to accommodate cultural diversity, Labadi (2013, p. 61) notes that the World Heritage list continues in its mode of 'privileging specific aesthetic and art historical points of view'.

Rau (2014) also highlights the potential negative impact of increased tourism and discusses the inherent contradiction in the position of UNESCO when they are aware of the dangers of increased promotion of a site, despite the damage that occurs. While it is mentioned in the Budapest Declaration that the UNESCO assignment is to promote 'an appropriate equitable balance between conservation, sustainability and development' (UNESCO, 2002) in UNESCO sites, UNESCO's overall objective is to preserve the cultural and natural (tangible and intangible) heritage for future generations. This threat can be considered when new visitor flows may seriously affect and damage the environmental and cultural integrity of destinations. These impacts could be traced to the overcrowding of sites, changes in use and appearance of buildings, commercialisation of local culture, the issue of management and conservation, compromised and corrupted cultural values, and 'tourismification' (Jimura, 2019; Nicholas, Thapa, & Ko, 2009; Daniel, 1996).

The role of local community

There is a strong relationship between heritage, identity, and community (Ballesteros & Ramírez, 2007). Simpson (2008) indicates the effect of community involvement and how it can be beneficial at all stages of tourism development. When WHS status is awarded to a site, to a certain degree, representation, control, and planning of the site are invariably removed from the local community, so that the locale becomes appropriated by national and international interests which may exclude the community from the conversation (Hall, 2006). In this regard, a major challenge is how to match the demands of tourism to local needs, while making it sustainable and viable. As a multifaceted industry, tourism has significant impacts, not only on the heritage sites themselves, but on the entire community and environment that surrounds the heritage site. These factors bring the threat of uncontrolled expansion of UNESCO cultural heritage sites to attention (Salazar, 2012).

Studies regarding the relationship between local community and tourism have been a feature of tourism research since the 1970s (Butler, 1980; Ap, 1992). Most of the literature regarding this issue suggests that an understanding and assessment of tourism development in local communities is fundamental to foster sustainable tourism (Johnson, Snepenger, & Akis, 1994; Diedrich & García-Buades, 2009). When it comes to tourism issues, direct and indirect impacts affect not only the cultural heritage site but the entire community and environment that surrounds it, so uncontrolled expansion can be considered a threat for the short and long-term sustainability of the site and the local community.

Local communities' attitudes towards tourism are a key component in the identification, measurement, and analysis of the changes caused by tourism, so that examination of these factors will help local decision-makers in terms of planning, developing, and managing of the current situation based on which the public could support the tourism industry (Hall & Piggin, 2002; Ryan & Montgomery, 1994; Pearce, 1980). Carmichael, Peppard, and Boudreau (1996) and Andereck and Vogt (2000) considered the important role of the local community and attitudes towards tourism and consider it vital that key local stakeholders have the opportunity to express their opinions in the decision-making process. They are those who ultimately decide which changes brought about by tourism are acceptable and which are not. Moreover, any site which is nominated for WHS status must have a detailed Management Plan and a strong legal framework as part of the Nomination Documents by its State Party (Hall, 2006; Shackley, 1998). In this regard, the management and conservation plan of the site must be improved throughout and after the nomination process as all WHSs need to uphold their management and conservation plan (Bianchi, 2002; Hall, 2006; Smith, 2002).

Beside the main role of the decision-makers (at all levels) in terms of planning and providing the infrastructure at the destination, local people would ideally need to be encouraged and educated about the preservation of the site, as their participation is a vital part of the mission of World Heritage (UNESCO, 2010). However, De Cesari (2010, p. 308) has noted that, because 'the 1972 Convention in fact authorises not only experts but also the nation-state and its representatives as the proper subjects of World Heritage', other interested parties, including local residents around the site, may not only be excluded, but may even become 'silenced in the process' (De Cesari, 2010). Tucker and Carnegie (2014), for example, discuss the ways in which local cultural values are subjugated to the supposed 'universal values' encompassed in the UNESCO World Heritage listings at a Turkish WHS. Further to this, according to Labadi (2013, p. 150), the content of World Heritage nominations often 'contains the seeds to fuel controversies, conflicts and the marginalization of whole sectors of populations'. It is therefore highly pertinent to consider the interplay between the UNESCO WHS global 'brand' and the local identity, or 'brand', otherwise exerted in and around sites in the WHS listings.

Iran's Cultural Heritage, Handicrafts and Tourism Organization, as a key tourism industry stakeholder in the country, has brought attention to the importance of local community engagement in cultural heritage management. Nevertheless, a lack of tourism experts, community consultation, and education, and ineffective strategies and policies are major challenges for many of Iran's destinations. For example, as Donato and Lohrasbi's (2017) study of Takht-e Soleyman WHS noted, the vital role of the local community in the development process of the site and destination was neglected despite a great desire for engagement from the community. Indeed, it is widely observed that if the advantages of tourism development are perceived to outweigh its disadvantages, the community will support and value tourism development, whilst failing community expectations will lead to negative reactions towards tourism development (Gursoy et al., 2002; Ye et al., 2014; Rasoolimanesh et al., 2015). This chapter therefore examines this interplay between the local community, World Heritage designation and tourism development in the case of Gonbad-e Qābus in Iran. The next section will outline how research for this case study was conducted.

Case study and methods

Based on previous studies regarding the effects of UNESCO site designation on a destination, the authors undertook an empirical survey in order to evaluate the interplay between an international brand and a local brand, in improving the image and fostering the tourism industry of a destination. The study was conducted in May 2019 in Gonbad, Iran, and was administered in a 'semi-structured interview' format in person by one of the authors (Shabani). Convenience sampling was used whereby 13 residents of Gonbad and 12 tourism experts with a minimum of ten years of working experience at ICHTO (Iran's Cultural Heritage, Handicrafts and Tourism Organization) of Golestan province branch were approached and asked if they were willing to take part in a short interview. Of the 25 respondents asked to participate, 20 were interviewed. Out of the ten experts who were interviewed, five of them were managers at ICHTO and the other five were ICHTO employees (archaeologists and heritage conservation specialists). Of the residents, five were souvenir shop owners around the UNESCO site and the other five were residents of Gonbad who were visiting the site. The residents' interviews lasted, on average, approximately 15 minutes each and the experts' interviews 25 minutes each.

The interviewees were open to express their ideas and were keen to help the improvement of the tourism industry of the region by taking part in the research. The interviews were conducted in Persian with the interviewees asked a series of questions on subjects including: the negative and positive points of Gonbad-e Qābus before and after WHS designation, the strengths, weaknesses, and potential of the tourism industry of Gonbad, and their views about the impact of WHS designation on the culture, economy, and overall image of the city as a destination. Interviewees were also asked about their ideas for increasing the level of awareness about the attractions of the city both nationally and internationally, and also their suggestions for improving tourism in the city. The respondents' answers to the interview questions were later translated into English and analysed for identifiable patterns with regard to what was considered 'meaningful' in relation to the subject of the role of the local brand (Turkmen culture) in comparison to an international one (UNESCO). While the study was limited in size and scope, it nonetheless yielded insightful information. These findings are organised around the role of the UNESCO brand as an international brand and, in comparing this to the role of the local brand, we discuss their implications for the destination.

The tallest brick tower in the world

Turkmen Sahra, which means Plain of Turkmens, is a region in Iran's Golestan Province south-east of the Caspian Sea that borders Turkmenistan and which is where the majority of the Turkmen ethnic peoples of Iran reside. Iranian Turkmen Ethnicity has for a long time represented a group of semi-nomadic tribes who are Sunni Muslim and have retained a fairly traditional way of life (Minorsky, 1953).

Gonbad-e Qabus is a city of Golestan province with a land area of 21 km^2 and a population of 151,910 in the north-east of Iran (Statistical Center of Iran, 2016; Gonbad Municipality, 2018). The history of the region (*Hyrcania* in Greek or *Varkâna* in Old Persian Language) dates back to 600 BC, but the city itself (reconstructed in 1934 by the order of Reza Shah, the first king of Pahlavi dynasty) takes its name from Qābus Ibn Voshmgir (Ziyarid ruler and literati, tenth–eleventh century), and is located near the ruins of the ancient city of Gorgan (also called Jorjan), the capital of the Ziyarid dynasty, which was destroyed during the Mongols' invasion of the fourteenth and fifteenth centuries (Governor of Golestan Informing Base, 2015). Gonbad-e Qābus Brick Tower is a 53 m high tomb which was built in AD 1006 for Qābus Ibn Voshmgir and was registered as a UNESCO WHS in 2012. This tower is one of the most iconic symbols of the ancient cultural exchange between Central Asian nomads and Iran and is considered an outstanding masterpiece of early Islamic brick architecture (UNESCO, 2012). It is believed that Gonbad-e Qābus Brick Tower is the only remaining evidence of the ancient city of Gorgan and is an outstanding and technologically innovative example of Islamic architecture that influenced sacred building in Iran, Anatolia, and Central Asia. The structural design (ten-pointed star) of this masterpiece is based on a geometric formula which achieved great height in load-bearing brickwork and makes this hollow cylindrical tower visible from great distances in the surrounding lowlands from all directions. Not only has its conical roofed form become a prototype for tomb towers and other commemorative towers in the region, but also it became an outstanding example of a commemorative tower whose design illustrates the exceptional development of mathematics and science in the Muslim world at the turn of the first millennium AD (UNESCO, 2012).

Besides the tower, the city has other attractions, including: the Great Wall of Gorgan; the longest brick wall in the world (c. 200 km) which was built from AD 420s to 530s by the Sasanid Empire (Sauer, Nokandeh, Rekavandi, & Wilkinson, 2013; UNESCO, 2017); the plain and wetlands (Alma Gol, Aji Gol, and Ala Gol); Turkmens' culture and customs; horse riding competitions (this city is the capital of horse riding in Iran); and the shrine of Imam Yahya bin Zaid. As a result, the city is among one of the most attractive tourism destinations in Iran and is the best representative of Turkmen culture (which is considered as the local brand for this destination) and is popular for their art and handicrafts. Apart from the history of Gonbad, Turkmen ethnicity (comprising more than 60 per cent of the population of the city) and culture are among the most important attractions in this region. Turkmen clothing, which is quite different from the country's usual dress, is also another attraction of this region; with both males and females wearing their traditional dress in public (Governor of Golestan Informing Base, 2015).

Local opinions in relation to WHS designation

For nearly all the residents interviewed (living in Gonbad for more than 20 years and hence remembering their visits to sites before and after the designation), the Brick Tower was considered among the top three attractions that the city was known for, followed by the Turkmen ethnicity and handicrafts. According to the residents, prior to Gonbad-e Qābus designation as a WHS site, it used to be an open space and a cultural centre bringing people together, although there was not much information or signage available for tourists. Tourism officials also stated that the site was one of the main areas of gathering for celebrations, festivals, and routine get-togethers. For example, one expert said: 'The cultural centre of the site was the best place for the younger generation to spend their free time'. Another respondent said: 'It used to be an open site that people could visit and enjoy anytime, no matter day or night'.

At the same time, respondents in both groups pointed out, in relation to the negative aspects of the site before designation, that there was previously a lack of an appropriate conservation programme for the site, as well as an unattractive and unsecure surrounding area, and a lack of standardised informing system for tourists such as available guides or informative signs. As one expert said: 'The site wasn't introduced well and no one even in the region knew about it, no protection and conservation program were considered for it'. Another resident said that: 'Nobody could control the safety and conservation of the site and the tower itself had suffered considerable damage'.

Following WHS listing, management became more systematic and people now needed to buy tickets for entry and the fund is used for maintenance and conservation purposes. The majority of the tourism officials interviewed believe this to be a positive development, due to additional funds for research and maintenance purposes and the opportunity for enhanced image and subsequent increased tourist visitation: 'A special protection team is now considered to do the studies and protecting the site, repairing the damaged part of the tower'. However, in the case of the residents, nearly all of them did not notice any significant difference, saying that 'Nothing important happened, just periodic conservation plans'. Another said: 'Just some informative signs in the site can be seen, but nothing major happened'.

On the other hand, residents were still pessimistic about the impacts of the WHS and stated the negative points about this designation, that the site has not benefited as expected with other UNESCO sites in other countries. Furthermore, residents believe that there have not been any major changes following its listing. Lack of attention to the site, limited efforts in advertising this WHS nationally and internationally, as well as lack of facilities are perceived to be the main weaknesses of the site from the residents' perspective. For example, one person said: 'I visited some of the UNESCO sites in other countries and their sites are not comparable with ours as the level of information and services for tourists are far better elsewhere'. Both groups highlighted what they saw as a lack of tourism experts at a managerial level, as well as weak city planning and infrastructure, limited accommodation (there are only two hotels in the city), and the absence of tour guides. It was pointed out, for example, that: 'The infrastructure is not ready for the tourists as there is no information and no suitable accommodation provided for tourists. Also, there is no expert at managerial level for tourism.' There appears to be lack of expertise on the tourism front with the majority of experts in the ICHTO having degrees and experience in archaeology and conservation, rather than tourism. Accordingly, the lack of a clear marketing strategy in order to make the site better known outside the region is considered a major issue: 'The UNESCO site is still unknown for the local people and also for the high rank decision makers of the region and there are still no informative plans for them'.

Simultaneously, the experts indicated that the WHS listing has caused disruption to the building development in the surrounding areas, with limited support and resolution from relevant government bodies. There is also awareness that WHS designation has caused the tightening of regulations for residents' properties around the site:

> As the site is under the control of UNESCO regulations, it has affected the neighbouring areas as the people who are living near the site are very dissatisfied because of UNESCO regulations that caused many strict limitations for constructing or renovating of their properties around it.

While the tourism experts accepted some of the neglect about planning, as well as the issue regarding providing information and services for tourists, they also appeared to lay some of the blame for the issues upon the fact that the local community do not consider this site as their own heritage and they have no sense of attachment to this monument. As one official explained: 'As the Turkmen ethnicity who is the majority of the population here don't really believe in this site as a part of their culture and they don't have any sense of belonging to this monument'. Another expert similarly commented: 'The people of the city do not consider the monument as a heritage for themselves and have no sense of belonging and they feel they have no control for managing the monument of their town as it is now under the control of UNESCO, somehow this made them disappointed'.

Both residents and experts stated that even the small number of visitors drawn by the WHS listing of the tower has affected the way that people are receiving the tourists and that this socialising with outsiders is having a positive effect on the community's culture. As one respondent stated: 'It had a great impact as there are many tourists visiting this city and people feel somehow proud that others are interested in their culture, and this will make them more open'. Another similarly remarked: 'It made people have more confidence and look at their own culture as a gift that others may want to know about it'.

WHS designation was considered to have only a limited effect on the local economy. As such, it had not made a tangible difference in the local community's daily life. Both interviewed groups said that they had expected more benefit from WHS designation. A common response was that: 'Maybe a little but not too much increase in the number of tourists brought some financial benefits to the local people but not that much as it was expected'. Example responses to the question about the main weaknesses of the tourism industry in Gonbad include a 'lack of planning for the tourism industry of the city and also the negligence of the main decision-maker of the province', and 'Infrastructures are not ready for the tourists as there are no information and no suitable accommodation provided for tourists. Also, there is no expert at managerial level for tourism.'

Interestingly, official statistics suggest a steady year-on-year decline since listing (Table 12.1), but this may be attributed to the recent sanctions and difficulty in travelling to the country. Despite this, both experts and

Table 12.1 Total number of visitors per year

Year	Total	International tourists	Domestic tourists
2007	95,943		
2008	104,037		
2009	129,363		
2010	193,454		
2011	115,641		
2012	139,685		
2013	102,764	368	102,396
2014	85,895	787	85,108
2015	101,698	594	101,104
2016	74,523	740	73,783
2017	63,203	459	62,744

Source: National Tourists Survey, Statistical Center of Iran, 2018.

residents suggest that there has been an increase in awareness towards the city and the site both nationally and internationally since WHS designation: 'Our culture and customs are now known nationally, and it had a great positive effect on other people's minds as we are Sunni and proved we are as hospitable as other ethnicities. Also, this caused many people even in Iran to know more about the site as they didn't hear about it before.' Another said that: 'The brand of the UNESCO has brought the name of the city to peoples' attention and I think this may provide more information about our city. Also, now the city and the Turkmen culture are more known among Iranians.' Similarly: 'For sure now chosen as the UNESCO site introduced the city globally and brought the name of the city to the attention of the tourism market. So, everyone wants to know more about this unique monument and also the Turkmen ethnicity.'

In order to better understand people's emotions about the city, the respondents were asked to describe the city as if it were a human being. It is interesting to note that the majority of interviewees (both residents and experts) used negative words such as: an old man, an ill/sick man, and depressed, although a few people described it as young, smart, and talented. This may be due to the fact that Gonbad, as a small city, is mainly comprised of minorities who have not received attention or financial incentives/investments over the past few decades, despite its great potential for development. Nevertheless, most people and experts believe that in the case of solving the tourism issues and providing the conditions for investment, the city has a great potential to become a major tourist destination due to its Turkmen cultural traditions and handicrafts, historical features (e.g. the Brick Tower, the Great Wall of Gorgan and the ancient Gorgan city), natural attractions (the wetlands around the city), religious sites (e.g. Yahya bin Zaid shrine) and sporting attractions (e.g. the most important horse riding competition in Iran). Respondents said, for example, that: 'This city has great potential to compete with famous cities in Iran but it needs to have tourism experts at the managerial level to understand the problems and issues of the city. Also, the government should provide the budget not only to the big cities but also for small cities like Gonbad.' It was also believed that: 'If the city improves all will benefit and also the opposite will happen if no one pays attention to it'.

Conclusion

It is clear from both groups of respondents that, as long as the local people are not well informed or involved in the tourism development and policies, or when they are not supportive or 'engaged' with the World Heritage brand, tensions will persist between the different brand levels. As Turkmens are among the minorities in Iran, both in terms of ethnicity and religion, they are sensitive about their own culture, and do not have strong identification with the World Heritage Site. Furthermore, the lack of tourism experts at the managerial level, an absence of comprehensive plans and marketing strategies, weak infrastructure, and insufficient budget and investment has discouraged the local community and made them believe that the WHS is nothing more than just a brand, despite the great potential of their city.

Iran, with its over 2,500-year history, has great potential in becoming one of the region's main heritage tourism destinations. WHS designation has brought both positive and negative impacts upon local communities in Gonbad. It has brought the city further exposure both nationally and internationally; however, the lack of educational and informative programmes has weakened the attachment of local communities towards this WHS. Moreover, the local community feel they have not been involved in developing their city's WHS site, so this has caused them to feel ignored and disappointed.

Based on the result of our study, both groups (residents and the tourism experts) have considered the local brand and image of their culture and city to have far more potential than the World Heritage brand. Furthermore, the officials have not been successful in capitalising on World Heritage listing to create a unique image of the city as a top destination in Iran. Accordingly, as for destination image, which is the most salient part of a destination brand, Turkmen culture and customs appear to be among the most important components of destination image for the region. Unfortunately, this issue exists not only for Gonbad but can be seen in many other WHSs in Iran. The majority of these sites have failed to reap the benefits of WHS listing due to lack of a clear marketing strategy and a master plan as well as limited information and expert guide availability in these sites.

Based on this study, there are three main factors which have failed to influence and encourage the local community in Gonbad since WHS listing. The first factor is the poor scale and pace of tourism development since WHS designation; this can be seen as a result of issues such as: the lack of tourism expertise at the managerial level, the absence of comprehensive urban planning and marketing strategies and weak infrastructure. The second factor is negligence by tourism decision-makers in educating and informing the local community and encouraging them to take an active role in developing tourism. The third factor is the great patriotic sense of being a Turkmen and strong beliefs in their own customs and culture that prevented them from accepting anything which is not part of their own culture, including World Heritage.

References

Abuamoud, I. N., Libbin, J., Green, J., & Alrousan, R. (2014). Factors affecting the willingness of tourists to visit cultural heritage sites in Jordan. *Journal of Heritage Tourism, 9*(2), 148–165.

Adie, B. A. (2019). *World Heritage and tourism: Marketing and management.* Abingdon: Routledge.

Adie, B. A., & Hall, C. M. (2017). Who visits World Heritage? A comparative analysis of three cultural sites. *Journal of Heritage Tourism, 12*(1), 67–80.

Adie, B. A., Hall, C. M., & Prayag, G. (2018). World Heritage as a placebo brand: a comparative analysis of three sites and marketing implications. *Journal of Sustainable Tourism, 26*(3), 399–415.

Alivizatou, M. (2012). *Intangible heritage and the museum: New perspectives on cultural preservation.* Walnut Creek, CA: Left Coast Press.

Andereck, K. L., & Vogt, C. A. (2000). The relationship between residents' attitudes toward tourism and tourism development options. *Journal of Travel Research, 39*(1), 27–36.

Ap, J. (1992). Residents' perceptions on tourism impacts, *Annals of Tourism Research, 19*(4), 665–690.

Ballesteros, E. R., & Ramírez, M. H. (2007). Identity and community – reflections on the development of mining heritage tourism in Southern Spain. *Tourism Management, 28*(3), 677–687.

Bianchi, R. V. (2002). The contested landscape of world heritage on a tourist island: The case of Garajonay National Park, La Gomera. *International Journal of Heritage Studies, 8*(2), 81–97.

Breakey, N. M. (2012). Study in of World Heritage visitors: The case of the remote Riversleigh fossil site. *Visitor Studies, 15*(1), 82–97.

Butler, R. W. (1980). The concept of a tourist area cycle of evolution: Implications for management of resources. *The Canadian Geographer, 21*(1), 5–12.

Carmichael, B., Peppard, B. D., & Boudreau, F. (1996). Megaresort on my doorstep: Local resident attitudes toward Foxwoods Casino and casino gambling on nearby Indian reservation land. *Journal of Travel Research, 34*(3), 9–16.

Caust, J., & Vecco, M. (2017). Is UNESCO World Heritage recognition a blessing or burden? Evidence from developing Asian countries. *Journal of Cultural Heritage, 27*, 1–9.

Correia, A., Kozak, M., & Ferradeira, J. (2013). From tourist motivations to tourist satisfaction. *International Journal of Culture, Tourism and Hospitality Research, 7*(4), 411–424.

Daniel, Y. P. (1996). Tourism dance performances: Authenticity and creativity. *Annals of Tourism Research, 23*(4), 780–797.

De Cesari, C. (2010) World Heritage and mosaic universalism: A view from Palestine. *Journal of Social Archaeology*, *10*(3), 299–324.

Diedrich, A., & García-Buades, E. (2009). Local perceptions of tourism as indicators of destination decline. *Tourism Management*, *30*(4), 512–521.

Di Giovine, M. (2009). *The heritage-scape: UNESCO, World Heritage, and tourism*. Lanham, MD: Lexington Books.

Donato, F., & Lohrasbi, A. (2017). When theory and practice clash: Participatory governance and management in Takht-e Soleyman. *Journal of Cultural Heritage Management and Sustainable Development*, *7*(2), 129–146.

Gonbad Municipality. (2018). *Gonbad City*. Retrieved from http://gonbadcity.ir/HomePage.aspx?TabID=4670&site=DouranPortal&lang=fa-IR.

Governor of Golestan Informing Base. (2015). Cultural heritage attractions of Gonbad-e Kavus County [in Persian]. Retrieved from https://www.en.golestanp.ir/.

Gursoy, D., Jurowski, C., & Uysal, M. (2002). Resident attitudes: A structural modelling approach. *Annals of Tourism Research*, *29*(1), 79–105.

Hall, C. M. (2006). Implementing the World Heritage Convention: What happens after listing? In A. Leask & A. Fyall (eds), *Managing World Heritage Sites* (pp. 46–60). Oxford: Butterworth-Heinemann.

Hall, C. M., & Piggin, R. (2002). Tourism business knowledge of World Heritage Sites: A New Zealand case study. *International Journal of Tourism Research*, *4*(5), 401–411.

Jimura, T. (2019). *World Heritage Sites: Tourism, local communities and conservation activities*. Wallingford: CABI.

Johnson, J. D., Snepenger, D. J., & Akis, S. (1994). Residents' perceptions of tourism development. *Annals of Tourism Research*, *21*(3), 629–642.

Labadi, S. (2013). *UNESCO, cultural heritage, and outstanding universal value: Value-based analyses of the World Heritage and Intangible Cultural Heritage Conventions*. Lanham, MD: AltaMira Press.

Landorf, C. (2009). Managing for sustainable tourism: A review of six cultural World Heritage Sites. *Journal of Sustainable Tourism*, *17*(1), 53–70.

Meskell, L. (2014). States of conservation: Protection, politics, and pacting within UNESCO's World Heritage Committee. *Anthropological Quarterly*, *87*(1), 217–243.

Minorsky, V. (1953). *Studies in Caucasian history*. Cambridge: Cambridge University Press.

Nicholas, L. N., Thapa, B., & Ko, Y. J. (2009). Residents' perspectives of a World Heritage Site: The Pitons Management Area, St. Lucia. *Annals of Tourism Research*, *36*(3), 390–412.

Pearce, J. A. (1980). Host community acceptance of foreign tourists: Strategic considerations. *Annals of Tourism Research*, *7*(2), 224–233.

Poria, Y., Butler, R., & Airey, D. (2003). The core of heritage tourism. *Annals of Tourism Research*, *30*(1), 238–254.

Poria, Y., Reichel, A., & Cohen, R. (2013). Tourists perceptions of World Heritage Site and its designation. *Tourism Management*, *35*, 272–274.

Rasoolimanesh, S. M., Jaafar, M., Kock, N., & Ramayah, T. (2015). A revised framework of social exchange theory to investigate the factors influencing residents' perceptions. *Tourism Management Perspectives*, *16*, 335–345.

Rau, K. (2014). Editorial: World Heritage and sustainable tourism, *World Heritage*, *71*. Retrieved from http://whc.unesco.org/en/review/71/.

Ryan, C., & Montgomery, D. (1994). The attitudes of Bakewell residents to tourism and issues in community responsive tourism. *Tourism Management*, 15(5), 358–370.

Saipradist, A., & Staiff, R. (2008). Crossing the cultural divide: Western visitors and interpretation at Ayutthaya World Heritage Site, Thailand. *Journal of Heritage Tourism*, 2(3), 211–224.

Salazar, N. B. (2012). Community-based cultural tourism: Issues, threats and opportunities. *Journal of Sustainable Tourism*, 20(1), 9–22.

Sauer, E. W., Nokandeh, J., Rekavandi, H. O., & Wilkinson, T. J. (2013). *Persia's imperial power in late antiquity: The Great Wall of Gorgan and frontier landscapes of Sasanian Iran*. Oxford: Oxbow Books.

Seyfi, S., & Hall, C. M. (eds) (2018). *Tourism in Iran: Challenges, development and issues*. Abingdon: Routledge.

Shabani, B., & Tucker, H. (2018). The role of socio-cultural events in rebuilding Iran's image. In S. Seyfi & C. M. Hall (eds), *Tourism in Iran: Challenges, development and issues* (pp. 144–157). Abingdon: Routledge.

Shackley, M. (1998). Conclusions: Visitor management at cultural World Heritage Sites. In M. Shackley (ed.), *Visitor management: Case studies from World Heritage Sites* (pp. 194–205). Oxford: Butterworth-Heinemann.

Simpson, M. C. (2008). Community benefit tourism initiatives – a conceptual oxymoron? *Tourism Management*, 29(1), 1–18.

Smith, M. (2002). A critical evaluation of the global accolade: The significance of World Heritage Site status for maritime Greenwich. *International Journal of Heritage Studies*, 8(2), 137–151.

Statistical Center of Iran. (2016). *Population statistics*. Retrieved from https://www.amar.org.ir/english/Statistics-by-Topic/Population.

Statistical Center of Iran. (2018). *National tourists survey*. Retrieved from https://www.amar.org.ir/english/Statistics-by-Topic/Culture-and-Tourism#287278-statistical-survey.

Su, M. M., & Wall, G. (2011). Chinese research on World Heritage tourism. *Asia Pacific Journal of Tourism Research*, 16(1), 75–88.

Timothy, D. J. (2011). *Cultural heritage and tourism: An introduction*. Bristol: Channel View Publications.

Timothy, D. J., & Boyd, S. W. (2006). Heritage tourism in the 21st century: Valued traditions and new perspectives. *Journal of Heritage Tourism*, 1(1), 1–16.

Tucker, H., and Carnegie, E. (2014). World Heritage and the contradictions of universal value. *Annals of Tourism Research*, 47(2), 63–76.

United Nations Educational, Scientific and Cultural Organization (UNESCO). (2002). *World Heritage Committee, The Budapest Declaration on World Heritage*. Retrieved from http://whc.unesco.org/en/decisions/1217/.

United Nations Educational, Scientific and Cultural Organization (UNESCO). (2003). *UNESCO convention for the safeguarding of the intangible cultural heritage*. Paris: UNESCO.

United Nations Educational, Scientific and Cultural Organization (UNESCO). (2010). *World Heritage*. Retrieved from http://whc.unesco.org/pg.cfm?cid¼160.

United Nations Educational, Scientific and Cultural Organization (UNESCO). (2012). *Gonbad-e Qābus*. Retrieved from https://whc.unesco.org/en/list/1398.

United Nations Educational, Scientific and Cultural Organization (UNESCO). (2017). *The Great Wall of Gorgan*. Retrieved from https://whc.unesco.org/en/tentativelists/6199/.

United Nations Educational, Scientific and Cultural Organization (UNESCO). (2019). *Iran (Islamic Republic of)*. Retrieved from http://whc.unesco.org/en/statesparties/ir.

Yang, C. H., Lin, H. L., & Han, C. C. (2010). Analysis of international tourist arrivals in China: The role of World Heritage Sites. *Tourism Management, 31*(6), 827–837.

Ye, B. H., Zhang, H. Q., Shen, J. H., & Goh, C. (2014). Does social identity affect residents' attitude toward tourism development? *International Journal of Contemporary Hospitality Management, 26*(6), 907–929.

13 Factors influencing residents' perceptions toward heritage tourism

A gender perspective

S. Mostafa Rasoolimanesh, Babak Taheri, Martin Gannon, and Hamid Ataeishad

Introduction

Tourism is responsible for 9 per cent of world GDP and 10 per cent job creation annually (World Tourism Organization (UNWTO), 2014). It is expected that worldwide international tourist numbers will reach 1.8 billion by 2030, complemented by a further five to six billion domestic counterparts (UNWTO, 2016). However, the growth of tourism is not always positive for host communities, with its potential negative impacts discussed widely across extant discourse (Rasoolimanesh & Jaafar, 2017; MacKenzie & Gannon, 2019). Nevertheless, it is well established that residents typically support development in their local area if they perceive that the positive impacts of tourism outweigh any drawbacks, whereas they will not support tourism development if they perceive the opposite as more likely (Andereck, Valentine, Knopf, & Vogt, 2005; Látková & Vogt, 2012). Recognising this, prior studies have focused on residents' perceptions toward tourism impacts, alongside the myriad factors likely to influence these perceptions in a variety of geographical contexts (Andereck et al., 2005; Gursoy, Jurowski, & Uysal, 2002; Látková & Vogt, 2012; Rasoolimanesh, Jaafar, Kock & Ramayah, 2015). To this end, the important role residents' perceptions play in achieving sustainable development has been established (Nicholas, Thapa, & Ko, 2009; Rasoolimanesh & Jaafar, 2017; Telfer & Sharpley, 2008).

From a gender perspective, some studies have examined whether differences exist in the perceptions and behaviours of male and female residents (Andereck & Nyaupane, 2011; Almeida-García, Peláez-Fernández, Balbuena-Vazquez, & Cortes-Macias, 2016; Harvey, Hunt, & Harris, 1995; Nunkoo & Gursoy, 2012; Nunkoo & Ramkissoon, 2010; Rasoolimanesh et al., 2015). However, few have investigated the discrepancy between male and female residents for the effects of influencing factors on their perceptions toward tourism development (Nunkoo & Ramkissoon, 2010). Addressing this gap is crucial in practical terms, as tourism planners and local authorities must first identify whether differences between the perceptions of female and male residents toward tourism impacts exist and, second, determine the key influencing factors for each group in order to gain support for tourism development from all local residents regardless of gender. Thus, by filling this gap, this study has the potential to provide significant theoretical contributions to extant resident perception literature alongside a number of practical implications for tourism planners in their quest for sustainable tourism development.

In order to do so, this chapter turns toward an under-researched yet emerging tourism market: Iran. Iran is home to a significant number of natural and cultural tourist attractions, with the quality of the country's cultural heritage recognised globally (Curran et al., 2018). Indeed, UNESCO have inscribed 22 World Heritage Sites (WHS), and 11 sources of World Intangible Heritage across Iran, with a further 68 cultural assets under consideration for future inscription (UNESCO, 2017a, 2017b). Iran is therefore endowed with the requisite cultural heritage assets necessary to grow and sustain a major tourism industry, with this offering a significant opportunity for economic growth more generally (Seyfi & Hall, 2018). To this end, coupled with easing international sanctions, inbound international tourism has steadily increased, rising from around three million visitors in 2010 to over 5.24 million visitors in 2015 (UNWTO, 2016).

Yet, despite growing interest in heritage attractions (Taheri, Gannon, Cordina, & Lochrie, 2018), outbound tourism (Gannon et al., 2017), and the nation's travel industry more generally (Taheri, Bititci, Gannon, & Cordina, 2019), residents' perceptions of tourism development and domestic growth within the Iranian context remain largely overlooked (Seyfi, Hall, & Kuhzady, 2019). As a result, this study turns to residents of one of Iran's most historic cities, Tabriz, in order to investigate the effects of influencing factors on residents' perceptions of tourism development, while also identifying whether differences exist in the perceptions of male and female residents.

Literature review

Theoretical framework

While several theories have been applied to frame investigations of residents' perceptions toward tourism development, Social Exchange Theory (SET) remains dominant (Ap, 1992; Gursoy et al., 2002; Rasoolimanesh et al., 2015). Emerson (1976) introduced SET to explain mutual exchange processes, with emphasis on exchanges where the benefits outweigh the costs (Thompson et al., 2018). Throughout tourism discourse, many studies adopt SET as the basis from which to explain the perceptions and support residents hold toward local tourism development. To this end, SET suggests that if residents perceive the benefits of inbound tourism exceed their associated costs, they will support tourism development in their community. In contrast, if residents perceive that inbound tourism will result in greater costs than benefits, they will not support it (Látková & Vogt, 2012; Nunkoo & Gursoy, 2012).

However, a number of studies question the utility of SET, suggesting that it may be of limited efficacy when attempting to justify the role antecedent factors play in shaping residents' perceptions (Rasoolimanesh et al., 2015; Ward & Berno, 2011; Woosnam, 2011). This stems from the assertion that SET cannot fully explain the reasons behind the effects of antecedents of positive and negative perceptions (Rasoolimanesh, Jaafar, Kock, & Ahmad, 2017b). In response, some studies combine SET with Weber's Theory of Rationality (Boley, McGehee, Perdue, & Long, 2014), whereas others contend that a revised SET framework can overcome these limitations (Rasoolimanesh et al., 2015; Rasoolimanesh, Taheri, Gannon, Vafaei-Zadeh, & Hanifah, 2019c). This revised framework draws upon six central rules (*reciprocity, rationality, altruism, group gain, status consistency,* and *competition*) to justify the reasons behind residents' support for tourism development and any positive and negative perceptions therein (Rasoolimanesh et al., 2015; Rasoolimanesh, Md Noor, & Jaafar, 2019a). Of these six rules, *status consistency* is typically considered the most suitable rule for justifying differences between the effects of influencing factors on residents' perceptions across gender. *Status consistency* refers to an individual's attachment to a particular group (e.g., ethnicity, culture, gender) and can shape perceptions. If residents believe that inbound tourism benefits the groups they align with, they will typically support tourism development. However, if tourism development is projected to harm their group, residents are typically unsupportive of tourism development in their community (Cropanzano & Mitchell, 2005; Rasoolimanesh, Jaafar, & Barghi, 2017a). This echoes identity theory, as applied by Nunkoo and Gursoy (2012), in explaining the effect gender may have on residents' perceptions more generally.

Residents' perceptions toward tourism development

Studies investigating the perceptions of residents toward tourism development have analysed data collected at a wide range of destinations (Andereck et al., 2005; Kim, Uysal, & Sirgy 2013; Nunkoo & Gursoy, 2012), with Iran proving no exception (Rasoolimanesh & Ataeishad, 2018; Rezaei, 2017; Zamani-Farahani & Henderson, 2014). Iran is not immune to the positive impacts of tourism, with previous studies identifying its role in job creation, boosting family incomes, and improving living standards (Abdollahzadeh & Sharifzadeh, 2014; Ghaderi & Henderson, 2012). Further, tourism development can encourage the private and public sectors to combine to improve recreational and entertainment facilities; facilitate an understanding of cultural identity; promote the preservation and revival of traditional arts, culture, and crafts; and encourage the local community to take pride in their culture (Rasoolimanesh & Ataeishad, 2018; MacKenzie & Gannon, 2019). Moreover, tourism development in historical areas can encourage the protection of heritage assets (Rezaei, 2017).

However, residents also perceive the negative impacts of tourism development. This includes increased living costs, commodification of local culture, increased crime and drug addiction, and the reduction in the quality of local handicrafts to minimise costs (Ghaderi & Henderson, 2012; Rezaei, 2017). As such, the extent to which residents perceive increased tourism as a positive or negative phenomenon can impact upon their support for tourist development in their community. However, residents' perceptions are not manifest in isolation, with extant research identifying a number of factors likely to influence their views on local tourism development (Andereck et al., 2005; Gursoy et al., 2002; Látková & Vogt, 2012; Rasoolimanesh et al., 2015; Rasoolimanesh, Roldán, Jaafar, & Ramayah, 2017c).

Factors influencing residents' perceptions and role of gender

Several studies have investigated how community attachment, community involvement, environmental and cultural attitudes, and economic gain shape residents' perceptions toward tourism development (Nicholas et al., 2009; Olya & Gavilyan, 2017; Tosun, 2002; Látková & Vogt, 2012; Rasoolimanesh et al., 2015). If residents feel a greater attachment and sense of belonging to their community, they typically hold more positive perceptions toward local tourism development (Látková & Vogt, 2012). Additionally, residents with higher cultural and environmental values and attitudes toward their community (including heritage and traditions therein) are more inclined to encourage inbound tourism. This is particularly apparent in heritage settings, where tourism has been viewed as a vessel through which tangible and intangible heritage assets can be promoted and preserved (Rasoolimanesh et al., 2017b; Woosnam, Draper, Jiang, Aleshinloye, & Erul, 2018; Zuo, Gursoy, & Wall, 2017).

Moreover, extant research highlights the positive effect economic gain can have over residents' perceptions toward tourism development (McGehee & Andereck, 2004; Rasoolimanesh et al., 2017c); those who believe they will benefit most from tourism are more typically more supportive of local tourism development (Rasoolimanesh et al., 2017b; Zuo et al., 2017). Community involvement can also shape residents' perceptions (Andereck & Nyaupane, 2011; Nicholas et al., 2009; Látková & Vogt, 2012). Those who are involved more in the process of tourism planning are often more supportive and positive about tourism development in their local area (Nunkoo & Ramikissoon, 2010; Rasoolimanesh, Md Noor, Schuberth, & Jaafar, 2017b; Zuo et al., 2017).

Previous studies have investigated differences between the perceptions of male and female residents toward tourism development more generally (Abdollahzadeh & Sharifzadeh, 2014; Almeida-García et al., 2016; Harvey et al., 1995; Nunkoo & Ramkissoon, 2010). A number of studies found significant gender discrepancies between residents' perceptions toward tourism development in their community (Nunkoo & Gursoy, 2012; Rasoolimanesh et al., 2015), whereas others found no noteworthy differences in male and female residents' perceptions (Almeida-García et al., 2016; Harvey et al., 1995; Rasoolimanesh & Jaafar, 2017).

Milman and Pizam (1988) found that male residents are more supportive and have more positive perceptions toward tourism impacts compared to female residents. Similarly, Pizam and Pokela (1985) found that female residents hold more negative perceptions of tourism impacts than male residents. However, whether the effects of influencing factors (community attachment, community involvement, environmental attitudes, cultural attitudes, economic gain) on residents' perceptions toward tourism development differ across gender groups is less clear. Nonetheless, female residents have been found to care more about the community and any negative environmental and/or social impacts stemming from increased tourism (Abdollahzadeh & Sharifzadeh, 2014; Nunkoo & Gursoy, 2012). As such, based on SET's *consistency rule*, there may be significant differences between the male and female residents for the effects of antecedent factors on residents' perceptions. Thus:

H1: There is a significant difference for the effect of community attachment on residents' perceptions between male and female residents.

H2: There is a significant difference for the effect of environmental attitude on residents' perceptions between male and female residents.

H3: There is a significant difference for the effect of cultural attitude on residents' perceptions between male and female residents.

H4: There is a significant difference for the effect of economic gain on residents' perceptions between male and female residents.

H5: There is a significant difference for the effect of community involvement on residents' perceptions between male and female residents.

Research methodology

Study area

The study sample was comprised solely of residents of the historic Iranian city of Tabriz. A cultural hotspot, Tabriz is home to a diverse collection of heritage assets, with some estimated at over 2,000 years old. Its portfolio of heritage sites includes: the Constitutional Revolution House; Qajar Museum; Bagmasha Gate; Blue Mosque; and the Aji Chay Bridge (Rasoolimanesh et al., 2019c). However, it is perhaps best known for its Bazaar Complex – a pillar of the historic Silk Road – inscribed as a UNESCO World Heritage Site in 2010 (Curran et al., 2018; UNESCO, 2019). Tabriz is also home to internationally recognised intangible heritage, best characterised by its indigenous handicrafts, traditional carpets, and distinctive rugs (Rasoolimanesh et al., 2019c).

Data collection

Data was collected using a questionnaire populated with items adapted from established sources. Items used to measure residents' perceptions, e.g., economic (4-items), environmental (3-items), and socio-cultural (4-items), were adapted from Jurowski, Uysal, and Williams (1997) and Rasoolimanesh et al. (2019c). Those measuzring community attachment (4-items), environmental attitudes (3 items), cultural attitudes (3-items), economic gain (3-items), and involvement (3-items) were also adapted from previous literature (Gursoy et al., 2002; Nicholas et al., 2009; Rasoolimanesh et al., 2015; Rasoolimanesh et al., 2017b). All participants were instructed to identify their agreement with the aforementioned items using a 5-point scale (1 'strongly disagree'; 5 'strongly agree'). Local researchers fluent in Farsi assisted the research team in ensuring the meaning and consistency of the questionnaire items via the process of back-translation (Gannon, Taheri, & Olya, 2019). Further, some statements were rephrased and/or deleted following feedback collected during an initial pilot test (five experts, 35 respondents).

Overall, 515 completed questionnaires were collected during early 2018 (January–March). In line with the objectives of this study, systematic cluster sampling was employed, with all respondents residing in Tabriz. With regard to gender, respondents were 58.6 per cent male and 41.4 per cent female. With regard to age, 11.7 per cent were 15–25, 39.2 per cent were 26–35, 31.3 per cent were 36–45, 12 per cent were 46–55, and 5.8 per cent were 56+. Further, 64.6 per cent of the 515 participants held a diploma/degree, and 17.3 per cent had completed postgraduate studies. The remaining 18.1 per cent were secondary school educated or held no recognised qualifications.

Data analysis

Partial least squares – structural equation modelling (PLS-SEM) using SmartPLS 3.2.8 (Ringle, Wende, & Becker, 2015) – was employed to assess the measurement and structural models. Moreover, Multi-Group Analysis (MGA) was performed to compare the effects of influencing factors on residents' perceptions across two gender groups: male and female. PLS-SEM was employed as the study framework is comprised of both formative and reflective constructs and, for performing MGA, non-parametric SEM is preferable (Hair, Hult, Ringle, & Sarstedt, 2017; Henseler, Ringle, & Sarstedt, 2016). The measurement invariance for composite (MICOM) approach (Henseler et al., 2016), using 5,000 permutations, was performed prior to MGA.

Results and findings

Model assessment using PLS-SEM

The proposed framework includes five reflective exogenous constructs: community attachment, environmental attitude, cultural attitude, economic gain, and involvement. Further, 'residents' perceptions' is characterised as an endogenous composite construct. This includes three reflective dimensions: economic perceptions, environmental perceptions, and socio-cultural perceptions. Thus, to assess the measurement model, the reliability and validity of all five exogenous constructs and the three reflective dimensions of 'residents' perceptions' were first assessed. Next, using a two-stage approach (Rasoolimanesh et al., 2019b), residents' perceptions were established as a second-order construct (Rasoolimanesh et al., 2019a). Finally, the measurement model was assessed by including five reflective exogenous constructs and one composite endogenous construct for female and male resident groups. Table 13.1 shows the measurement model assessment results. It demonstrates that composite reliability (CR) and average variance extracted (AVE) is above 0.7 and 0.5 respectively, indicating acceptable reliability and convergent validity for both gender groups (Hair et al., 2017). Discriminant validity for female and male residents was checked using the heterotrait-monotrait (HTMT) approach (Henseler, Ringle, & Sarstedt, 2015), which proved acceptable for both groups.

After establishing residents' perceptions as a second order composite using a two-stage approach, multi-collinearity was assessed via variance inflation factors (VIF) and significance of outer weights. The results for both female and male residents showed that VIF were <3.3, with significant outer weights for all underlying items (Table 13.1). Moreover, acceptable reliability, convergent validity, and discriminant validity were established for all reflective constructs.

Measurement invariance must be tested prior to comparing the path coefficients between two groups (e.g., male and female residents), using MGA to test the proposed hypotheses (Henseler et al., 2016; Rasoolimanesh et al., 2017c). The measurement invariance of composites approach (MICOM) was employed, as per recent literature (Henseler et al., 2016). MICOM contains three steps: (1) configural invariance assessment, (2) compositional invariance assessment, and (3) the assessment of equal means and variances (Rasoolimanesh et al., 2017c). Using MICOM, partial measurement invariance was established via configural and compositional invariance – a requirement for MGA (Rasoolimanesh et al., 2019c). Further, MICOM demonstrated equal means for all constructs (e.g., community attachment, environmental attitude, cultural attitude, economic gain, and involvement), alongside residents' perceptions, for both the male and female resident groups.

Table 13.1 Measurement model assessment results

Construct/associated items	Loading/weight		CR		AVE	
	Male	Female	Male	Female	Male	Female
Community attachment			0.827	0.852	0.545	0.592
I have positive feelings for my city.	0.757	0.763				
I feel a sense of belonging to my city.	0.708	0.821				
I have an emotional attachment to this place- it has meaning to me.	0.788	0.833				
I am willing to invest my talent or time to make this an even better place	0.695	0.645				
Environmental attitude			0.832	0.843	0.624	0.641
The diversity of heritage must be valued and protected.	0.771	0.766				
Community environment must be protected now and in the future.	0.821	0.835				
The development of infrastructure and public facilities, as well private sector, should not damage heritage areas	0.776	0.800				
Cultural attitudes			0.813	0.891	0.592	0.732
Local and traditional culture should be preserved.	0.723	0.801				
The lifestyle of local residents should be protected.	0.757	0.908				
My traditions and culture are very important for me.	0.825	0.855				
Economic gain			0.838	0.871	0.636	0.693
Increasing the number of visitors effects my current household income.	0.910	0.867				
A high percentage of my income comes from the money spent by visitors.	0.762	0.824				
Most of the income of the company I work for (or business I own) comes from the tourist trade.	0.707	0.806				
Involvement			0.848	0.895	0.585	0.682
Residents have been involved in the management of heritage.	0.656	0.830				
Residents have been involved in the process of tourism development and planning.	0.686	0.821				

(*Continued*)

Table 13.1 Continued

Construct/associated items	Loading/weight		CR		AVE	
	Male	Female	Male	Female	Male	Female
Most of the time, my opinions have been asked regarding planning and development of tourism.	0.894	0.865				
Most of the time, my opinions have been asked regarding heritage conservation projects.	0.801	0.786				

			P-value		VIF	
			Male	Female	Male	Female
Residents' perception						
Economic perceptions	0.506	0.398	<0.01	<0.01	1.343	1.412
Environmental perceptions	0.326	0.396	<0.01	<0.01	1.345	1.546
Socio-cultural perceptions	0.426	0.426	<0.01	<0.01	1.436	1.724

Note
Items of Economic Perceptions, Environmental Perceptions, and Socio-cultural Perceptions:
Economic Perceptions
ECO_RP1 Tourism development creates more jobs for my community.
ECO_RP2 Tourism development attracts more investment to my community.
ECO_RP3 Our standard of living increases considerably because of tourism.
ECO_RP4 Tourism development provides more infrastructures and public facilities (roads, shopping malls, etc.).
Environmental Perceptions
ENV_RP1 Tourism development helps to preserve the natural environment.
ENV_RP2 Tourism development helps to preserve the historical buildings.
ENV_RP3 Tourism development improves the area's appearance.
Socio-Cultural Perceptions
SCUL_RP1 Tourism development preserves the cultural identity of host residents.
SCUL_RP2 Tourism development promotes cultural exchange.
SCUL_RP3 Tourism development facilitates meeting visitors and educational experiences.
SCUL_RP4 Tourism development increases recreation facilities and opportunities.

Hypothesis testing

Table 13.2 shows the results of hypothesis testing and MGA for both gender groups. Two nonparametric approaches were applied to test the proposed hypotheses: Henseler's MGA (Henseler, Ringle, & Sinkovics, 2009) and the permutation test (Chin & Dibbern, 2010). This facilitated the comparison of the effects of community attachment, environmental attitude, cultural attitude, economic gain, and involvement on residents' perception toward tourism development between male and female respondents. The results show the positive effects of community attachment, economic gain, and environmental attitude for both male and female residents. However, the results do not support the effects of cultural attitudes and involvement on residents' perceptions for both gender groups. Further, the MGA results only identify a

Table 13.2 Hypothesis testing results

Hypothesis	Relationships	Path coefficient		Confidence interval (95%) Bias corrected		P-value difference		Supported
		Male	Female	Male	Female	Henseler's MGA	Permutation test	
H1	Community attachment → Residents' perceptions	0.167	0.296	[0.006, 0.267]	[0.117, 0.474]	0.119	0.225	NO/NO
H2	Environmental attitude → Residents' perceptions	0.451	0.203	[0.345, 0.561]	[0.049, 0.340]	0.997	0.011	YES/YES
H3	Cultural attitude → Residents' perceptions	0.010	0.056	[−0.125, 0.116]	[−0.092, 0.220]	0.335	0.675	NO/NO
H4	Economic gain → Residents' perceptions	0.275	0.308	[0.176, 0.372]	[0.167, 0.460]	0.354	0.705	NO/NO
H5	Community involvement → Residents' perceptions	0.021	0.062	[−0.169, 0.099]	[−0.83, 0.191]	0.345	0.632	NO/NO

Note
In Henseler's MGA method, p values lower than 0.05 or higher than 0.95 indicate significant differences between specific paths at the 5 per cent level.

significant difference between the effect of environmental attitude on residents' perceptions between male and female residents, with this effect stronger for male residents (H2). Thus, the results support H2. However, as the results do not identify significant differences between males and females for the effects of other antecedents on residents' perceptions, the remaining hypotheses (H1, H3, H4, H5) are not supported.

Importance–Performance Analysis

Recent tourism research has applied Importance–Performance Analysis (IPA) to gain further insight from collected data and to highlight both the importance and performance of antecedent factors in achieving study outcomes (Boley, McGehee, & Hammett, 2017). Ringle and Sarstedt (2016) employed IPA in order to improve the interpretation of PLS-SEM results by generating Importance–Performance Map Analysis (IPMA). In this study, IPMA was used to identify the importance and performance of community attachment, environmental attitude, cultural attitude, economic gain, and involvement in establishing perceptions toward tourism development for both male and female Tabriz residents. According to the results of the IPMA, economic gain was identified as the most important antecedent for female residents. Nonetheless, the performance of this antecedent factor is low. For male residents, economic gain holds the highest importance (after environmental attitude), but its performance is also low. The performance of community attachment is high for both gender groups, but its importance is higher for participating female residents. Finally, the IPMA results demonstrate the low importance attached to cultural attitudes and involvement for both gender groups.

Discussion

This study investigated whether the perceptions of residents toward tourism development differ across gender by examining the effects of influencing factors. Significant differences between male and female residents with regard to the effects of community attachment, environmental attitudes, cultural attitudes, economic gain, and involvement on their perceptions toward tourism development were hypothesised, underpinned by SET's *status consistency* rule. However, the results largely did not support any differences between the perceptions of male and female residents toward tourism development. This is perhaps unsurprising as previous studies remain contradictory. For example, some identify significant discrepancies between gender groups (Nunkoo & Gursoy, 2012; Rasoolimanesh et al., 2015), whereas others contend that the perceptions of male and female residents towards tourism development are broadly similar (Almeida-García et al., 2016; Harvey et al., 1995; Rasoolimanesh & Jaafar, 2017).

The results did not support H1, H3, H4, or H5, suggesting that there were no significant differences between the effects of community attachment, cultural attitudes, economic gain, and involvement on residents' perceptions toward tourism development across gender groups. The effects of community attachment and economic gain were high for both male and female residents, whereas the effects of cultural attitude and involvement were insignificant for both groups. Research has identified the positive effects of community attachment and economic gain on perceptions of residents toward tourism development (Jurowski et al., 1997; Látková & Vogt, 2012; McGehee & Anderck, 2004; Rasoolimanesh et al., 2015), consistent with the results of this study. However, no significant differences between male and female residents were observed. The results only identified a significant difference between male and female residents for the effect of environmental attitudes on perceptions toward tourism development, with this effect proving stronger for male residents. However, this is inconsistent with extant literature, which contends that female residents care more about community and are more worried about any negative environmental and social impacts of tourism (Abdollahzadeh & Sharifzadeh, 2014; Nunkoo & Gursoy, 2012).

Additionally, IPA was performed for both groups. The results show environmental attitudes hold the highest performance among all antecedents for both male and female residents, while the level of importance is higher for male residents. This echoes the MGA results. The IPMA shows economic gain as the most important antecedent of perceptions toward tourism development for female residents. However, its performance is very low. Economic gain is identified as the second most important antecedent for male residents. However, the performance of this factor is also low, consistent with their female counterparts. As such, the results suggest that Tabriz residents do not perceive any economic value from tourism development and, for female residents in particular, their expectation is to therefore gain greater benefit from inbound tourism in the future.

Conclusion

This study investigated discrepancies between the perceptions of male and female residents toward tourism development, alongside differences in the effects of influencing factors on these perceptions across these two gender groups. This nascent study is therefore one the first to examine differences in the effects of influencing factors on residents' perceptions across gender, with this serving as its core theoretical contribution. However, the study was limited to one city in Iran. In order to address this limitation, future studies should conduct comparative research across different types of destinations (e.g., urban/rural; developed/developing). Nonetheless, this study proffers several practical implications for tourism planners and the local authority within the historic city of Tabriz.

The MGA and IPMA results demonstrate that environmental attitude has the highest effect and importance on male residents' positive perceptions toward tourism development. This concept should be considered and improved upon in order to gain the support of male residents. This factor is also an important antecedent for female residents. However, the most important factor to improve the positive perceptions of female residents and gain their support for the process of tourism development remains economic gain. Yet, the female residents of Tabriz believed that the potential economic benefit derived from tourism was very low. Therefore, local authorities must focus on improving the economic gain derived from tourism for female in order to improve their perceptions of, and support for, tourism development more generally. Nonetheless, the results also demonstrate a low level of economic gain derived from tourism from male residents. Therefore, local authorities must also develop initiatives that increase the economic benefits male residents derive from tourism, despite its lower importance when compared to female residents.

References

Abdollahzadeh, G., & Sharifzadeh, A. (2014). Rural residents' perceptions toward tourism development: A study from Iran. *International Journal of Tourism Research*, *16*(2), 126–136.

Almeida-García, F., Peláez-Fernández, M. Á., Balbuena-Vazquez, A., & Cortes-Macias, R. (2016). Residents' perceptions of tourism development in Benalmádena (Spain). *Tourism Management*, *54*, 259–274.

Andereck, K., & Nyaupane, G. (2011). Exploring the nature of tourism and quality of life perceptions among residents. *Journal of Travel Research*, *50*(3), 248–260.

Andereck, K., Valentine, K., Knopf, R., & Vogt, C. (2005). Residents' perceptions of community tourism impacts. *Annals of Tourism Research*, *32*(4), 1056–1076.

Ap, J. (1992). Residents' perceptions on tourism impacts. *Annals of Tourism Research*, *19*(4), 665–690.

Boley, B. B., McGehee, N. G., & Hammett, A. T. (2017). Importance–Performance Analysis (IPA) of sustainable tourism initiatives: The resident perspective. *Tourism Management*, *58*, 66–77.

Boley, B. B., McGehee, N. G., Perdue, R. R., & Long, P. (2014). Empowerment and resident attitudes toward tourism: Strengthening the theoretical foundation through a Weberian lens. *Annals of Tourism Research*, *49*, 33–40.

Chin, W. W., & Dibbern, J. (2010). A permutation based procedure for multi-group PLS analysis: Results of tests of differences on simulated data and a cross cultural analysis of the sourcing of information system services between Germany and the USA. In V. Esposito Vinzi, W. W. Chin, J. Henseler, & H. Wang (eds), *Handbook of partial least squares: Concepts, methods and applications* (pp. 171–193). Heidelberg, Germany: Springer-Verlag.

Cropanzano, R., & Mitchell, M. S. (2005). Social exchange theory: An interdisciplinary review. *Journal of Management*, *31*(6), 874–900.

Curran, R., Baxter, I., Collinson, E ... & Yalinay, O. (2018). The traditional marketplace: Serious leisure and recommending authentic travel. *Service Industries Journal*, *38*(15–16), 1116–1132.
Emerson, R. M. (1976). Social exchange theory. *Annual Review of Sociology*, *2*(1), 335–362.
Gannon, M. J., Baxter, I. W., Collinson, E., Curran, R., ... & Maxwell-Stuart, R. (2017). Travelling for Umrah: Destination attributes, destination image, and post-travel intentions. *The Service Industries Journal*, *37*(7–8), 448–465.
Gannon, M., Taheri, B., & Olya, H. (2019). Festival quality, self-connection, and bragging. *Annals of Tourism Research*, *76*, 239–252.
Ghaderi, Z. & Henderson, J. C. (2012). Sustainable rural tourism in Iran: A perspective from Hawraman Village. *Tourism Management Perspectives*, *2–3*, 47–54.
Gursoy, D., Jurowski, C., & Uysal, M. (2002). Resident attitudes: A structural modeling approach. *Annals of Tourism Research*, *29*(1), 79–105.
Hair, J., Hult, G., Ringle, C., & Sarstedt, M. (2017). *A primer on partial least squares structural equations modeling (PLS-SEM)* (2nd edn). Los Angeles, CA: Sage.
Harvey, M. J., Hunt, J., & Harris Jr, , C. C. (1995). Gender and community tourism dependence level. *Annals of Tourism Research*, *22*(2), 349–366.
Henseler, J., Ringle, C. M., & Sarstedt, M. (2015). A new criterion for assessing discriminant validity in variance-based structural equation modeling. *Journal of the Academy of Marketing Science*, *43*(1), 115–135.
Henseler, J., Ringle, C., & Sarstedt, M. (2016). Testing measurement invariance of composites using partial least squares. *International Marketing Review*, *33*(3), 405–431.
Henseler, J., Ringle, C. M., & Sinkovics, R. R. (2009). The use of partial least squares path modeling in international marketing. In R. R. Sinkovics & P. N. Ghauri (eds), *Advances in International Marketing* (Vol. *20*, pp. 277–320). Bingley, UK: Emerald.
Jurowski, C., Uysal, M., & Williams, D. R. (1997). A theoretical analysis of host community resident reactions to tourism. *Journal of Travel Research*, *36*(2), 3–11.
Kim, K., Uysal, M., & Sirgy, M. (2013). How does tourism in a community impact the quality of life of community residents? *Tourism Management*, *36*, 527–540.
Látková, P., & Vogt, C. (2012). Residents' attitudes toward existing and future tourism development in rural communities. *Journal of Travel Research*, *51*(1), 50–67.
MacKenzie, N., & Gannon, M. (2019). Exploring the antecedents of sustainable tourism development. *International Journal of Contemporary Hospitality Management*, *31*(6), 2411–2427.
McGehee, N., & Andereck, K. (2004). Factors predicting rural residents' support of tourism. *Journal of Travel Research*, *43*(2), 131–140.
Milman, A., & Pizam, A. (1988). Social impacts of tourism on central Florida. *Annals of Tourism Research*, *15*(2), 191–204.
Nicholas, L., Thapa, B., & Ko, Y. (2009). Residents' perspectives of a World Heritage site: The Pitons Management Area, St. Lucia. *Annals of Tourism Research*, *36*(3), 390–412.
Nunkoo, R., & Gursoy, D. (2012). Residents' support for tourism: An identity perspective. *Annals of Tourism Research*, *39*(1), 243–268.
Nunkoo, R., & Ramkissoon, H. (2010). Modeling community support for a proposed integrated resort project. *Journal of Sustainable Tourism*, *18*(2), 257–277.

Olya, H. G. T., & Gavilyan, Y. (2017). Configurational models to predict residents' support for tourism development. *Journal of Travel Research*, *56*(7), 893–912.

Pizam, A., & Pokela, J. (1985). The perceived impacts of casino gambling on a community. *Annals of Tourism Research*, *12*(2), 147–165.

Rasoolimanesh, S. M., & Ataeishad, H. (2018). Residents' perceptions towards heritage tourism development: A case of historical City of Kashan, Iran. In S. Seyfi & C. M. Hall (eds), *Tourism in Iran: Challenges, development and issues* (pp. 127–143). London: Routledge.

Rasoolimanesh, S. M., & Jaafar, M. (2017). Sustainable tourism development and residents' perceptions in World Heritage Site destinations, *Asia Pacific Journal of Tourism Research*, *22*(1): 34–48.

Rasoolimanesh, S. M., Jaafar, M., & Barghi, R. (2017a). Effects of motivation, knowledge and perceived power on residents' perceptions: Application of Weber's theory in World Heritage Site destinations. *International Journal of Tourism Research*, *19*(1), 68–79.

Rasoolimanesh, S. M., Jaafar, M., Kock, N., & Ahmad, A. G. (2017b). The effects of community factors on residents' perceptions toward World Heritage Site inscription and sustainable tourism development. *Journal of Sustainable Tourism*, *25*(2), 198–216.

Rasoolimanesh, S. M., Jaafar, M., Kock, N., & Ramayah, T. (2015). A revised framework of social exchange theory to investigate the factors influencing residents' perceptions. *Tourism Management Perspectives*, *16*, 335–345.

Rasoolimanesh, S. M., Md Noor, S., & Jaafar, M. (2019a). Positive and negative perceptions of residents toward tourism development: Formative or reflective. In S. Rezaei (ed.), *Quantitative tourism research in Asia: Current status and future directions*. Singapore: Springer.

Rasoolimanesh, S. M., Md Noor, S., Schuberth, F., & Jaafar, M. (2019b). Investigating the effects of tourist engagement on satisfaction and loyalty. *The Service Industries Journal*, *39*(7–8), 559–574.

Rasoolimanesh, S. M., Roldán, J. L., Jaafar, M., & Ramayah, T. (2017c). Factors influencing residents' perceptions toward tourism development: Differences across rural and urban World Heritage sites. *Journal of Travel Research*, *56*(6), 760–775.

Rasoolimanesh, S. M., Taheri, B., Gannon, M., Vafaei-Zadeh, A., & Hanifah, H. (2019c). Does living in the vicinity of heritage tourism sites influence residents' perceptions and attitudes? *Journal of Sustainable Tourism*, *27*(9), 1295–1317.

Rezaei, N. (2017). Resident perceptions toward tourism impacts in historic center of Yazd, Iran. *Tourism Geographies*, *19*(5), 734–755.

Ringle, C. M., & Sarstedt, M. (2016). Gain more insight from your PLS-SEM results: The Importance–Performance Map *Analysis*. *Industrial Management & Data Systems*, *116*(9), 1865–1886.

Ringle, C., Wende, S., & Becker, J. (2015) *SmartPLS 3 (version 3.2.3, computer software)*. Boenningstedt, Germany: SmartPLS GmbH.

Seyfi, S., & Hall, C. M. (eds) (2018). *Tourism in Iran: Challenges, development and issues*. London: Routledge.

Seyfi, S., Hall, C. M., & Kuhzady, S. (2019). Tourism and hospitality research on Iran: Current state and perspectives. *Tourism Geographies*, *21*(1), 143–162.

Taheri, B., Bititci, U., Gannon, M., & Cordina, R. (2019). Investigating the influence of performance measurement on learning, entrepreneurial orientation and performance in turbulent markets. *International Journal of Contemporary Hospitality Management, 31*(3), 1224–1246.

Taheri, B., Gannon, M., Cordina, R., & Lochrie, S. (2018). Measuring host sincerity: Scale development and validation. *International Journal of Contemporary Hospitality Management, 30*(8), 2752–2772.

Telfer, D., & Sharpley, R. (2008). *Tourism and development in the developing world.* London: Routledge.

Thompson, J., Baxter, I. W., Curran, R., Gannon, M. J., Lochrie, S., Taheri, B., & Yalinay, O. (2018). Negotiation, bargaining, and discounts: Generating WoM and local tourism development at the Tabriz bazaar, Iran. *Current Issues in Tourism, 21*(11), 1207–1214.

Tosun, C. (2002). Host perceptions of impacts: A comparative tourism study. *Annals of Tourism Research, 29*(1), 231–253.

UNWTO (2014). *UNWTO Tourism Highlights, 2014* Edition. Madrid, Spain: UNWTO.

UNWTO (2016). *UNWTO Tourism Highlights, 2016 Edition.* Madrid, Spain: UNWTO.

UNESCO (2017a). *Iran. (Islamic Republic of).* Retrieved from http://whc.unesco.org/en/statesparties/ir.

UNESCO (2017b). *Iran (Islamic Republic of) and the 2003 Convention. UNESCO, Intangible Cultural Heritage Lists.* Retrieved from https://ich.unesco.org/en/state/iran-islamic-republic-of-IR.

UNESCO (2019). *Tabriz Historic Bazaar Complex. UNESCO World Heritage list.* Retrieved from https://whc.unesco.org/en/list/1346.

Ward, C., & Berno, T. (2011). Beyond social exchange theory: Attitudes toward tourists. *Annals of Tourism Research, 38*(4), 1556–1569.

Woosnam, K. M. (2011). Testing a model of Durkheim's theory of emotional solidarity among residents of a tourism community. *Journal of Travel Research, 50*(5), 546–558.

Woosnam, K. M., Draper, J., Jiang, J., Aleshinloye, K. D., & Erul, E. (2018). Applying self-perception theory to explain residents' attitudes about tourism development through travel histories. *Tourism Management, 64*, 357–368.

Zamani-Farahani, H., & Henderson, J. C. (2014). Community attitudes toward tourists: A study of Iran. *International Journal of Hospitality and Tourism Administration, 15*(4), 354–375.

Zuo, B., Gursoy, D., & Wall, G. (2017). Residents' support for red tourism in China: The moderating effect of central government. *Annals of Tourism Research, 64*, 51–63.

14 Climate change threats to cultural and heritage tourism in Iran

Jennifer M. Fitchett and Gholamreza Roshan

Introduction

Iran has a rich heritage spanning more than 5,000 years, a function of the continuity of civilisations and the geographic importance of the region (Zamani-Farahani & Musa, 2008; Baum & O'Gorman, 2010; Rastegar, 2010). The country hosts 23 UNESCO World Heritage Sites, and countless archaeological, historical, and architectural heritage attractions (Rastegar, 2010), distributed across both major cities and small towns. Heritage and cultural tourism therefore represents the primary tourism attractions in the country, and an important consideration for economic growth (Zamani-Farahani & Musa, 2008). Efforts to increase tourism flow to Iran therefore rely heavily on promoting visits to these cultural heritage sites (Rastegar, 2010).

Climate is considered to be a key determinant in the destination tourists choose to visit, the timing and duration of their vacation, and their enjoyment of the activities they partake in (Gössling, Scott, Hall, Ceron, & Dubois, 2012). For this reason, significant concern has been raised regarding the threats that climate change poses to the future climatic suitability of tourist destinations across the world (Kaján & Saarinen, 2013). Although some destinations may experience an improvement in climate and come out as 'winners', increases in temperature, changes in precipitation, wind, and humidity, and an increased severity of extreme events will make many regions 'losers' (Scott, McBoyle, & Schwartzentruber, 2004). For Iran in particular, heat stress has been identified as the primary threat to tourism and tourist satisfaction (Farajzadeh & Matzarakis, 2009; Akbarian Ronizi, Roshan, & Negahban, 2016), while wind and heavy precipitation are cited as secondary threats (Roshan, Yousefi, & Fitchett, 2016).

As many cultural and heritage attractions globally are indoors, often in climate-controlled buildings to protect the exhibits, good weather is not considered a prerequisite for tourists to visit a destination, for them to enjoy the attraction, or a factor that would limit the duration of a visit. However, for much of the developing world, cultural and heritage tourism not only involve outdoor areas, but the outdoors often forms an integral part of the experience. For this reason, many of the climate change threats to outdoor

Climate change threats 219

tourism attractions, such as beaches and nature reserves, apply equally to these destinations. There is thus a need to critically evaluate the threats of climate change to heritage and cultural tourism. More recently, a special issue of the *Journal of Heritage Tourism* on 'Heritage, Tourism and Climate Change' has reflected the challenges climate and climate change pose to the subsector (Hall, 2016; Hall, Baird, James, & Ram, 2016), but with no focus there or in subsequent literature on the Iranian context. This is a stark gap in the literature, as Iran is one such country, where many of the cultural and heritage attractions involve outdoor components, and where indoor components are seldom climate-controlled.

This chapter makes a first estimation of the climate and climate change threats to heritage and cultural tourism in Iran, through biometeorological calculations using the Tourism Climatic Index (TCI) (Mieczkowski, 1985) and the Universal Thermal Climate Index (UTCI) (Blażejczyk et al., 2013). This is intended to provide initial grounds from which to encourage further research into the climate threats to particular heritage and cultural tourism attractions in the Middle East and North Africa.

Study region

Iran covers a terrestrial area of 1,648,000 km^2 (Nazemosadat & Ghasemi, 2004). Approximately half of this land area is mountainous (Figure 1.1); the Zagros Mountains extending along the west of the country and the Alborz Mountains located in the north, resulting in an altitudinal range from –20 masl in the Caspian Lowlands to 5,860 masl in the Alborz Mountains (Rasuly, Babaeian, Ghaemi, & ZawarReza, 2012). The country borders large water bodies with the Caspian Sea to the north and the Persian Gulf to the south (Haftlang, 2003). Iran is classified amongst the drier regions of the world, with over 60 per cent of the country experiencing precipitation of less than 50–350 mm annually (Modarres & da Silva, 2007). Precipitation varies from over 1,800 mm over the west Caspian Lowlands to less than 50 mm over the eastern inland desert regions (Rasuly et al., 2012). With a predominantly Mediterranean climate governed by the Siberian High, Westerly Depressions, and South Westerly Monsoon, 70 per cent of the country experiences rainfall during the winter months spanning October and March (Rasuly et al., 2012). Temperature in Iran varies considerably, from winter temperatures as low as –20°C to summer temperatures reaching 50°C (Ghasemi & Khalili, 2008), driven by a combination of latitude, altitude, and proximity to the coast.

Iran hosts a rich cultural and historical heritage spanning 5,000 years, and leisure and environmental attractions, which attract a diverse group of tourists who visit widely distributed locations (Farajzadeh & Matzarakis, 2009). Iran has a total of eight World Heritage Sites, including ancient historical sites and towns and religious sites (Baum & O'Gorman, 2010; Seyfi, Hall, & Fagnoni, 2019). The city of Shiraz, a World Heritage Site located at the foot of the Zagros Mountains, is one of Iran's oldest cities, visited primarily by tourists from nearby Islamic countries (Aref, Redzuan, & Gill, 2009). The province of Kermanshah in western Iran similarly attracts visitors through its collection of historical monuments dating back to AD 226 (Mohmmadi, Khalifah, & Hosseini, 2010). The coastal area of Ramsar, located 291km from Tehran, attracts predominantly leisure tourists from the region and further abroad (Eshiki & Kaboudi, 2012). In addition to cultural and leisure tourism, Iran also has a long history of business tourism (Baum & O'Gorman, 2010). Despite the large number and variety of tourism attractions in Iran, the country currently attracts fewer than two million arrivals annually and receives only 5 per cent of the Islamic tourism market (Morakabati, 2011).

For the purpose of exploring the climate threats to heritage and cultural tourism in Iran, a selection of 38 cities were identified across the country (Figure 14.1), each of which hosted at least two heritage and/or cultural heritage attractions (Table 14.1) and had an active meteorological station managed by the Iranian Meteorological Organization. These cities provide a reasonable spatial distribution across the country, with a notable paucity north-east of the Zagros Mountains. This region comprises the Central Iran Desert, one of the hottest regions on earth (Mildrexler, Zhao, & Running, 2011). The cultural and heritage sites are varied, including but not limited to

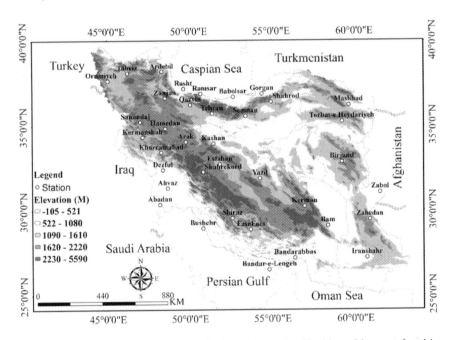

Figure 14.1 Map of Iran indicating the location of the 38 cities of interest for this study.

Climate change threats 221

Table 14.1 Heritage and cultural tourism attractions at the 38 Iranian locations of interest in this study

City	Heritage and/or cultural tourism attractions		
Abadan	Rangooniha Mosque	Abadan refinery	
Ahvaz	Remains of the Historic City of Hormuz Ardeshir	Eight Bungalows and Railroad	White Bridge
	Moninatjar Monument	Spinning and Knitting Factory	Black Bridge
		Amari Mosque	
Anzali	Mid Stacker Palace	Maryam Holy Church	Ghasem House
	Clock Tower	Qa'miyya Mosque Minaret	Golzagh Bridge
	Music Building		
Arak	Arak Bazaar	Historic Bath of Four Seasons	Mesrop Church
	Historical Home and Handicraft Museum of Hasanpour	Sultan Abad museum	Caravanserai Monument
		Museum of Fine Arts	Museum of Anthropology
Ardebil	Sheikh Safi al-Din Khānegāh and Shrine Ensemble	Museum of the Monastery and Tomb of Sheikh Safiuddin Ardebili	Saidabad Bath
	Ibrahim Abad Bath	Archaeological Museum	Mansoorieh Bath
	Pearzer Bath	The Bathhouse of Mollaadi	Sheikh Historical Bath
			Ardabil Artistic Handicrafts Museum
Babolsar	The Tomb of Imamzadeh Ibrahim	Soganfar Foulad Kola	Soganfar Armej Kola
	Sculpture Square	Soganfar Jazin	Sotogh Bath
	Kafir Kathi Hill	Soganfar Sharmakla	The Old Clock tower
	The Cotton Factory	Suspension Bridge Babolsar	The Barracks Complex
	The Building of the Township		
Bam	Bam Citadel (Argh)	Bam Argh Mosque	
Bandarabas	Golestar Mosque	Dezak Mosque	Shah Hoseini Warehouse
	Delmasha Mosque	Red Dome	Fin Dam
	Hindu temple	Golchin Caravanserai	Castle Fin

(*Continued*)

Table 14.1 Continued

City	Heritage and/or cultural tourism attractions		
	Golmar Dormition	Golcharvar Caravanserai	
Bandarlenge	Khaledi Mosque	Ancient City of Harire	Sheikh Ahmad Sarhan's Tomb
	Old Lengeh Mosque	Stone Tower	Old Cong Tree Collection
	Farouk's House	Porta Castle	Elite Kish Palace
	Ahmad Ibn Hanbal Mosque	Bastaki House	Marjan Palace Kish
Birjand	Birjand Museum of Anthropology	Pardlily House	Akbarieh Garden and Mansion House
	Birjand Heritage Museum	Haghiabad Arg	Four Tree Mosque
	Birjand Archaeological Museum	Amir Abad Garden and Mansion	Chahar Barat Bath (Pahlavani Museum)
	Birjand Participatory Museum of Anthropology	Birjand Castle	Garden and Manor House
	Masoumiyeh Garden and Mansion	Old Post Building	Baharestan Church
Bushehr	Imamzadeh Abdolmayiman Bushehr	Dehdashti Mansion	Malek Mansion
	Imamzadeh Mirmam Dashti	Tangestani Mansion	Golshan Mansion
	Shoghab Cemetery	Bushehr Church	Holy Church of the Holy Ghost of Bushehr
	Germany Abad Bushehr	Church of the Rising of Christ	
Dezful	Grand Mosque of Dezful	Shahrkoddin Baths	Old Bazaar of Dezful
	Baths of Crenation (Anthropology Museum)	Livs Village	Chaghamshid Baths
	Shahrankuddin Baths	Qaa Yaqoub Layts Safari	Old Dezful Castle
Esfahan	Shrine of Esfahan	The Sheikholeslum House	The Qaiserie Bazaar
	The Palace of the Eight Paradises	Chehelsotun Palace	The Monarjbanan
	Minarets of Isfahan in the Early Islamic era	Khaju Bridge (Shahi Bridge)	Abbasi Mosque
	The Shaykh Lotfollah Mosque	Decorative Arts Museum	The Supreme Qapu Palace

(*Continued*)

Climate change threats 223

City	Heritage and/or cultural tourism attractions		
	Persian Gardens	Vank Cathedral	Naghshe Jahan Square
Ghazvin	The Old Mosque Al-Nabi Mosque	Tower of Barajin	Old Tehran Gate
	Panjeh Ali Mosque	Cantor Church	Alamut Castle
	Senseid Mosque	Armenian Church	Tomb of the Head of Al-Mujahideen
	Atiq Jami Mosque	Sepahdar Mansion	Tomb of Hamdollah Mostofi
	Asurian Church		
Gorgan	Tomb of Imamzadeh Noor	Gorgan Museum Palace	Gorgan Great Wall
	Tomb of Imamzadeh Abdollah	Palace of Agha Mohammad Khan Qajar	Ancient City of Gorgan
	Nalbandan Bazaar	Gorgan Constitutional House	Gorgan Archaeology Museum
Hamedan	Tomb of Bu-Ali Sina	Asadabad Museum	Anjeli Church
	Tomb of Baba Taher	Abu Ali Sinah Museum of Traditional Medicine	Gregory Church of Stepan - Hazrat Maryam
	Ghorban Tower	Shahsangi Bridge	Holy Defense Museum
	Alavian Dome	Mohajer Bridge	Tomb of Imamzadeh Khezr
	Alavian Mosque	Paul Abashineh	Hegmataneh Archaeology Museum Sharifieh Caravanserai
	Hamedan Mosque	Hossein Khani Caravanserai	Tomb of Imamzadeh Yahya
	Tomb of Imamzadeh Ismail		
Iranshahr	Castle of Nasseri	Bampour Castle	Speech Cemetery
Kashan	Fin Garden	Al-Yasin Historical House	Tabatabai Historical House
	Fountain of Sulaimaniyah	Bazaar Historical Complex	Jalali Castle and Seljuk Hesar
	Tomb of Imamzadeh Prince Ibrahim	Tombs of Mohtasham Kashani	Agha Big Mosque and School

(*Continued*)

224 J. M. Fitchett and G. Roshan

Table 14.1 Continued

City	Heritage and/or cultural tourism attractions		
	Borujerdi Historic House	Tomb of Imamzadeh Haroon ibn Musa ibn Ja'far (pbuh shah)	Historical house of Manouchehri
	Ameri Historic House		Center for Crafts and Traditional Arts
	Historical monuments of Abbasids		
Kerman	Jebel Ali Dome	Zarestan Museum	Mozafari Kerman Mosque
	Ganjali Khan Bath	Shahid Bahonar Museum	Kerman Vakil's Mosque
	Ridge Citadel	Harandi Museum Garden	Contemporary Industrial Museum
	Holy Defense Museum	Shah Nematollah Vali Museum	Coin Museum
Kermanshah	Bistoon	Jame Mosque	Haj Shahbaz Khan Mosque
	Taq Bostan	Emad Doldah Mosque	Dolshah Mosque
	Anahita Temple	Shahzadeh Mosque	Artillery Bazaar
	Traditional Bazaar		
Khoramabad	Museum of Anthropology of the Province	Minaret Brick	Stone-Writing - Khorram Abad
	Khorramabad Natural Science Museum	Babatiehar Tomb	Monument to Imam Zadeh Zayd bin Ali Mirza Sayed Reza Caravanserai
	Falak Al-Falak Castle	Mir Miras Miras Building	
Mashhad	Historical Complex of the tomb of Nader Shah Afshar	Naderi Museum	Hesar and Taj Mahal Tabarran Toos
	Khadj-e-Khaste	Naderi Gallery	Tomb of Hakim Abolghasem Ferdowsi
	Historical complex of Ferdowsi's Tomb	Khorasan Grand Museum	Haroonia Building
	Green Dome	Mashhad Moslem Historical Complex	Tomb of Khaje Rabi

(*Continued*)

City	Heritage and/or cultural tourism attractions		
Nushahr	Botanical Garden	Bath of Kouhper Oliya	Tomb of Darvish Amir
	Building of Imamzadeh Noah	Bath of Taher and Motahar	Imamzadeh Jafar ibn Musa
	Castle of Malek Kiumars	Kandilus Bath	Imamzadeh Mohammad's Tomb
	Emamzadeh Hamza Reza Tomb		
Orumiyeh	Three Orphanage Dome Tombs	Sardar Mosque	Neda Maryam Church
	Monument to Castle Barduk	Hedayat Mosque	
Ramsar	Ramsar Cultural Complex	Ramsar Garden	Memorial Martyrs of Dalkhani Forest
	Castle of Marco		
Rasht	Loth Caravanserai	Silk House	Jamshj Mosque
	Rasht Places of Worship	Amin Dawlah House	Samadkhan Mosque
	Paul Lishavandan	Small Chapel Caravanserai	Mirza Shrine Tomb
	Rasht National Library	Old House of Sayyid Ali Moghimi	Mausoleum of Master Poor Davood
	Chamarsara Bridge		
Sanandaj	The Museum of Anthropology of Kurd at Asif Divan Mansion	Khosrowabad Mansion	Old Mansion Tomb
	Khan Bath	Moshir Divan Mansion	Sanandaj Jewish Synagogue
	Habibi Museum	Imamzadeh Tomb Hajar Khatoon	Asif Mansion
	Sanandaj bazzar	Tomb of Imam Zaman	Sanandaj Museum
Semnan	Gate of the Citadel Bazshikh Alaoddoleh	Pegmbaran Region Semnan bazzar	Tymcheh Hazrat Great bazaar
	Tedin House (Mohammadiyya)	Mehr Museum and Semnan Coin	Museum of Shahr
Shahrekord	Mosque of Ekbatan	Qarchakhshahr Castle	Emamzadeh Halimeh Khatoon
	Ghale Yousef Khan	Shoreshjan Mosque	Chaleshtar Castle
	Parvizgar Baths	Kakalak Bath	Armenian Circus
	Castle of Smsam Al-Saltanah	Tomb of Agha Seyed Mohammad	Chaleshtar Mosque

(*Continued*)

Table 14.1 Continued

City	Heritage and/or cultural tourism attractions		
	Castle of Yousef Khan	Shahrekord Archaeology Museum	
Shahroud	Shahroud Museum	Shahrood bazaar	Shahroud Water Museum
	Shahroud Museum of Orientalism	Yaghami Museum	Bastam Temple
Shiraz	Ali Akbar Mosque Gate of Quran, Lawyer's Bath	Delgosha Garden Eram Garden	Sibouee Tomb Shiraz Atiq Jami Mosque
	Hafiz Tomb	Achaemenid Museum	Tomb of Sayyed Ala'ddin Hussein
	Karim Khan Zand Tomb	Karim Khan Zand Museum	Shah Cheragh Tomb
	Khatun Shrine Tomb	Persepolis	Khajavi Tomb of Kermani
Tabriz	Babakouhi Tomb Museum of the Azerbaijan Republic	Sadi Tomb Tabriz bazaar	Archaeological Museum of Khoravan
	Constitutional Museum	Tomb of Sahibamar	Mosque Tabriz
	Quran Museum and Book	Tomb of Seyyed Ebrahim	Tomb and Mosque of Seyyed Hamzeh
	Museum of Muharram	Tomb of the Two Kamal	Rashidi Quarter
	Museum of Contemplation	Iligli or Shahgoli	The Ravandi's Tomb in Khosroshah
	Qajar Museum	Azeri Museum	The Khosroshah Jami Mosque
	Ethiopian Museum of Arts	Tabriz Churches	Maqbar al-Sha'ra
	Tabriz Museum of Excellence	The Tomb Mosque	The Khalatpushan Tower
Tehran	Tehran Museum of Contemporary Art	Imperial Palace Mansion	Reza Khan House
	Tomb of Malek Al-MotaKelmin	Kazemi Mansion	Moghadam House and Museum
	Yousef Abad Small Mill	Niavaran Palace	Hojjatieh Mosque
	Tehran's Historical Citadel	Orthodox Church	Malekoltjar Mosque
	Imamzadeh Yahya's Tomb	St. Peter's Church	Masjid Dawla System

(*Continued*)

City	Heritage and/or cultural tourism attractions		
	Darband Garden	Hermitage Church	Qasr Prison
	Oudlajan Neighborhood	Mary the Great Church	Mansion of Hormoz
	Adrian Temple	Armenian Cemetery	Al-Saltanah Mansion
	Pars Theater Culture Hall	Tajrish Bazaar	Azadi Tower
Torbat-e-Heidarieh	The Four Arches of the Horea Range	The Haji Bathhouse	The Old Mosque
	The Tomb of Bibi Husseinieh	National Garden of Torbat-e-Heidarieh	Tabasi Caravansary
	Paul Kaskak	The Tomb of Sheikh Abolqasem Gurkani	The Fire Temple of Hawr
Yazd	Garden of Dolatabad Yazd	Taft Anthropology Museum	Abarkuh Museum of Anthropology
	Yazd Museum of Fine Arts and Culture	Yazd Chapel Museum	Abarkuh Mosque, Abarkuh Mosque
	Qazareinha Museum	Meybod Zilu Museum	Abkouh Mosque House
	Yazd Lori House	Meybod Dome	Aqa Abarkuh House Ana Sayyid Ali Aqa Abarkuh
	Yazd Coin Museum	Yazd Castle	House of Muhammad Ali Shadeh
	Yazd Mosque	Museum Meybod Wildlife	Attar Meybod
	Yazd Water Museum	Museum of Anthropology	Museum of Natural Sciences Yazd
	Yazd Zoroastrian Temple Museum	Yazd Museum of Art (South Factory	
	Yazd Marquez Museum	Anthropology Museum of Takzar	
Zabol	Zabol Museum of Anthropology	Haj Agha Sadr Seminary	Zabol Bazaar
Zahedan	Southern Regional Museum	Sistan's Anthropology	Zahedan's Arts and Crafts and Museums Old Building of Justice
	Southwestern Handicrafts and Communications	Shams Old House	

(*Continued*)

Table 14.1 Continued

City	Heritage and/or cultural tourism attractions		
Zanjan	Imamzadeh Seyed Ebrahim	Zolfaghari Mansion	Chehel Soton Mosque
	Jame Mosque (Seyed Mosque) in Zanjan	Successful Building	Grand Mosque of Hosseiniyeh Zanjan
	Mirza'i Mosque	Zanjan Bazaar	Laundromat Building
	Khanum Mosque	Caravanserai	Bridge Haj Mirb al-din
	Sardar Bridge		

museums, mosques and churches, baths, ruins, and remains of ancient cities, and historical buildings (Table 14.1).

Methods

A range of climatic variables have been argued to affect the suitability of a given location for tourism, including thermal heat, wind speed, sunshine hours, and rainfall. The Tourism Climatic Index, developed by Mieczkowski (1985) and adapted for data availability by Perch-Nielsen, Amelung, and Knutti (2010), is amongst the most widely used approaches that incorporates these variables to quantify climatic suitability for tourism at monthly to annual timescales. The combination of these variables is of greatest importance to outdoor attractions, of which there are many that comprise the heritage and cultural tourism offerings in Iran. The TCI is calculated monthly for each of the 38 locations for the historical period spanning the period 1961–2010, using raw data obtained from the Iranian Meteorological Organization, and for the period 2020–2040 from General Circulation Model (GCM) projections for each climate variable. Standard TCI calculations and classifications are performed, as detailed by Roshan et al. (2016).

For indoor attractions, rainfall, sunshine hours, and wind speed are of lesser consequence. These factors will likely influence the total number of visitors, as they would be affected by adverse or favourable to transport to and from such attractions. They will not, however, contribute significantly to the experience of the attraction itself. Heat stress will, however, remain important, particularly where attractions do not have air conditioning, as is most often the case in Iran. Therefore, we additionally calculate the heat stress using the Universal Thermal Climate Index (UTCI) for the 38 locations. The UTCI (Błażejczyk et al., 2013) is modelled to represent heat stress to humans, as a function of the air and radiant temperature, wind speed, and humidity. The UTCI is calculated with daily climate data obtained from the

Iranian Meteorological Organization for the period 1995–2014. Details of the calculation and classification are detailed by Roshan and Nastos (2018). We use the output values to produce risk maps for Iran indicating the level of risk for cold and heat stress, categorising into five classes spanning very low risk through very high risk on the basis of the number of days during this period that are classified as having experienced 'moderate' cold stress and 'moderate' to 'very high' heat stress (Roshan & Nastos, 2018, p. 306).

Results

Tourism Climatic Index

The majority of locations have mean annual TCI scores in the range of very good to good calculated from both the historical record and future projections (Table 14.2). The exceptions are for the towns of Rasht and Anzali, each of which have mean TCI scores in the range of acceptable for both the historical and future models with scores of 59 and lower. The highest mean annual TCI scores are calculated for Kerman and Zahedan, with both the historical and future scenarios in excess of 78. For two cities, Ramsar and Kerman, there is a change in classification between historical and future. For 11 stations, there is no calculated change in the TCI score between historical and future models. For 14 stations, a decrease in climatic suitability for tourism between the historical record and future models is calculated. These reductions in suitability are the most severe for Abadan, Bushehr, and Rasht at three TCI units each. For the remaining 13 locations, slight improvements in climatic suitability between the historical and future variables are modelled, with a maximum change of 2 units. For Kerman this is an improvement from the category of 'good to very good' to 'excellent', albeit only a two unit change. For Ramsar, a depreciation from 'good to very good' to 'acceptable' is projected, although similarly by a very small margin of only one unit.

Scott and McBoyle (2001) propose value in classifying inter-annual TCI scores into seasonal brackets. A winter peak in climatic suitability is calculated for six locations (Table 14.2), representing all of the stations on the coast of the Persian Gulf, and those inland of the coast (Figure 14.1). For eight locations – Bam, Dezful, Gorgan, Kashan, Kerman, Yazd, Zabol, and Zahedan – the distribution that Scott and McBoyle (2001) classify as a 'Bimodal-Shoulder Peak' is calculated, with peaks in approximately the spring and autumn months. These stations, with the exception of Zabol, are located in the foothills of mountainous regions in the interior of the country. For the remaining stations (24), a summer peak in climatic suitability for tourism is calculated. No change in the seasonal distribution is observed between the historical and future models. This represents a reasonable annual distribution of climate resources across the country, which could

Table 14.2 Mean annual and monthly TCI scores for 38 locations in Iran, calculated from historical data spanning the period 1961–2010 and future projections for 2020–2040

Stations	Jan H	Jan F	Feb H	Feb F	Mar H	Mar F	Apr H	Apr F	May H	May F	Jun H	Jun F	Jul H	Jul F	Aug H	Aug F	Sep H	Sep F	Oct H	Oct F	Nov H	Nov F	Dec H	Dec F	Ann Avg H	Ann Avg F	
Abadan	68	69	81	83	89	87	76	75	52	51	43	36	52	50	41	37	44	40	59	52	85	81	75	73	64	61	↓
Ahvaz	64	65	79	80	85	86	75	71	53	50	44	40	53	52	43	41	46	41	63	57	84	83	71	70	63	61	↓
Anzali	38	45	40	41	45	42	61	59	82	79	77	78	82	86	59	49	63	60	64	61	47	55	39	43	58	58	-
Arak	47	47	53	54	58	59	74	77	88	93	83	85	88	85	74	71	89	83	87	84	63	65	51	55	71	71	-
Ardebil	46	39	49	55	52	58	70	74	82	81	91	90	82	85	87	88	87	85	66	71	52	55	46	42	67	69	↑
Babolsar	48	49	51	50	53	47	72	68	88	88	75	76	88	89	56	45	61	58	73	73	59	64	48	52	64	63	↓
Bam	71	72	80	85	88	86	87	91	67	67	56	45	67	66	59	43	69	67	88	88	90	92	78	78	75	73	↓
Bandarabas	82	82	85	87	81	79	70	61	46	43	41	38	46	45	43	39	40	40	50	49	79	77	85	85	62	60	↓
Bandarlenge	84	85	87	88	87	83	74	68	51	50	42	41	51	52	44	42	42	36	57	55	83	81	87	84	66	64	↓
Birjand	58	55	61	47	71	73	86	86	89	90	73	85	89	93	76	69	88	85	90	92	80	86	62	60	77	77	-
Bushehr	68	69	78	77	86	87	82	82	59	55	48	47	59	49	43	37	44	35	63	55	85	83	74	76	66	63	↓
Dezful	58	63	72	75	79	83	76	80	56	66	46	45	56	52	44	37	50	49	64	67	77	82	65	61	62	63	↑
Esfahan	60	55	64	60	70	73	87	93	94	96	76	80	94	95	70	65	87	85	90	92	71	76	61	56	77	77	-
Ghazvin	50	53	53	52	58	59	76	85	88	89	83	88	88	94	71	78	87	85	86	89	64	66	52	43	71	73	↑
Gorgan	56	58	56	57	56	63	77	77	78	75	65	64	78	80	52	47	65	55	78	76	71	73	57	55	66	65	↓
Hamedan	41	37	45	55	54	57	68	74	86	87	89	93	86	84	75	75	90	92	83	87	59	59	46	43	68	70	↑
Iranshahr	82	84	86	89	84	84	68	65	52	54	44	45	52	50	44	37	53	48	69	60	88	91	86	90	67	66	↓
Kashan	58	60	65	60	76	69	86	82	78	71	62	57	78	82	56	60	72	68	87	89	76	83	62	60	71	70	↓
Kerman	58	57	62	73	72	78	87	96	91	95	74	80	91	92	77	71	88	88	89	82	81	83	63	67	78	80	↑
Kermanshah	45	36	49	55	54	62	73	85	88	84	77	80	88	90	65	67	83	83	84	89	64	66	50	42	68	70	↑
Khoramabad	51	44	56	52	62	67	79	85	85	80	70	63	85	87	61	59	73	66	85	87	72	66	53	57	69	68	↓
Mashhad	52	47	54	54	57	55	78	80	89	90	80	82	89	90	78	80	91	90	87	83	68	69	56	55	73	73	-
Noshahr	47	47	48	49	48	51	63	63	81	83	75	76	81	80	54	47	62	59	64	65	50	52	46	67	60	62	↑
Orumiyeh	48	42	50	47	54	60	65	74	82	80	92	92	82	87	85	87	90	88	76	85	56	57	48	42	69	70	↑
Ramsar	48	47	47	47	47	43	60	59	79	78	75	74	79	79	59	57	61	55	66	67	52	55	48	52	60	59	↓
Rasht	42	43	44	45	47	47	69	65	80	81	71	69	80	65	53	42	59	51	64	65	52	53	44	47	59	56	↓
Sanandaj	44	43	48	57	54	50	71	78	86	87	82	89	86	89	69	70	86	92	84	81	61	57	50	43	68	70	↑
Semnan	57	62	61	60	69	66	87	81	86	78	70	73	86	89	63	61	81	86	90	92	73	64	59	64	73	73	-
Shahrekord	49	47	55	52	59	49	72	75	89	88	85	85	89	95	79	84	89	91	87	95	64	66	52	51	72	73	↑
Shahroud	52	50	57	48	63	57	82	83	91	91	86	87	91	90	80	88	91	95	88	90	67	69	55	58	75	75	-
Shiraz	54	57	62	67	72	70	87	88	89	92	70	78	89	89	65	62	77	71	92	90	82	86	60	53	75	75	-
Tabriz	42	37	48	55	53	59	64	60	85	89	94	93	85	85	81	83	95	96	81	87	60	63	48	45	70	71	↑
Tehran	52	55	55	56	63	57	83	79	94	90	75	82	94	97	67	56	86	83	90	90	68	68	55	57	73	73	-
Torbat-e-Heidarieh	51	44	54	56	61	53	80	83	92	93	84	87	92	95	85	88	91	88	87	88	69	66	56	59	75	75	-
Yazd	61	59	69	66	80	83	91	94	83	87	65	70	73	72	65	57	76	70	92	92	82	84	65	59	75	74	↓
Zabol	65	65	75	77	86	84	82	83	63	66	50	50	63	63	52	49	65	67	89	88	87	85	70	71	71	71	-
Zahedan	61	69	68	73	83	87	93	93	82	82	68	69	82	81	70	66	85	82	91	92	87	88	68	70	78	79	↑
Zanjan	45	46	48	45	54	61	66	65	83	87	92	95	83	87	83	90	91	93	81	77	57	59	49	40	69	70	↑

H: historical (1961–2010)
F: Future (2020–2040)

- 80–100 excellent
- 60–79 very good - good
- 50–59 acceptable
- 20–49 unfavourable
- 0–19 extremely unfavourable - impossibe

facilitate year-round tourism income for the country. However, for each location, this reveals a strong seasonality in the suitability for tourism, with scores in the excellent range during the peak, and scores in the unfavourable range during the worst months (Table 14.2).

Exploring the individual monthly TCI scores for each of the 38 locations, there are 85 instances in which the difference between those derived from historical record and the future projections that change the suitability classification to either a better or a worse category (Table 14.2). These are of a higher magnitude than the changes in the mean annual TCI scores, with maximum changes of 10 units more for 11 instances and in excess of 15 for Rasht for July and for Bam for August. For the February scores for Birjand a change of 14 units results in a change by two classes. The much lower difference in the mean annual scores for each of these stations both increases and decreases TCI scores. There is no net pattern regarding either an improvement or reduction in the climatic suitability of a given location in either the season of best or worse TCI scores for the 2020–2040 projection horizon. However, these large changes to monthly scores between the historical and future projections should be monitored in planning for tourism at these destinations in those months.

Universal Thermal Comfort Index

UTCI modelling for Iran reveals distinct spatial variability in the thermal stress, segregating the country into regions that are prone to cold stress, which are predominantly located in the north-east, and regions that are prone to moderate to strong heat stress, which broadly comprise the central to south-eastern region. Detailed maps presenting the UTCI classes are presented in Roshan and Nastos (2018). Of particular interest to heritage tourism in the region is the frequency of days in which heat and cold stress have occurred over the study period, and hence the threat of such thermal stress to persons visiting cities in each region.

The highest risk of heat thermal stresses is modelled for the coastal areas of southern Iran with an occurrence threshold of 4,080–6,780 days (Figure 14.2a). A classification of very high risk applies to the cities of Bandarabas, Bandarlenge, and Bushehr. Abadan and Ahvaz are classified as having the lower category of high heat risk. Among the factors affecting the maximum occurrence of thermal stress in this region is the low latitude. The proximity of these areas to the Persian Gulf and the Oman Sea, and the injection of moisture from these water bodies exacerbate the occurrence of thermal stresses in this area, particularly during the hot summer months. In winter months, the region experiences a lower influence of the westerlies. These cities do, however, experience the lowest occurrence of cold stress, at 1–214 days of cold stress, classifying them as a very low cold risk (Figure 14.2b).

The majority of the eastern half of the country is classified as having a medium to high risk of heat thermal stress. However, the north-east of Iran

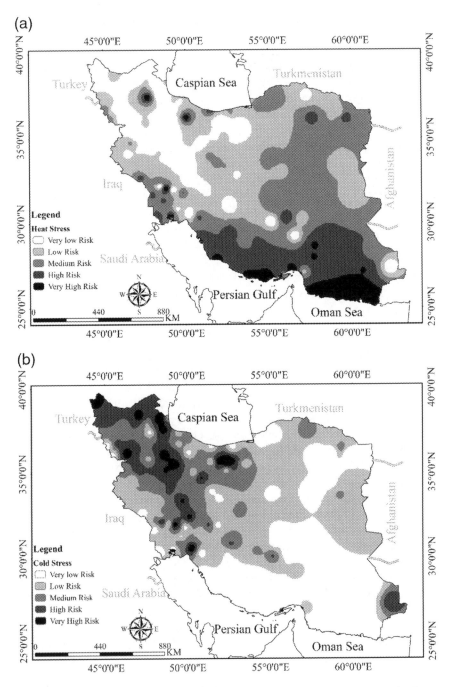

Figure 14.2a–b UTCI calculated risk maps for heat and cold thermal stress for Iran: a) Heat stress, b) Cold stress.

during summer is affected by the warm conditions which penetrate the Turkmen desert and extend into this area. Central Iran is characterised as one of the hottest regions of the world, experiencing high thermal stresses during the warm seasons and dry, desert conditions (Mildrexler et al., 2011). The northern region of Iran, which includes the southern shores of the Caspian Sea, are predominantly classified as having a low risk for cold stress and medium risk for heat stress. This is as a result of the moderating effect of the Caspian Sea. The cities of this area include Rasht, Ramsar, Babolsar, and Gorgan. Many of these regions rely on outdoor tourist attractions.

The cities in the west and north-west of Iran experience the lowest risk of heat stress for the country. The frequency of heat stress days for some cities in this area, such as Tabriz, Ardebil, Sanandaj, and Orumiyeh span a large range of 342–3,050 days during the period 1995–2014. However, this region has the highest risk of the occurrence of cold stress, with a prevalence of between 1,090 and 2,630 days during the study period. This is a result of the mountains in the region, and the influence of the westerly systems in the region. These combine to increase the minimum temperatures and the wind chill effect.

Overall, the UTCI outputs for the period 1995–2014 indicate a much greater incidence of heat stress than cold stress for Iran. A far greater proportion of the country is classified as having a high to very high risk of heat stress than the proportion classified as high to very high risk of cold stress. Under continued climate change the area at risk of cold stress is likely to contract, while the region under risk of heat stress will expand. The areas currently at very high risk of heat stress, comprising the south-eastern corner of Iran, and smaller isolated regions across the north of the country, will likely experience a higher incidence of heat risk days, which compromises the sustainability of tourism offerings in these regions.

Discussion

There is a fair level of agreement between the outputs of the TCI and the UTCI calculations for the 38 stations considered in this study. Regions along the coast of the Persian Gulf have a high heat risk, and the most favourable TCI scores during the winter months, when cooler temperatures fall within a more optimal range. Regions at the foothills of the Zagros Mountains have low to medium heat and cold risk, and a bi-modal shoulder peak distribution in the TCI scores. This is important in understanding the significance of heat stress in contributing to the climatic suitability of cities across the country for tourism, in line with previous studies undertaken for specific regions of the country (cf. Farajzadeh & Matzarakis, 2009; Akbarian Ronizi et al., 2016). These threats of heat stress in particular are important given the projected significant increases in heat risk for the Middle East and Africa (Lelieveld et al., 2016). Heat risk in the tourism context is important as it will affect the necessity for climate control indoors, the suitability of outdoor attractions, and the comfort of tourists travelling to and from a destination. Where cultural practices involve outdoor activities, these may be compromised by extreme heat conditions, and artefacts that cannot be sufficiently protected through climate control may be at risk of degradation.

While the UTCI is calculated to model human physiological heat stress, the same input factors can be indicative of threats to many cultural and heritage artefacts and historic buildings (Portal et al., 2014). In particular, increases in indoor temperature and relative humidity under climate change have been modelled to pose considerable threat to paintings and wooden artefacts (Huijbregts et al., 2012), and to the materials that comprise historical buildings (Portal et al., 2014). The threats of worsening indoor climate can arguably be mitigated through the installation of climate control such as air conditioning (Tétreault, 1994), where cost and heritage requirements allow. Outdoor climates, which are often more extreme than their indoor counterparts due to passive climate control intrinsic in the buildings themselves (Fitchett et al., 2019), are less easy to mitigate. These artefacts and attractions would also be subjected to additional climatic stress resulting from rain, wind, and exposure to sunlight, each of which would likewise change in nature under climate change.

The outdoor cultural and heritage sites that are situated within the regions of greatest heat stress include Persepolis in Shiraz, Bam Citadel in Bam, Golcharvar and Golchin Caravanserai in Bandarabbas, the Castle of Nasseri in Iranshahr, Shoghab Cemetary in Busher, and the Remains of the Historic City of Hormuz Ardeshir in Ahvas. Cultural and heritage tourism sites that are either completely or partially indoors which are located in regions of severe heat stress include the Spinning and Knitting Factory in Ahvaz, the Hindu Temple in Bandarabbas, the Holy Defense Museum and Contemporary Industrial Museum in Kerman, Zabol Museum of Anthropology in Zabol, Sistan's Anthropology Museum in Zahedan, and Karim Khan Zand Museum in Shiraz. While many of these indoor attractions run air conditioning during the summer months, the operation of air conditioning at times of severe heat stress places considerable demand on the energy network (Fallahi, 2019). Indeed, this energy network has been under considerable stress over the past decade and is subject to frequent and prolonged power cuts (Byrd & Matthewman, 2014; Fallahi, 2019), during which time these indoor attractions would not benefit from any amelioration of temperature or humidity.

The TCI results do reveal significant variation. For the season of peak TCI scores, these reveal excellent climatic suitability for tourism for the majority of the 38 locations. Given that these stations include summer, winter, and bimodal shoulder peak annual distributions in TCI scores, successful year-round tourism in Iran is possible, if managed carefully (Roshan et al., 2016). This requires advertising and tour operators to package destinations for the months of suitable climate (Zamani-Farahani & Musa, 2008), and to discourage tourists from visiting locations during the season of lowest climatic suitability (Rastegar, 2010). For more than half of the cities, the season of lowest TCI scores is classified as having unfavourable climatic conditions for tourism. Visits during this period, particularly if tourists have not been warned, may result in disgruntled visitors who detract future tourists via word of mouth (Fitchett & Hoogendoorn, 2018). It is promising, however, that calculations of projected TCI scores do not indicate a significant change in the mean annual score, nor in the seasonal distribution. Therefore, strategies implemented now to improve tourism visitation through accurate advertising of the climate would not be at threat of imminent changes under climate change. The larger departures in suitability index values for particular months should, however, be carefully monitored.

Finally, of course the effective management of climate resources to promote tourism in the most suitable months would not be sufficient alone to improve the very low number of tourists visiting Iran. Despite hosting such a large array of heritage and cultural tourism attractions, a lack of marketing has meant that the country is largely 'obscure to the outside world' (Zamani-Farahani & Musa, 2008, p. 1234), requiring direct intervention from the government and tourism operators (Baum & O'Gorman, 2010). Danger to tourists in the form of road accidents, injury of pedestrians, violent attacks and kidnappings are cited as a deterrent to regional and international tourists (Baum & O'Gorman, 2010). Furthermore, the history of war and political instability has had a significant impact in reducing visitor numbers (Baum & O'Gorman, 2010). However, this further underlines the importance of ensuring that the existing tourist market remain satisfied by their visit, and that efforts to market the destination are made with consideration for the current and future climate resources.

Summary and conclusion

Iran host a wealth of cultural and heritage tourism attractions. The output of the TCI and UTCI calculations reveal that climate and climate change do pose threats to tourism in Iran. As many of these attractions are either in part or whole outdoors, the climate threats apply to this subsector. As heat stress plays a significant role in the threats to climatic suitability, this may affect not only tourist enjoyment of a destination, but the number of destinations that they will have the energy to visit in a given trip. Heat and cold stress may also affect certain exhibits or cultural practices which form a key component of the cultural and heritage attractions for the region, while changes in humidity, temperature, and other aspects of climate pose a threat to artefacts and structures. However, the data also reveal significant climate resources for tourism in the region, which, coupled with effective marketing that considers the seasonal and spatial distribution of such resources, could facilitate an improvement in tourist visitor numbers both internationally and locally. Moreover, as heat stress forms a primary concern for the region, adaptation should be targeted towards ensuring indoor temperatures within comfort levels to ensure the sustainability of these destinations for future tourist visitation.

Iran has a highly heterogeneous climate, and consequently a large range in the TCI and UTCI derived model outputs reflecting climatic suitability. The findings for the country therefore indicate likely threats to the North African and Middle East region, where many of the microclimates are similar to those of a given location in Iran. The broad threats and opportunities revealed from the biometeorological analyses for Iran poses an urgent need for attention to the climate change threats to cultural and heritage tourism, particularly where efforts are being placed on increasing visitor numbers and upgrading facilities. However, these results themselves are highly spatially and temporally heterogeneous, thus requiring urgent future research to quantify the nature and extent of the climate threats to tourism in the rest of the region.

References

Akbarian Ronizi, S. R., Roshan, G. H., & Negahban, S. (2016). Assessment of tourism climate opportunities and threats for villages located in the northern coasts of Iran. *International Journal of Environmental Research, 10*(4), 601–612.

Aref, F., Redzuan, M., & Gill, S. S. (2009). Community perceptions toward economic and environmental impacts of tourism on local communities. *Asian Journal of Social Science, 5*(7), 130–137

Baum, T. G., & O'Gorman, K. D. (2010). Iran or Persia: What's in a name, the decline and fall of a tourism industry? In R. Butler & W. Suntikul (eds), *Tourism and political change* (pp. 175–185). Oxford: Goodfellow Publishers.

Błażejczyk, K., Jendritzky, G., Bröde, P., Fiala, D., Havenith, G., Epstein, Y., Psikuta, A., & Kampmann, B. (2013). An introduction to the Universal Thermal Climate Index (UTCI). *Geographica Polonica, 86*(1), 5–10.

Byrd, H., & Matthewman, S. (2014). Exergy and the city: The technology and sociology of power (failure). *Journal of Urban Technology, 21*(3), 85–102.

Eshiki, S. A., & Kaboudi, M. (2012). Community perception of tourism impacts and their participation in tourism planning: A case study of Ramsar, Iran. *Social and Behavioural Science, 36*, 333–341

Fallahi, E. (2019). Iran electricity issue: Should we expect blackouts again? *Tehran Times, 21 May 2019.* Retrieved from https://www.tehrantimes.com/news/436178/Iran-electricity-issue-should-we-expect-blackouts-again.

Farajzadeh, H., & Matzarakis, A. (2009). Quantification of climate for tourism in the northwest of Iran. *Meteorological Applications, 16*(4), 545–555.

Fitchett, A., Govender, P., & Vallabh, P. (2019). An exploration of green roofs for indoor and exterior temperature regulation in the South African interior. *Environment, Development and Sustainability.* DOI:10.1007/s10668-019-00413-4.

Fitchett, J. M., & Hoogendoorn, G. (2018). An analysis of factors affecting tourists' accounts of weather in South Africa. *International Journal of Biometeorology, 62*(12), 2161–2172.

Ghasemi, A., & Khalili, D. (2008). The effect of the North Sea-Caspian Pattern (NCP) on winter temperatures in Iran. *Theoretical and Applied Climatology, 92*(1–2), 59–74.

Gössling, S., Scott, D., Hall, C. M., Ceron, J. P., & Dubois, G. (2012). Consumer behaviour and demand response of tourists to climate change. *Annals of Tourism Research*, *39*(1), 36–58.

Haftlang, K. K. (2003). *The book of Iran: A survey of the geography of Iran.* (A. Rajabi, Trans.) Tehran: Center for International Cultural Studies.

Hall, C. M. (2016). Heritage, heritage tourism and climate change. *Journal of Heritage Tourism*, *11*(1), 1–9.

Hall, C. M., Baird, T., James, M., & Ram, Y. (2016). Climate change and cultural heritage: Conservation and heritage tourism in the Anthropocene. *Journal of Heritage Tourism*, *11*(1), 10–20.

Huijbregts, Z., Kramer, R. P., Martens, M. H. J., Van Schijndel, A.W. M., & Schellen, H. L. (2012). A proposed method to assess the damage risk of future climate change to museum objects in historic buildings. *Building and Environment*, *55*, 43–56.

Kaján, E., & Saarinen, J. (2013). Tourism, climate change and adaptation: A review. *Current Issues in Tourism*, *16*(2), 167–195.

Lelieveld, J., Proestos, Y., Hadjinicolau, P., Tanarhte, M., Tyrlis, E., & Zittis, G. (2016). Strongly increasing heat extremes in the Middle East and North Africa (MENA) in the 21st century. *Climatic Change*, *137*(1–2), 245–260.

Mieczkowski, Z. (1985). The tourism climate index: A method of evaluating world climates for tourism. *Canadian Geographer*, *29*(3), 220–233.

Mildrexler, D. J., Zhao, M., & Running, S. W. (2011). Satellite finds highest land skin temperature on earth. *Bulletin of the American Meteorological Society*, *92*, 855–860.

Modarres, R., & da Silva, V. (2007). Rainfall trends in arid and semi-arid regions of Iran. *Journal of Arid Environments*, *70*(2), 344–355.

Mohmmadi, M., Khalifah, Z., & Hosseini, H. (2010). Local people perceptions toward social, economic and environmental impacts of tourism in Kermanshah (Iran). *Asian Journal of Social Science*, *6*(11), 220–225.

Morakabati, Y. (2011). Deterrents to tourism development in Iran. *International Journal of Tourism Research*, *13*(2), 103–123.

Nazemosadat, M., & Ghasemi, A. (2004). Quantifying the ENSO-related shifts in the intensity and the probability of drought and wet periods in Iran. *Journal of Climate*, *17*(20), 4005–4018.

Perch-Nielsen, S. L., Amelung, B., & Knutti, R. (2010). Future climate resources for tourism in Europe based on the daily Tourism Climate Index. *Climate Change*, *103*(3–4), 363–381.

Portal, N. W., Van Schijndel, A. W. M., & Kalagasidis, A. S. (2014). The multi-physics modeling of heat and moisture induced stress and strain of historic building materials and artefacts. *Building Simulation*, *7*(3), 217–227.

Rastegar, H. (2010). Tourism development and residents' attitude: A case study of Yazd, Iran. *Tourismos: An International Multidisciplinary Journal of Tourism*, *5*(2), 203–211.

Rasuly, A. A., Babaeian, I., Ghaemi, H., & ZawarReza, P. (2012). Time series analysis of pressure of the synoptic pattern centres affecting on seasonal precipitation of Iran. *Geography and Development*, *27*, 18–21.

Roshan, G., & Nastos, P. T. (2018). Assessment of extreme heat stress probabilities in Iran's urban settlements, using first order Markov chain model. *Sustainable Cities and Environment*, *36*, 302–310.

Roshan, G., Yousefi, R., & Fitchett, J. M. (2016). Long-term trends in tourism climate index scores for 40 stations across Iran: The role of climate change and influences on tourism sustainability. *International Journal of Biometeorology*, *60*(1), 33–52.

Scott, D., & McBoyle, G. (2001). Using a 'tourism climate index' to examine the implications of climate change for climate as a natural resource for tourism. In A. Matzarakis & C. de Frietas (eds), *Proceedings of the First International Workshop on Climate, Tourism and Recreation*, International Society of Biometeorology, Commission on Climate, Tourism and Recreation, Halkidiki, Greece, 5–10 October, pp. 69–88.

Scott, D., McBoyle, G., & Schwartzentruber, M. (2004). Climate change and the distribution of climatic resources for tourism in North America. *Climate Research*, *27*, 105–117.

Seyfi, S., Hall, C.M., & Fagnoni, E. (2019). Managing World Heritage Site stakeholders: A grounded theory paradigm model approach. *Journal of Heritage Tourism*, *14*(4), 308–324.

Tétreault, J. (1994). Display materials: The good, the bad and the ugly. *Exhibition and Conservation*, *1*, 79–87.

Zamani-Farahani, H., & Musa, G. (2008). Residents' attitudes and perception towards tourism development: A case study of Masooleh, Iran. *Tourism Management*, *29*(6), 1233–1236.

15 Conclusion
The futures of cultural heritage tourism in the MENA countries

C. Michael Hall and Siamak Seyfi

Constructing heritage

Heritage is usually defined in terms of the things we want to keep. Common to many definitions of heritage is the reference to a 'form of collective memory, a social construct shaped by the political, economic and social concerns of the present' (Graham & Howard, 2008, p. 2). However, the process of keeping memories and its relationship to identity and the 'we' raises difficult questions about which identities, memories, and heritages are celebrated, and those that are ignored or, at worst, suppressed – issues that are very much at the forefront of the politics of heritage tourism in MENA countries (Isaac, Hall, & Higgins-Desbiolles, 2016; Seyfi & Hall, 2019a, 2019b). Indeed, in many ways tourism is integral to the political economy of heritage whereby economic value becomes a justification to conserve and promote heritage even though the memories behind heritage may be flattened or even erased in official accounts of cultural heritage so as to serve particular national interests. For example, the Armenian heritage in parts of Turkey is promoted in the absence of accounts of the Armenian genocide (Watenpaugh, 2014; Törne, 2015); biblical and Jewish heritage in Israel is used to press claims to place in the absence of acknowledgement of the Palestinian exodus (the Nakba) and heritage (Butler, 2009; Gori, 2013; Zayad, 2018); while, simultaneously, the forced and voluntary movement of Jews to Israel around the MENA region as a result of colonial independence, and the creation of and opposition to the state of Israel has resulted in the loss of cultural memories of Jewish space in many cities of the region (Lafi, 2015). Such a situation reflects understandings of the different uses of heritage (Smith, 2006). Accordingly, heritage provides 'a point of validation or legitimization for the present in which actions and policies are justified by continuing references to representations and narratives of the past that are encapsulated through manifestations of tangible and intangible' (Graham & Howard, 2008, p. 6). Shifting the perception of the past can also become 'a resource for identity-building, in the politics of remembering and, more recently, in the value attributed to the past as economic factor' (Riedel, 2015, p. 225).

Importantly, heritage is socially and politically constructed. While all of us engage in heritage making and we all have our own personal notion of the things we would like to keep for reasons of memory and identity, the heritage that this book focuses on is institutionalised heritage. That is:

> heritage is heritage because it is subjected to the management and preservation/conservation process, not because it simply 'is'. This process does not just 'find' sites and places to manage and protect. It is itself a constitutive cultural process that identifies those things and places that can be given meaning and value as 'heritage', reflecting contemporary cultural and social values, debates and aspirations (Smith, 2006, p. 3).

Such 'official' heritage construction is undertaken for a range of reasons, including the perceived economic benefits of heritage tourism, the promotion of national and regional discourses on identity; nation-building and place promotion as well as conservation and management purposes. For example, given Jordan is not a country with rich natural resources or other industries, the country depends highly on the earnings from tourism and the earnings from tourism are a major contributor to the state's finances (Riedel, 2015). However, the promoting of Jordanian heritage sites for the economic value of tourism and their perceived value to the state's economy and the way they have been developed has been subject to substantial debate (Addison, 2004; Daher, 2005; Abu-Khafajah, Al Rabady, & Rababeh, 2015; Abu-Khafajah & Miqdadi, 2019), with questions raised about the ranking of Jordanian sites in terms of their value and the subsequent implications this has for management (Riedel, 2015).

In the Iranian context the use of heritage as an international representation of national identity brings another perspective on heritage identity and highlights the selective promotion of heritage by the state. Although the glorification of Persian history and civilisation as a means of celebrating the country's cultural heritage was on the agenda of the Shah's administration, the Islamic republic mainly promotes the Islamic heritage of the country (Seyfi, Hall, & Fagnoni, 2019; Seyfi & Hall, 2018a). As Saleh and Worrall (2015, p. 73) argued, despite some external perceptions in the West, 'Iran is a multi-ethnic state which has long had difficulty in incorporating different identities into mainstream, Persian dominated, discourses of Iranian identity'. Seyfi et al. (2019) also commented that in its revolutionary zeal, Islamic identity has become the paramount identity and Persian identity has been given less attention particularly by the conservative elements in the ruling elite. Defining the national identity in Iran has been subject to debate and the contestation between the Islamic/Shiite identity and the Persian ethnolinguistic identity has been a constant theme in modern Iranian politics (Saleh & Worrall, 2015). When it comes to heritage promotion, the hardliners and conservative elements in the ruling elite perceive the great number of ancient sites in Iran belonging to the pre-Islamic era as 'inconsistent' with Islamic values and identities. For Saleh and Worrall (2015) these contractions and the ensuing identity problematique stem from the fact that 'nationalist discourses in Iran are built upon the glorification of pre-Islamic heritage which is consistently portrayed as the authentic source of Iranian identity, this ties the notion of Iran to a specific territory, a specific sense of self and a knowledge of former greatness' (2015, p. 74). As a consequence, the contradictions between heritage recognition and tourism development have also aroused significant concerns in the general public. Hence as Seyfi et al. (2019, p. 4) conclude, 'given domestic politics and the ruling elite's ideological priorities, public sector support for heritage tourism, particularly in internationally recognized sites does not always match the willingness of NGOs and the private sector to foster cultural heritage development'. Nevertheless, given the current domestic politics in the country, it is also argued that nationalism (in the form of glorification of Persian identity) and Islamism (highlighting Islamic/Shia identity) will remain the two main components in the definition of Iran's national identity, with many implications for the shaping and orientation of the country's tourism industry.

Heritage, heritage tourism, and the ongoing politics of identity

Several chapters in this volume have demonstrated that there appears to be increasing use of cultural heritage tourism to attract international visitors and the foreign exchange and employment they generate as well as contributing to improvements in destination branding and positioning at an international level while also serving to fulfil domestic and diasporic political agendas. For example, Thani and Hennan (Chapter 10, this volume) noted the way in which the United Arab Emirates' cities of Abu Dhabi and Dubai are using heritage, including the development of museums, institutions, and events, to present a particular interpretation of Arabism to Western tourists. Adie (Chapter 6, this volume) similarly suggests that the selection of World Heritage Sites in Morocco is undertaken both with tourism in mind and the conveyance internationally of selected representations of national identity. Interestingly, a similar use of World Heritage is also undertaken in Turkey with respect to the Safranbolu World Heritage Site (Tataroglu, Chapter 4, this volume). However, here a Romantic discourse shared by many Turkish cultural conservatives has been developed surrounding the values of the city in relation to the impacts of modernity on Turkish cultural life. Such an ideology is very much in keeping with those of the Erdogan government (Büyüksaraç, 2004; Whitehead & Bozoğlu, 2016) and reflects that cultural heritage management has been constantly and systematically influenced by political concerns in Turkey. As a result, 'the discrepancy between the state's cultural identity, on the one hand, and the "foreign" nature of cultural heritage, on the other' (Eldem, 2015, p. 67) has been a major issue in the domestic discourse of both the Ottoman Empire and its successor state the Republic of Turkey, with both having been confronted in various ways by 'the notion of heritage and to the pressure of a growing western interest for the material traces of the past lying on their territories' (Eldem, 2015, p. 67).

Various elements of Ottoman and Turkish heritage have therefore suffered from the powerful and often abusive grasp of politics. Eldem (2015) observes that, 'This mismatch has led to a containment of mainstream archaeology and museology within the logic of a civilizational mission, while new avenues were explored that might allow for a greater overlap between heritage and political identity' (Eldem, 2015, p. 67). As a result, the cultural heritage of Turkey has become dominated by different tendencies (development of Islamic and Ottoman archaeology, the valorisation of Anatolian and Near Eastern civilisations, and the secular Kemalism):

> which, depending on time, context, or agency, may compete or simply overlap in opportunistic fashion in the definition of cultural policies and of cultural heritage as a whole. To this, one should add the very influential impact exerted by western perceptions of the same process, either at scholarly level or, more widely, at the demotic level of mass tourism (Eldem, 2015, p. 68).

More recently, this can be seen in the pursued ideology of the Erdogan government and its neo-Ottomanism approach, and help illustrate the ties between political power and the maintenance and portrayal of heritage and the official discourses that surround it (Ekber Doğan, 2020; Whitehead & Bozoğlu, 2016; Zencirci, 2014). However, such uses of heritage are not new. Atakuman (2010, 2017) observes that:

> Turkish heritage has been used for chauvinistic displays of national identity throughout the course of Turkey's relationship with Europe. In the context of this reactionary response that was mainly directed at Europe, heritage in Turkey has been constructed and continues to be perceived as 'things' to be protected for their value in terms of international prestige and touristic consumption, while the problems at the core of Turkey's cultural policy remain unresolved (Atakuman, 2010, p. 108).

Över (2016) also explores the ways in which states manage their national identity through cultural tourism policy. Drawing on archival and ethnographic data, Över (2016) focused on the opening of the Armenian Cathedral of the Holy Cross, a medieval Armenian Apostolic cathedral, in Akhtamar, Turkey to cultural tourism and religious services for the first time since the Armenian genocide. However, the reopening and restoration in 2007 was fraught with controversy, as the building was reopened as a museum rather than as a place of worship and Armenian groups lobbied very strongly to have religious symbols put in place and also to be able to hold services.

> Beginning in 2010, it was also opened for an annual religious ceremony in the context of the 'Faith Tourism' program. While the Faith Tourism program placed emphasis on the multi-religious composition of Anatolia and aimed to present Turkey as the homeland of a tolerant nation-state, the restriction of religious ceremony at Akhtamar and the state's resistance to place across atop the church during its restoration were recognized as signs of intolerance. One party interpreted the opening of the Akhtamar as a move for political benefit in the genocide recognition debate and as a superficial effort to remove the stigmas associated with the nation-state's identity. Others viewed it as a symptom of a deeper change in the state-definition of national identity and condemned it as a sign of a decline in ethnic Turkish nationalism (Över, 2016, p. 174).

Based on narrative evidence from the disputes among various actors with conflictual constructions of history, Över (2016) found that cultural tourism was being used by the state to produce multiple articulations of national identity and that these articulations were being governed in accordance with state interests.

> The presence of multiple stages of tourism policy and the time and space bounded nature of interaction at each stage allow for the production of multiple images in different interaction situations. At the same time, the discourse of economic development associated with cultural tourism allows state actors to insulate themselves from criticism in disputes over national identity (Över, 2016, p. 173).

States clearly use cultural heritage tourism to create national identity even in the case of complex histories. 'Turkey's history with heritage policy demonstrates that when speaking of diversity and tolerance in the country, it has always been best to display "fossilized" sites in the hope of obscuring fundamental problems at the living sites of contestation, which is where heritage as well as human rights policies begin to disintegrate' (Atakuman, 2010, p. 125). Nevertheless, it would be vastly unfair to suggest that this action is undertaken by Turkey alone, although the country serves as a good example of the ways in which the state actively uses heritage and heritage tourism as a means of achieving broader political goals. As noted throughout this volume, the use of heritage sites and heritage tourism to promote particular discourses and ideas of identity, including religious identity (see Timothy, Chapter 2, this volume; Olsen & Emmett, Chapter 3, this volume), appears inseparable from the use of institutionalised heritage in the MENA region.

World Heritage

One of the most notable forms of institutionalised heritage is the nomination and promotion by countries of World Heritage sites. As Atakuman (2010, p. 10) notes, the World Heritage List 'has long been and continues to be one of the most important venues for the display of national prowess'. There has been increasing interest in the WHS nomination, as it is a commonly promoted view that WHS status increases visitor numbers and that acts as a 'brand' for marketing sites, promoting tourism, and attracting visitors (Frey & Steiner, 2011; Adie, Hall, & Prayag, 2018). For example, Adie (Chapter 6, this volume) notes their importance for tourism in Morocco as well as their use as international representations of national identity. For Palestine, the World Heritage nomination process is regarded as a means to reinforce its state status in the international arena while simultaneously also using heritage to promote a national identity and tourism (Isaac, Chapter 8, this volume). However, the nomination of World Heritage sites may not always be in keeping with local understandings of heritage. For example, Adie (Chapter 6, this volume) highlights how Moroccan World Heritage sites are an emblematic example of the reiteration of the French colonial narrative of heritage, and which also remain important tourist markets. She notes that Moulay Idriss Zerhoun has been on the Moroccan World Heritage Tentative List since 1995 and would appear to, given its spiritual importance to Moroccans, be of greater cultural significance than the Roman city of Volubilis, which receives only limited local visitation (Adie & Hall, 2017). While Volubilis was, briefly, Moulay Idriss's capital, it seems that, potentially due to the official discourse about the site, which stresses its Roman connections, Volubilis is of greater interest for European, and particularly French, tourists. However, by putting Volubilis forward as a World Heritage site, Morocco has in essence nationally promoted a site which, until the French colonial period, was used as a source of cut stones with which to build Moulay Idriss Zerhoun, an arguably much more significant location both spiritually and from the perspective of national identity. From such a perspective, the interpretation of World Heritage sites such as Göbekli Tepe (Rıza Manci, Chapter 9, this volume) and Safranbolu (Tataroglu, Chapter 4, this volume), both in Turkey, take on new meaning. Indeed, the issue of MENA heritage being framed by European heritage concerns as well as heritage discourses, particularly including those surrounding World Heritage, which will undoubtedly remain a focal point for institutionalised cultural heritage in the region, is well contextualised by Atakuman (2010, p. 10):

> Ultimately, in a country where there are more mosques (over 85,000) than schools (under 70,000), the majority of the public is interested neither in Anatolian heritage nor in nominations to the World Heritage List. Those who do attach a value to this international display often

place their evaluation in the context of chauvinistic displays of symbolic conquest, like that of Turkey's victories in the Eurovision song contest or the European soccer cup. Within this context, the fact that most sites on the inscribed list consist of 'pre-Islamic' places, is easily subsumed within a vantage point that speaks of the conquest of Europe through the possession of things perceived to be important to Europe.

Furthermore, in Iran, as noted above, given the dual Persian and Islamic/Shia identities, World Heritage listing has also followed the ideological views of the ruling elite. Although, the Shad administration focused on World Heritage as a means for the country's national image and Persian glorification, the theocratic governance that replaced the monarchy ignored any listing and the process of the inscription of properties on the WHL was interrupted in the aftermath of the 1979 revolution. It was only in 2003 during the administration of President Khatami (1997–2005) when there was again a focus on Persian identity and cultural heritage in the tentative listing inventory process, and the tourism organisation recommenced nominating Iranian heritage sites to the UNESCO list (Seyfi, Hall, & Fagnoni, 2019).

Beyond World Heritage

A major area of future research in the MENA region is comparing the relative importance attached to heritage sites by tourists from outside the region and the perspectives of local people as to what constitutes heritage to them as opposed to an economic resource. Nevertheless, substantial differences as to what constitutes heritage also occurs at other scales. For example, with respect to Tel Ashkelon in Israel, Ram (Chapter 7, this volume) found that locals and the park authorities hold different perspectives as to what is important, locals are less satisfied with places that do not represent their personal heritage and desire simply for somewhere to barbeque, and plans are managed in a top-down manner. Similarly, in Tunisia there has historically been a focus on some coastal areas and particular types of heritage, while other regions and more intangible heritage traditions have often been ignored by official bodies (Dhaher et al., Chapter 5, this volume). Meanwhile, in Iran stresses arise between the promotion of Islamic and Persian identities in heritage tourism management (Seyfi & Hall, 2019a, 2019b; Seyfi et al., 2019). Thus, these differences in values and interests among stakeholders and the dissonance, may create a conflict in heritage preservation and management. Such tensions between different framings of what constitutes official heritage are unlikely to go away, especially as the understanding of heritage in the MENA gradually develops a more indigenous focus as opposed to what is considered appropriate by either ruling elites or Western heritage and tourism development experts. Nevertheless, even as such changes occur there will be a continued need to try to manage and accommodate the range of different heritage interests and values that exist.

Destruction of heritage

An extreme version of heritage management is dealing with the deliberate destruction of heritage sites. Since the beginning of the armed conflicts and public uprisings that accompanied and followed the 'Arab Spring', cultural heritage sites have been exposed to the destruction and damage by different perpetrators (Munawar, 2019) which has had 'a direct impact on the collective memory and cultural identity of the nations concerned' in the MENA region (Munawar, 2019, p.157).

Violent conflicts have limited access to as well as damaged heritage sites as diverse as Sana'a, a mountain city in the Yemen; the Roman city of Leptis Magna in Libya; and Palmyra in Syria, all sites inscribed on the World Heritage List. Sana'a and Leptis Magna are caught in violent civil wars, while Palmyra, including the main Temple of Bel (also known as Baal or Ba'al) which was blown up, was deliberately targeted by ISIS (Islamic State of Iraq and Syria; also known as ISIL (Islamic State of Iraq and the Levant); and *Daesh* or *Daish*). Palmyra was being visited by 150,000 tourists each year until war broke out in Syria in 2011 (Jeffries, 2015). Significantly, Palmyra was being destroyed by ISIS not only for religious reasons, but also to raise funds by supplying the archaeological black market as well as for reasons of publicity (Jeffries, 2015). Under the Ummayyad caliphate that existed in Palmyra in the seventh century AD, part of the Temple of Bel was used as a mosque, meaning by its actions ISIS was erasing not just pre-Islamic culture but Islamic heritage as well (Jeffries, 2015). Munawar (2019) observes that:

> The destruction of monuments, including those considered to be material representations of a nation's identity, does not inevitably mean the end of the lifecycle of those monuments. Rebuilding cultural heritage in the aftermath of war should not be taken for granted, and the focus should first be on the semantics and motives of the destruction—*i.e.* how and why these heritage sites and monuments were built and later damaged, and what reasons lay behind the targeting of historic cities by state or non-state actors (Munawar, 2019, p. 158).

Since heritage in the post-war period is usually a reconstruction of some image of the past rather than preservation of the original, many countries in the region that have been exposed to heritage destruction have difficulties in any reconstruction given the lack of a unified nation or tradition of historical preservation. The situation is only being further complicated by limited financial support (Borneman, 2015). Soufan (2018) also argued that authenticity is associated with ideological understandings of heritage in the Syrian context and therefore hard to attain in future post-war reconstruction, and commented that:

> The reconstruction and development of cultural heritage is closely linked to how different Syrian groups perceive their pasts and their

futures. Although specific items of the past might be recovered, Syrian society is politically deeply divided along religious, ethnic, and other lines. Each of these divided groups is characterised by both distinct political aspirations for the future and distinct understanding of the authentic past (Soufan, 2018, p. 1).

Nevertheless, 'cultural heritage has been subject to appropriation, looting, and destruction throughout history and continues to be an ongoing problem' (Zayad, 2018, p. 81). Cheikhmous Ali, of the Association for the Protection of Syrian Archaeology, regarded ISIS's actions in Palmyra as 'a way to pressure and torture the local population – to suppress their history and their collective memory' (quoted in Jeffries, 2015). Iconoclasm, the politically and/or religiously related deliberate destruction of religious icons and monuments, is an issue throughout the MENA region given the centrality of religion to many heritage sites and monuments and presents an ongoing management problem, especially when state and religious interests are intermixed (Hall & Prayag, 2019; Seyfi & Hall, 2019b). Acceptance of religious and political differences and the willingness to acknowledge the heritage values of others is made more difficult when people are subject to stress and insecurity.

The contemporary conflicts in Iraq, Syria, Libya, Yemen, and Mali, and the displacement of people as well as extensive damage to, and destruction of, cultural heritage in these countries, have also highlighted the need to translate into practice the rules of national and international legal framework for protecting cultural property in armed conflict (Cunliffe, Muhesen, & Lostal, 2016). Nevertheless, many criticisms have been raised about the effectiveness of the existing frameworks such as the *1954 Hague Convention* and the *World Heritage Convention* and the role of the international heritage community in protecting the cultural properties in conflicts. Cunliffe et al. (2016) argue that:

> Given the lack of (or perhaps the impossibility of) the national or international enforcement of these frameworks during conflict, it must be concluded that they are inadequate for cultural property protection. Even after the conflict, enforcement will undoubtedly remain problematic, and it is doubtful to what extent, if any, prosecutions would act as a deterrent, particularly given that those involved in such war crimes are often involved in worse atrocities against the people whose heritage it belongs to, for which there does exist a body of prosecutions as precedent (Cunliffe et al., 2016, p. 22).

National laws have also been criticised for their ineffectiveness in providing a legal framework for protection of cultural properties in conflicted areas. For instance, Bowker, Goodall, and Haciski (2016) argued that despite having domestic laws to prohibit the looting and destruction of antiquities, both Iraq and Syria are overextended by the armed conflict with ISIS and simply unable to effectively enforce their own laws, and they further recommend external assistance, robust international collaboration, and intervention to combat the devastation of cultural property in these countries. This can be seen in the attitude of the international community to cultural heritage and the UNESCO effort in 2015 when 50 countries adopted UN Security Council Resolution 2199 under the binding Chapter VII of the United Nations Charter, which prohibited trade in cultural property coming from Iraq and Syria (UNESCO, 2015). Furthermore, a gendered approach may be critical to the successful development of a cultural rights framing of heritage where women should be involved in protecting and promoting heritage assets, through professional or volunteer roles (Matthews et al., 2020). By taking the example of practices that implemented UNESCO Conventions in Nigeria and Vietnam, Mathews et al. (2020) emphasised that the participation and engagement of women in the post-conflict negotiation process is 'essential to enhance the protection of cultural diversity through the voices of women survivors such as in the case of the Yazidi minority in northern Iraq' (Matthews et al., 2020, p. 136).

Climate change

In the MENA countries a major source of stress, and arguably a driver behind the civil war in Syria (Gleick, 2014), is climate change (Hall, 2019). Although the precise role of climate change in increasing conflict risk remains a topic of debate (Adams et al., 2018; Selby et al., 2017), it is clear that water is becoming securitised in the region (King, 2015; Weinthal, Zawahri, & Sowers, 2015). From a tourism perspective, conflict and political instability obviously have a major impact on visitor numbers, with terrorism and the Arab Spring being a significant backdrop to many of the chapters in this volume. The combination of already stressed fresh water resources and rapid population growth substantially increases the vulnerability of the region to future climate change (Chenoweth et al., 2011). Potential reductions in water availability as a result of climate change, and industry and population pressures, mean that there could be 30 to 70 per cent less water per person by 2025 (Sowers et al., 2011). Such a situation is expected to create increased tensions between tourism and other sectors for available water resources, given that tourism is a major direct and indirect water user (Hall, 2019).

Sea level rise is also a potentially significant issue for MENA states which not only affects coastal resort areas but can also have a significant impact on tourism resources, especially cultural heritage, while other aspects of climate change such as extreme weather events and changes in humidity are also significant for heritage conservation (Hall, 2016; Hall et al., 2016). Nevertheless, coastal cultural landscapes and built environments are particularly at risk (Hall, 2018; Hall & Ram, 2018). Although there is growing awareness of the potential implications of climate change for tourism in the MENA region (Fitchett & Roshan, Chapter 14, this volume), there are many unknowns with respect to the capacity of tourists and attractions to adapt, especially with respect to heat waves and photochemical air pollution in urban centres. The potential of such pressures on flagship heritage projects, such as new museums and attractions, in the Gulf States, Saudi Arabia, and Egypt may be substantial. As Lelieveld et al. (2014, p. 1947) observe, 'Considering the multiple environmental stresses in metropolitan areas, including confounding factors such as the urban heat island effect and growing air pollution, the cities in this region will become true hot spots of climate change'. Yet, in 'a future that is full of technological, political, social, and economic uncertainty, climate change is a relative certainty that can be considered and planned for by policy makers' (Chenoweth et al., 2011, p. 17). However, despite the clear interests of government to promote tourism in the region as an economic development mechanism, there is no matching attention to encourage tourism-related adaptation and mitigation (Hall, 2019).

Conclusion

Despite the development of international Westernised mass tourism and the growth of halal tourism, cultural heritage tourism will likely be a mainstay of the industry in the MENA region in the foreseeable future. Nevertheless, as the various chapters in this volume have indicated, heritage and heritage tourism are subjects surrounded by substantial political and economic issues that are only likely to become more contested over the coming decades. Critical to resolving some of the issues will be the development of a stronger sense of indigenous heritage in institutional heritage management that reflects the concerns of local people and the wider community rather than elites and European heritage concerns. Significant in this will be encouraging the growth of domestic cultural heritage tourism. Although such a development may not meet some of the economic motivations of state tourism and heritage policies, it would help contribute to more sustainable local tourism developments and stronger relationships between communities and heritage sites that acknowledge and reflect the wide range of interests and values associated with sites at multiple levels. Perhaps most importantly of all, such a shift in cultural heritage tourism thinking may help counter the ongoing use of heritage and cultural heritage tourism by governments and political and religious elites to satisfy their own narrow and, often selfish, interests rather than expansive idea of the 'we' in the things we want to keep.

References

Abu-Khafajah, S., Al Rabady, R., & Rababeh, S. (2015). Urban heritage 'space' under neoliberal development: A tale of a Jordanian plaza. *International Journal of Heritage Studies*, *21*(5), 441–459.

Abu-Khafajah, S., & Miqdadi, R. (2019). Prejudice, military intelligence, and neoliberalism: Examining the local within archaeology and heritage practices in Jordan. *Contemporary Levant*, *4*(2), 92–106.

Adams, C., Ide, T., Barnett, J., & Detges, A. (2018). Sampling bias in climate–conflict research. *Nature Climate Change*, *8*(3), 200–203.

Addison, E. (2004). The roads to ruins: Accessing Islamic heritage in Jordan. In Y. Rowan & U. Baram (eds), *Marketing heritage: Archaeology and the consumption of the past* (pp. 229–248). Walnut Creek, CA: Rowman Altamira.

Adie, B. A., & Hall, C. M. (2017). Who visits world heritage? A comparative study of three cultural sites. *Journal of Heritage Tourism*, *12*(1), 67–80.

Adie, B. A., Hall, C. M., & Prayag, G. (2018). World Heritage as a placebo brand: A comparative analysis of three sites and marketing implications. *Journal of Sustainable Tourism*, *26*(3), 399–415.

Atakuman, Ç. (2010). Value of heritage in Turkey: History and politics of Turkey's World Heritage nominations. *Journal of Mediterranean Archaeology*, *23*(1), 107–131.

Atakuman, Ç. (2017). Shifting discourses of heritage and identity in Turkey: Anatolianist Ideologies and beyond. In A. de Francesco (ed.), *Search of pre-classical antiquity: Rediscovering ancient peoples in Mediterranean Europe (19th and 20th c.)* (pp. 166–181). Leiden: Brill.

Borneman, J. (2015). Heritage sites after war: Germany 1945, Syria now. In D. Haller, A. Lichtenberger, & M. Meerpohl (eds), *Essays on heritage, tourism and society in the MENA region* (pp. 237–248). Munich: Verlag Ferdinand Schöningh.

Bowker, D., Goodall, L., & Haciski, R. (2016). Confronting ISIS's war on cultural property. *American Society of International Law*, *20*(12).

Butler, B. (2009). 'Othering' the archive—from exile to inclusion and heritage dignity: The case of Palestinian archival memory. *Archival Science*, *9*(1–2), 57.

Büyüksaraç, G. B. (2004). Conquering Istanbul: The controversy over the Taksim Mosque project. *Anthropology in Action: Journal of Applied Anthropology*, *11*, 22–31.

Chenoweth, J., Hadjinicolaou, P., Bruggeman, A., Lelieveld, J., Levin, Z., Lange, M. A., Xoplaki, E., & Hadjikakou, M. (2011). Impact of climate change on the water resources of the eastern Mediterranean and Middle East region: Modelled 21st century changes and implications. *Water Resources Research*, *47*, W06506.

Cunliffe, E., Muhesen, N., & Lostal, M. (2016). The destruction of cultural property in the Syrian conflict: Legal implications and obligations. *International Journal of Cultural Property*, *23*(1), 1–31.

Daher, R. F. (2005). Urban regeneration/heritage tourism endeavours: The case of Salt, Jordan 'local actors, international donors, and the state'. *International Journal of Heritage Studies*, *11*(4), 289–308.

Ekber Doğan, A. (2020). The construction of Erdogan autocracy: Balancing hegemonic crisis with promises of accumulation regime. *Critique*, *48*(1), 95–111.

Eldem, E. (2015). Cultural heritage in Turkey: An eminently political matter. In D. Haller, A. Lichtenberger, & M. Meerpohl (eds), *Essays on heritage, tourism and society in the MENA region* (pp. 67–91). Munich: Verlag Ferdinand Schöningh.

Frey, B. S., & Steiner, L. (2011). World Heritage List: Does it make sense? *International Journal of Cultural Policy*, *17*(5), 555–573.

Gleick, P. H. (2014). Water, drought, climate change, and conflict in Syria. *Weather, Climate, and Society*, *6*(3), 331–340.

Gori, M. (2013). The stones of contention: The role of archaeological heritage in Israeli–Palestinian conflict. *Archaeologies*, *9*(1), 213–229.

Graham B., & Howard, P. (2008). Introduction: Heritage and identity. In B. Graham & P. Howard (eds), *The Ashgate research companion to heritage and identity* (pp. 1–18). Aldershot: Ashgate.

Hall, C. M. (2016). Heritage, heritage tourism and climate change. *Journal of Heritage Tourism*, *11*(1), 1–9

Hall, C. M. (2018). Climate change and its impacts on coastal tourism: regional assessments, gaps and issues. In A. Jones & M. Phillips (eds), *Global climate change and coastal tourism: Recognizing problems, managing solutions, future expectations* (pp. 48–61). Wallingford: CABI.

Hall, C. M. (2019). Tourism and climate change in the Middle East. In D. Timothy (ed.), *The Routledge handbook of tourism in the Middle East and North Africa* (pp. 109–209). Abingdon: Routledge.

Hall, C. M., & Ram, Y. (2018). Israel: Coastal tourism, coastal planning and climate change in Israel. In A. Jones & M. Phillips (eds), *Global climate change and coastal tourism: Recognizing problems, managing solutions, future expectations* (pp. 263–272). Wallingford: CABI.

Hall, C. M., & Prayag, G. (eds) (2019). *The Routledge handbook of halal hospitality and Islamic tourism*. Abingdon: Routledge.

Hall, C. M., Baird, T., James, M., & Ram, Y. (2016). Climate change and cultural heritage: Conservation and heritage tourism in the Anthropocene. *Journal of Heritage Tourism*, *11*(1), 10–24.

Isaac, R. K., Hall, C.M., & Higgins-Desbiolles, F. (eds) (2016). *The politics and power of tourism in Palestine*. Abingdon: Routledge.

Jeffries, S. (2015). Isis's destruction of Palmyra: 'The heart has been ripped out of the city'. *The Guardian*, 2 September. Retrieved from https://www.theguardian.com/world/2015/sep/02/isis-destruction-of-palmyra-syria-heart-been-ripped-out-of-the-city.

King, M. D. (2015). The weaponization of water in Syria and Iraq. *The Washington Quarterly*, *38*(4), 153–169.

Lafi, N. (2015). The nature of Jewish spaces in Ottoman Algiers. In A. Gromova, F. Heinert, & S. Voigt (eds), *Jewish and non-Jewish spaces in the urban context* (pp. 83–99). Berlin: Neofelis Verlag.

Lelieveld, J., Hadjinicolaou, P., Kostopoulou, E., Giannakopoulos, C., Pozzer, A., Tanarhte, M., & Tyrlis, E. (2014). Model projected heat extremes and air pollution in the eastern Mediterranean and Middle East in the twenty-first century. *Regional Environmental Change*, *14*(5), 1937–1949.

Matthews, R., Rasheed, Q. H., Palmero Fernández, M., Fobbe, S., Nováček, K., Mohammed-Amin, R., ... & Richardson, A. (2020). Heritage and cultural healing: Iraq in a post-Daesh era. *International Journal of Heritage Studies*, 1–22.

Munawar, N. A. (2019). Competing heritage: Curating the post-conflict heritage of roman Syria. *Bulletin of the Institute of Classical Studies*, *62*(1), 142–165.

Över, D. (2016). Cultural tourism and complex histories: The Armenian Akhtamar Church, the Turkish state and national identity. *Qualitative Sociology*, *39*(2), 173–194.

Riedel, A. (2015). Which past is worthy to preserve? Case studies from Jordan. In D. Haller, A. Lichtenberger, & M. Meerpohl (eds), *Essays on heritage, tourism and society in the MENA region* (pp. 225–235). Munich: Verlag Ferdinand Schöningh.

Saleh, A., & Worrall, J. (2015). Between Darius and Khomeini: exploring Iran's national identity problematique. *National Identities*, *17*(1), 73-97.

Selby, J., Dahi, O. S., Fröhlich, C., & Hulme, M. (2017). Climate change and the Syrian civil war revisited. *Political Geography*, *60*, 232–244.

Seyfi, S., & Hall, C. M. (eds.) (2019a). *Tourism in Iran: Challenges, development and issues*. Abingdon: Routledge.

Seyfi, S., & Hall, C. M. (2019b). Deciphering Islamic theocracy and tourism: Conceptualization, context and complexities. *International Journal of Tourism Research*, *21*(6), 735–746.

Seyfi, S., Hall, C. M., & Fagnoni, E. (2019). Managing World Heritage Site stakeholders: A grounded theory paradigm model approach. *Journal of Heritage Tourism*, *14*(4), 308–324.

Smith, L. (2006). *Uses of heritage*. Abingdon: Routledge.

Soufan, A. (2018). Post-war teconstruction, authenticity and development of cultural heritage in Syria. In *ICOMOS University Forum* (pp. 1–18). ICOMOS International.

Sowers, J., Vengosh, A., & Weinthal, E. (2011). Climate change, water resources, and the politics of adaptation in the Middle East and North Africa. *Climatic Change*, *104*, 599–627.

Törne, A. (2015). 'On the grounds where they will walk in a hundred years' time' – struggling with the heritage of violent past in post-genocidal Tunceli. *European Journal of Turkish Studies. Social Sciences on Contemporary Turkey*, *20*.

UNESCO (2015). *A historic resolution to protect cultural heritage*. Retrieved from https://en.unesco.org/courier/2017nian-di-3qi/historic-resolution-protect-cultural-heritage.

Watenpaugh, H. Z. (2014). Preserving the medieval city of Ani: Cultural heritage between contest and reconciliation. *Journal of the Society of Architectural Historians*, *73*(4), 528–555.

Weinthal, E., Zawahri, N., & Sowers, J. (2015). Securitizing water, climate, and migration in Israel, Jordan, and Syria. *International Environmental Agreements: Politics, Law and Economics*, *15*(3), 293–307.

Whitehead, C., & Bozoğlu, G. (2016). Protest, bodies, and the grounds of memory: Taksim Square as 'heritage site' and the 2013 Gezi protests. *Heritage & Society*, *9*(2), 111–136.

Zayad, L. (2018). Systematic cultural appropriation and the Israeli-Palestinian conflict. *DePaul Journal of Art, Technology & Intellectual Property Law*, *28*, 81–125.

Zencirci, G. (2014). Civil society's history: New constructions of Ottoman heritage by the Justice and Development Party in Turkey. *European Journal of Turkish Studies. Social Sciences on Contemporary Turkey*, *19*.

Index

Abrahamic religions 10, 26, 34, 40, 41, 42, 43, 44; *see also* Christianity, Islam, Judaism
Abu Dhabi 157–9, 161–7; *see also* United Arab Emirates
Afghanistan 2, 36
Algeria 23, 24, 40, 88; competitiveness 22; civil war xi; country profile 3; international tourism receipts 21; international visitor arrivals 20; World Heritage 14
antiquities 90, 172, 176; artefact recording 177; looting and trafficking xii, 15, 131, 178, 247
Arab–Israeli conflict xi, 23
Arab culture and civilization 159, 162; authenticity 162
Arab Spring xii, 12, 23, 246, 248; geopolitics 12; impacts on Egyptian tourism 171
Arab World 2, 90, 157, 160, 165–7; relationship to MENA region 90; and orientalism 165–7
Arabian Peninsula 20
archaeology 41, 116, 126, 131; and economic objectives 18, 24; and political objectives 18–19, 49, 131, 134, 138, 242; religious 49, 55
Armenian heritage 239; Armenian Cathedral of the Holy Cross 242–3; churches 39, 223
Armenian Christians 43
Armenian genocide 239, 242–3
Association for the Protection of Syrian Archaeology 247
Atlantic Ocean 6, 9
attractions *see* tourist attractions
authenticity 55, 79, 82, 84, 87, 91, 116, 158, 164, 165, 179; and ideology 246; meaning 56; and religious heritage 56–9
aviation hub 13, 157, 164, 167

Bábism 37
Baha'i Faith 36, 37, 43, 44, 65; Haifa 44, 45, 65; Mount Carmel 43, 65
Bahrain 12; competitiveness 22; country profile 3; diplomatic relations with Qatar 13; geopolitics 12; international tourism receipts 21; international visitor arrivals 20; World Heritage 14
Brigham Young University (BYU) Jerusalem Center 65–6
business tourism 220
Byzantine 58, 59, 63, 73

Caspian Sea 233
Christianity 34, 35, 36; *see also* pilgrimage
Church of Jesus Christ of Latterday Saints 47, 65–6
churches 35, 36, 38–9, 41, 57, 58
civil war xi; Syria 12, 16, 248; Lebanon 18
City of David (Jerusalem Walls) National Park 19–20
climate change 26, 218–38, 248–9; human physiological heat stress 234; pressure on energy network 234; sea level rise 248
Cold War 1, 23
collective memory 15, 17, 18, 75, 84, 239, 246
commoditisation 2, 7
community development 116, 171
Comoros 13

Convention Concerning the Protection of the World Cultural and Natural Heritage, see World Heritage
Convention on the Protection and Promotion of the Diversity of Cultural Expression 95, 189
Convention for the Protection of Cultural Property in the Event of Armed Conflict 130; and conservation of cultural heritage in Palestine 130–1
Convention for the Safeguarding of the Intangible Cultural Heritage 189
conservatism 11, 83–4, 157, 240; cultural 83, 159; Islamic 5; religious 11; Romantic 84
cultural consumption 95, 97
cultural festival 94
cultural heritage tourism 2, 10, 94, 170–2, 180, 183–4, 241–3, 249; marketing 179; themed hotels and resorts 166; *see also* cultural tourism, heritage tourism
cultural heritage planning 170–1, 191
cultural property 15, 92, 130; destruction 15–20, 130, 247–8
cultural tourism 5, 116, 170, 188; Egypt 173; Iran 218–9; Morocco 10; religious heritage 50; policy 242–3; Tunisia 92, 94; Turkey 242–3; *see also* cultural heritage tourism, heritage tourism, intangible heritage

Daesh *see* ISIS
Dead Sea Scrolls 132
de-historification 103
Democracy 13, 61
diplomacy 1
Disneyfication 161–7
Djibouti 2
domestic tourism 14; Iran 47; Morocco 108; Saudi Arabia 5; Tunisia 96
Druze 37
Dubai 157–9, 161–7; *see also* United Arab Emirates

economic development 1, 6, 14, 23, 88, 96, 173, 176, 183, 249; discourse 243; local 176; threat to heritage 17
economic diversification 5, 166
Egypt 13, 23, 38; Abu Mena 173; archaeology 39; Cairo 42, 175, 177, 179, 180, 181, 182–3; competitiveness 22; country profile 3; cultural heritage tourism 153, 158, 170–86; Giza plateau 174, 180–3; Grand Egyptian Museum 181; Great Pyramids 174, 180–2; international tourism receipts 21; international visitor arrivals 20; Luxor 173–4, 180; Mount Sinai 41; pilgrimage 47; Sphinx International Airport 182–3; World Heritage 14; *see also* Ministry of Antiquities
employment generation 5, 6, 11, 25, 107, 241
Eurocentrism 1, 88, 189
Eurovision Song Contest 245
Exoticism 91, 104

faith *see* religion
falconry 165
Far East 1
foodscape 46
France 6, 35, 87, 88, 108, 111; colonial policy 105–6

Gastronomy 7, 10; *see also* foodscape
Gaza Strip *see* Palestine
gender 121, 202–17; segregation 45
genocide 239, 242, 243; recognition debate 243
geographical fixity 2
geopolitics 1, 12
globalism 90
governance 24, 172; Egyptian antiquities 172; Sahara 24; theocratic 245
greater Middle East 2
green space 115–16, 121–5
Gulf Cooperation Council (GCC) 3–4, 13, 20
Gulf states 12, 249

Hague Convention (*Hague Convention for the Protection of Cultural Property in the Event of Armed Conflict*) 130, 247; and conservation of cultural heritage in Palestine 130–1
Hajj 5, 36, 46–7; *see also* Islam, pilgrimage
halal 45; tourism 249
heritage 2, 11, 72–4, 239–45; definition 239; destruction and representation in MENA region 15–20, 23–4, 246–8; religious dimensions 34–70; social and

cultural construction of 26, 74–84, 102–12, 239–45; *see also* natural heritage, World Heritage
heritage conservation 8, 18, 19, 72, 74–5, 77, 91, 95, 136, 171, 180; and climate change 248; discourse 82; negotiated meanings 75; and tourism 142
heritage interpretation 18, 19, 56, 57, 66, 72, 143, 148, 158, 175, 244; defined 56; interpretation circuits 108; visitor centres 180; and visitor satisfaction 151, 158
heritage management 18–19, 72, 136, 170–1, 175, 191, 246, 249; legal frameworks 17, 60–1, 95, 116, 130, 135–8, 158, 189; political dimensions 18, 55–6, 59–66, 131–8, 241; site management 126, 175
heritage planning 170–86
heritage policy *see* policy
heritage tourism xi, 2, 11, 141, 153, 158, 187, 235–6, 239; Egypt 171–4, 179–84; MENA context 13–15, 20–2, 26, 239, 249; Morocco 102–12; Tunisia 87–97; United Arab Emirates 158–67
heritagescape 188; *see also* cultural tourism, cultural heritage tourism
hiking 7, 48; *see also* trails
Holy Land 36, 40, 41, 42, 45–6, 47, 59, 63; authenticity 58; trails 48
human mobility 1
human rights 134; Palestine 134; Turkey 61, 243

Iberian Peninsula 36
Identity: cultural identity 9, 15, 24, 54, 74, 83, 94–5, 97, 103, 109, 160, 187, 204, 241, 248; heritage identity 76, 80; local identity 19, 191; national identity 25, 89, 90, 103, 105, 112, 157, 160, 240–3, 244; political identity 242; politics of identity 103, 241–3; religious identity 54, 243; social identity 74
inclusive tourism 97
India 103–4
Indonesia 36
insecurity 247
intangible heritage 10, 11, 87, 189, 205, 245; economic significance 90, 93, 107; intangible culture 45; Iran 203; Morocco 107; Tunisia 90, 93

International Centre for the Study of the Preservation and Restoration of Cultural Property (ICCROM) 16, 136
International Charter of Venice 158
International Council on Monuments and Sites (ICOMOS) 16, 110; definition of cultural heritage 116; International Charter of Venice 158
International Court of Justice 134
International Monetary Fund (IMF) 2, 4
international tourism xi, 11, 21, 171, 187, 203
interpretation *see* heritage interpretation
Iran 2, 11, 37, 38, 39, 49; climate change 218–36; competitiveness 22; country profile 3; and geopolitics 12, 13; Gonbad-e Qābus Brick Tower 187–201; identity 240–1, 245; international tourism receipts 21; international visitor arrivals 20; and regional rivalry with Saudi Arabia 12; religious tourism 47, 54; and Shia Islam 5, 47; Tabriz 206–14; World Heritage 14, 187–201, 203, 218, 220, 245
Iran Cultural Heritage, Handcraft and Tourism Organization (ICHTO) 191, 194
Iraq xi, 1, 5, 12, 38, 39, 44, 240–1; archaeology 40, 44; competitiveness 22; country profile 3; cultural heritage destruction 15, 49, 247–8; and geopolitics 1, 12; international tourism receipts 21; international visitor arrivals 20; pilgrimage 47–8; and Shia Islam 5; World Heritage 14
ISIL (Islamic State of Iraq and the Levant) *see* ISIS
ISIS 1, 15, 246–7; Syrian armed conflict and its impact on cultural heritage 15–18
Islam 5, 11, 34, 35–6, 44, 46, 105, 110; Ibadi 5; Shia 5, 47, 241, 245; Sunni 5, 47, 192, 196; Wahhabism 163; *see also* hajj, Islamic tourism
Islamic tourism 10–11, 220; conservative position of the OIC 11; *see also* hajj
Israel 2, 5, 13, 38, 39, 45, 59, 62–3, 65–6, 115–16, 118–26, 129, 239; archaeology and national narratives 19–20; Ashkelon 115–16, 118–26;

competitiveness 22; country profile 3; international tourism receipts 21; international visitor arrivals 20; Nazareth 61–2; pilgrimage 47–8; religious meals 45–6; sacred hills and mountains 43; Tiberius 62; War of Independence 23; World Heritage 14; *see also* Jerusalem, Judaism, Palestine
Israel Antiquities Authority 20
Israel Lands Authority 62
Israel Nature and Parks Authority 20, 115, 118, 119, 121–6

Jerusalem 43, 44, 45, 48, 49, 66, 129, 132, 137; Al-Aqsa Mosque 37; City of David (Jerusalem Walls) National Park 19–20; Church of the Holy Sepulchre 38; Mount of Olives 41, 44; old city 131; separation barrier/wall 49, 134; Wailing Wall 48, 63–4
Joint Comprehensive Plan of Action (JCPOA) 13; US withdrawal 13
Jordan 19, 23, 38, 44, 158; competitiveness 22; country profile 3; Holy Land 47, 49, 58–9; importance of heritage tourism 240; international tourism receipts 21; international visitor arrivals 20; Petra 153; World Heritage 14
Jordan River 55, 58; Baptism Site Al-Maghtas 40, 59; competing baptismal sites 58–9
Jordan Valley 129, 134
Judaism 3, 34, 35, 36, 37; description 35; archaeological sites 39; museums 40–2; synagogues 39

Kemalism 242
kosher 45
Kurds 3, 4, 5; Turkish aggression against xi
Kuwait: competitiveness 22; country profile 3; international tourism receipts 21; international visitor arrivals 20; World Heritage 14

Lebanon 5, 18, 38, 39, 48; archaeology 18–19; Beqa'a Valley 19; competitiveness 22; conflict xi; country profile 3; geopolitics 12; international tourism receipts 21; international visitor arrivals 20; World Heritage 8, 14
Libya 15, 38, 88; competitiveness 22; conflict 15, 246, 247; country profile 3; World Heritage 14; international tourism receipts 21; international visitor arrivals 7, 20
List of World Heritage in Danger 16, 49–50, 173; Abu Mena 173; *see also* World Heritage
looting xii, 15, 172, 247; Arab Spring 171; Egypt 175, 178; Palestine 133; strategy to combat looting 178; Syria 16

Maghreb xi, 6, 87, 88; tourism 88, 91
Malaysia 103
Mandaenism 37
Manichaeism 37
Mashriq xi, 2
mass tourism 88, 161, 163, 242, 249; Tunisia 88, 96–7
Mauritania 13, 23, 88, 110
Mediterranean 1, 10, 20, 21, 35, 87, 107, 110
Mediterranean climate 219
Mediterranean diet 8
Mediterranean Sea 6, 9, 115
MENA xi, 1–23, 239–49; climate change 248–9; cultural and heritage tourism 13–14, 239–45; defined 2–5; destruction of cultural property and heritage 15, 18–20, 246–8; geopolitics 12–13, 22–23; significance of tourism 6, 10–11, 20–22
MENAP (Middle East, North Africa, Afghanistan, and Pakistan) 2
MENAT (Middle East, North Africa, and Turkey) 2
Ministry of Antiquities (Egypt) 172, 175, 176, 177–9; artefact recording and documentation 177–8; cultural heritage tourism marketing 179; strategy to combat looting 178
modernity 7, 74, 82, 84, 91, 104, 106, 160–1; discourse of heritage against modernity 78–80, 241
mosques 34, 37–8, 40, 41, 47, 87, 174, 244
Morocco 6–10, 39, 44, 48, 88, 102, 105–12; colonialism 105–7, 109; competitiveness 22; country profile 3;

Fez 106; heritage tourism 108–12; international tourism receipts 21; international visitor arrivals 20; tourism policy 107–89; Volubilis 110–12; World Heritage 14, 110–12, 241, 244
Mount Sinai 41
museums 40–41, 55, 95, 171, 228, 241, 249; Egypt 172, 175, 179, 181; Grand Egyptian Museum 181; Morocco 7–9; Nazareth 62; religious heritage 38, 40–42; Tunisia 95; UAE 157, 159–60, 162

national identity 90, 241; Iran 240–1; Morocco 105, 112; Tunisia 89, 90; Turkish 25, 242–3; UAE 157, 160
national parks 11, 119; Askelon 115–16, 119, 122; Jerusalem Walls 19–20; Morocco 8
nationalism 64, 166, 241; competing 64; cultural 160; Iranian 241; religious 41; Turkish 243; United Arab Emirates 166
natural gas 5
natural heritage 82, 134, 136–8; discourse 82
NAWA (North Africa–West Asia) 2
Nazareth 2000 Project 62–3
Near East 1, 41, 42

oil 5, 12, 23, 24, 157, 166; diversification from 5, 166; geopolitics 12; reserves in MENA region xi, 5
Oman 5, 103, 158; competitiveness 22; country profile 3; international tourism receipts 21; international visitor arrivals 20; World Heritage 14
Oman Sea 231
Organisation for Economic Co-operation and Development (OECD); MENA country membership 3–4
Organisation of Islamic Cooperation (OIC) 10; MENA country membership 3–4; perspective on Islamic tourism 10–11
Organization of Petroleum Exporting Countries (OPEC) 5; *see also* oil
Orientalism 102–6, 112
Oslo Accords 62, 129–30
Ottoman architecture 62, 87
Ottoman empire 60, 242

Ottoman heritage 62, 74, 76, 76, 83, 242
over-tourism 49–50; in Jerusalem 49

Pakistan 2, 36
Palestine 5, 13, 19, 47, 129–40, 244; al Nakba 23; Bethlehem 62, 133, 137; competitiveness 22; country profile 3; existence before Jewish presence 132; Gaza Strip 12, 129, 130, 135, 137; Hebron 63–5; illegal Israeli settlements and roads 132–3; impact of the Israeli military occupation on conservation of cultural heritage 130–5; international tourism receipts 21; international visitor arrivals 20; Jericho 135; Nablus 133; religion 37, 38, 42, 43, 45, 66; segregation wall 133–4; trails 49, 137; UNESCO membership 135–8, 244; World Heritage 14, 135–8; *see also* Jerusalem
Palestine War (al-Nakba) 23
Palestinian National Authority 135
peace 131; Jordan–Israel peace agreement 59; Oslo Peace Accords 62, 129–30, 135; President Trump's 'peace plan' 13
Persians 5, 115, 240–1, 245; history 240
Persian Gulf 23
pilgrimage 35, 36, 37, 46–48, 54–5, 111; Abrahamic religion 10; Baha'i 44; Christian 35, 38–9, 47, 59, 62, 133; Coptic 38; gardens 44; Islamic 5, 36, 44, 46–7; Judaism 35, 48; Orthodox 38; secular 5; war sites 5; *see also* hajj
place attachment 88, 118, 119–21, 126; *see also* sense of place
policy 1, 94, 121, 126, 136; actors 93; climate change 249; colonial policy 105–6, 111; cultural policy 242; heritage policy 91, 136, 243; tourism policy 102, 112, 242–3
Polisario Front 23; *see* Western Sahara
post-colonialism 102–6, 109, 112

Qatar 13; competitiveness 22; country profile 3; Doha 42; international tourism receipts 21; international visitor arrivals 20; Saudi sanctions against 13; World Heritage 14
Qatar Airlines 13

Red Sea 38, 170
religion 3–4, 34–71, 247; archaeological sites 40; main religions of MENA countries 3–4; museums 42; originating in the Middle East 37; sacred hills and mountains 43
religious freedom 61
resident perceptions 203
Russia 12; and civil war in Syria 12

sacred space 34, 36, 37, 45, 46–8, 55, 58; Mount Gerizim 41–2; Mount of Olives 44; Mount Sinai 41; sacred hills and mountains 42–44; Saint Catherine area 40
Safranbolu'da Zaman [*Safranbolu: Reflections of Time*] 74–83; *see also* sense of place, World Heritage
Sahara 6, 9, 24; *see also* Western Sahara
Saharawi/Sahrawi 24
Sahrawi Arab Democratic Republic (SADR) 23; *see* Western Sahara
Samaritanism 36, 37, 41; Mount Gerizim 41
Saudi Arabia 11, 12, 47, 158, 249; competitiveness 22; country profile 3; international tourism receipts 21; international visitor arrivals 20; Jeddah 38; Mecca 35, 36, 42; Medina 35, 44; regional conflict with Iran xii, 12; sanctions against Qatar 13; tourism as economic diversification 5; World Heritage 14
Saudi Commission for Tourism and National Heritage (SCTH) 5
Sea of Galilee 62
seasonality 89, 231
security 1, 22–3, 44, 49, 89, 129, 174; as excuse for confiscation of Palestinian water and land 133, 136; management 64, 171, 175, 178; perception of MENA region 12
sense of place 72–84; defined 72; and heritage discourse 72–3, 74; *see also* place attachment
Shabakism 36
Sharjah 42, 160, 163–4, 166; *see also* United Arab Emirates
Shia Islam *see* Islam
Silk Road 206
Six-Day War 23, 58, 59

social change 80–1
Somalia 2
Spain: and Morocco 6–7, 105, 108; and Western Sahara 23
Spanish Sahara *see* Western Sahara
spectacle 157, 159, 163; Dubai 159, 163
Strait of Hormuz 12
Sudan 2
Sunni Islam *see* Islam
sustainable development 97, 107, 170, 174, 181, 202; UN 2030 Agenda for Sustainable Development 137
sustainable tourism 96–7, 190, 203
synagogues 34, 37, 39, 48; Djerba Synagogue 39
Syria 1, 23, 38, 39, 44, 47, 158; Aleppo 17; civil war xi, 1, 246, 248; competitiveness 22; country profile 3; cultural heritage destruction 15, 16–17, 49, 246–7; Damascus 44; international tourism receipts 21; international visitor arrivals 20; Palmyra 18, 246–7; World Heritage 14, 44, 246–7

terrorism 47, 90, 248
Thomas Cook 47
totalitarianism 90
tourism competitiveness 21, 22, 88, 142, 183
tourism demand 5
tourism development 6–7, 165, 202–5; in Iran 189–91; in Morocco 103, 107; in Tunisia 87–9, 92–3; in United Arab Emirates 165
tourism marketing 103–4, 153, 172, 235; cultural heritage 179; Iran 235
tourism policy *see* policy
tourist attractions 1, 40, 41, 44, 95, 159, 161, 203; and climate change 233; synagogues 39; war sites 5
trafficking xii, 15
trails 48–9; Abraham Path 49; Gospel Trail 48; Jesus Trail 48; Nativity Trail 48–9
Tunisia 87–100, 245; competitiveness 22; complexities of heritage tourism development 92–3; country profile 3; historical and archaeological sites 92; importance of heritage 89–92, 93–6; international tourism receipts 21; international visitor arrivals 20; Jewish heritage 39, 48; tourism

development 87–9, 92–3; World Heritage 14, 92
Turkey 12, 38, 72–86, 141–56, 240, 241–3; Anatolia 73, 141, 193, 243; Armenian genocide 239, 242; Armenian heritage 239, 242–3; competitiveness 22; country profile 4; Göbekli Tepe 141–55; Hagia Sophia 60–1; heritage and political identity 241–3; international tourism receipts 21; international visitor arrivals 20; Istanbul 38, 42, 60; in MENA 2; Safranbolu 72–85; World Heritage 14, 72–85, 141–55
Turkmen 188, 195, 197; culture 188, 192, 193, 196, 197, 233
Turkmenistan 192

Ummayyad caliphate 246
United Arab Emirates (UAE) 157–67; Abu Dhabi 157–9, 161–7; competitiveness 22; country profile 4; Dubai 157–9, 161–7; international tourism receipts 21; international visitor arrivals 20; relations with Qatar 13; Sharjah 42, 160, 163–4, 166; World Heritage 14
United Nations 2030 Agenda for Sustainable Development 137; *see also* sustainable development
United Nations Development Programme (UNDP) 2; MENA region 2–4
United Nations Education, Scientific and Cultural Organization (UNESCO) 8–9, 16–17, 94, 130, 158–9; intangible cultural heritage 8; Palestinian membership 135–8; *see also* World Heritage
United Nations Institute for Training and Research (UNITAR) 16
United Nations Security Council 248
United Nations World Tourism Organization (UNWTO) 20; MENA region 20–2
United States 13, 129; Jews in 35; opposition to Palestinian World Heritage listings 64, 135; withdrawal from treaty with Iran 13
United States Commission on International Religious Freedom (USCIRF) 61

United States Agency for International Development (USAID) 19
urban parks 117–126; visitor satisfaction 117–18

visiting friends and relatives/relations (VFR) 7, 10; in Morocco 7
visitor satisfaction 117–18, 141, 142, 179; at Göbekli Tepe 146, 151; and urban parks 117–18

Wahhabism 163
WANA (West Asia and North Africa) 2
war crimes 15, 247; and destruction of cultural property 15, 247
water availability 248
West Bank *see* Palestine
Western Sahara 23–4; archaeology in 24; independence from Morocco 23–4; tourism in 24
westernization 90
World Economic Forum (WEF) 22, 158; competitiveness index 22
World Heritage 72–85, 102–113, 187–90, 244–5, 247; Abu Mena 173; brand 186, 191, 197; Göbekli Tepe 141–155; Gonbad-e Qābus Brick Tower 190–200; in Iran 187–200, 203; in MENA region by country 14; in Morocco 102–113; religion-associated archaeological sites 40; Sana'a 40, 246; Safranbolu 72–85; in Syria 16, 246; World Heritage in Danger 16, 49–50, 173
World Monuments Fund 173–4
World Travel and Tourism Council (WTTC) 89

Yardenit Baptismal Site 58–9
Yarsanism 37
Yazidism 37
Yemen 12, 13, 39, 49; competitiveness 22; conflict in xii, 12, 246, 247; country profile 4; destruction of cultural heritage 15, 246; international tourist arrivals 20; international tourist receipts 21; Jewish heritage 39, 48; Sana'a 40, 246; World Heritage 14, 40, 246

Zoroastrianism 37

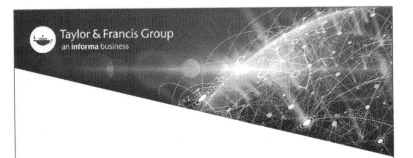

Printed in the United States
By Bookmasters